JOHN WILLIS'

DANCE WORLD

1975

Volume 10

1974-1975 SEASON

CROWN PUBLISHERS, INC.
419 Park Avenue South
New York, N.Y. 10016

To
MARY ANN NILES

a great talent, a beautiful person, and a wonderful friend to "gypsies," animals, and me.

CONTENTS

EDITOR: JOHN WILLIS

Assistant Editor: Stanley Reeves

Staff: Alberto Cabrera, Frances Harwood, Jack Moore, Don Nute,
Evan Romero, Robert Van Cleave

Staff Photographers: Ron Reagan, Lyn Smith, Van Williams

Left: GELSEY KIRKLAND and MIKHAIL BARYSHNIKOV
in American Ballet Theatre's "Coppelia"

Left:
Martha Swope Photo

DANCE PROGRAMS ON BROADWAY

ALVIN THEATRE
Opened Monday, October 14, 1974.*
Richard Barr and Charles Woodward present:

THE PAUL TAYLOR DANCE COMPANY

Artistic Director-Choreographer, Paul Taylor; Administrator, Neil S. Fleckman; Musical Director, John Herbert McDowell; Wardrobe Supervisor, Kathi Horne; Rehearsal Mistress, Bettie de-Jong; Assistant to the Producers, William Martin

COMPANY

Paul Taylor	Bettie deJong
Carolyn Adams	Eileen Cropley
Ruby Shang	Nicholas Gunn
Monica Morris	Elie Chaib
Lila York	Greg Reynolds
Ruth Andrien	Michael Deane

GUEST ARTIST: Rudolf Nureyev

REPERTOIRE: *NY Premiere* of "Sports and Follies" (Erik Satie, Paul Taylor; Costumes, George Tacit; Lighting, Jennifer Tipton), "Post Meridian" (Tape by Evelyn Lohoefer DeBoeck; Costumes, Alex Katz), "Churchyard" (Cosmos Savage; Costumes, Alec Sutherland), "Aureole" (Handel; Costumes, George Tacit), "American Genesis: The Creation (Bach), Before Eden (Haydn), So Long Eden (Fahey), West of Eden (Bohuslav Martinu), The Flood (Gottschalk)"

General Manager: Michael Kasdan
Company Manager: Jack Damios
Press: Meg Gordean, Howard Atlee
Stage Manager: Perry Cline

*Closed Oct. 19, 1974 after limited engagement of 8 performances.

Kenn Duncan, Jack Mitchell Photos

**Left: The Paul Taylor Dance Company
(Paul Taylor top center)**

Bettie deJong (c) in "Churchyard"

Eileen Cropley, Paul Taylor, Bettie deJong
in "Churchyard"

Ruby Shang, Elie Chaib, and top with Monica Morris,
Carolyn Adams, Eileen Cropley, Nicholas Gunn,
Elie Chaib in "Sports and Follies"

Nicholas Gunn
in "Sports and Follies"

Eileen Cropley, Ruby Shang, Nicholas Gunn,
Greg Reynolds Top: Paul Taylor in
"American Gothics"

Carolyn Adams, Top: Bettie deJong, Paul
Taylor in "American Genesis"

THE PAUL TAYLOR DANCE COMPANY

Eileen Cropley, Paul Taylor
in "Aureole"

URIS THEATRE
Opened Thursday, December 26, 1974.*
Hurok presents:

NUREYEV AND FRIENDS

Conductor, Jacques Beaudry; Lighting Supervision, Gilbert V. Hemsley, Jr.; Production under the supervision of John Taras; General Manager, Lee Walter; Dance Coordinator, Simon Semenoff; Production Assistant, Duane Schuler; Wardrobe, Stephanie Cheretun

COMPANY

Rudolf Nureyev	Nicholas Gunn
Carolyn Adams	Merle Park
Lisa Bradley	Mimi Paul
Eileen Cropley	Ruby Shang
Louis Falco	Lynda Yourth

PROGRAM: "Apollo" (Stravinsky, Balanchine), "Flower Festival in Genzano Pas de Deux" (Halsted, Erik Bruhn after Bournonville), "Aureole" (Handel, Paul Taylor), "The Moor's Pavane" (Purcell, Jose Limon)

Company Manager; John H. Wilson
Press: Sheila Porter, Lillian Libman, Robert E. Weiss
Stage Manager: William Hammond

*Closed Jan. 25, 1975 after limited engagement of 38 performances.

Left: Nureyev in "Apollo"

Rudolf Nureyev in "The Moor's Pavane"

Louis Falco, Rudolf Nureyev, Lisa Bradley, Merle Park in "The Moor's Pavane"
Top: Louis Falco, Merle Park in "The Moor's Pavane"

Lisa Bradley, Lynda Yourth, Rudolf Nureyev, Merle Park in "Apollo"
Top: Merle Park, Rudolf Nureyev

DANCE THEATRE OF HARLEM

Directors, Arthur Mitchell, Karel Shook; Music Director-Conductor, Tania Leon; Assistant Music Director, David Gagne; Concert Master, Harry Cykman; Lighting, Gary Fails; General Manager, Theatre Now; Ballet Master, William Scott; Coordinator, Lorenzo James; Wardrobe, Andrea Ross, Charles Sullivan, John Wainright; Costumes, Zelda Wynn

COMPANY

Lydia Abarca, Laura Brown, Karen Brown, M. Elena Carter, Brenda Garrett, Yvonne Hall, Virginia Johnson, Laura Lovelle, Susan Lovelle, Gayle McKinney, Melva Murray-White, Sheila Rohan, Roslyn Sampson, Karen Wright, Homer Bryant, Roman Brooks, Ronald Perry, Walter Raines, Paul Russell, Allen Sampson, William Scott, Samuel Smalls, Mel Tomlinson, Derek Williams, Joseph Wyatt

REPERTOIRE

"Holberg Suite" (Grieg, Arthur Mitchell), "Don Quixote Pas de Deux" (Minkus, Karel Shook), "Agon" (Stravinsky, George Balanchine), "Dougla" (Music, Choreography and Costumes, Geoffrey Holder), "Design for Strings" (Tchaikovsky, John Taras), "Bugaku" (Mayuzumi, Balanchine; Staged by Rosemary Dunleavy), "Forces of Rhythm" (Traditional-Contemporary, Louis Johnson), and *WORLD PREMIERE* Friday, April 25, 1975 of "Every Now and Then" (Quincy Jones, William Scott; Costumes, Hutaff Lennon, Jack Cunningham; Lighting, Gary Fails) danced by Sheila Rohan, Homer Bryant and entire company

Company Managers: Robert Frissell, Richard A. Gonsalves, Lorenzo James
Press: Winfrey Sampson, Karyn Taylor, Merle Debuskey, Susan L. Schulman
Stage Managers: Jerome King, Gary Fails

* Closed May 11, 1975 after limited engagement of 24 performances.

Martha Swope Photos

Top Right: Virginia Johnson, Paul Russell in "Don Quixote Pas de Deux"

Ronald Perry, Lydia Abarca

Laura Brown, Paul Russell in "Le Corsaire"

13

Roman Brooks, Samuel Smalls, Walter Raines in "Every Now and Then"
Top (L) Lydia Abarca in "Bugaku" (R) "Dougla"
Martha Swope Photos

Lydia Abarca, Derek Williams in "Agon"
Top: "Holberg Suite"

Virginia Johnson
in "Forces of Rhythm"
Martha Swope Photos

DANCE THEATRE OF HARLEM

Susan Lovelle, Derek Williams in "Agon"
Top: "Bugaku"

Paul Russell, Virginia Johnson, Homer Bryant
in "Holberg Suite" Above: "Agon"
Anthony Crickmay Photo

"Forces of Rhythm" Above: "Agon"
Marbeth Photo

Gayle McKinney, Homer Bryant in "Forces of Rhythm"
(Marbeth Photo) Top: "Every Now and Then"

DANCE THEATRE OF HARLEM

DANCE PROGRAMS AT LINCOLN CENTER

METROPOLITAN OPERA HOUSE
Opened Tuesday, June 18, 1974.*
S. Hurok presents:

MOISEYEV DANCE COMPANY

Artistic Director-Choreographer, Igor Moiseyev; Music Director, Anatoli Gusti; Conductor, Alexander Radzhetski; Guest Conductor, Arthur Lief; Production Manager, Irving Sudrow; Dance Coordinator, Simon Semenoff

COMPANY

SOLOISTS: Tatiana Afonina, Yuri Alexandrov, Boris Arutyunov, Alla Berezina, Boris Berezin, Alla Biryukova, Nelli Bondarenko, Evgeni Butov, Galina Eliseyeva, Fedor Enikeyev, Anatoli Fedorov, Lev Golovanov, Tatiana Ivanova, Eliza Iveleva, Igor Kalugin, Rudi Khodzhoyan, Nikolai Kosogorov, Vladimir Kotovski, Ludmila Kudreyavtseva, Stanislav Kulikov, Valentina Kulikova, Victor Lavrukhin, Victor Nikitushkin, Anatoli Novikov, Boris Petrov, Tatiana Salakova, Boris Sankin, Vassily Savin, Yuri Shumilin, Alexander Sinitsyn, Victor Sokolov, Alexander Strelkov, Elena Turkanova, Vladimir Yleyanov, Grigori Zhakharov

PROGRAM

"Summer," "The Three Shepherds," "Polka over the Leg," "Zhok," "Old City Quadrille," "Polovetsian Dances from Prince Igor" (Borodin), "Partisans," "Festival at Kirghizia," "Yourta," "Dance of the Seven Maidens," "Kalmyk Dance," "Platter Dance," "Catch the Maiden," "Gypsies," "Venzelya," "Gaucho," "Gopak"

Company Manager: Peter Inkey
Press: Sheila Porter, John Gingrich

* Closed July 20, 1974 after limited engagement of 40 performances to tour U.S.

**Left: "Prince Igor" Above: Igor
Moiseyev and "Prince Igor" dancers**

"Gopak"

"Prince Igor" Above: "Summer" Top: "Zhok"   "Summer" Above: "Zhok"

NEW YORK STATE THEATER
Opened Tuesday, July 2, 1974.*
Ballet Theatre Foundation (Sherwin M. Goldman, President) in association with City Center of Music and Drama (Norman Singer, Executive Director) presents:

AMERICAN BALLET THEATRE

Directors, Lucia Chase, Oliver Smith; Associate Director, Antony Tudor; General Manager, Daryl Dodson; Principal Conductor, Akira Endo; Conductor, David Gilbert; Regisseurs, Dimitri Romanoff, Enrique Martinez; Ballet Masters, Scott Douglas, Michael Lland; Ballet Mistresses, Patricia Wilde, Fiorella Keane; Lighting Designer, Nananne Porcher; Production Assistant, Dana Bruce; Wardrobe, Robert Holloway, May Ishimoto, Robert Boehm

COMPANY

PRINCIPALS: Karena Brock, Eleanor D'Antuono, Carla Fracci, Cynthia Gregory, Jonas Kage, Ted Kivitt, Daniel Levins, Natalia Makarova, Bruce Marks, Ivan Nagy, Dennis Nahat, Terry Orr, Marcos Paredes, John Prinz, Zhandra Rodriguez, Martine Van Hamel, Sallie Wilson, Gayle Young
SOLOISTS: Buddy Balough, Fernando Bujones, William Carter, David Coll, Warren Conover, Deborah Dobson, Nanette Glushak, Kim Highton, Ian Horvath, Keith Lee, Bonnie Mathis, Hilda Morales, Marianna Tcherkassky, Maria Youskevitch
CORPS: Elizabeth Ashton, Carmen Barth, Amy Blaisdell, Betty Chamberlin, Mona Clifford, Rory Foster, Rodney Gustafson, Kevin Haigen, Melissa Hale, Cristina Harvey, Kenneth Hughes, Marie Johansson, Susan Jones, Rhodie Jorgenson, Francia Kovak, Linda Kuchera, Charles Maple, Dennis Marshall, Sara Maule, Ruth Mayer, Jolinda Menendez, Michael Owen, Kirk Peterson, Janet Popelskii, Leigh Provancha, Cathryn Rhodes, Giselle Roberge, Richard Schafer, Kevin Self, Janet Shibata, Frank Smith, Clark Tippet, Gaudio Vacacio, Charles Ward, Denise Warner, Patricia Wesche, Sandall Whitaker, Apprentices: Sheila Bridges, Roman Jasinski

REPERTOIRE

"Apollo" (Stravinsky, Balanchine), "Billy the Kid" (Copland, Loring), "Coppelia" (Delibes, Martinez), "Etudes" (Riisager, Lander), "Fancy Free" (Bernstein, Robbins), "Giselle" (Adam, David Blair), "Intermezzo" (Brahms, Eliot Feld), "Jardin aux Lilas" (Chausson, Tudor), "The Moor's Pavane" (Purcell, Limon), "Napoli" (Paulli, Bournonville), "Petrouchka" (Stravinsky, Fokine), "Pillar of Fire" (Schoenberg, Tudor), "The River" (Ellington, Ailey), "Some Times" (Ogerman, Dennis Nahat), "Swan Lake" (Tchaikovsky, Blair), "Tales of Hoffmann" (Offenbach, Darrell), "Theme and Variations" (Tchaikovsky, Balanchine), "Three Virgins and a Devil" (Respighi, deMille), "Undertow" (Schuman, Tudor), and *New Productions* of "The Sleeping Beauty Act III" (Tchaikovsky, David Blair after Petipa) on July 2, 1974, "La Bayadere" (Minkus, Natalia Makarova after Petipa) on July 3, 1974, and "Le Baiser de la Fee" (Stravinsky-Tchaikovsky, John Neumeier) on July 4, 1974.

Company Manager: Herbert Scholder
Press: Virginia Hymes, Irene Shaw, Joan Ehrlich-White
Stage Managers: Jerry Rice, Richard Thorkelson

* Closed Aug. 10, 1974 after limited engagement of 41 performances. Re-opened at City Center Monday, Dec. 23, 1974 for 48 performances, closing Feb. 2, 1975. Additions to the company were Mikhail Baryshnikov, Michael Denard, and Gelsey Kirkland, and guest artist Rudy Bryans. Additions to the repertoire were "La Fille Mal Gardee" (Hertel, Romanoff), "Concerto" (Shostakovich, MacMillan), "La Sylphide" (Loewenskijold, Bruhn after Bournonville), "Les Patineurs" (Meyerbeer, Ashton), "Le Jeune Homme et la Mort" (Bach, Petit), "Pas de Quatre" (Pugni, Dolin-Perrot), "At Midnight" (Mahler, Feld), "Dark Elegies" (Mahler, Tudor), "Fall River Legend" (Gould, deMille), "Harbinger" (Prokofiev, Feld), "Unfinished Symphony" (Schubert, VanDyk), and on Jan. 23, 1975 the *PREMIERE* of "Gemini" (Hans Werner Henze, Glen Tetley; Sets and Costumes, Nadine Baylis) On Saturday, Jan. 11, 1975 the company celebrated its 35th anniversary with a Gala Performance. (See separate listing)

**Cynthia Gregory, Ivan Nagy
in "La Bayadere"**

Martha Swope Photos

Martine Van Hamel in "Concerto"
Top: Natalia Makarova, Mikhail Baryshnikov in "Coppelia"

Eleanor D'Antuono, Warren Conover in "La Fille Mal Gardee"
Top: (L) Marcos Paredes, Sallie Wilson in "Pillar of Fire"
(R) Cynthia Gregory, Ivan Nagy in "Le Baiser de la Fee"

ia Chase, Gayle Young, Sallie Wilson in "Fall River Legend"
Top: Zhandra Rhodriguez, Terry Orr, Karena Brock in
"Les Patineurs"

Ted Kivitt, Eleanor D'Antuono
in "Napoli"

23

AMERICAN BALLET THEATRE

Natalia Makarova, Ivan Nagy in "Apollo"
Top: Terry Orr, Marianna Tcherkassky in "Billy the Kid"

Cynthia Gregory in "Swan Lake"
Top: Dennis Nahat in "Three Virgins and a Devil"

Cynthia Gregory in "Le Baiser de la Fee"
Top: David Coll, Dennis Wayne, Fernando
Bujones in "Fancy Free"

Eleanor D'Antuono, Ted Kivitt
in "Theme and Variations"

Natalia Makarova, Mikhail Baryshnikov in "La Bayadere"
Above: Cynthia Gregory, Jonas Kage in "Apollo"

Cynthia Gregory, Gayle Young in "Concerto" Above:
Eleanor D'Antuono, Fernando Bujones in "Napoli" To
Ivan Nagy, Natalia Makarova in "La Fille Mal Gardee

Mikhail Baryshnikov, Gelsey Kirkland in "La Fille Mal Gardee" Top: (L) Cynthia Gregory, Richard Schafer in "Undertow" (R) Keith Lee, Ivan Nagy, Sallie Wilson in "The Moor's Pavane"

AMERICAN BALLET THEATRE

METROPOLITAN OPERA HOUSE
Opened Tuesday, July 23, 1974.*
S. Hurok presents:

THE NATIONAL BALLET OF CANADA

Founder, Celia Franca; Artistic Director, David Haber; General Manager, Gerry Eldred; Resident Producer, Erik Bruhn; Conductor-Musical Director, George Crum; Assistant Conductor, John Goss; Conductor, Aubrey Bowman; Assistant Artistic Director, Betty Oliphant; Concert Master, Jesse Ceci; Ballet Master, David Scott; Ballet Mistress, Joanne Nisbet

COMPANY

PRINCIPALS: Vanessa Harwood, Mary Jago, Karen Kain, Nadia Potts, Veronica Tennant, Frank Augustyn, Winthrop Corey, Tomas Schramek, Sergiu Stefanschi, Hazaros Surmeyan
SOLOISTS: Victoria Bertram, Andrea Davidson, Linda Maybarduk, Sonia Perusse, Wendy Reiser, Gailene Stock, Jacques Gorrissen, Charles Kirby, Andrew Oxenham
CORPS: Yolande Auger, Carina Bomers, Deborah Castellan, Gerre Cimino, Christy Cumberland, Ann Ditchburn, Norma Fisher, Lorna Geddes, Kathryn Joyner, Jennifer Laird, Daphne Loomis, Cynthia Lucas, Gloria Luoma, Esther Murillo, Patricia Oney, Jennifer Orr, Heather Ronald, Katherine Scheidegger, Mavis Staines, Barbara Szablowski, Karen Tessmer, Kathleen Trick, Charmain Turner, Valerie Wilder, Jane Wooding, Ronald Alexander, David Allan, Brian Armstrong, John Aubrey, Richard Bowen, Daniel Capouch, Victor Edwards, Miguel Garcia, David Gornik, Stephen Greenston, James Kudelka, Michael Matinzi, William Meadows, Thomas Nicholson, Constantin Patsalas, Chester Roberts, David Roxander
GUEST ARTIST: Rudolf Nureyev

REPERTOIRE

"The Sleeping Beauty" (Tchaikovsky, Rudolf Nureyev after Petipa); Scenery and Costumes, Nicholas Georgiadis; Lighting, David Hersey), "Swan Lake" (Tchaikovsky, Erik Bruhn), "Giselle" (Adam, Peter Wright), "La Sylphide" (Loewenskijold, Bruhn after Bournonville), "Le Loup" (Dutilleux, Roland Petit), "The Moor's Pavane" (Purcell, Jose Limon)
* Closed Aug. 10, 1974 after limited engagement of 24 performances.

Veronica Tennant, Rudolf Nureyev Above: Rudolf Nureyev, Veronica Tennant in "Sleeping Beauty"

Veronica Tennant Top Left: Rudolf Nureyev, Nadia Potts in "Sleeping Beauty"

Winthrop Corey, Mary Jago, Rudolf Nureyev in "Moor's Pavane" Top: (L) Tomas Schramek,
Vanessa Harwood in "Le Loup" Below: Rudolf Nureyev, Winthrop Corey, Mary Jago in
"Moor's Pavane" (R) Winthrop Corey, Rudolf Nureyev

Rudolf Nureyev in "La Sylphide"
Top: Karen Kain, Frank Augustyn in "Giselle"
Judy Cameron Photos

Sergiu Stefanschi, Veronica Tennant in "Giselle"
Above: "Giselle" (also top)

NATIONAL BALLET OF CANADA

Karen Kain Above: "Swan Lake" Top: Karen Kain
in "Swan Lake"

Veronica Tennant, Tomas Schramek in "Le Loup"
Above: Vanessa Harwood, Rudolf Nureyev in "Swan Lake"

31

NEW YORK CITY BALLET

Director, Lincoln Kirstein; Ballet Masters, George Balanchine, Jerome Robbins, John Taras; Musical Director-Principal Conductor, Robert Irving; Associate Conductor, Hugo Fiorato; Costume Execution, Barbara Karinska; Lighting, Ronald Bates; Wardrobe, Sophie Pourmel, Leslie Copeland, Dorothy Fugate, Larry Calvert; General Manager, Betty Cage; Make-up, Michael Arshansky; Hairstylist, James Brusock; Company Manager, Zelda Dorfman; Press, Virginia Donaldson, Larry Strichman; Stage Managers, Ronald Bates, Kevin Tyler, Roland Vazquez

COMPANY

PRINCIPALS: Jacques d'Amboise, Karin von Aroldingen, Anthony Blum, Jean-Pierre Bonnefous, Suzanne Farrell, Allegra Kent, Sara Leland, Patricia McBride, Peter Martins, Kay Mazzo, Francisco Moncion, Helgi Tomasson, Violette Verdy, Edward Villella
SOLOISTS: Susan Hendl, Deni Lamont, Teena McConnell, Robert Maiorano, Marnee Morris, Shaun O'Brien, Frank Ohman, Susan Pilarre, Carol Sumner, Robert Weiss
CORPS: Muriel Aasen, Merrill Ashley, Debra Austin, Tracy Bennett, James Bogan, Bonita Borne, Elyse Borne, Vicki Bromberg, Maria Calegari, Victor Castelli, Hermes Conde, Bart Cook, Gail Crisa, Richard Dryden, Penelope Dudleston, Daniel Duell, Gerard Ebitz, Renee Estopinal, Nina Fedorova, Elise Flagg, Wilhemina Franfurt, Jean-Pierre Frolich, Judith Fugate, Kathleen Haigney, Linda Homek, Richard Hoskinson, Dolores Houston, Elise Ingalls, Sandra Jennings, William Johnson, Deborah Koolish, Catherine Morris, Peter Naumann, Colleen Neary, Alice Patelson, Elizabeth Pawluk, Delia Peters, Bryan Pitts, Terri Lee Port, Lisa de Ribere, Christine Redpath, David Richardson, Francis Sackett, Paul Sackett, Stephanie Saland, Lilly Samuels, Marjorie Spohn, Carol-Marie Strizak, Richard Tanner, Nolan T'Sani, Sheryl Ware, Heather Watts, Garielle Whittle, Sandra Zigars

REPERTOIRE

(All choreography by George Balanchine, except where noted) "Brahms-Schoenberg Quartet" (Brahms), "Bugaku" (Mayuzumi), "The Concert" (Chopin, Robbins), "Concerto Barocco" (Bach), "Cortege Hongrois" (Glazounov), "Dances at a Gathering" (Chopin, Robbins), "Divertimento from Le Baiser de la Fee" (Stravinsky), "Donizetti Variations" (Donizetti), "Don Quixote" (Nabokov), "Duo Concertant" (Stravinsky), "Dybbuk Variations" (Bernstein, Robbins), "Episodes" (Webern), "Jewels" (Faure-Stravinsky-Tchaikovsky), "The Goldberg Variations "(Bach, Robbins), "Harlequinade" (Drigo), "Monumentum pro Gesualdo" (Stravinsky), "Movements for Piano and Orchestra" (Stravinsky), "The Nutcracker" (Tchaikovsky), "Pas de Deux" (Tchaikovsky), "Prodigal Son" (Prokofiev), "Pulcinella" (Stravinsky, Balanchine-Robbins), "Raymonda Variations" (Glazounov), "Saltarelli" (Vivaldi, Jacques d'Amboise), "Scenes de Ballet" (Stravinsky, John Taras), "Scherzo Fantastique" (Stravinsky, Robbins), "Scotch Symphony" (Mendelssohn), "Serenade" (Tchaikovsky), "La Sonnambula" (Rieti), "Stravinsky Violin Concerto" (Stravinsky), "Swan Lake" (Tchaikovsky), "Symphony in C" (Bizet), "Symphony in Three Movements" (Stravinsky), "Tarantella" (Gottschalk-Kay), "Tchaikovsky Concerto #2" (Tchaikovsky), "Tchaikovsky Suite #3" (Tchaikovsky), "Variations pour Une Porte et un Soupir" (Henry), "Western Symphony" (Kay), "Who Cares?" (Gershwin-Kay)

Company Manager: Zelda Dorfman
Press: Virginia Donaldson, Larry Strichman
Stage Managers: Ronald Bates, Kevin Tyler, Roland Vazquez

* Closed Feb. 16, 1975 after 56 performances in repertory, 40 performances of "The Nutcracker" (Dec. 5, 1974–Jan. 5, 1975), and 14 performances of "Don Quixote" (Feb. 6–16, 1975). Suzanne Farrell returned to the company and gave her first performance on Jan. 16, 1975 in "Symphony in C." A new production of "Coppelia" (Leo Delibes, George Balanchine-Alexandra Danilova after Petipa; Costumes and Scenery, Rouben Ter-Arutunian) was premiered on Nov. 20, 1974. Thursday, Jan. 9, 1975 was the *WORLD PREMIERE* of "Sinfonietta" (Paul Hindemith, Jacques d'Amboise; Designed by John Braden; Lighting, Ronald Bates; Conductor, Robert Irving) with Christine Redpath, Bart Cook, Colleen Neary, Francis Sackett, Catherine Morris, Stephanie Saland, Hermes Conde, Paul Sackett, and ensemble.

The company opened its 62nd season Tuesday, Apr. 29, 1975 and closed June 29, 1975 after 72 performances, including 24 performances of a "Ravel Festival" (May 15–May 31, 1975), and 7 performances of "A Midsummer Night's Dream" (June 25–29, 1975). Additions to the repertoire were "An Evening's Waltzes" (Prokofiev, Robbins), "Afternoon of a Faun" (Debussy, Robbins), "Agon" (Stravinsky), "Divertimento #15" (Mozart), "Firebird" (Stravinsky, Balanchine-Robbins), "Four Bagatelles" (Beethoven), "In the Night" (Chopin, Robbins), "Irish Fantasy" (Saint-Saens, d'Amboise), "Ivesiana" (Ives), "Meditations" (Ravel) "Scherzo a La Russe" (Stravinsky), "La Source" (Delibes), "Stars and Stripes" (Sousa-Kay), "Valse Fantaisie" (Glinka), "Watermill" (Ito, Robbins).

The Ravel Festival included "La Valse," "The Spellbound Child" (Balanchine-Robbins), and *WORLD PREMIERES* of "Piano Concerto in G" (Robbins) on Thursday May 15, 1975; Thursday, May 22, 1975: "Mother Goose" (Robbins), "Scheherazade" (Balanchine), "Tzigane" (Balanchine), "Gaspard de la Nuit" (Balanchine), "Daphnis and Chloe" (John Taras); Thursday, May 29, 1975: "Sarabande and Danse" (d'Amboise), "Alborada del Gracioso" (d'Amboise), "Introduction and Allegro" (Robbins), "Sonatine" (Balanchine), "Le Tombeau de Couperin" (Balanchine), "Rapsodie Espagnole" (Balanchine)

Additions to the company were Jilise Bushling, Stephen Caras, Jay Jolley, Lourdes Lopez, Laurence Matthews, Kyra Nichols

Martha Swope Photos

Top Right: Jacques d'Amboise, Suzanne Farrell in "Diamonds" from "Jewels" Below: Violette Verdy, Anthony Blum in "Jewels"

Jean-Pierre Frolich, Delia Peters in "Symphony in C" Above: Edward Villella in "Watermill" Peter Martins, Patricia McBride in "Cortege Hongrois" *Martha Swope Photos*

Muriel Aasen, Peter Schaufuss in "The Nutcracker" Above: Anthony Blum, Kay Mazzo in "Bugaku" Top: Helgi Tomasson, Karin von Aroldingen in "The Prodigal Son"

Suzanne Farrell, Peter Martins (C) in "Symphony in C" Top: (L): Sara Leland, Helgi Tomasson in "Tarantello" (R) Jean-Pierre Bonnefous, Teena McConnell in "Cortege Hongrois"

NEW YORK CITY BALLET

Bart Cook, Karin von Aroldingen in "Violin Concerto"
Above: Tracy Bennett, Paul Sackett, Colleen Neary
in "Concerto #2" Top: Merrill Ashley, Jacques
d'Amboise in "Irish Fantasy"

Patricia McBride, Shaun O'Brien Top: Patricia
McBride, Helgi Tomasson in "Coppelia"

Helgi Tomasson in "Dybbuk"
Top: Debra Austin in "Sinfonietta"

Colleen Neary, Bart Cook in "Episodes"
Martha Swope Photos

NEW YORK CITY BALLET

Jean-Pierre Bonnefous, Kay Mazzo in "Don Quixote" Top: (L) Sara Leland in "The Concert" (R) Suzanne
Farrell, Colleen Neary in "Concerto Barocco"

NEW YORK CITY BALLET

Peter Martins, Nina Federova in "Daphnis and Chloe"
Above: "Le Tombeau de Couperin" Top: Suzanne
Farrell in "Tzigane"

Helgi Tomasson, Patricia McBride in "Introduc
and Allegro" Above: "L'Enfant et les Sortileg
Top: Daniel Duell, Muriel Aasen in"Mother Go

"HOMMAGE A RAVEL"
May 15 - 31, 1975

Martha Swope Photos

Martins, Suzanne Farrell in "Concerto in G"   Above:
T'Sani, Karin von Aroldingen in "Rapsodie Espagnole"
Violette Verdy, Jean Pierre Bonnefous, in "Sonatine"

Martha Swope Photos

Suzanne Farrell in "Albavada del Gracioso" Above:
Colleen Neary in "Gaspard de la Nuit" Top: Kay
Mazzo, Edward Villella in "Scheherazade"   **39**

NEW YORK CITY BALLET

HARKNESS THEATRE
Opened Monday, March 31, 1975.*
The Jose Limon Dance Foundation presents:

JOSE LIMON DANCE COMPANY

Artistic Director, Ruth Currier; Assistant Artistic Director, Clay Taliaferro; Production Manager, John Toland; Wardrobe Supervisor, Allen Munch; Lighting, William Otterson; Management, H. I. Enterprises

COMPANY

Mark Ammerman, Bill Cratty, Robyn Cutler, Matthew Diamond, Christopher Gillis, Laura Glenn, Ryland Jordan, Gary Masters, Fred Mathews, Carla Maxwell, Marjorie Philpot, Jennifer Scanlon, Louis Solino, Risa Steinberg, Clay Taliaferro, Ann Vachon, Nina Watt For "Missa Brevis": Richard Ammon, Peggy Hackney, Susan Hogan, Hannah Kahn, Robert Kahn, Tonia Shimin

REPERTOIRE

"Brandenburg Concerto No. 4" (Bach, Doris Humphrey-Ruth Currier; Setting, Doris Humphrey; Costumes, Pauline Lawrence), "Night Spell" (Priaulx Rainer, Humphrey; Costumes, Pauline Lawrence), "The Shakers" (Traditional, Humphrey; Costumes, Pauline Lawrence), "Choreographic Offering" (Bach, Jose Limon; Costumes, Pauline Lawrence), "The Moor's Pavane" (Purcell, Limon), "The Traitor" (Gunther Schuller, Limon), "Carlota" (Jose Limon; Costumes, Charles Tomlinson), "There Is a Time" (Dello Joio, Limon), "Emperor Jones" (Dello Joio, Limon), "Missa Brevis" (Zoltan Kodaly, Limon), "Homage to Federico Garcia Lorca" (Sylvestre Revueltas, Anna Sokolow; Poetry, Garcia Lorca; Costumes, Jose Coronado), and on Monday, April 7, 1975, the *WORLD PREMIERE* of "Phantasmagoria 1975" (Ilhan Kemaleddin Mimaroglu-Alban Berg-Charles Ives, Ruth Currier)
General Manager: Theatre Now
Press: Tom Kerrigan

* Closed Apr. 12, 1975 after limited engagement of 15 performances

Martha Swope, Susan Cook Photos

Left: Risa Steinberg, Robyn Cutler, Nina Watt, Carla Maxwell, Gary Masters in "Carlota"

Jennifer Scanlon, Clay Taliafero in "Moor's Pavane"

Gary Masters, Fred Mathews in "Brandenburg Concer†

Clay Taliaferro in "Emperor Jones" Top: Ruth
Currier (L) and Jose Limon Company

Risa Steinberg, Louis Solino in "Night Spell"

Clay Taliaferro in "The Traitor" Top: Bill Cratty,
Louis Solino, Nina Watt in "Night Spell"

Marjorie Philpot, Robyn Cutler, Laura Glenn in
"Missa Brevis" Top: "Missa Brevis"

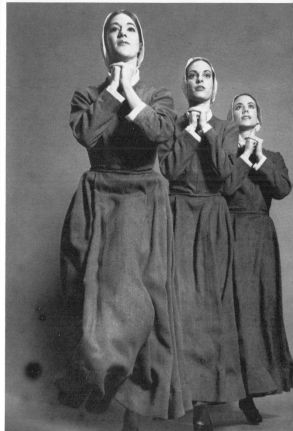

Christopher Gillis, Ryland Jordan, Bill Cratty
Top: Gary Masters, Carla Maxwell,
Risa Steinberg in "The Shakers"

Mark Ammerman, Jennifer Scanlon, Laura Glenn
Top: Robyn Cutler, Laura Glenn, Marjorie
Philpot in "The Shakers"

METROPOLITAN OPERA HOUSE
Opened Monday, April 22, 1975.*
Hurok presents:

BOLSHOI BALLET

Artistic Director-Principal Choreographer, Yuri Grigorovich; Designer, Simon Virsaladze; Conductors, Algis Zhyuraitis, Alexander Kopylov; Ballet Director, Piotr Khomutov; Technical Director, Viktor Zavitayev; Tour Director, Kiril Molchanov; Lighting, Boris Lelyukhin; Ballet Masters/Repetiteurs, Galina Ulanova, Nikolai Simachov; Technical Coordinator, Mario de Maria; Dance Coordinator, Simon Semenoff

SOLOISTS

Natalia Bessmertnova, Nina Timofeyeva, Nina Sorokina, Ludmila Semenyaka, Tatiana Golikova, Elena Kholina, Larisa Dmitrieva, Vladimir Vasiliev, Mikhail Lavrovsky, Yuri Vladimirov, Maris Liepa, Boris Akimov, Vyacheslav Gordeyev, Alexander Bogatyrev, Mikhail Gabovich, Vladimir Levashev, Shamil Yagudin, Anatoli Simachov, Yuri Papko

REPERTOIRE

"Giselle" (Adolphe Adam, Coralli-Perrot-Petipa reproduced by Leonid Lavrovsky), *U.S. PREMIERES* of "Spartacus" (Aram Khatchaturian, Yuri Grigorovich; Costumes and Scenery, Simon Virsaladze), "Ivan the Terrible" (Serge Prokofiev, Yuri Grigorovich; Scenery and Costumes, Simon Virsaladze), "The Sleeping Beauty" (Piotr Tchaikovsky, Grigorovich after Petipa; Scenery and Costumes, Simon Virsaladze), "Swan Lake" (Piotr Tchaikovsky, Yuri Grigorovich after Gorsky-Ivan-ov-Petipa; Scenery and Costumes, Virsaladze)

General Manager: John H. Wilson
Company Manager: Peter Inkey
Press: Sheila Porter, Lillian Libman, Robert Weiss
Stage Managers: Alexander Sokolov, Yuri Ignatov, Robert D. Currie, Michael J. Maurer

* Closed May 24, 1975 after limited engagement of 38 performances.

Vladimir Vasiliev, Natalia Bessmertnova in "Ivan the Terrible"
Top Left: Natalia Bessmertnova, Yuri Vladimirov in "Ivan the Terrible"

Vladimir Vasiliev in "Ivan the Terrible"
Top: Liudmila Semenyaka in "Sleeping Beauty"

"Sleeping Beauty"

Natalia Bessmertnova, Mikhail Lavrovsky in "Swan Lake"
Top: Liudmila Semenyaka in "Sleeping Beauty"

Natalia Bessmertnova, Mikhail Lavrovsky
in "Swan Lake"

Natalia Bessmertnova in "Swan Lake"
Top: "Swan Lake"

THE BOLSHOI BALLET

Vladimir Vasiliev in "Spartacus" Top Left: Maris Liepa, Nina Timofeyeva in "Spartacus" Top Right: Nina Sorokina, Yuri Vladimirov in "Spartacus"

THE BOLSHOI BALLET

Boris Akimov in "Spartacus"
Top: Mikhail Lavrovsky in "Spartacus"

Natalia Bessmertnova, Mikhail Lavrovsky
in "Spartacus"

Natalia Bessmertnova, Mikhail Lavrovsky in "Giselle"
Top: Nina Timofeyeva in "Giselle"

Vladimir Vasiliev in "Giselle"
Above and Top: "Giselle"

THE BOLSHOI BALLET

METROPOLITAN OPERA HOUSE
Opened Tuesday, May 27, 1975
Hurok presents by arrangement with the Wuerttemberg State Theatre
(Hans Peter Doll, General Administrator; George Zoller, Administrative Director):

THE STUTTGART BALLET

Director-Choreographer, Glen Tetley; Assistant Director, Anne Wooliams; Conductors, Stewart Kershaw, Friedrich Lehn, Jacques Beaudry (Guest Artist); Manager, Dieter Grafe; Ballet Masters, Alan Beale, Alex Ursuliak; Choreologist, Georgette Tsinguirides; Technical Director, Josef Frey; American Production Supervisor, Gilbert V. Hemsley, Jr.

COMPANY

PRINCIPALS: Marcia Haydee, Birgit Keil, Judith Reyne, Joyce Cuoco, Minka Knapp, Egon Madsen, Richard Cragun, Heinz Clauss, Jan Stripling, Vladimir Klos, Reid Anderson, Ruth Papendick, Hella Heim, Lucia Isenring, Jean Allenby, Gudrun Lechner, Betsy Wistrich, Marilyn Trounson, Dieter Ammann, David Sutherland, Jiri Kylian, Barry Ingham, Marcis Lesins
CORPS: Franca Barchiese, Sabine Bartels, Sylviane Bayard, Karen Bieling, Ludmilla Bogart, Wileen Brady, Suzanna Brooks, Jacqui Cully, Brigitte Erdweg, Megan Hintz, Elke Holle, Lise Houlton, Hilde Koch, Gudrun Kranz, Sabine Kupferberg, Melissa Lyons, Maria Moldoveanu, Teresina Mosco, Melinda Witham, Marie Luise Kersten, Dale Brannon, Peter Connell, Ulf Esser, Christian Fallanga, Gunther Falusy, William Forsythe, Jurgen Heiss, Carl Morrow, Patrice Montagnon, Mark Neal, Peter Rille, Ronald Thornhill, Michael Wasmund, Guy Pontecorvo, Christopher Boatwright

REPERTOIRE

"Eugene Onegin" (Tchaikovsky, John Cranko), "Romeo and Juliet" (Prokofiev, Cranko), "Swan Lake" (Tchaikovsky, Cranko), "Brouillards" (Debussy, Cranko), "Initials R.B.M.E." (Brahms, Cranko), "The Taming of the Shrew" (Kurt-Heinz Stolze after Scarlatti, Cranko)
AMERICAN PREMIERES: "Voluntaries" (Francis Poulenc, Glen Tetley; Designs, Rouben Ter-Arutunian) and "Arena" (Morton Subotnick, Glen Tetley; Set, Paul Thek), on Wednesday, June 4, 1975, "Daphnis and Chloe" (Maurice Ravel, Glen Tetley; Designed by Willa Kim) on Thursday, June 12, 1975

General Manger, John H. Wilson
Manager: Lee Walter
Press: Sheila Porter, Robert Weiss, Rima Corben
Stage Managers: Gerd Praast, Robert Crawley, E-Ping Nie

* Closed June 21, 1975 after limited engagement of 29 performances.

Marcia Haydee, Richard Cragun (also top right) in "The Taming of the Shrew"

Marcia Haydee, Heinz Clauss Above: Birgit Keil, Reid Anderson in "Eugene Onegin"

Jan Stripling, Birgit Keil, Reid Anderson
Top: Marcia Haydee, Richard Cragun in "Voluntaries"

Marcia Haydee, Richard Cragun in "Daphnis and Chloe"
Above: "Daphnis and Chloe" Top: "Voluntaries"

THE STUTTGART BALLET

Vladimir Klos, Birgit Keil, Heinz Clauss in "Brouillards"
Top: (L) Marcia Haydee, Richard Cragun in "Romeo and Juliet"
(R) Joyce Cuoco, Egon Madsen in "Romeo and Juliet"

Birgit Keil, Bernd Berg, Reid Anderson
in "Initials R.B.M.E." Top: Birgit Keil
Richard Cragun in "Swan Lake"

Marcia Haydee, Heinz Clauss in "Initials R.B.M.E."
Top: Vladimir Klos, Birgit Keil in "Swan Lake"

THE STUTTGART BALLET

TONY WHITE

A one-man show: A Dance Suite in Four Parts

Right: Tony White

LIBRARY & MUSEUM OF PERFORMING ARTS
Wednesday & Thursday, September 25 & 26, 1974
The New York Public Library at Lincoln Center presents:

THE LAURA VELDHUIS DANCE COMPANY

Director-Choreographer, Laura Veldhuis; Technical Consultant-Designer, Joop Veldhuis; Guest Musicians, Peter Isaacson, John Isaacson

COMPANY

Gary Davis
Charles Meyers
Brigitta Mueller

Ellen Pundyk
Henry Smith
Laura Veldhuis

PROGRAM: "The Mind's Garden" (Benjamin Britten), "Walk Softly" (Stan Kenton), "Original Songs" (Peter and John Isaacson), "Green Mountain Suite" (Peter and John Isaacson), "Blue Eyes," "Green Mountain Boy"

Myra Armstrong Photo

Right: Laura Veldhuis, Henry Smith in "The Mind's Garden"

LIBRARY & MUSEUM OF PERFORMING ARTS
Thursday, January 23, 1975*

THE PHILIPPINE DANCE COMPANY OF NEW YORK

Artistic Director-Choreographer, Ronnie Alejandro; Assistant Director, Ching Valdes; Executive Director, Bruna P. Seril; Technical Director, Chuck Golden; Stage Manager, Lee Horsman; President, Salvador Zapanta

COMPANY

Ronnie Alejandro, Sonny Zapanta, Cesar Villanueva, Tony Parel, Ramon de Luna, Mel Chionglo, Benny Felix, Eddie Sese, Noel Valdes, Nardz Peji, Gloria Sambat, Evelyn de Luna, Trudl Pinon, Ching Valdes, Rosemarie Valdes, Dulce Valdes, Sherry Valdes, Vicky Valdes, Kathy Serio, Vicky Tiangco, Ruth Malabrigo, Eugene Domingo, Beth Padua, Melen Acaac, Tessie Antonio

PROGRAM

BIGHANI—Portrait of the Philippine Dance: (All choreography by Ronnie Alejandro) "Polkabal (Traditional-Kasilag), "Timawa," "Panuelo de Amor (Traditional-Kasilag), "Paypay de Manila" (Traditional-Kasilag), "Jota Cavitena" (Traditional-Kasilag), "Malong" (Kasilag), "Tarjata Sin Kagukan" (Dadap), "Singkil," "Apayao Maidens" (Traditional-Kasilag), "Kalinga Wedding Dance" (Kasilag), "Anihan" (Gonzalez), "Binasuan," "Itik-Itik", "Subli", "Pandanggo sa Ilaw", "Tinikling"
* This program was also presented at the American Museum of Natural History Oct. 26, 1974, Governor's Island Dec. 21, 1974, and at International House Jan. 10, 1975.

Philippine Dance Company

JUILLIARD THEATER
April 26–28, 1975 (3 performances)
The Juilliard School presents:

JUILLIARD DANCE ENSEMBLE

Production Director, Martha Hill; Production Supervisor, Joe Pacitti; Stage Manager, Lee Schlosberg; Costume Supervisor, William MacDugald; Headdresses, Timothy Miller; Sound Technician, Stanley Thomas; Wardrobe Mistress, Ruth Thomason; Administrative Assistant for Production, Mary Chudick; Costumes, Robert Yodice; Lighting, Joe Pacitti

PROGRAM
(All Premiere Performances)

"THE WALDSTEIN SONATA" (Beethoven, Jose Limon-Daniel Lewis; Pianist, Emanuel Krasovsky) danced by Roxolana Babiuk, Dian Dong, Virginia Hulburt, Dianne Hulburt, Pierre Barreau, William Belle, Robert Swinston, Leigh Warren, on Apr 27: Shirley Brown, Linda Spriggs, Catherine Sullivan, Colette Yglesias, Anthony Balcena, William Belle, Hsueh-Tung Chen, Barry Weiss
"MASK OF NIGHT" (George Crumb, Kazuko Hirabayashi; Conductor, David Ramadanoff) danced by Janice Carp, Virginia Edmands, Janell Hollingsworth, Dianne Hulburt, Susan Osberg, Linda Spriggs, Pierre Barbeau, Hsueh-Tung Chen, Robert Swinston, Leigh Warren, Barry Weiss
"RIDE THE CULTURE LOOP" (Teo Macero, Anna Sokolow; Projections, Robert Yodice; Conductor, Teo Macero) danced by Deborah Allton, Marilyn Banks, Yael Barash, Leslie Brown, Shirley Brown, Trude Cone, Helen Castillo, Yveline Cottez, Dian Dong, Thelma Drayton, Martina Ebey, Elizabeth Fisher, Mary Ann Golick, Nancy Hill, Janell Hollingsworth, Lisa Kerr, Ann Kohn, Marie Lind, VV Dachin Matsuoka, Elizabeth McCarthy, Andrea Morris, Rosemary Newton, Valencia Ondes, Maria O'Neill, Revei Paul, Patrice Regnier, Ayala Rimon, Robin Somers, Linda Spriggs, Elizabeth Sung, Jill Wagoner, Anthony Balcena, Pierre Barbeau, William Belle, Sam Berman, Hsueh-Tung Chen, Mercie Hinton, John Jackson, Allen Maniker, Andrew Miller, John Seaman

Juilliard Dance Ensemble in "Ride the Culture Loop"
Milton Oleaga Photo
Top: in "The Waldstein Sonata"
Jane Rady Photo

JUILLIARD THEATER
Wednesday, May 21, 1975 (2 performances)
The New York City Ballet Guild presents the tenth annual workshop performance of the:

SCHOOL OF AMERICAN BALLET

President of the Board, Lincoln Kirstein; Chairman, George Balanchine; Co-ordinator of Workshop Performances, Mrs. Peter A. Ralston; Conductor, Christian Badea

PROGRAM

"KONSERVATORIET—Excerpts from Part I" (H. S. Paulli, Bournonville; Staged by Stanley Williams) danced by Leslie Brown, Nichol Hlinka, Marco Carrabba, Hillary Aiges, Toni Bentley, Elizabeth Carr, Florence Fitzgerald, Sophie Grzibowski, Dana Lewis, Diane Partington, Leslie Roy, Beverly Tucker, Kevin Donnelly, Joseph Duell, Richard Fritz, John Grensback, David Otto, Bruce Padgett, Denise Greenbaum, Patrice Hemsworth
"SLEEPING BEAUTY—Excerpts from Act I" (P. I. Tchaikovsky, Patipa; Staged by Alexandra Danilova) danced by Elizabeth Carr, Siobhan DePrima, Lisa Dosne, Jana Fugate, Florence Fitzgerald, Jeanna Gailar, Shirley Kirstein, Barbara Leach, Diane Partington, Sarah Smith, Susan Soddy, Lesley Troy, John Bass, Kevin Donnelly, Joseph Duell, David Everitt, Richard Fritz, John Grensback, Tom Helm, James Lane, Bruce Padgett, Peter Schetter, Wade Walthall, Ian Walton, Nora Heiber, Vicki Marsen, Sheila Schwartzbart, Carol Shultz, Hillary Aiges, Carole Divet, Lisa Hess, Lisa Rooney, Michelle Bailey, Bernadette Erlon, Mandy Gates, Pamela Giardino, Vicky Lykiardopoulous, Regina Maximilien, Corinne Merz, Melissa Pittman, Wendy Rosenberg, Lindy Roy, Susan Strain, Lisa Torcicolla, Lauren Huaser
"CONCERTO BAROCCO" (J. S. Bach, George Balanchine; Staged by Suki Schorer) danced by Nichol Hlinka, Joseph Duell, Lisa Hess, Toni Bentley, Karen Crepps, Carole Divet, Dana Lewis, Diane Partington, Lisa Rooney, Leslie Roy, Noelle Shader
"COUNTRY DANCES FROM ENGLAND AND AMERICA" (Staged by Ronald Smedley and Robert Parker) danced by Michelle Bailey, Mandy Bennett, Elizabeth Brown, Dianthe DeBuys, Pamela Giardino, Julie Hays, Jillana Hess, Regina Maximilien, Corinne Merz, Melissa Pittman, Lindy Roy, Sharon Solik, Susan Strain, John Bass, Ames Beals, Marco Carrabba, Kevin Donnelly, Joseph Duell, David Everitt, Richard Fritz, Tom Helm, James Lane, Bruce Padgett, Peter Schetter, Ian Walton, Wade Walthall

Leslie Brown in "Concerto Barocco" Above: Lauren Hauser, Joseph Duell in "Sleeping Beauty"
(School of American Ballet)

Martha Swope Photos

56

DANCE PROGRAMS AT CITY CENTER

CITY CENTER 55th STREET THEATER
Tuesday, October 1–6, 1974 (8 performances)
Hurok presents:

SLASK

Polish Folk Song and Dance Ensemble

Director-Choreographer, Elwira Kaminska; Manager, Janusz Maciejowski; Artistic Manager, Stainslaw Hadyna; Conductors, Alina Ilnicka, Czeslaw Pietruszka; Technical Manager, Czeslaw Leniec; Stage and Production Manager, Franciszek Klimek; Dance Coordinator, Simon Semenoff; Press, Sheila Porter, James Murtha, Robert Weiss; Company Manager, Kurt Neumann

PROGRAM

"Trojak," "A Girl in a Forest," "Taniec Chustkowy," "Maids from Rzeszow," "Kujawiak with Oberek," "Kujawiaczek," "Carnival in Wilamowice," "Taniec z Batami," "Kolomajki," "Call to the Moon," "The Robbers' Ballad," "Tatra Dances," "Polonaise," "A Girl and a Soldier," "When Margaret Went Dancing," "Play to Me Music!," "Suite from Zywiec," "Hello! Hello! Helen," "Dance of the Two Michaels," "Cracow Suite"

CITY CENTER 55th STREET THEATER
Opened Wednesday, October 9, 1974.*
The Foundation for American Dance (Anthony A. Bliss, Chairman) in
association with City Center of Music and Drama presents:

CITY CENTER JOFFREY BALLET

Artistic Director, Robert Joffrey; Associate Director, Gerald Arpino; General Administrator, William Crawford; Assistant Administrator, Jane Hermann; Music Director, Seymour Lipkin; Associate Conductor, Sung Kwak; Guest Conductor, Roy Rogosin; Lighting Designer, Jennifer Tipton; Ballet Master, Basil Thompson; Wardrobe, John Allen, Dorothy Coscia; Assistants to Mr. Joffrey, William Leighton, Scott Barnard, Diane Orio; Administrative Assistant, Edith Jerell; Production Assistant, Alan Gerberg; Press Consultant, Isadora Bennett

COMPANY

Charthel Arthur, Diana Cartier, Francesca Corkle, Donna Cowen, Starr Danias, Ann Marie De Angelo, Erika Goodman, Jan Hanniford, Alaine Haubert, Nancy Ichino, Denise Jackson, Krystyna Jurkowski, Janey Kawaguchi, Pamela Nearhoof, Diane Orio, Beatriz Rodriguez, Trinette Singleton, Rebecca Wright, Adix Carman, Gary Chryst, Richard Colton, Donn Edwards, Robert Estner, Tom Fowler, Larry Grenier, Phillip Hoffman, Christian Holder, Gregory Huffman, Jeffrey Hughes, Kevin McKenzie, Ted Nelson, Russell Sultzbach, Paul Sutherland, Robert Talmage, Burton Taylor, Robert Thomas, Edward Verso, Dennis Wayne, William Whitener

REPERTOIRE

"Pulcinella" (Stravinsky, Leonide Massine; Decor and Costumes, Pablo Picasso, re-created by Rouben Ter-Arutunian), "As Time Goes By" (Haydn, Twyla Tharp), "N.Y. Export, Op. Jazz" (Robert Prince, Jerome Robbins; Re-staged by Wilma Curley), "Viva Vivaldi!" (Vivaldi, Gerald Arpino), "Remembrances" (Wagner, Robert Joffrey), "Trinity" (Alan Raph-Lee Holdridge, Arpino), "The Relativity of Icarus" (Gerhard Samuel, Arpino), "Kettentanz" (Strauss, Arpino), "William Tell Variations" (Rossini, Bournonville), "The Clowns" (Hershy Kay, Arpino), "Monotones" (Satie, Frederick Ashton; Staged by Faith Worth), "Secret Places" (Mozart, Arpino), "The Moor's Pavane" (Purcell, Jose Limon), "Evening Dialogues" (Robert Schumann, Jonathan Watts), "Le Beau Danube" (Strauss, Massine), "The Dream" (Mendelssohn, Ashton), "Confetti" (Rossini, Arpino), "The Green Table" (Cohen, Jooss), "Interplay" (Gould, Jerome Robbins), "Moves" (none, Robbins), "Parade" (Satie, Massine), "Sacred Grove on Mt. Tamalpais" (Ralph, Arpino), "Square Dance" (Corelli-Vivaldi, Balanchine), "Valentine" (Druckman, Arpino), "Weewis" (Walden, Sappington) *NEW YORK PREMIERES:* "Pulcinella," "Evening Dialogues," "The Relativity of Icarus"

Company Managers: Hans Hortig, Stan Ware
Press: Robert Larkin, Ruth Hedrick
Stage Managers: Dan Butt, Penelope Curry

* Closed Nov. 3, 1974 after limited engagement of 32 performances. Returned for spring season (Wednesday, Feb. 28, 1975–March 23, 1975; 31 performances) with 4 additions to the repertoire: "Deuce Coupe II," a revised "Deuce Coupe" (Beach Boys, Twyla Tharp), "Pas des Deesses" (John Field, Robert Joffrey), *NY PREMIERE* of "The Big City" (Alexander Tansman, Kurt Jooss), and "Jeu de Cartes" (Stravinsky, John Cranko; Staged by Georgette Isinguirides, and re-staged by Hiller Huhn).
Additions to the company were Ingrid Fraley, Miyoko Kato, Gay Wallstrom, Dermot Burke, and Michael Tipton. Beatriz Rodriguez was on leave, and Dennis Wayne left to join ABT

Herbert Migdoll, Martha Swope Photos

Top Left: Charthel Arthur, William Whitener in "The Big ◀
Below: Russell Sultzbach, Ted Nelson in "The Relativit
of Icarus"

"Deuce Coupe II"

"Trinity" Above: "Pulcinella" Top: Charthel Arthur,
Denise Jackson, Burton Taylor, Francesca Corkle
in "Pas des Deesses"

"The Green Table"
Top: "The Clowns"

"Jeu de Cartes" Top: (L) Christian Holder, Burton Taylor, Beatriz Rodriguez, Jan Hanniford in "The Moor's Pavane"
(R) Denise Jackson, Gregory Huffman in "Remembrances"

CITY CENTER JOFFREY BALLET

Donna Cowen, Dennis Wayne in "Secret Places"
Top: "Interplay"

Rebecca Wright, Christian Holder in "Valentine"

Kevin McKenzie, Pamela Nearhoof, Robert Thomas in "Monotones" Top: (L) Charthel Arthur in
"William Tell Variations" (R) Denise Jackson, Paul Sutherland in "Kettentanz"

CITY CENTER JOFFREY BALLET

Burton Taylor, Rebecca Wright in "Monotones"
Gregory Huffman, Starr Danias in "Le Beau Danube"

Ann Marie DeAngelo in "The Relativity of Icarus"

"Parade" *Fred Fehl Photo* **Top:** "Moves" *Herbert Migdoll Photo*

CITY CENTER JOFFREY BALLET

CITY CENTER 55th STREET THEATER
Opened Tuesday, November 19, 1974.*
Hurok presents:

THE ROYAL SWEDISH BALLET

Artistic Director, James Moore; Conductors, Bjorn Hallman, Thomas Schuback; Administrator, Veit Bethke; Ballet Master, Frank Schaufuss; Ballet Mistress, Jean Geddis-Zetterberg; Artistic Advisers-Repetiteurs, Yvonne Brosset, Berit Skold; Choreologist, Agneta Stjerniof; Technical Manager, Jan Johansson; Pianists, Emil Lasko, Julius Jacobsen; Lighting Director-Production Supervisor, Gilbert V. Hemsley, Jr.

COMPANY

PRINCIPALS: Gerd Andersson, Yvonne Brosset, Maria Lang, Kerstin Lidstrom, Berit Skold, Astrid Struwer, Walter Bourke, Jens Graff, Nils-Ake Haggbom, Verner Klavsen, Per Arthur Segerstrom

SOLOISTS: Anneli Alhanko, Lillemor Arvidsson, Ella-Britt Hammarberg, Hervor Sjostrand, Markku Heinonen, Istvan Kisch, Peder Lewn, Aulis Peltonen, Klas Rickman, Nisse Winquist

CORPS: Viola Aberle, Ing-Marie Bjurstrom, Isobell Bude, Ann-Catherine Bystrom-Videau, Barbro Carles, Maria Ericson, Karin Grimma, Rosy Jauckens, Karin Jekell, Pia Kuumola, Kristin Kage, Lisbeth Larsson, Elina Lehto, Margareta Lindstrom, Annika Lof, Mia Loof, Helena Nydahl, Helene Perback, Margareta Reini, Marie-Louise Sid, Charlotte Stalhammer, Ann-Berit Sorensen, Marie-Louise Waldenstrom, Birgitta Wisth, Solange MacArthur, Rolf Andersson, Serge Bonnafoux, Dmitry Cheremeteff, Ingemar Gustafsson, Par Isberg, Nils Johansson, Jeremy N. Leslie-Spinks, Charles Mudry, Pasi Nieminen, Guy Pontecorvo, Tino Rellos, Niels Siemonsen, Matz Skoog, Per-Birger Stenudd, Vasil Tinterov, Mats Wegmann

REPERTOIRE

"The Consort" (Elizabeth Songs, Eliot Feld), "Miss Julie" (Ture Rangstrom, Birgit Cullberg), "Gaite Parisienne" (Jacques Offenbach, Leonide Massine), "Swan Lake" (Tchaikovsky, Natalie Conus after Petipa-Ivanov), "Konservatoriet" (H. S. Paulli, August Bournonville), "Pas de Deux for Grand Tarantella" (Louis Gottschalk, Walter Bourke), "Pas de Deux for Romeo and Juliet" (Prokofiev, Kenneth MacMillan), "Embrace Tiger and Return to Mountain" (Morton Subotnick, Glen Tetley), "The Sleeping Beauty Act III" (Tchaikovsky, Ulf Gadd-Bjorn Homgren)

Company Manager: John H. Wilson
Press: Sheila Porter, Robert Weiss, Ruth Cage
Stage Managers: Per Mankeus, Staffan Sollscher, David Thurow

* Closed Nov. 24, 1974 after limited engagement of 8 performances.

"The Consort" Top Right: **Markku Heinonen, Gerd Andersson in "Miss Julie"**

Kerstin Lidstrom, Jens Graff, Maria Lang in "Konservatoiret" Top: (L) Maria Lang, Walter Bourke in "Grand Tarantella" (R) Gerd Andersson, Nils-Ake Haggbom in "Embrace Tiger"

ROYAL SWEDISH BALLET

Kerstin Lidstrom. Klas Rickman in "Gaite Parisienne" Top: (L) Per Arthur Segerstrom, Anneli Alhanko in "Sleeping Beauty" (R) Gerd Andersson, Per Arthur Segerstrom in "Gaite Parisienne"

Lillemor Arvidsson, Per Arthur Segerstrom, Ann-Berit Sorencen in "Swan Lake" Top: (L) Maria Lang, Nils-Ake Haggbom in "Swan Lake" Below: "Swan Lake" (R) Maria Lang, Nils-Ake Haggbom in "Swan Lake"

ROYAL SWEDISH BALLET

ALVIN AILEY CITY CENTER DANCE THEATER

Artistic Director-Choreographer, Alvin Ailey; General Manager, Ivy Clarke; Associate Artistic Director-Ballet Master, Ali Pourfarrokh; Assistant Ballet Master, Dudley Williams; Musical Director-Conductor, Howard Roberts; Associate Conductor, Tibor Pusztai; Lighting Supervisor, Chenault Spence; Wardrobe, Gloria Scott, Duane Talley; Administrative Assistant, Lois Framhein

COMPANY

Charles Adams, Nerissa Barnes, Enid Britten, Masazumi Chaya, Ulysses Dove, Judith Jamison, Melvin Jones, Mari Kajiwara, Linda Kent, Bernard Lias, Jodi Moccia, Michihiko Oka, Kenneth Pearl, Cynthia Penn, Kelvin Rotardier, Beth Shorter, Warren Spears, Estelle Spurlock, Clive Thompson, Sylvia Waters, Elbert Watson, Dudley Williams, Donna Wood, Peter Woodin, Sara Yarborough, Tina Yuan
GUEST ARTISTS: Brother John Sellers, George Tipton, Cynthia Clarey, Alan Baker, John Morrison

REPERTOIRE

"Fanga" (Traditional, Pearl Primus), "Blues Suite" (Traditional, Ailey), "The Wedding" (Traditional, Primus), "Cry" (Coltrane-Nyro-Voices of Harlem, Ailey), "Rainbow 'Round My Shoulder" (Arranged, McKayle), "Revelations" (Traditional, Ailey), "Choros" (Gagliano, Dunham), "The Road of the Phoebe Snow" (Ellington-Strahorn, Beatty), "Streams" (Kabelac, Ailey), "Journey" (Ives, Trisler), "Carmina Burana" (Orff, Butler), "Dance for Six" (Vivaldi, Trisler), "Missa Brevis" (Kodaly, Limon), "Hidden Rites" (Sciortino, Ailey), "According to Eve" (Crumb, Butler), *Company Premieres* of "Feast of Ashes" (Surinach, Ailey; Costumes, Jac Venza; Lighting, Thomas Skelton) on Dec. 10, 1974, "Portrait of Billie" (Songs of Billie Holiday, John Butler; Costumes, Normand Maxon; Lighting, Shirley Prendergast) on Dec. 3, 1974. *WORLD PREMIERE* of "Nocturne" (Yusef Lateef, John Jones; Costumes, John Jones; Lighting, Chenault Spence) on Dec. 12, 1974.

Production Manager: William Hammond
Press: Howard Atlee, Meg Gordean
Stage Managers: William Burd, Donald Moss

* Closed Dec. 22, 1974 after limited engagement of 24 performances. Returned Tuesday, April 15, 1975 for 24 performances, closing May 4, 1975. Additions to the company were Sarita Allen and Christopher Aponte. Additions to the repertoire were: "Love Songs" (Selected, Ailey), *Company Premiere* of "After Eden" (Lee Hoiby, John Butler) on Apr. 17, 1975.
WORLD PREMIERES: On April 15, 1975 "The Mooche" (Duke Ellington, Alvin Ailey; Costumes, Randy Barcelo; Decor, Rouben Ter-Arutunian; Lighting, Chenault Spence); on Apr. 22, 1975 "Night Creature" (Duke Ellington, Alvin Ailey; Costumes, Jane Greenwood; Lighting, Chenault Spence)

Kenn Duncan, Johan Elbers, Fred Fehl, Jack Mitchell Photos

Estelle Spurlock, Judith Jamison, Sarita Allen, Sara Yarborough in "The Mooche" Top Right: Judith Jamison, Kelvin Rotardier in "Portrait of Billie"

Clive Thompson, Sara Yarborough in "Feast of Ashes"

Sarita Allen, Masazumi Chaya, Enid Britten, Tina Yuan, Estelle Spurlock in "Night Creature" Top: (L) Sara Yarborough in"Cry" (R) Kelvin Rotardier, Tina Yuan, Dudley Williams in "Night Creature"

ALVIN AILEY CITY CENTER DANCE THEATER

Tina Yuan, Donna Wood, Ulysses Dove
in "Feast of Ashes" Top: "Missa Brevis"

Sara Yarborough, Judith Jamison
in "Carmina Burana"

71

Elbert Watson, Melvin Jones, Michihiko Oka, Ulysses Dove in "Rainbow Round My Shoulder" Top: (L) "Rainbow . . (R) "Revelations"

ALVIN AILEY CITY CENTER DANCE THEATER

azumi Chaya, Donna Wood, Kenneth Pearl in "Blues Suite" Top: (L) Clive Thompson, Tina Yuan in "Hidden Rites" (R) Charles Adams, Masazumi Chaya, Jodi Moccia, Michihiko Oka in "Feast of Ashes"

35th ANNIVERSARY GALA

Director, Donald Saddler; Conductors, Akira Endo, David Gilbert; Lighting, Nananne Porcher; Chairman, Mrs. William Zeckendorf, Jr.; Stage Managers, Dan Butt, Jerry Rice, Bentley Roton

PROGRAM

Overture: "Polonaise" by Frederic Chopin
"*Nocturne from Les Sylphides*" (Chopin, Fokine) danced by Karena Brock, Hilda Morales, Marianna Tcherkassky, John Prinz, and Amy Blaisell, Janet Shibata, and Misses Ashton, Frazer, Harvey, Johansson, Jones, Kovak, Kuchera, Maule, Mayer, Popeleski, Provancha, Rhodes, Warner, Wesche
"*Grand Pas de Deux from Don Quixote*" (Minkus, Petipa) danced by Eleanor D'Antuono and Ted Kivitt
"*Fancy Free*" (Bernstein, Robbins) danced by Fernando Bujones, Buddy Balough, Terry Orr
"*Rose Adagio from Princess Aurora*" (Tchaikovsky, Dolin-Petipa) danced by Cynthia Gregory and Igor Youskevitch, Andre Eglevsky, Scott Douglas, Gayle Young
"*Three Virgins and a Devil*" (Respighi, deMille) danced by Sallie Wilson, Ruth Mayer, Hilda Morales, Yurek Lazowski, William Carter
"*Concerto*" (Shostakovich, MacMillan) danced by Natalia Makarova and Ivan Nagy
"*The River*" (Ellington, Ailey): "Vortex" danced by Eleanor D'Antuono, "Riba (Mainstream)" danced by Kirk Peterson, Rodney Gustafson, Kenneth Hughes, Charles Maple, Dennis Marshall, Michael Owen, Kevin Self, Clark Tippet, Melissa Hale, Cynthia Harvey, Francia Kovak, Sara Maule, Leigh Provancha, Cathryn Rhodes, Giselle Roberge, Sandall Whitaker
Miss Agnes de Mille
"*Etudes*" (Riisager, Lander) Opening Barres danced by Deborah Dobson, Ruth Mayer, Maria Youskevitch, Elizabeth Ashton, Melissa Hale, Susan Jones, Linda Kuchera, Sara Maule, Jolinda Menendez, Leigh Provancha, Cathryn Rhodes, Patricia Wesche
"*Grand Pas de Deux from The Nutcracker*" (Tchaikovsky, Ivanov) danced by Marianna Tcherkassky and Fernando Bujones
"*Prologue from Romeo and Juliet*" (Delius, Tudor) danced by Sono Osato and Hugh Laing
"*Miss Julie*" (Rangstrom, Cullberg) "Kitchen Scene" danced by Cynthia Gregory, Erik Bruhn and Sallie Wilson
"*Pas de Deux from Le Corsaire*" (Adam, Nureyev after Petipa) danced by Gelsey Kirkland and Mikhail Baryshnikov
"*Pillar of Fire*" (Schoenberg, Tudor) danced by Lucia Chase, Nora Kaye, Antony Tudor, Hugh Laing, Elizabeth Ashton and Company
"*Spring Waters Pas de Deux*" (Rachmaninov, Messerer) danced by Natalia Makarova and Ivan Nagy
"*Etudes*" (Finale) danced by Eleanor D'Antuono, Ted Kivitt, Jonas Kage, and Company

**Top Right: Hilda Morales, Ruth Mayer, Agnes de Mille
Below: Elizabeth Ashton, Lucia Chase, Nora Kaye**

Scott Douglas, Igor Youskevitch,
Cynthia Gregory, Andre Eglevsky

Hugh Laing, Sono Osato Above: Fernando Bujones, Ter
Orr, Buddy Balough, Jerome Robbins, John Kriza, Harold

CITY CENTER 55th STREET THEATER
Opened Tuesday, February 11, 1975.*
Hurok presents:

BALLET FOLKLORICO OF MEXICO

General Director-Choreographer, Amalia Hernandez; Director, Norma Lopez Hernandez; Artistic Coordinator, Jose Villaneuva; Costumes, Delfina Vargas, Dasha, Jose Gomez Rosas, Carlos Ochoa; Scenic Design, Robin Bond, Jose Gomez Rosas; Lighting Design, Gilbert V. Hemsley

DANCERS

Fatima Alonso, Argel Alvarado, Maria Del Carmen Cardenas, Maria Teresa Chong, Elsa Maria Garcia, Patricia De Lima, Maria Elia Macias, Haydee Maldonado, Maria de Carmen Molina, Maria Morales, Aida Polanco, Eva Rodriguez, Christine Stegar, Esther Vizcarra, Jose Santa Cruz, Miguel Cano, Nestor Castelan, Emilio Ceron, Francisco Cruz, Salvador Delgado, Alfredo Espinoza, Jose Manuel Esquivel, Canuto Garcia, Mario Gardia, Jorge Francisco Garduno, Carlos Ochoa, Guillermo Pensado, David Rodriguez, Eduardo Valasquez

PROGRAM

"Los Concheros," "Chiapas," "The Zacatecans," "Fiesta in Veracruz," "Los Matachines," "Juegos," "El Venado," "Jalisco"

Company Manager: Kurt Neumann
Press: Sheila Porter, Robert Weiss
Stage Manager: David Thurow

* Closed Feb. 24, 1975 after limited engagement of 16 performances.

Right: "Zacatecas" Top: "Los Matachines"

Elizabeth Keen

DOWNSTAIRS AT CITY CENTER
February 15–16, 21–22, 1975 (4 performances)
Directional Concepts Dance Theatre Foundation presents:

ELIZABETH KEEN DANCE COMPANY

Director-Choreographer, Elizabeth Keen; Technical Director, Jim Harrison; Costumes, Whitney Blausen

COMPANY

Elizabeth Keen

Janis Ansley
Avi Davis
Jennifer Donohue

Dalienne Majors
Michael Rivera
Ted Striggles

PROGRAM: "Open Parentheses," "Pale Cool—Pale Warm" (Meyer Kupferman), "Close Parentheses," "A Polite Entertainment for Ladies and Gentlemen" (Stephen Foster): Gentility, Regret, Patriotism, Adoration, Sweetness, Sobriety, Coquetry, Civility, Beauty, Camaraderie, "Dancing to Records" (Elton John): The Choreographer Speaks, The Basic Pulse, The Intrinsic Meaning, The Cultural Roots, Societal Roles, The Sincere Truth

DANCE PROGRAMS AT BROOKLYN ACADEMY OF MUSIC

BROOKLYN ACADEMY OF MUSIC
November 14–17, 1974*
The Brooklyn Academy of Music and the Pennsylvania Ballet Association present:

PENNSYLVANIA BALLET

Founder-Executive Artistic Director, Barbara Weisberger; Associate Artistic Directors-Choreographers, Benjamin Harkarvy, Robert Rodham; Music Director, Maurice Kaplow; Ballet Mistress, Fiona Fuerstner; Lighting Designer, Nicholas Cernovitch; President-General Manager, Richard E. LeBlond, Jr.; Associate General Manager, Timothy Duncan; Press, Craig Palmer, Elizabeth Clure, Carol Jennings; Stage Managers, Jane Clegg, David K. H. Elliott; Costume Supervisor, E. Huntington Parker; Wardrobe Mistress, Lillian Avery; Production Assistant, Peter Dudley; Assistant Conductor, Daniel Forlano.

COMPANY

PRINCIPALS: Alba Calzada, Joanne Danto, Fiona Fuerstner, David Kloss, Michelle Lucci, Keith Martin, Lawrence Rhodes, Barbara Sandonato
SOLOISTS: Marcia Darhower, Dane LaFontsee, Laurence Matthews, Gretchen Warren
CORPS: Sandra Applebaum, Dana Arey, Christina Bernal, Enid Britten, Karen Brown, Kimberly Dye, David Jordan, Barry Leon, Remus Marcu, Barbarajean Martin, Anya Patton, Reva Pincusoff, Richard Rein, Ramon Rivera, Constance Ross, Janek Schergen, Missy Yancey, Linda Zettle
GUEST ARTISTS: Gelsey Kirkland, Mikhail Baryshnikov

REPERTOIRE

"Serenade" (Tchaikovsky, Balanchine), "Zig Zag" (Stravinsky, Lubovitch), "The Moor's Pavane" (Purcell, Limon), "Concerto Barocco" (Bach, Balanchine), "Grand Pas Espagnol" (Harkarvy), "Time Passed Summer" (Tchaikovsky, Harkarvy), *NY PREMIERES* of "The American Rhapsody" (George Gershwin, Robert Rodham), "Solo for Voice I" (John Cage, Hans van Manen), and on Nov. 16, 1974 Guest Artists Mikhail Baryshnikov and Gelsey Kirkland danced the "Don Quixote Pas de Deux."
* The company returned March 13–16, 1975 performing "Madrigalesco" (Vivaldi, Harkarvy), "Concerto Grosso" (Handel, Charles Czarny), "Recital for Cello and Eight Dancers" (Bach, Harkarvy), "Opus Lemaitre" (Bach, van Manen), "After Eden" (Lee Hoivy, John Butler), "Scotch Symphony" (Mendelssohn, Balanchine), and *NY PREMIERE* of "Adagio Hammerklavier" (Beethoven, Hans van Manen)

Right: "Time Passed Summer"
Above: Lawrence Rhodes, Alba Calzada
in "Grand Pas Espagnol"

Mikhail Baryshnikov, Gelsey Kirkland

"Concerto Barocco"

BROOKLYN ACADEMY OF MUSIC
November 7–10, 1974 (4 performances)

HOUSE PARTY
with
THE AMONG COMPANY

Choreography, Carolyn Brown; Film, James Klosty; Sound, Maggi Payne; Lighting, Richard Nelson; Masks, Carl Hecker; Stage Manager, Kitzi Becker

COMPANY

Jumay Chu	Joyce Morgenroth
Ellen Cornfield	Ellen Saltonstall
Ann Darby	Wendy Rogers
Ellen Likwornik	Ellen Webb

James Klosty Photo

"House Party"

Anne Sahl, Eva Gruber, Laurie McKirahan, Rudy Perez in "New Annual" Above: Anne Sahl, Steve Witt, Barbara Roan in "Arcade"

BROOKLYN ACADEMY OF MUSIC
November 21–24, 1974 (4 performances)
The Brooklyn Academy of Music presents:

RUDY PEREZ DANCE THEATER

Direction, Choreography, Sound Collages, Rudy Perez; Lighting Designer-Production Stage Manager, Chip Largman; Assistant to Mr. Perez, David Varney; Technical Assistants, Ken Merkel, Ruis Woertendyke; Audio, John Moore; Press, Charles Ziff

COMPANY
Rudy Perez

Barbara Roan	David Varney
Laura McKirahan	Anne Sahl
Steve Witt	Fern Zand
Eva Grubler	Bill Bass

REPERTOIRE: "Running Board for a Narrative," "Monumental Exchange," "Panorama," "Arcade," "New Annual", and *NY PREMIERE* of "Pedestrian Mall"

Johan Elbers Photos

BROOKLYN ACADEMY OF MUSIC
February 27–March 2, 1975
The Brooklyn Academy of Music presents:

KEI TAKEI'S MOVING EARTH
in
LIGHT

A Series of Nine Works; Choreographed by Kei Takei; Music by Geki Koyama (Part II), Lloyd Ritter (Parts III, IV, VII, VIII), Marcus Parsons III (Parts V, VI), Jacques Coursil (Part VI), Maldwyn Pate (Part VII); Technical Director, Vincent Lalomia; Management, Richard Brown, Mara Greenberg, Mathias Thim; Lighting Design, Vincent Lalomia; Set, Maxine Klein; Executive Producer, Maldwyn Pate; Stage Managers, Vincent Winter, Richard Hoover

COMPANY

Abel, Margo Bassity, Amy Berkman, Carmen Belichat, Tone Blevins, Alice Duskey, Ellen Feder, Janna Jensen, Richmond Johnstone, Yukiko Iino, Michael Kasper, Kathy Kramer, Regine Kunzle, John de Marco, Elsi Miranda, Barbara Mitsueda, Wendy Osserman, John Parton, Maldwyn Pate, Joe Ritter, Joan Schwartz, Kei Takei, Laurie Uprichard, Howard Vichinsky, John Vinton, Annetta Wade

Kei Takei in "Light"

BROOKLYN ACADEMY OF MUSIC
April 3–6, 1975

The Brooklyn Academy of Music presents:

LAURA DEAN and DANCE COMPANY
STEVE REICH and MUSICIANS
in
"Drumming"

(Names of company not submitted)

Left Center: Laura Dean and Company in "Drumming" (Babette Mangolte Photo)

BROOKLYN ACADEMY OF MUSIC
Sunday, May 25, 1975
Destiné Dance Foundation Ltd. presents:

JEAN-LÉON DESTINÉ
AFRO-HAITIAN DANCE COMPANY

Artistic Director-Choreographer, Jean-Léon Destiné; Costumes, Ellie Antoine, Ajaibo Walrond; Wardrobe-Technical Assistant, Barbara Fielding; Audio Assistant, Ernest Destiné; Headpieces, Georges Mills

COMPANY

Ajaibo Walrond, Marianne Marvellia, Audrey Mason, Benjamin Sterlin, Louines Louinis, Carolyn Clemons, Linda Lindsey, Melvada Hughes, Priscilla Lenes, Laverne Wood, Melvina Diggs, drummers Alphonse Cimber, Louis Celestin, Jacques Succes, percussionists Albert Louisjeune, Jean Remy
GUEST ARTISTS: Gerald Dupervil, Le Super Jazz des Jeunes, Myriam Dorisme, Carlo Destiné

PROGRAM

"Village Festival," "Baptism of the Drum," "Spider Dance," "Yoruba Bakas," "African Suite," "Brazilero," "Caribbean Bamboche," and PREMIERE of "Le Serment du Bois Caiman"

Jean-Leon Destine in "Le Serment"

CHARLES WEIDMAN
and
THEATRE DANCE COMPANY

EXPRESSION OF TWO ARTS THEATRE
Performances on weekends for 48 weeks during the year
Artistic Director-Choreographer, Charles Weidman; Administrative Assistant, Dennis Kear; Sound, Paul Spong; Stage Manager, Lee Hopkins; Costumes, Charles Weidman, Janet Towner; Lighting, Patrika Brown

COMPANY

Charles Weidman, Janet Towner, Barry Barychko, Robert Kosinski, Karen Mullin, Elyse Chaskes, Jerianne Heimendinger, Catlin Cobb, Pamela Valente, Dennis Kear, Debbie Carr, Irene Porretto, Nina Cohen, Joenine Roberts, Max Schufer, Martha Karess, Scott Volk, Rebecca Kelly, Joanne Kaczynsky, Roger Robichaud

REPERTOIRE

"Adagio for Strings," "Opus 51," "Fables for Our Time" (Miller), "Submerged Cathedral," "Bargain Counter," "Christmas Oratorio" (Bach), "Lynchtown" (Engel), "Letter to Mrs. Bixby" (Hindemith-Nowak), "Easter Oratorio" (Bach), "St. Matthew's Passion" (Bach), "A House Divided" (Lionel Nowak), "Gymnopedies Suite" (Satie), "Soledad," "Brahms Waltzes," "Dialogue—Situation Two" (Bloch), and *PREMIERE* of "Visualization or From a Farm in New Jersey" (A Tribute to Ruth St. Denis)

Andy Sealfon Photos

**Right: Charles Weidman as Lincoln
in "A House Divided"**

"St. Matthew's Passion"

Janet Towner, Barry Barychko
in "Visualization. . . ."

CHOREOGRAPHERS THEATRE (CT)
ChoreoConcerts & Critiques

Director, Laura Foreman; Administrative Coordinators, Donna Moore, Jane D. Schwartz; Lighting Designer, Cheryl Thacker; Stage Manager, Lauren Barnes; Electrician, Nancy Offenhauser; Sound, Hank O'Neal; Technical Assistant, Charles Hyman; Program Coordinators, Laura Foreman, Phyllis Lamhut; Discussion Coordinators, Frances Alenikoff, Dick Bull, Phyllis Lamhut, Gus Solomons, Jr.

NEW SCHOOL FOR SOCIAL RESEARCH
(All-premiere-all-commissioned series)
Saturday, October 12, 1974

"postludes" (John Watts, Laura Foreman-Graciela Torino) danced by Judy Pisarro, Nancy Salmon, Satoru Shimazaki; "Late Show" choreographed and danced by Phyllis Lamhut; "Cloister" (Choreography, Emery Hermans) danced by Susan Creitz, Emery Hermans, Fred Myers; "Station" (Stephen Smoliar, Cliff Keuter; Costumes, Karla Wolfangle, John Dayger) danced by Joan Finkelstein, Ellen Jacob, Ellen Kogan, Elina Mooney, Karla Wolfangle, John Dayger, Bill DeYoung, Ernest Pagnano
Saturday, October 19, 1974

"geode" (James Buckley, Sara Shelton) danced by Bob Beswick, Christine Eccleston, Reenie Linden, Patrick Ragland; "Untitled Duet" (Choreography, Phoebe Neville) danced by Edward Spena and Phoebe Neville; "Chapter One" (Sound and Choreography, Gus Solomons, Jr.; Costumes, Eva Tsug) performed by Santa Aloi, Ruedi Brack, Douglas Nielsen, Gus Solomons, Jr. as Martinez; "Octopus - 1. Whale, 2. Hubbahubba & the Boohoos" (Tape, Fanny Logos; Choreography, Douglas Dunn) performed by Douglas Dunn, Epp Kotkas, Sara Rudner, Howard Vichinsky, David Woodberry
Saturday, October 26, 1974

"In the Courtyard, singing low songs . . . and even thinking . . . dancing" (Choreography, Janet Soares; Lighting, Astrid Garcia; Costumes, Meg Kozera, Dalienne Majors) danced by Emily Andrews, Shaw Bronner, Jessica Fogel, Jane Hedal, Carol Hess, Kate Johnson, Hannah Kahn, Linda Roberts, Martha Wiseman; "I Don't Want to Kiss Your Mouth of Salt" (Choreography, Frances Alenikoff; Set, Ray Grist; Costumes, Sharon Weaver) danced by Frances Alenikoff, Carol-rae Kraus, Dalienne Majors; "The Terrible Fate of an Ill-Begotten Muse" a fantasy by Carolyn Lord realized with Gordon Bressac; "Pale-Cool, Pale-Warm" (Meyer Kupferman, Elizabeth Keen) danced by Janis Ansley, Avi Davis, Jennifer Donohue, Dalienne Majors, Michael Rivera, Roger Preston Smith
Saturday, November 2, 1974

"Domaine" (Essay, F. M. Esfandiary; Choreography, Stuart Hodes) danced by Michael Bluc Aiken, Erica Eigenberg, Lorn MacDougal, Cynthia May, and students from NYU School of the Arts Dance Department; "The Universe on the Head of a Pin" (Pachelbel, Sally Bowden) danced by Sally Bowdon, Scott Caywood; "The Journey" (Choreography, Deborah Jowitt) performed by Peggy Hackney, Irene Meltzer, Vicki Shick, Maris Wolff; "Small Step Giant Leap" (Bull-NASA, Richard Bull) danced by Cynthia Novack, Susannah Payton

Oleaga Photos

Top Right: Judy Pisarro, Satoru Shimazaki in "postludes" Below: Phyllis Lamhut in "Late Show"

Cynthia Novack, Susannah Payton
in "Small Step Giant Leap"

CHOREOGRAPHERS THEATRE
ASSOCIATED PRODUCTIONS

HENRY STREET SETTLEMENT
June 11–14, 1974 (5 performances)

Sara Shelton & Company in "The Rosenfelds" (Choreography, Sara Shelton; Technical Director, C. Richard Mills) performed by Sara Shelton, Christine Eccleston, Jeff Eichen Wald, Reenie Linden, Jeff Maer, Patrick Ragland, Philip Tietz

NYU SCHOOL OF THE ARTS
August 29 & 30, 1974 (4 performances)

The Ad Hoc Teacups Dance Company in "After the Teacups" (Choreography, Stuart Hodes; Assistant, Barbara Boyle; Technical Director, William Kleinsmith; Music, Francis Thorne) performed by Gary Cowen, Louise Frank, Edward Bilanchone, Barbara Boyle, Esther Chaves, Linda Diamond, Michael Ebbin, Judith Jenkins, Ceth Walsh, Jack Walsh; "Abyss" (Margo Richter, Stuart Hodes) performed by Jerel Hilding, Jody Wintz, Michael Bjerknes, Philip Jerry, Andrew Levinson

AMERICAN THEATRE LAB
March 7–9, 1975 (4 performances)

The Laura Foreman Dance Theatre (Director-Choreographer, Laura Foreman; Associate Director, Graciela Torino; Company Manager, Donna Moore; Lighting, Cheryl Thacker; Stage Manager, Rachel Lampert; Sound, Hank O'Neal) in "postludes" (Sound, John Watts) danced by Judy Pisarro, Nancy Salmon, Satoru Shimazaki; "a deux" danced by David Malamut, Satoru Shimazaki; "glass and shadows" (Sound-Film, Hank O'Neal; Costumes, Sharon Weaver) danced by Diane Grumet, Leslie Innis, Judy Pisarro, Nancy Salmon, Satoru Shimazaki, Carol Volanth, Susan Whelan

AMERICAN THEATRE LAB
March 14–16, 1975 (4 performances)

Dances by Beverly Brown (Choreography, Beverly Brown; Lighting, Cheryl Thacker; Stage Manager, Kate Elliott), "Morning Call" choreographed and danced by Anthony LaGiglia and Beverly Brown; "Glympses of When" (Frank Martin) danced by Beverly Brown; "Season of Earth Hush" (Eleanor Hovda; Costumes, Raya; Paintings, Ray Said) danced by Natalie Richman, Lillo Way, Beverly Brown; "Life in a Drop of Pond Water" (Skip LaPlante, Beverly Brown; Design, Raya) danced by Debbie Andres, Ruth Botchan, Whit Carman, Eli Pollack, Sara Vogeler, Beverly Brown, "Cloudspeed" (Gerald Lindahl) danced by Eli Pollack and Beverly Brown

AMERICAN THEATRE LAB
March 21–23, 1975 (4 performances)

Dances/Janet Soares (Choreography, Janet Soares; Sound, Hank O'Neal; Lighting, Jennifer Herrick Jebens; Stage Manager, Francis Roefaro): "Hannah, Bill, Jessica, Jane" (Milton Babbitt, Janet Soares; Costumes, Meg Kozera; Premiere) danced by Jessica Fogel, Jane Hedal, Hannah Kahn, William Belle; "Workprints" (Sound, Mark Seiden; Janet Soares) danced by Carol Hess, Kate Johnson, Hannah Kahn, Linda Roberts; "Bentwood Pieces" (Beethoven, Soares) danced by Carol-rae Kraus, Leigh Warren; "singing low songs . . . and even thinking . . . dancing" (Janet Soares) danced by Emily Andrews, Shaw Bronner, Jessica Fogel, Carol Hess, Kate Johnson, Hannah Kahn, Linda Roberts, Martha Wiseman

Oleaga Photos

Top Right: Sara Vogeler, Ruth Botchan, Debbi Andres in "Life in a Drop of Pond Water" Below: Satoru Shimazaki, Leslie Innis, Carol Volanth, Nancy Salmon, Diane Grumet in "glass and shadows"

Bottom: Emily Andrews, Shaw Bronner, Jessica Fogel, Jane Hedal, Carol Hess, Kate Johnson, Hannah Kahn, Linda Roberts, Martha Wiseman in "singing low songs . . . and even thinking . . . dancing"

THE CUBICULO

Artistic Director, Philip Meister; Managing Director, Elaine Sulka; Program Director, Maurice Edwards, Pamela Hare; General Manager, Albert Schoemann; Resident Designer, Brian Jayne, Press, Pamela Hare

THE CUBICULO
June 3–4, 1974
AN EVENING OF DANCE BY LIANNE STOFSKY with Gail Kachadurian, Judith Schmukler, Michael Feinman, Marina Pricci, Martha Rzasa, Tom Wetmore, performing "Eternity's Faces" (Telleman), "Perimeter" (Tom Johnson-Laura Brittain) choreographed and danced by Laura Brittain, "Some Say Sour.ds Seek Significance," "Tweet for Two" (Bayla), "Edge of the Abyss" (John Gilbert)
June 5–7, 1974 (5 performances)
"Zero Sum" (Choreographed by Frances Alenikoff) and danced by Frances Alenikoff, Kenneth Boys, Kenneth Fischer, Carol-Rae Kraus
June 6–7, 1974
JORGE SAMANIEGO AND DANCE COMPANY: Jorge Samaniego, Christine Ham, Coleen Morse, Kenneth MacDonald, Norma de Luca, Lynn Letko, performing "Energies" (Villa-Lobos-Bachianas), "For Those Who Wear Tunics, and Capezio Dance-Wear" (Balakirev Islamey), "Brahminical" (David Fanshawe)
June 11–12, 1974
SANDRA JAMROG/KEDZIE PENFIELD dancing "Earth Sun Air" (Sheldon-Berde, Carol Boggs) performed by Peggy Hackney, Sandra Jamrog; "Dream until Your Dreams Come True" (Richard Abba) choreographed and performed by Kathy Robens; "Ragtime Dance" (Scott Joplin, Sandra Jamrog) performed by Gail August and Sandra Jamrog; "Two/Three" (Cage, Jamrog) danced by Frederick McKitrick and Sandra Jamrog; "Inside and Out-Entropy" (Joanne Tanner Cooper, Kedzie Penfield) performed by Marilyn Baker, Peggy Hackney, Kedzie Penfield; "Hymn" (Nightingale, Sandra Jamrog)
June 17–18, 1974
SIN CHA HONG choreographed and danced in "Rite," "3, 14159265" Music by Meredith Monk; "Crossroad" danced by Satoru Shimazaki, Ted Dalbotten; "Representing America" (John Lennon, Shelley Dearth) danced by Shelley Dearth, Faye Waisbrot, Richard Arbach, Gabrielle Lansner, Marian Lizzio, Emily Samton; Choreography by Victoria Larrain and danced by Victoria Larraine, Julie Maloney, Jeanne Edelman, Shelly Dearth, Candy Cristaros, Kathy Buchanan, Jeanne Alsen
June 24–25, 1974
LAURA FOREMAN DANCE COMPANY: "a deux" danced by Timothy Haynes and Satoru Shimazuki; WETZIG DANCE COMPANY: Meryl Green, Evelyn Shepard, Judy Lasko, Kathryn Woglom, Betsy Wetzig performing "Bring Your Child" (Wetzig), "Inbetween (a dream of me)" (Carl Michaelson, Wetzig), "Space Cycle" (Wetzig), "Beginning" (Michaelson, Wetzig)
July 1–2, 1974
LAURA FOREMAN DANCE COMPANY: Timothy Haynes, Satoru Shimazaki, Betty Martyn, Risa Steinberg, Fred Mathews, Louis Solino, Frank Colardo dancing "a deux", "Clouds" (Horn, Foreman), "Chasm" (Martinero, Mathews), "Klompy Dance" (Ravel, Martyn), "Moving" (Manchester, Betty Martyn), "The Keepers" (Varese, Mathews)

**Jose Coronado, Rick Hood, Peter Lawrence
in "Vigil"** *(Louis Peres Photo)*

**Hank O'Neal, Satoru Shimazaki, Timothy
Haynes in "a deux"** *(Oleaga Photo)*

THE CUBICULO
July 8–9, 1974
JUDE MORGAN in "Jumpin' Biz," "Held for 8 Years by Telephone," "Box Piece," "Mattock," "Orenda,"
JACK SCALICI In "Walks," "Fisherman," "Girl in the Park"
Wednesday, July 10, 1974
SUMATHY KAUSHAL dancing "Sabhavandana," "Jatiswaram," "Taranga Nritya," "Tillana," "Kalapam," "Ahalya," "Meera Bhajan"
July 12–13, 1974
BRUCE PACOT AND DANCERS: Felice Dalgin, Ellen Ducker, Erica Herman, Nancy Mapother, George Giroiud, dancing "Slow Walking Steps" (Vivaldi), "Trash," "Wheatfields" (Collage tape)
July 19–20, 1974 Cubiculo Dance Theatre VI Part I
LAURA FOREMAN DANCE COMPANY featuring Timothy Haynes and Satoru Shimazaki in "a deux";
RISA STEINBERG and FRED MATHEWS dancing "Chasm" (Martinero, Mathews) and "The Keepers Part II" (Varese, Mathews), KAREN BARRELL and ROLANDO JORIF in "Movie" (Faure, Jorif); DALIENNE MAJORS In "Palindrome" (Tape and Choreography, Majors); "THE EDGE" (Traditional-Eddie Goldman, Anya Allister) danced by Agnes Denis, Linda Dingwall, Gary Easterling, Marjorie Philpot
July 22–23, 1974 Cubiculo Dance Theatre VI Part II
JUDE BARTLETT in "Dedicated" (Traditional, Bartlett); BETSY WETZIG in "Inbetween (My World—My Dream)" (Michaelson, Wetzig); JUDE MORGAN in "Orenda" (Morgan) with Barbra Clay; "Spill" (Evans, Hannah Kahn) danced by Kate Johnson, Dalienne Majors, Catherine Sullivan; THOMAS HOLT DANCERS: Betsy Baron, Lucinda Gehrke, Thomas Holt, Ann Moser, Geraldo Rosario, Allan Seward, Karen Sing, Paulette Taylor, Phillip Tietz, John Wilson, performing "Afterhours in Wonderland"
Wednesday, July 23, 1974
RITHA DEVI dancing "Pushpanjali," "Batu Nritya," "Ashtapadi," "Path-Pallavi," "Ashtapadi," "Gati-Vilasa-Pallavi," "Mahasati"
July 26–27, 1974 Cubiculo Dance Theatre VI Part III
JAN WODYNSKI DANCE COMPANY: Robert Kosinsky and Mike Wodynski in "Tudo" (Jan Wodynski); PEGGY CICIERSKA with David Hill, Ericka Berland in "Vacuum" (Pink Floyd-Martirano, Cicierska); PHOEBE NEVILLE with Christopher Beck, Alison Bradford, Ed Spence in "Cartouche" (Purcell, Neville), and "Memory" (Environment, Neville) with Maurice Edwards; CHRISTOPHER BECK in "Dying Away" (None, Beck); JOSE CORONADO with Peter Lawrence, Ilona Copen, Rich Hood in "Vigil" (Penderecky-Bach, Coronado)
September 23–24, 1974
BEGAM NAJMA AYASHAH dancing "Ganesh Vandana," "Thaat," "Salaami," "Amaad," "Parans," "Thumri," "Ghazal," "Tatkar," "Gath," "Paran"
September 30–October 1, 1974
JOSE CORONADO AND DANCERS: Seth Goldstein, Betsy Baron, Ilona Copen, Jerel Hilding, dancing "Solo from Vigil," "Solo from 3 Pieces for Ellen," "Rose Wound" (Olivas), "The Arena" (Blomdahl) "In a Bed of Faded Roses" (Reynolds), "So Was/So Is/So Be" (Ives)

THE CUBICULO
October 3–5, 1974

THE GREENHOUSE DANCE ENSEMBLE: Beverly Brown, Carol Conway, Nada Reagan, Natalie Richman, Lillo Way, Robert Yohn, dancing "The Product of the Sides" (Choreographed by Carol Conway), "Tryptych" (Amy, Lillo Way), "Windwing" (Choreography, Natalie Richman), "Blued Spaces" (Whiteside, Nada Reagan), "Day in the Lee of April" (Rundle, Robert Yohn)
October 7–8, 1974

BARBARA BERGER AND BETTY SALAMUN DANCE WORKS: "Fleeting/Feeling" (Karlin, Berger) danced by Barbara Berger, Anita Feldman, Betty Salamun; "Laquered Nests" (Collage, Salamun) danced by Betty Salamun; "Dream 1 into 2" (Bach-Elton John, Berger); "Horizon" (Collage, Salamun); "Thunderhead" (Avi Davis, David HB Drake); "Heat Lightning" (Zien, Salamun); "Dusk" danced by Avi Davis, David HB Drake, Betty Salamun
October 10–12, 1974

JAN WODYNSKI DANCE COMPANY: Kathy Eaton, Joanne Edelmann, John Kelly, Robert Kosinski, Julie Maloney, Madeleine Perrone, Jan Wodynski, Mike Wodynski, performing "koreotroniks," "freekwensi," "pit-stop," "five minutes more" (Choreography and Costumes, Jan Wodynski)
October 14–15, 1974

MANJUSRI dancing "Rudra-Madhur," "Lai Harouba," "Gostha Pareng," "Padam," "Navaraska Sloka," "Visva Veena," "Pujarini"
October 17–19, 1974

THE OCTOBER PARADE (Choreographed by Barbara Roan) with members of Dance Works, Inc., and The Blue Mountain Paper Parade, including Irene Feigenheimer, Robert Marinaccio, Laurie Uprichard, Hollyce Yoken, Janna Jensen, Paul Sanchez, Ellen Robbins, Dennis Florio, Michael Kasper, Mary Benson, Jude Bartlett, Tommy Wilkinson, Barbara Roan, Karla Wolfangle, Ruedi Brack, Connie Brunner, Jane Goldstein, Abby Child
October 21–22, 1974

SARA SHELTON AND SIN CHA HONG with Bob Beswick, Christine Eccleston, Patrick Radand, Reenie Linden, Sara Shelton, Bill Bass, Bill Kirkpatrick, John Sillings, Lisa Nalven, Irene O'Brian, Phylis Richmond, dancing "Sketches from Geode" (Shelton), "Solo" (Monk, Hong), "Crossroad" (Licciardello, Hong), "Work in Progress" (Quintiere, Hong)
October 24–26, 1974

SOLO DANCES BY TOBY ARMOUR: "Rattlesnake" (Dupree, Armour), "Winter Pavilion" (Sims, Lois Ginandes), "Trio A" (Yvonne Rainier), "Last News of a Morning Cruise" (Collage, Armour), "Moonlight Sonata" (Beethoven, James Waring), "Heads", "Continued" and "Social Dancing" (all by Armour)
November 18–19, 1974

ROLANDO JORIF DANCE COMPANY: David Lee, Janis Roswick, Rolando Jorif, Maria Bueno, dancing "le violin d'Ingres" (Chopin, Jorif), "Landscape" (Ravel, Jorif), "Luxury I" (Ravel, Jorif)

Rod Rodgers

THE CUBICULO
November 21–23, 1974

ROD RODGERS DANCE COMPANY: Shirley Rushing, Noel Hall, Lynne Elze, Carl Rowe, Thomas Pinnock, Lillie Andrews, Rose Auslander, Joy Graham, Tamara Guillebeaux, Beverly Mann, Sheryl Sedlecek, Stephanie Terry, Sharon Wong, performing "Consumation" (Gladys Knight and the Pips-Nina Simone, Noel Hall), "Star's Dance" (Ringo Starr, Rael Lamb), "Fetish" (Miles Davis, Shirley Rushing), "Intervals" (Percussion, Rod Rodgers), "Survivors" (Jules Moss, Jeanne Moss), "Creature" (Herbie Hancock, Shirley Rushing), "Butterfly" (Subotnick, Rael Lamb)
November 25–26, 1974

PRISCILLA COLVILLE In "Epiphanies" with Ramon Colon and Hannah Kahn, performing "Loss" (T. S. Eliot), "Dirge without Music" (Edna St. Vincent Millay), "Watercurrents," "Dover Beach" (Ives-Mathew Arnold), "rut" (Lewis Carroll), "Scavenger" (Collage-Edna St. Vincent Millay), "Seasons, an Impression" (Bach) (Choreography by Priscilla Colville)
November 28–30, 1974

KATHERINE LITZ DANCE COMPANY: Janice Ansley, Jill Coghlan, Marion DuBois, Grethe Holby, Jeannie Hutchins, Scott Caywood, Bill Maloney, Katherine Litz, dancing "Blood of the Lamb" (Nicolast), "Twilight of a Flower" (Ravel), "Marathon" (Ashley), "Suite Oblique" (Handel), "Daughter of Virtue" (Rachmaninoff), "Fir in the Snow" (Beethoven), "Territory" (Prideaux), "The Fall of the Leaf" (Gottschalk)
February 6–8, 1975
Tuesday, January 28, 1975

DANCES BY VIRGINIA LAIDLAW & ALICE TEIRSTEIN with Jill Feinberg, Kathy Heath, Elissa Kirtzman, Gale Ormiston, Frank Pistritto, Edward Marsan, Valerie Bergman, Linda Caruso Haviland, Kathy Robens, Mei Hsueh Guobis, Raymond Maguire, Marilyn Mazur, Luisa Moore, Mariam Solan, dancing "What's a Nice Girl like you? (Hole in the Wall, Laidlaw), "Trio" (Vivaldi, Teirstein), "Circadian" (Nonesuch, Laidlaw), "Nexus" (Early Brown, Teirstein), "Leisure Dances" (John Lewis-Sergei Natla-Ruth White-Gwendolyn Watson, Teirstein), "Parts" (Sesame Street, Laidlaw) January 30 - February 1, 1975

EMERY HERMANS & DANCERS: Jim Cave, Susan Creitz, Mark Esposito, Beth Goren, Emery Hermans, Carl Pellegrini, Patrick Ragland, Jeanette Stoner, Konstantino Tzoumas, Judy Yardley, dancing "Rooms" (Isham Jones, Hermans), "Moth Danse" (Electronic, Hermans), "The Pallid Horse" (Bach-Cage-Medieval, Hermans)

Katherine Litz

February 3–4, 1975

CANDICE CHRISTAKOS, KATHLEEN HEATH, KATHER-
INE LIEPE with Janis Brenner, Deborah Glaser, Gael Stepanek,
Dianne Bryan, Elyssa Paternoster, Kathleen Colihan, Denise Fer-
retti, Carl Pellegrini, Donna Evans, Rich Hood, performing "Clear
Song" (Hot Tuna, Christakos), "Fritz" (Terry Riley, Heath),
"Aqua" (Hovhaness-Watkins, Liepe), "To Helen a Salute" (Wolf
Cries, Heath), "Journey Two" (Handel, Heath), "Knot" (Balanese,
Liepe), "Firefly" (Collage, Christakos), "Explorations" (Messian,
Liepe), "The Garden Spot" (Villa-Lobos, Liepe)

February 6–8, 1975

JOHN CWIAKALA, GAY DELANGHE, CAROL RICHARD,
SUZANNE WHITE with Holly Bruback, Jan Bufkins, Beth Corn-
ing, Sharon Flack, Army Gincberg, Laura Knott, Carol Richard,
Elizabeth Rogers, Elizabeth Swain, Judy Cassidy, Doe Hughe,
Nancy Powers, Ann Wanamaker, Suzanne White, Sylvie Pinard
Lambert, Ken Marko, David Marshall, Lynn Slaughter Rosenfeld,
Lenore Delanghe, August Delanghe, dancing "Cop de la Bop"
(Charlie Parker, Carol Richard), "Sweet Landskip" (Tape, Suzanne
White), "Brewed" (Terry Riley, John Cwiakala), "Tears or Learning
in the Living Room" (Kenton-Purcell-Telemann, Gay Delanghe)
WORKS BY SUE BARNES-MOORE/MARLEEN PENNISON
with Conni Brunner, Laurie Gittelman, John Moore, Barbara
Salmon, Dede Greene, Susan Okuhara, Jo Susser, Tommy Wilkin-
son, dancing "Bethena" (Scott Joplin, Pennison), "Circumference"
(Sounds, Barnes-Moore), "Solo for an Interrupted Afternoon" (Col-
lage, Barnes-Moore), "Don't Step on the Pavement Cracks" (Tape,
Pennison), "The Keeper" (Tape, Pennison), "Myth" (Hindemith,
Barnes-Moore)

February 13–15, 1975

REYNALDO ALEJANDRO'S SAYAW SILANGANI with Lei
Lynne Doo, Betty Salamun, Ching Valdes, Reynaldo Alejandro,
dancing "Morang Tarjata," "Urduja," "Josephine Bracken" (Stockhausen), "Sisa," "Donya Victorina" (Mackenzie), "Gabriela Silang"
(Harrison)—all choreography by Reynaldo Alejandro

February 17–18, 1975

CHOREOGRAPHY BY FRED MATHEWS: with Christopher
Gillis, Amanda Kreglow, Louis Solino, Risa Steinberg, Fred Math-
ews, dancing "A Siege of Herons Part III" (Xenakis), "Quietus,"
"Chasm" (Martirano), "Amoroso" (Donald Litaker), "Sang-Froid"
(Litaker), "The Keepers" (Varese)

March 25–26, 1975

CHOREOGRAPHY BY SUSAN CREITZ and ANNE MARIE
RIDGWAY with Timothy Crafts, Carl Pellegrini, Gael Stepanek,
Naomi Weinstein, Richard Biles, Janet Katzenberg, Diane Markham, dancing "Singleton" (Max Neuhaus, Creitz), "Ahtram ½mv
²" (Subotnick-Czajkowski, Ridgway), "Sanatana" (Arranged, Rid-
way), "A CREATURE FEATURE piece" (Janet Lemansky,
Creitz)

March 28–29, 1975

CONSORT DANCE ENSEMBLE: Selby Beebe, Myra Hushansky,
Miriam Kenig, Donna Mondanaro, Margaret O'Sullivan, Bobbi
Silvera, and guest reader Rolando Policastro, performing "Millen-
nium" (Collage, Donna Mondanaro), "Stroll" (Ussachevsky, Myra
Hushansky), "Odyssey" (Otto Luening-Halim el Dabh, Mon-
danaro), "Paper Clowns" (Music and Choreography, Donna Mon-
danaro), "Song" (Arnold Schoenberg, Mondanaro), "Encounters"
(Ussachevsky-Xenakis, Hushansky)

March 31, April 1, 1975

CHOREOGRAPHY BY PEGGY CICIERSKA with Erika Ber-
land, Peggy Cicierska, Hedy Weiss, Maris Wolff, Kim Arrow, Vicki
Shick, dancing "Glass" (Philip Glass), "End of Time" (Messiaen),
"Going Going Gone" (Bob Dylan), "Vacuum" (Salvatore Mar-
tirano-Pink Floyd), "Andante Amoroso" (Alban Berg, Anna Sokolow), "The Shoppers" (Chick Corea), "Walking on Gravel"
(Collage), "The Unanswered Question" (Charles Ives)

THE CUBICULO

Friday, April 4, 1975

MAYA KULKARNI and JANAK KHENDRY (Mukta Rathra,
Narrator) dancing "Stotra," "Dasha Avtara," "Jathiswaram,"
"Varnam," "Padam," "Varugalamo," "Thillana," "Kuchipudi,"
"Bhama Kalapam," "Manduka Shabdam"

April 7–8, 1975

NEW YORK MIME DUET (Louis Gilbert and Rene Houtrides)
performing "Balloon," "People and Animals," "Tightrope Walkers,"
"Invitation to the Voyage," "Baseball," "Ocean," "Football," "The
Lion Tamer and the Lion," "Images of Rain"

April 10–12, 1975

CHOREOGRAPHY BY SALLY GROSS with Sally Gross, Sidonia
Gross, Toby Glanternik, Carol Ritter, Jerome Rothenberg (vocal-
ist), performing "Nonesuch," "Bells," "Rope II," "It's O. K.,"
"Sticks I, II, III" (10th Horse), "Transitivity" (Terry Riley), "Small
Visions" (Satie)

Sue Barnes-Moore, John Moore in "Myth"
JFM Studio Photo

Fred Mathews, Risa Steinberg in "Keepers"
Barry Bell Photo

Janak Khendry
O. E. Nelson Photo

DANCE UPTOWN
Fifteenth Series

Director, Janet Soares; Lighting Designer, Dennis Parichy; Stage Managers, Jennifer Herrick Jebens, Sylvia Yoshioka, Mary Bush; Sound, Mark Seiden, Bob Dedrick; Sponsored by Barnard College Theatre Company

MINOR LATHAM PLAYHOUSE
Thursday, September 19, 1974

THE NEW YORK IMPROVISATION ENSEMBLE: Martha Bowers, Dian Dong, Colette Yglesias, Nancy Mapother, Anne Woods, Michael Cava (musician), performing "Focus/Wispen/-Rondo/Daisies Won't Tell" (Direction, Doris Rudko; Founders, Doris Rudko, Noah and Marianna Creshevsky)
September 20–21, 1974

"Fanfare for a Solo Dancer" (Gerard Schwarz, Lillo Way; Costume, Beth Burkhardt) performed by Lillo Way, "Common Ground" (Charles Madden, David Lusby) danced by Janis Ansley and David Lusby, "Spill/Quell" (Bill Evans-Jim Hall, Hannah Kahn; Costumes, Dalienne Majors) danced by Carol Hess, Kate Johnson, Jane Lowe, Catherine Sullivan, "Rags" (Berlin-Mozart-Schubert-Joplin, Linda Roberts) danced by Carol Beskinger, Mary Bruen, June Flanagan, Carla Litvany, Andy Jannetti, George Macaluso, Jim Van Treuren, Martin Van Treuren, Ted Dalbotten
September 27–28, 1974

"Fanfare for a Solo Dancer," "Spill/Quell," The New York Improvisation Ensemble performing "Focus/Wispen/12 Midnight, Rochester, N.Y., October 7, 1973/Rondo" (Noah Creshevsky, Doris Rudko), "Common Ground," "Rags"
Friday, October 4, 1974

Janet Soares and Dancers: Hannah Kahn, Linda Roberts, Jessica Fogel, Carol Hess, Kate Johnson, Martha Wiseman, Jane Hedal, Shaw Bronner, Emily Andrews, Janet Soares, performing "singing low songs . . . and even thinking . . . dancing" (Cat Stevens, Soares; Costumes, Meg Kozera, Dalienne Majors)
Thursday, September 26, 1974

Hannah Kahn and Dancers: Kate Johnson, Dalienne Majors, Catherine Sullivan, Jane Lowe, performing "Spill/Quell" (Evans-Hall, Kahn)
October 2 & 4, 1974

"Wyeth Study" (Sound, Burt Alcantara; Costume, Melissa Greenberg) choreographed and danced by Jennifer Muller, "Apollo and Dionysos: Cheek to Cheek" (Choreographers, James Cunningham, Lauren Persichetti, Costumes, William Florio) performed by James Cunningham and The Acme Dance Company: Raymond Dooley, Barbara Ellman, William Holcomb, Lauren Persichetti, Ted Striggles, Linda Tarney, and friends: Pat Baidi, Jennifer Barr, Robin Becker, Valarie Bergman, Lori Blaustein, Mary Broaddus, Mary Jo Buhl, Linda Cohen, Ruth Diamond, Drew Dreeland, Ellen Ducker, Deborah Dutton, Deborah Kumba Edwards, Felicia Freed, Candace Gilles-Brown, Debbie Glass, Mei Gropus, Melida Gross, Jeffrey Harris, Sally Hechinger, Laurie Herzig, Julie Hymen, Page Jackson, Yvonne Jayne, Bill Kilpatrick, Dawn Klausner, Marion Kwartler, Martha Lask, Claire Le Claire, Lisa Lehman, Holly Ann Lipton, Mei-Ling Louie, Viviane Marescor, Rita Marquez, Sue McDonough, Margaret Palca, Lesley Pratt, Lynn Ritchie, Lisa Salvani, Julie Salwen, Barbara Straus, Rosalind van Stolk, Davida Witaman
October 3 & 5, 1974

"Water Pieces" (Choreography , Deborah Jowitt) danced by Peggy Hackney, Lee Olsen, Vicki Schick, Maris Wolff, Debra Zalkind, Jessica Chao, Susan McDonough, Ruth Susser, Laura Woodard, "No Strings" (Gabriel Faure-David Rose, Daniel Lewis) danced by Teri Weksler, Leigh Warren, Daryl Bratches, Dianne Hulbert, Nancy Scattergood, Andrew Miller, "singing low songs . . . and even thinking . . . dancing" (Stevens, Soares), "Union" (Text, Langston Hughes-Margaret Walker, Dianne McIntyre) danced by Phillip Bond, William Donald, Lonnetta Gaines, Bernadine Jennings

Top Right: Shaw Bronner, Jane Hedal, Hannah Kahn, Kate Johnson, Linda Roberts, Martha Wiseman, Carol Hess in "singing low songs . . . and even thinking . . . dancing" *(Johan Elbers Photo)*

Lauren Persichetti in "Apollo and Dionysos"
Gerry Goodstein Photo

85

MISCELLANEOUS NEW YORK DANCE PROGRAMS

WOLLMAN AUDITORIUM
Saturday, June 1, 1974
The Tagore Society of New York in association with Kazuko Hillyer
International presents:

MANJUSRI CHAKI-SIRCAR

with
Pallabi Bhattacharyya
Gail Gilkey
Ranjabati Sircar
Shikha Roy Choudhury
Ari Darom

PROGRAM: "Songs of Tagore," "Nataraj Bandana," "Nri-
tyargha," "Navarasa Sloka," "Vasudha Bandana," "Pujarini"

Manjusri Chaki-Sircar
Myra Fine Photo

DONNELL LIBRARY CENTER
Tuesday, June 4, 1974*

THE LAURA VELDHUIS DANCE COMPANY

Director-Choreographer, Laura Veldhuis; Designer-Technical
Consultant, Joop Veldhuis

COMPANY

Laura Veldhuis Patrick Hayden
Henry Smith Brigitta Mueller
Ellen Ashcraft Eve Saxon

PROGRAM: "The Mind's Garden" (Britten, Veldhuis), "Walk
Softly" (Stan Kenton, Veldhuis), "The Story of Daniel" (12th Century, Veldhuis; Poetry, W. H. Auden)

* On Thursday, June 13, 1974 the program was repeated at Central
Park Mall Bandshell

Laura Veldhuis in "The Mind's Garden"
Myra Armstrong Photo

THEOSOPHICAL SOCIETY
Wednesday, June 5, 1974*

INDRA-NILA

performing "Mudra—Hands of the Gods," "Maha Ganapati,"
"Shiva Slokam," "Ananda Natanam," "Allarrippu," "Vrittam,"
"Jugath Janani"

* Program was repeated Friday, June 7, 1974 at Wagner College,
and on Friday, June 28, 1974 at Meher Baba House

Indra-nila

JAPAN HOUSE
Wednesday, June 5, 1974
Japan Society presents:

SAEKO ICHINOHE AND COMPANY

Director-Choreographer, Saeko Ichinohe; Lighting Designer-Stage Manager, Edward M. Greenberg; Costumes, Masaaki Kawashima, Dalienne Majors; Pianist, Paul Epstein

COMPANY
Saeko Ichinohe

Peter Sparling	Salli Sillman
Victor Vargas	Diane Reiko Lam
Alma Swartz	Lauren Dong

PROGRAM: An Evening of Modern Dance Inspired by the Japanese Tradition: "Evocation" (Arne Nordheim), "Blue Granite Mappings" (Paul Epstein, Peter Sparling), "Goza" (Alessandro Marcello), "Woman Who Loved Worms" (Katsuyuki Osaka; Poem, Colette Inez; Recited by Julie Polly), "Luna Park" (Otto Luening-Vladimir Ussachevsky-Tod Dockstader)

Top Right: Saeko Ichinohe in "Woman Who Loved Worms"

Gudde Dancers

ST. CLEMENT'S CHURCH
June 5,–9, 1974

GUDDE DANCERS

Director-Choreographer, Lynda Gudde; Assistant, Silvia De La Rosa; Costume Designer, Lizbeth Fullemann; Lighting, Jon D. Andreadakis, Michael Carson; Stage Manager, Mike LeRoy, Music Tape, Corey Kaup; Company Manager, Patricia Fogarty

COMPANY

Lynda Gudde, Jim Akers, Eligio Alvino, Margarita Ballesteros, Audrey De La Rosa, Silvia De La Rosa, Betsy Feldman, John Mass, Shelly Pressley, Janet Schoenfeld, Brenda Singleton, Janice Singleton, Melvin Bruce Singleton, Margaret Smith, Linda Torrey, Lola Wayles

PROGRAM

"Ancient Voices of Children" (George Crumb), "Delvaux" (Hovhaness), *World Premieres* of "Sketches of the Old South" (Leadbelly), "Feathers of Death" (Bach)

AMERICAN THEATRE LAB
June 7–10, 1974*
Directional Concepts Dance Theatre Foundation presents:

THE SOLOMONS COMPANY/DANCE

Director-Choreographer, Gus Solomons, Jr.; Technical Director-Lighting Designer, Ruis Woertendyke; Costumes-Decor, Eva Tsug

COMPANY

Santa Aloi	Randall Faxon
Ruedi Brack	Valerie Hammer
John Cwiakala	Douglas Nielsen
Ben Dolphin	Gus Solomons, Jr.

PROGRAM: "Par/Tournament," *NY Premieres* of "Yesterday" (Poetry, Ethan Ayer), "Randdance" (Elton John), "A Shred of Prior Note" (Words, Martinez), "Molehill" (Bartok), and *WORLD PREMIERE* of "Stoneflesh" (Jimi Hendrix)
* March 12–17, 1975 the company gave 7 performances of "Steady Work" at Larry Richardson's Dance Gallery. Additions to the company were Jack Apffel, John Turner. (No photos available)

Joel Gordon Photo

Ruedi Brack, Santa Aloi, Ben Dolphin, Valerie Hammer, Douglas Nielsen, Randall Faxon, Gus Solomons (on floor)

Saturday, June 8, 1974
The 92nd Street YM-YWHA presents:

THE MOSHE ARIEL DANCE COMPANY

Director-Choreographer, Moshe Ariel; Costumes, Evelyn Ozer; Lighting Designer, Ira Landau

COMPANY

Erika Berland, Wendy Levin, Barbara Ryba, Hedy Weiss, Moshe Guri, Susan Spiegel, Stacey Sperling

PROGRAM: "From Song of Songs" (Chen-Admon-Amiran-Levy), "Ruth" (Paul Ben Haim), "Yemenite Wedding" (Traditional), "Shabbat Sholom" (Satie), "Israel Chai" (Ernest Bloch-Claude Debussy-Folk Music-Paul Ben Haim)

**Left: Moshe Ariel Dance Co.
in "Ruth"**

WASHINGTON SQUARE CHURCH
June 9, 10, 11, 1974

THOMAS HOLT DANCE ENSEMBLE

Director-Choreographer, Thomas Holt; Lighting Design, Joanna Schielke; Sound, John Wilson; Stage Managers, Debbie LePaye, Rhonda Zhawm

COMPANY

Thomas Holt

Betsy Baron	Ann Moser
Cameron Burke	Allan Seward
Lucinda Gehrke	Karen Sing
John Killacky	Paulette Taylor

PROGRAM: "Arienata" (Vivaldi, Holt), "Afterhours in Wonderland" (Holzman-Jefferson Airplane-Pfeiffer-Hiller-Exuma, Holt), "Duet for Summer" (Lee Holdridge, Holt), "Love Quartet" (Choreography by Lucina Kathmann), and *PREMIERE* of "There Ain't No Leaves" (Cameron-Brooks-Ruby-Morton-Gershwin-Ellington, Gary McKay)

**Right Center: Thomas Holt as the White Rabbit
in "Afterhours in Wonderland"**

JAPAN HOUSE
Tuesday & Wednesday, June 11–12, 1974

PHYLLIS ROSE DANCE COMPANY

Director-Choreographer, Phyllis Rose; Lighting Designer, Deanna Weiner; Costumes, Terry Leong; Stage Manager, Dave Schulz; Production Assistants, Nicholas Grant, Caesar Napier; Stage Artist, Cathy Skopic; Manager, Virginia Page; Props, Ned Hallick

COMPANY

Ricky Davenport	Elizabeth Price
Esther Farmer	Phyllis Rose
Erick Hodges	Diana Simkin
Pat Masters	J. Edward Sydow

PROGRAM: (The First Beatrice Wolff Anderson Memorial Concert) "Cycle" (Pink Floyd, Nicholas Grant), "Trio for Four" (Percussion Score-Jimmy Erwin, Phyllis Rose), "Journey in Satchidananda" (Traditional, Ricky Davenport), "Santanna" (Isaac Hayes-Santanna, Erick Hodges), and *PREMIERES* of "Gotham Boogie" (Bette Midlar, Diana Simkin), "Interweave" (Conga Drums-Raymond Rojas, Phyllis Rose), "The Mourner" (Choreography, Phyllis Rose)

**Phyllis Rose Dance Company
in "Santanna"**

The Frances Alenikoff (standing center) Dance Theater Co. in "Notes for a Moon Calendar"

AMERICAN THEATRE LAB
June 13, 14, 15, 1974
Choreographers Theatre presents:

THE FRANCES ALENIKOFF DANCE THEATRE COMPANY

Director-Choreographer, Frances Alenikoff; Costumes, Jose Coronado; Lighting Design-Production Manager, Edward I. Byers; Mask and Set Design, Ray Grist; Technical Assistant, Tina Charney; Management, Judith Liegner Artists Management

COMPANY

Frances Alenikoff, Carol-Rae Kraus, Dalienne Majors, Myrna Packer, Janis Beaver, Scott Fields, John De Marco, Irene Meltzer, Elsi Miranda, Wendy Osserman, Joan Schwartz
GUEST ARTISTS: Deborah Jowitt, Andrew Bolotowsky, and Charlie Morrow and The New Wilderness Preservation Band

PROGRAM

"The One of No Way" (Charlie Morrow), "Terns in Place" (Scott Fields-John DeMarco), and *PREMIERES* of "Fingers" (Bruce Ditmas), "Flutewind" (Robert Shaughnessy), "Notes for a Moon Calendar" (a work in progress)
Don Manza Photos

THEATRE OF THE RIVERSIDE CHURCH
June 13–16, 1974

THE GREENHOUSE DANCE ENSEMBLE

Manager, Ron Reagan; Lighting Designer, Paul Butler; Stage Manager, Eiko Levitch; Technical Director, Lee Goldman; Crew, Kristen Peterson, Alan Lynes, Arlene Kennedy, Checker Ives, Judy Davis; Costumes, Raya, Karen Sargeant, Kristen Peterson, Natalie Richman, Ruth Miller, Jim Pelletier, Judith Brusseau; Sets, Jim Pelletier, Ned Hallick, Daryl McConnell

COMPANY

Beverly Brown
Carol Conway
Nada Reagan
Natalie Richman
Lillo Way
Robert Yohn
with Anthony LaGiglia, Cathy Ward, Brian Webb

REPERTOIRE: "Wind" (Sergio Cervett, Carol Conway), "Windwing" (Natalie Richman), "Summer Settings" (J. Miller, Nada Reagan), "Encyphered" (Gerard Schwarz, Lillo Way), "Fire Fall" (Eleanor Hovda, Beverly Brown), *NY Premiere* of "Day in the Lee of April" (Robert Yohn), and *WORLD PREMIERES* of "Morning Call" (Beverly Brown-Anthony LaGiglia), "Tryptych" (Gilbert Amy, Lillo Way), "Duelle" (Sergio Cervetti, Carol Conway), "Blued Spaces" (David Whiteside, Nada Reagan), "Fifth Avenue Pigeon" (Michael Willens, Natalie Richman)

Cathy Ward, Nada Reagan, Carol Conway in "Summer Settings" *(Ron Reagan Photo)*

LA MAMA
Saturday & Sunday, June 15–16, 1974
Performing Arts Foundation presents:

REYNALDO ALEJANDRO & DANCERS

Director-Choreographer, Reynaldo Alejandro; Production Design-Director, Cecile Guidote; Lighting, Chuck Golden, Madeleine Abalos; Music, Mutya Gener; Stage Manager, Marilyn Abalos; Sculpture and Masks, Kap Soon Park; Props, Din Pajaron; Production Assistant, Luisa Reyes; Costumes, Linda Pichon, Inday Refi, Ching Valdes; Puppeteers, Nemi Gardon, Aurora Ramos; Consultants, Lutgardo Labad, Moreno Requisa

COMPANY

Reynaldo Alejandro, Enrico Labayen, Dianne Lam, Ching Valdes, Cesar Villanueva, Rene Domingo, Rosemarie Valdes, Kathy Serio, Melinda Acaac, Vicky Tiangco, Beth Padua, Ramon de Luna, Nardz Peji, Tony Parel, Eddie Sese

PROGRAM

SIBOL: "Tausog Variations" (Lutgardo Labad-Lucrecia Kasilag), "Anak," "Malong," "Matapang," "Enigambara-Ulan," "Tausog"

Ching Valdes in "Tausog Variations"

NEW YORK UNIVERSITY THEATRE

June 20–23, 27–29, 1974
The Mary Anthony Dance Theatre Foundation presents:

MARY ANTHONY DANCE THEATRE

Artistic Director-Choreographer, Mary Anthony; Associate Director, Ross Parkes, Administrative Director, Ray Steehler; Assistant to Choreographers, Ellen Tittler; Stage Manager, Barbara Rosoff; Lighting Supervisor, Arden Fingerhut; Sound, Marjorie Horne; Costumes, Daniel Maloney, Anne Wattenberg, Susan McPherson, Leor C. Warner II, William Sherman

COMPANY

Mary Anthony	Ross Parkes
Daniel Maloney	Murial Cohan
Tonia Shimin	Patrick Suzeau
Gwendolyn Bye	Linda Hayes
Michael Bruce	Elaine Anderson
Jacqulyn Buglisi	Evelyn Shepard
Carl Paris	Beth Shorter

REPERTOIRE: "Antiphon" (Louis Calabro, Mary Anthony), "Rooms" (Kenyon Hopkins, Anna Sokolow), "Power" (Earth, Wind and Fire, Daniel Maloney), "In the Beginning" (Peter Sculthorpe, Anthony), "Tides" (Ralph Vaughan Williams, Ross Parkes), "Threnody" (Benjamin Britten, Anthony), "Cain and Abel" (Peter Sculthorpe), "1 2 3 4 5" (Samuel Barber, Parkes)

PREMIERES: "Four Glances" (Valerie Simpson-Dorothy Morrison-Gloria Spencer-Edwin Hawkins Singers; Costumes, Daniel Maloney, Anne Wattenberg; Lighting, Arden Fingerhut), "Chasm" (Karel Husa, Mary Anthony; Costumes, Anne Wattenberg; Lighting, Arden Fingerhut), "Renascent Visions" (Ralph Vaughan Williams, Daniel Maloney; Costumes, Daniel Maloney, Anne Wattenberg; Lighting, Arden Fingerhut)

Lewis Brown Photos

Michael Bruce, Linda Hayes, Tonia Shimin, Gwendoly Bye, Patrick Suzeau, Ross Parkes in "Rooms" Top: Ross Parkes, Mary Anthony in "Threnody" Left Center: Pat Thomas, Daniel Maloney in "Power"
Lois Greenfield Photo

Manju Prasad

SUMMERGARDEN

Friday & Saturday, June 21–22, 1974*
The Museum of Modern Art presents:

MANJU PRASAD

in a program of classical and light Indian dances includin "Bharata Natyam," "Alaripu," "Varnam," "Padam," "Kathak"

* Program was repeated July 27, at the Brooklyn Museum, an April 5 & 6, 1975 at the American Museum of Natural Histor

AMERICAN MUSEUM OF NATURAL HISTORY
Sunday, June 30, 1974*
Performing Arts Foundation, Inc. presents:

THE PHILIPPINE DANCE COMPANY OF NEW YORK

Artistic Director-Choreographer, Ronnie Alejandro; Assistant Director, Ching Valdes; Executive Director, Brun P. Seril; Technical Director, Chuck Golden; Stage Manager, Lee Horsman; President, Salvador Zapanta

COMPANY

Ronnie Alejandro, Ching Valdes, Vicky Tiangco, Kathy Serio, Dulce Valdes, Ruth Malabrigo, Tony Parel, Sonny Zapanta, Ramon de Luna, Benny Felix, Eugene Domingo

PROGRAM

(All choreography by Ronnie Alejandro) SULYAP—A Glimpse of Philippine Culture through Dance: "Jota Cavitena (Traditional-Kasilag), "Paypay de Manila" (Traditional-Kasilag), "Tarjata Sin Kagukan" (Dadap), "Subli" (Traditional), "Pandanggo sa Ilaw" (Traditional), "Tinikling" (Traditional)
* This program was repeated Aug. 4, 18, 1974, Jan. 5, 1975, Feb. 9, 1975, Mar. 16, 1975, Apr. 13, 1975, May 11, 1975, and at Grant's Tomb Sept. 8, 1974, International House Oct. 13, 17, 1974.

Philippine Dance Company of New York
Lori Weinless Photo

ASTORIA PARK
Saturday, July 6, 1974*
Foundation for the Advance of Dance presents:

EDITH STEPHEN DANCE COMPANY

Artistic Director-Choreographer, Edith Stephen; Design Consultant, Richard Abrams; Production Assistant, Helen Daphnis; Visuals, Maxine Haleff; Video, Marlene Franks; Personal Management, Edward Kapel

COMPANY

Edith Stephen

Kathy Gargan	Ralph M. Thomas
Candace Gilles-Brown	Annabella Gonzalez
Beverly Mann	Paula Schapiro
Gernot Petzold	Theadore Jamison
Anthony Barbato	Stephanie Nightingale
Frederick Courtney	Jean Galle
Meredith Evans	Steven Pope

PROGRAM: "The Lopsided People" (Dana McCurdy), and environmental happening in four parts: "Some of my best friends are numbered," "The Concrete Heart," "Battle of the Sexes," "Dream of the Wild Horse"
* Repeated Prospect Park July 14, Brooklyn Museum July 21, Boro Hall Aug. 2, Lincoln Center Aug. 21, 1974.

Edith Stephen Dance Company

SOUTH STREET SEAPORT THEATER
Friday, Saturday, Sunday, September 20–22, 1974

AMERICANA PIE

Conceived and Performed by Ballet Classics. (no other details available)

NYU SCHOOL OF EDUCATION
Friday & Saturday, September 20–21, 1974

JAMES CUNNINGHAM
and
THE ACME DANCE COMPANY

Director-Choreographer, James Cunningham; Lighting Design, Raymond Dooley; General Manager, Peter Levitan; Stage Manager, Raymond Dooley; Films by Harold Kalishman, Kirk Smallman, Hiroaki Tanaka, John Zingraff; Costumes, Bill Florio

COMPANY

James Cunningham
Barbara Ellmann
Lauren Persichetti
Ted Striggles
Linda Tarnay

PROGRAM: "Lauren's Dream" (conceived, choreographed and performed by James Cunningham and Lauren Persichetti), *NY Premiere* of "Dancing with Maisie Paradocks"

Joel Gordon Photo

front: **Ted Striggles, Linda Tarnay, William Holcomb,**
back: **Barbara Ellmann, James Cunningham, Lauren Persichetti in "Maisie Paradocks"** **91**

THEATRE OF RIVERSIDE CHURCH
October 4–6, 1974
The Theatre of the Riverside Church in association with Dance Theatre Worshop presents:

MIKI WAKAMATSU
in
"Five Interpretations of Love"

Choreography, Miki Wakamatsu, assisted by Ikuko Tsuda; Music, Koh-ici Hattori; Lighting Designer, Nicholas Wolff Lyndon; Sound, Koji Sumino; Electrician, Rachel Lampert; Sound, Koji Sumino

DANCERS

Miki Wakamatsu
Erin Martin
Ikuko Mimachi
Minako Manita

PROGRAM: "Love Realized," "Love Lost," "Love's Zenith," "Love Today," "Love Yesterday"

Miki Wakamatsu

HARKNESS HOUSE FOR BALLET ARTS
Tuesday, October 8, 1974
The Harkness Ballet Foundation presents the Harkness Ballet Trainees in:

THE PERFECT FOOL

Music by Gustave Holst; Choreography by Eric McCullough

COMPANY

Eric McCullough, Rachel Westlake, Kathy McNurney, Sylvester Dolinar, Larry Leritz, Lyndsey Jones, Martha Boyle, Lori MaRose, Suzanne Nadeau, Ellen Kulik, Melinda Bronson, Laura Cutler, Cynthia Hanrahan, Steve Maynard, Bill Sterner, Eric Weichardt (No photos available)

AMERICAN THEATRE LAB
October 11, 12, 13, 1975

NEW CHOREOGRAPHY BY VALERIE HAMMER

Performed by The New York Dance Collective: Livia Blankman, Gary Cowan, Valerie Hammer, Jonathan Hollander, Clarice Marshall, Idelle Packer, Victoria Uris, Debra Wanner; Lighting Designer, Ruis Woertendyke

PROGRAM

"In the Meantime" (Leo Kottke), "Clearance" (Urszula Dudziak), "Faded" (George Harrison; Costumes, Jim Corry; Text adapted from articles by Tom Wolf)

"Faded" by Valerie Hammer
Johan Elbers Photo

CATHEDRAL OF ST. JOHN THE DIVINE
Sunday, October 20, 1974

WENDY HILTON BAROQUE DANCE COMPANY

Artistic Director-Choreographer, Wendy Hilton; Costumes, Cheryl Lovett

COMPANY

Eileen Cropley
Elizabeth Haberer
Charles Garth
Nicholas Gunn
Haynes Owens

PROGRAM: Dances of the 17th Century: "Canzona" (Frescobaldi), "Pavan Matthei" (Anonymous), "Gagliarda" (Frescobaldi), "Sonata" (Castello), "Amarilli Mia Bella" (Caccini), "Lavolta" (Frescobaldi), "English Country Dances" (Playford) "Grand Ritournelle" (Couperin), "L'Allemande" (Campra), "Le Menuet" (Campra), "Gavotte" (Marais), "La Forlana" (Campra), "Passepied a Quatre" (Couperin)

Wendy Hilton

EPIPHANY AUDITORIUM
Wednesday, October 23, 1974*

NEW YORK DANCE ENSEMBLE

Larry Leritz
Justis Skaye
Betteanne Terrell
Anne Wilson

PROGRAM: "The Ballet Story," "Dying Swan," "Billy the Kid"
* On Dec. 3, 1974 the company with Eloise Carrigan, Lindsay Jones, Linda Griffin, Barbara File, Kye McWilliams, Ron Pratt, and Carol Binney performed at P. S. 40 with "Brahm's Waltzes" and "Firebird" added to the program.

**Right: Betteanne Terrell, Justis Skaye
in "Firebird"**

HUNTER COLLEGE PLAYHOUSE
Wednesday & Thursday, October 30–31, 1974*

PEOPLE/DOROTHY VISLOCKY DANCE THEATRE

Choreography, Dorothy Vislocky; Lighting Design, Dorothy Vislocky; Stage Manager, Carol Indianer; Technical Director, Michael Richardson; Company Manager, JoAnne Barone

COMPANY

JoAnne Barone
Jana Feinman
Cheryl Hahn

Frances Lucerna
Barbara Mahler
Pamela Tait

PROGRAM: "Overture" (McDowell-Denby), "Karmal—Streets," "Avabahda—Walking Perception" (McDowell), "Santosa—Peace" (Pachelbel-McDowell; Dedicated to the memory of Ethel Griegas and Desiree Magnus)
* Performed May 17, 1975 at Waterside Plaza.

Right: Dorothy Vislocky Dance Theatre

WESTSIDE CENTER
October 31, November 1 & 2, 1974*

LES BALLETS TROCKADERO DE MONTE CARLO

Artistic Directors, Antony Bassae, Natch Taylor, Peter Anastos; General Director, Eugene McDougle; Ballet Mistress, Elenita Licklider; Scenic Designers, Richard Strahan, Joseph DeAngelis; Stage Manager, Peter Fusco; Lighting and Technical Director, Druth McClure

COMPANY

Tamara Karpova, Natasha Veceslova, Suzina LaFuzziovitch, Olga Tchikaboumskaya, Veronika-Malaise du Mer, Cypriana Nubianovitch, Pichka Melba, Vera Namethatunova, Malinkaya Lubyanka, Eugenia Repelski, Zamarina Zamarkova, Kapmeh Dolguzhina, Tyatya Nougatchoutchou, Maya Mayakovskaya, Nina Oblongatova, D. Zayre, Marfa Boraksovna, Alexis Ivanovitch Lermontov, Random Foch, Tino Xirau-Lopez, Medulli Lobotomov

REPERTOIRE

"Swan Lake Act II" (Tchaikovsky, Tamara Karpova), "Go For Barocco" (Bach, Peter Anastos), "Don Quixote" (Minkus, Anastos), "Pas de Quatre" (Pugni, Trutti Gasparinetti), "Loie Flutter" (Poncielli, Marian Horosko)
Program was repeated at the Touchstone Theatre Nov. 8–10, 15–17, 1974; Dec. 19–22, 26–29, 1974, Jan. 2–5, 1975 the company performed "The Nutcracker" at the Touchstone. March 7–30, 1975 the company danced at the Vandam Theatre where the following were included in the repertoire: "Siberiana" (Tchaikovsky, Anastos), "Marzipan" (Tchaikovsky, Antony Bassae), "Ecole de Ballet" (Pastiche, Anastos), "Trepak" (Tchaikovsky, Bassae), "Firebird" (Stravinsky, Horosko), "Choreo" (Les Baxter, Bassae), "The Queen's Revenge" (Purcell, Bassae)
John L. Murphy Photos

Zamarina Zamarkova, Suzina LaFuzziovitch, Tamara Karpova, Olga Tchikaboumskaya in "Pas de Quatre"

The Allnations Company

NEW YORK UNIVERSITY THEATRE
Friday & Saturday, November 15–16, 1974
N. Y. U. School of Education Dance Program presents:

THE WASHINGTON SQUARE REPERTORY DANCE COMPANY

Director-Choreographer, Laura Brittain; Lighting and Technical Director, Charles Miller; Stage Manager, Rebecca Dinin; Sound, Bonnie Robbins; Wardrobe, Jeannie Radoczy, Rochelle Anixt; Press, Joyce Meyerson; Stage Assistants, Amy Weiss, Linda Del Zio Zoffer, Richard Cabezas, Bonnie Rosenstock, Darryl Brittain

COMPANY

Pipper Armel   Elaine Perlmutter
Maxine Lee Booth   Marie Pintauro
Laurie Kane   Victorianne Pizzuta
Susan Mandel   Leslie Seaman
Guest Soloist: Gail Kachadurian
AUXILIARY COMPANY: April Brooks, Mara Lewis, Mary Manly, Joyce Meyerson, Caren Rosenthal, Barbara Sherman, Roberta Wein, Julinda Williams, Elin Benson, Pamela Renner, Jane Silverman
PROGRAM: "Anticipate, The Go" (Brahms, Sally Balen), "Air Swum" (Hovhaness, Kelly Hogan), "Perimeter" (Tom Johnson, Laura Brittain), "The Edge" (Webern, Martha Rzasa), "Progression of Blue" (Pink Floyd, Linda Kohl), "For Dali" (Three Surrealists, Jane Silverman), "Disengage" (Villa-Lobos, Laura Brittain), "Four Squares" (Robert Sallier, Kathy Duncan)

Ekaterina Sobechanskaya

55 BETHUNE STREET
Saturday & Sunday, November 2–3, 1974

DANCES BY KATHRYN BERNSON

Performed by Kathryn Bernson, Robert Bonfiglio, Ellen Cornfield, Morgan Ensminger, Stormy Mullis, Monica Solem, Mitch Kamen, Merrilee Wallbrunn, Lyman Maynard Stowe, Jr.

PROGRAM: "The Flying Zucchinis" (Martin H. Healey), "No Watering" (Robert Bonfiglio), "Real Costumes" (Robert Bonfiglio), "Board Dance"
(No photos available)

COOPER UNION GREAT HALL
Thursday, November 7, 1974
The Performing Arts Foundation, Inc. presents:

THE ALLNATIONS COMPANY

Producer, Herman Rottenberg; Artistic Director, Chuck Golden; Technical Director, Leonard Buggs

COMPANY

Reynaldo Alejandro, Pierre Barreau, Larry Bianco, Richard Clairmont, Jose Coronado, Linda Cuneo, Natasha Grishin, Noel Hall, Lee Harper, Sachiyo Ito, Robert Owens Jones, Nomi Katzir, Louines Louinis, Sun-Ock Lee, Peter Lobdell, Sumiko Murashima, Rick Ornellas, Antonio Parel, Maldwyn Pate, Joyce Pierre-Louis, Kathy Serio, Hope Sherman, Gertrude Sherwood, Simion Timlichman, Ching Valdes, Dulce Valdes, Rosemarie Valdes, John Van Buskirk

PROGRAM: "Joy in Every Land" in two parts.

Gail Kachadurian and Washington Square Repertory Dance Co. in "The Edge"

TRUCK & WAREHOUSE THEATRE
November 15–December 15, 1974*

EKATHERINA SOBECHANSKAYA DANCES

with THE TROCKADERO GLOXINIA BALLET COMPANY Mariana Bublittschskaya, Olga Plushinskaya, Ludmila Samoilov, Yvonne Terekova, Fedora Popovich, P. Phunck, Onna Gatti, Svetlana Kamargo, Mala Feminova, Lohr Wilson

Director, Larry Ree; Ballet Mistress, Carolyn Lord; Stage Manager, George Ritter; Lighting, Charles Embry; Sound, Guy Bishop, Jr.; Wardrobe Mistress, Zenubia Gaborgias; Press, Fran Schmitt; Costumes, Lohr Wilson, Jose Coronado

REPERTOIRE

"Russian Snowflakes" (Tchaikovsky), "Four Spirits" (Prokofiev), "Tragic Heart of Gloom and Despair" (Gould), "Dragonfly" (Kreisler), "Roses and Butterflies" (Drigo), "Red" (Offenbach), "Dance of the Liberation of the American People" (Tchaikovsky), "Raymonda Act III" (Glazounov), "Surprise" (Strauss), NY Premiere of "Die Puppenfee" (Bayer), and World Premieres of "Dance of the Liberation of the Russian People" (Tchaikovsky, Plushinskaya), and "Classe de Perfection" (Arranged, Marian Horosh; Costumes, Kiki)
* Performed April 3–6, 1975 at La Mama Annex.

AMERICAN THEATRE LAB
Saturday & Sunday, November 16–17, 1974
Dance Theatre Workshop presents:

ART BERGER/DORIS GINSBERG/HOLLY SCHIFFER

with Maris Wolff, Valerie Pullman, Lenore Latimer; Lighting Design, Suzanne Joelson; Sound, Joseph Popper; Technical Director, John Beven

PROGRAM

"Tremble Lake" (Sound Collage, Art Berger), "Broken Flight, In Ink" (Vivaldi, Doris Ginsberg), "Two Songs" (Jay Ash, Holly Schiffer), "Crossings" (Larry Coryell, Doris Ginsberg), "Deep-mouthed Figure" (Sound effects from the Kabuki, Doris Ginsberg)

Left: Doris Ginsberg, Holly Schiffer, Art Berger

CARNEGIE HALL
Tuesday, November 19, 1974
The Performing Arts Program of the Asia Society presents:

HEEN BABA AND HIS DANCE ENSEMBLE

PROGRAM: Ceremonial Opening, "Magul Bera," "Pooja Netuma," "Gajaga Vannama," "Gahaka Vannama," "Uddekki Dance," "Naga Vannama," "Samanala Vannama," "Bera Tharangaya," "Pantheru Dance," "Ukkussa Vannama," "Udhara Vannama," "Thuranga Vannama," "Drum Improvisation," "Ves"

Heen Baba in "Ves Dance"

Gale Ormiston in "Take 3"
Tom Caravaglia Photo

LOUIS D. BRANDEIS AUDITORIUM
November 20, 21, 22, 1974
Circum-Arts Foundation presents:

GALE ORMISTON DANCE COMPANY

Director-Choreographer, Gale Ormiston; Lighting Designer-Stage Manager, Jon Garness; Technical Assistant, William Campbell; Production Assistant, K. S. Tartt

COMPANY

Gale Ormiston
Luise Wykell
Richard Biles
Karen Levin
Lynn Ruthenberg

PROGRAM: "RePLAY" (Arranged, Ormiston), "Quintumbcylrhomp" (Arranged, Richard Biles), "Take 3" (New Vaudeville Band-Slugger Ryan, Ormiston), "Rondo" (Pachabel, Ormiston; a work in progress), and *PREMIERES* of "Reciprocity" (Monk, Luise Wykell), "Syzygy" (Arranged, Ormiston)

LIBRARY & MUSEUM OF PERFORMING ARTS
Thursday, November 21, 1974

INDRA-NILA

performing "A Family Portrait of the God of Dance": Nataraj Shiva, Parvati, Ganapati, Kartikeya, and "Other Indian Inspirations"

Left: Indra-nila

AMERICAN THEATRE LAB
November 22–24, 1974 (4 performances)
Castalia Enterprises presents:

JOSE CORONADO AND DANCERS

Director-Choreographer, Jose Coronado; Lighting Design, Edward Greenberg

COMPANY

Jose Coronado

Betsy Baron	Rick Hood
Lisa Brodsky	Kathy Kepler
Ilona Copen	Peter Lawrence
Judith Epstein	Joselyn Lorenz
Robin Goldstein	Nancy Mikota
Seth Goldstein	Suzan Rike

PROGRAM: "Saeta" (J. Homs), "In a Bed of Faded Roses" (R. Reynolds), "O Beautiful Dreamer" (C. Ives), "Mujeres" (Handel), "The Arena" (Blomdahl), "Vigil" (Penerecki-Bach)

Left: Jose Coronado in "Saeta"
Nina Melis Photo

GRAMERCY ARTS THEATRE
Opened Tuesday, November 26, 1974.*
Spanish Theatre Repertory Company (Gilberto Zaldivar, Producer) presents:

PILAR RIOJA AND COMPANY

A Spanish Dance program with poetry by Federico Garcia Lorca. Choreography, Pilar Rioja; Lighting Designer, Tony Quintavalla; Production Assistant, Lillian Love; Associate Producer, Robert Federico

COMPANY

Pilar Rioja

Antonio De Cordoba	Lorenzo Fernandez
Simon Garcia	Roberto Antonio
Isabel Segovia	Patricia Triana
Jose Juan Baldini	

REPERTOIRE: "Allegro Assai" (Bach), "Folia" (Corelli), "Moto Perpetuo" (Paganini), "Grave Assai y Fandango" (Boccherini), "El Cafe de Chinitas" (Garcia Lorca), "El Vito," "Sevillanas del Siglo XVIII" (Lorca), "Lorquiana" (Lorca), "Anda Jaleo" (Lorca), "Tangos Del Piyayo," "Baladilla de los Tres Rois," "Farruca," "Siguiriya," "Cinco Siglos de Danza Espanola," "Teoria y Juego de Duende, de Federico Garcia Lorca," "Danzas Barrocas Populares y Espanolas"

Press: Marian Graham
* Closed Dec. 22, 1974 after limited engagement of 20 performances. Re-opened Tuesday, April 23, 1975 and closed May 1975 for an additional 24 performances.

Pilar Rioja

NYSF PUBLIC/NEWMAN THEATER
Opened Friday, November 29, 1974.*
Original Ballets Foundation Inc., in cooperation with the New York
Shakespeare Festival, presents:

ELIOT FELD BALLET

Director-Choreographer, Eliot Feld; Music Coordinator, Herbert
Harris; Scenic Production Supervisor, Santo Loquasto; Wardrobe
Master, Frank Green; Audio Master, Roger Jay; Administrator,
Cora Cahan; Assistant to Mr. Feld, Elizabeth Lee; Lighting, Jennifer
Tipton, Thomas Skelton

COMPANY

Betty Chamberlin, Helen Douglas, Richard Fein, Valerie Feit, Eliot
Feld, Richard Gilmore, Michaela Hughes, Laurie Ichino, Charles
Kennedy, Edmund LaFosse, Elizabeth Lee, Remus Marcu, Linda
Miller, George Montalbano, Lawrence Rhodes, Christine Sarry, Jeff
Satinoff, Naomi Sorkin, John Sowinski

REPERTOIRE

"Sephardic Song" (Traditional), "The Gods Amused" (Debussy),
"Tzaddik" (Copland), "At Midnight" (Mahler), "Intermezzo"
(Brahms), a *Company Premiere* of "Embrace Tiger and Return to
Mountain" (Morton Subotnick, Glen Tetley), *NY Premiere* of re-
vised "The Consort" (Dowland-Neusidler-and others; Arranged and
Conducted by Michael Jaffee; Choreography, Eliot Feld; Costumes,
Carrie F. Robbins; Lighting, Thomas Skelton), and *WORLD PRE-
MIERE* Saturday, Dec. 7, 1974 of "The Real McCoy" (George
Gershwin, Eliot Feld; Setting and Costumes, Rouben Ter-
Arutunian; Lighting, Thomas Skelton)

Press: Merle Debuskey, Susan L. Schulman
Stage Managers: Richard Thorkelson, John H. Paull III, Joseph
Ligammari

* Closed Jan. 5, 1975 after limited engagement of 38 performances.

Thomas Victor Photos

**Right: Christine Sarry, Lawrence Rhodes, Elizabeth
Lee in "The Gods Amused" Top: "Embrace Tiger and
Return to Mountain"** *(Martha Swope Photo)*

**Richard Gilmore, John Sowinski, Eliot Feld
in "Tzaddik"**

Lawrence Rhodes in "At Midnight"

November 26, 1974*
The Leonard Davis Center for the Performing Arts presents:

DANIEL NAGRIN
in
"CHANGES"

A retrospective of solo dances 1948–1974.
Stage Manager: Michael Hunold
* This program was performed at the Studio-Theatre on Saturday, March 15, 1975. On March 14, Mr. Nagrin performed "Jazz Changes," a retrospective of solo jazz dances and dances set to jazz scores from 1948 to 1974.

Right: Daniel Nagrin

KAUFMANN CONCERT HALL
Sunday, December 1, 1974
The 92nd Street Young Men's & Young Women's Hebrew Association presents:

THE LAURA VELDHUIS DANCE COMPANY

Director-Choreographer, Laura Veldhuis; Designer-Technical Consultant, Joop Veldhuis; Lighting Designer, Harvey Mette; Stage Manager, Civia Zoe; Press, Elaine Hyams; Technical Director, Diane Smith; Production Coordinator, Bob Keil; Technician, Peter Matusewitch

COMPANY

Gary Davis	Brigitta Mueller
Diana Gregory	Ellen Pundyk
David Koch	Laura Veldhuis

Guest Artists: Peter and John Isaacson

PROGRAM: "March" (Charles Ives), "Green Mountain Suite" (Peter and John Isaacson), "The Mind's Garden" (Benjamin Britten)

Left: Alan D'Angerio, Laura Veldhuis in "The Mind's Ga▸
Myra Armstrong Photo

HUNTER COLLEGE PLAYHOUSE
Tuesday & Wednesday, December 3–4, 1974
The Classics Department of Hunter College presents:

THE CHIANG CHING DANCE COMPANY

Artistic Director-Choreographer, Chiang Ching; Production Manager, Yoshio Kishi; Stage Manager, Patricia Spargo; Lighting Designer, David Kissel; Costumes, Chiang Ching; Sound, Radford Polinski

COMPANY

Chiang Ching	Charlotte Coady Christon
Chou Wen-Chung	Lynette Chun
Tsai	Linda Dobson
Chinary Ung	Lily Gee
Joyce Trisler	Oliver Tessier
Chih-Ming Lu	Benton Wong

Part I: From Classical Chinese Repertory, Part II: After the Music of Chou Wen-Chung, with a *PREMIERE* of Joyce Trisler's "Soliloquy of a Bhiksuni," Part III: An Adventure in Sculpture, Music and Dance, with the *PREMIERE* of "Pien" choreographed by Chiang Ching

Si-Chi Ko Photo

Chiang Ching Dance Co.

TOWN HALL

Wednesday, December 4, 1974
Town Hall Interludes presents:

LAR LUBOVITCH DANCE COMPANY

Artistic Director-Choreographer, Lar Lubovitch; Administration, Margaret Wood Performing Artservice

COMPANY

Robert Besserer	Mari Ono
Gerri Houlihan	Aaron Osborne
Elaine Kudo	Rebecca Slikin
Lar Lubovitch	Susan Weber
Debbie Nigro	Janet Wong

PROGRAM: "Zig Zag" (Stravinsky), "Prelude in C Minor" (Bach), "The Time before the Time after (after the Time Before) (Stravinsky)

Top Right: Lar Lubovitch
Dina Makarova Photo

EXCHANGE THEATER

December 5–7, 1974
Exchange Theater in association with Dance Theater Workshop presents:

HAVA KOHAV AND DANCE COMPANY

Director-Choreographer, Hava Kohav; Lighting and Stage Design, Hayman-Chaffey; Costume Designs, S. Guida, Lavinia Nielsen, Hava Kohav; Technical Assistants, Gale Freeman, Polly Adams; Stage Manager, P. J. Hayman-Chaffey

COMPANY

Bruce Bloch
Ilona Copen
Sarah Edgett
Peggy Harrer
Bill Kirkpatrick
Hava Kohav
Ronald Young

PROGRAM: Reflections: "Moments" (H. Alpert D. Standen), "Mist" (P. Horn), "Moon Passage" (DeCabezon-DeMudarra-Dufay-Busnoys-DePlata-Anonymous), "A Dance" (Scarlatt-Purcell), and *PREMIERE* of "Gwendolyn" (Traditional and Popular, Hava Kohav)

Johan Elbers Photo

**Right Center: Hava Kohav, Ronald Young
in "Gwendolyn"**

CARNEGIE HALL

Saturday & Sunday, December 7–8, 1974
Hurok Concerts presents:

RAJKO HUNGARIAN GYPSY DANCERS AND ORCHESTRA

A company of 24 musicians and 10 dancers. Names of staff and performers not available; Press, Sheila Porter, Robert Weiss

PROGRAM

"Czardas" (Vdady), "Memory of Lavotta" (Farkas), "Hungarian Dances" (Brahms-Szirmai), "Love Songs" (Terez Kariko, Soloist), "Haiduk Dance" (Szirmai-Vadady), "Hungarian Rhapsody No. 2" (Liszt), "Gypsy Dance" (Somogyi), "Gypsy Songs" (Sarasate), "Hungarian Folk Songs," "Pastoral Dance" (Somogyi), "The Choppy Lake Balaton" (Hubay), "Hungarian Songs" (Terez Kariko, Soloist), "Bottle Dance" (Szirmai), "Free and Easy" (Tinar), "Czardas" (Monti), "Lark" (Dinicu), "Gypsy Dances and Songs" (Szirmai)

Rajko Hungarian Gypsy Dancers

Phoebe Neville in "Ladydance"
Philip Hipwell Photo

NEW YORK UNIVERSITY THEATRE
Opened Saturday, December 20, 1974.*
Chimera Foundation presents:

MURRAY LOUIS DANCE COMPANY

Director-Choreographer, Murray Louis; Production Coordinator, Ruth Grauert; Manager, William Bourne; Technical Director, Peter Koletzke; Stage Manager, Anthony Micocci; Costume Director, Frank Garcia; Press, Nigel Redden

COMPANY
Murray Louis

Michael Ballard	Jerry Pearson
Richard Haisma	Sara Pearson
Helen Kent	Robert Small
Anne McLeod	Marcia Wardell

REPERTOIRE: "Chimera" (Alwin Nikolais), "Hoopla" (Nikolais), "Calligraph for Martyrs" (Nikolais), "Continuum" (Corky Siegel Blues Band-Alwin Nikolais), "Proximities" (Brahms), "Porcelain Dialogues" (Tchaikovsky), "Personnae" (Free Life Communication), "Index (to necessary neuroses. . . .)" (Oregon Ensemble), "Scheherezade, a dream" (Rimsky-Korsakov/Alwin Nikolais/Free Life Communication), and *PREMIERE* of "Geometrics" (Alwin Nikolais, Murray Louis; Costumes, Frank Garcia; Lighting, Alwin Nikolais) on Dec. 20, 1974.

* Closed Jan. 5, 1975 after limited engagement of 17 performances.

Left: "Personnae"	**Below: "Continuum"**
David Shaw Photo	*Milton Oleaga Photo*

Top: "Scheherezade"

WASHINGTON SQUARE METHODIST CHURCH
Friday & Saturday, January 10–11, 1975
Washington Square United Methodist Church in association with Dance Theater Workshop presents:

PHOEBE NEVILLE
New and Recent Dances

Choreography, Phoebe Neville; Lighting Design, Cheryl Thacker; Sound, Curt Ostermann; Set, Edward Spena; Stage Manager, Lauren Barnes

COMPANY

Phoebe Neville	Lorn MacDougal
Lee Connor	Susan Okuhara
Anthony LaGiglia	Marlene Pennison
Ellen Likwornik	Edward Spena

PROGRAM: "Ladydance" (Hovhaness), "Canto" (Environmental Sounds), "Cartouche" (Purcell), and *PREMIERE* of "Oracles" (Eleanor Hovda)

KAUFMANN CONCERT HALL
January 6, 8, 11, 13, 1975
92nd Street Young Men's and Young Women's Hebrew Association presents the World Premiere of:

THE POSSESSED
(in three acts)

Choreography, Pearl Lang; Based on "The Dybbuk" by S. Ansky; Music and Sound Score, Meyer Kupferman, Joel Spiegelman; Lighting Design, Ken Billington; Scenic Design, Stuart Wurtzel; Projections, Virginia Hochberg; Costumes, A. Christina Giannini

CAST

Leye	Pearl Lang
Channon	William Carter
Messenger/Tsaddik	Bertram Ross
Sender	Alexander Mintz
Prospective Groom	Andrew Krichel
His Mother	Deborah Zalkind
His Father	Richard Arbach

(No photos available)

Peggy Hackney, Jeffrey Maer, Micki
Goodman in "Unrequited Love"
Lois Greenfield Photo

HENRY STREET SETTLEMENT
January 23–26, 1975
The Henry Street Settlement Arts for Living Center in association with
Dance Theater Workshop presents:

UNREQUITED LOVE AND OTHER STATES OF MIND

Choreography by Micki Goodman; Lighting Design, Cheryl
Thacker; Set, Micki Goodman, Peggy Hackney, Jeffrey Maer, Sally
Locke; Costumes, Micki Goodman, Joe Napodano; Tapes, John
Moore; Technical Director, C. Richard Mills; Sound, Brad Wil-
liams; Masks, Joan Goodman

COMPANY

Micki Goodman
Peggy Hackney
Jeffrey Maer

PROGRAM: "Plastic Dance" (Tape), "Unrequited Love" (Beetho-
ven/Villa-Lobos/Telemann), "Mandala" (Watazumido-Shuso; In
memory of Jose Limon)

CARNEGIE HALL
Monday, January 27, 1975
The Carnegie Hall Corporation by arrangement with The Asia Society
Performing Arts Program presents:

CHHAU

The Masked Dance of Bengal
Asutosh Bhattacharyya, Director

Primitive dancers in conventional costumes from the district of
Purulia in West Bengal, India performing "The Killing of the Buffa-
lo-Demon Mahisha," "The Death of the Demoness Tadaka," "The
Bow Contest," "The Last Day of Lord Krishna," "The Tragic End
of Abhimanyu"

Right Center: Masked Dancers of Bengal

AMERICAN THEATRE LAB
January 31–February 2, 1975 (4 performances)*
The American Theatre Laboratory presents:

PAUL WILSON'S THEATREDANCE ASYLUM

Artistic Director-Choreographer, Paul Wilson; Technical Design,
Daniel Potucek, Technical Assistant, Ellen Skinner, Ned Hallick;
Production Manager, George Bennett; Tapes, Scott Volk, Michael
Wodynski; Incidental Songs, Gary Castelluccio; Sets and Costumes,
Paul Wilson

COMPANY

Paul Wilson	Francis Witkowski
Joanne Edelmann	John Kelly
Rebecca Kelly	Martha Karess
Joanne Kaczynski	Scott Volk
Joenine Roberts	Penelope Vane
Julie Maloney	Joan Witkowski

PROGRAM: "Dancing on a Grave" (Joe Schwarzenberger, Paul
Wilson), "Releasing" (Gary Castelluccio, Wilson), "Night Migra-
tions" (Walter Carlos, Rebecca Kelly), "The American Dream"
(Mozart, Wilson), "Show 'N' Tell" (Paul Wilson-Francis Witkow-
ski), "Rambling" (Ralph Towner, Wilson), "Conversation" (Donald
Erb, Julie Maloney), "Freshfruit" (Gary Castelluccio, Wilson)

* Program was repeated March 7–8, 14–15, 1975 at Choreground,
  assisted by Ron Paul and Keith Rahner

Joanne Edelmann, Joanne Kaczynski, Scott Volk
John Kelly, Kathy Eaton in "The American Dream"
Tom Maloney Photo

CONSTRUCTION COMPANY DANCE STUDIO
February 1–17, 1975 (9 performances)
Theater/Dance Associates presents:

DIVINE COMEDIES BOOK III

with
Barbara Gardner
Beth Eisenberg

Choreography, Barbara Gardner; Lighting, Joanna Schielke; Technical Assistants, Stage Managers, Jenny Ball, Linnea Pearson; Decor, Dorothy Podber, Jack Champlain, Barbara Gardner, Richard Michaels

Bruce Fields Photo

Right: Barbara Gardner in "The Gift" from "Divine Comedies Book III"

Lar Lubovitch Dance Company in "Whirligogs"
Oleaga Photo

AMERICAN THEATRE LAB
February 6–9, 13–16, 1975
The Lubovitch Dance Foundation presents:

FIVE DANCES BY LAR LUBOVITCH

Danced by the Lar Lubovitch Dance Company; Artistic Director-Choreographer, Lar Lubovitch; Lighting Designer, Beverly Emmons; Stage Managers, Maxine Glorsky, Kitzi Becker; Company Manager, Margaret Wood

COMPANY

Rob Besserer	Mari Ono
Cameron Burke	Aaron Osborne
Gerri Houlihan	Rebecca Slifkin
Willa Kahn	Leslie Watanabi
Lar Lubovitch	Susan Weber
Sarah Neece	Janet Wong

PROGRAM: "Whirligogs" (Luciano Berio), "The Time before the Time after (after the Time before)" (Stravinsky), "Scherzo Part I" (Ives), "Prelude in C Minor" (Bach), "Zig Zag"

TEARS
February 7–8, 14–15, 21–22, 1975
Tears in association with Dance Theater Workshop presents:

THE LAURA PAWEL DANCE COMPANY

Director-Choreographer, Laura Pawel; Lighting Designer, Joseph P. Maceda; Costumes, Desi Koslin

COMPANY

Jim Finney
Pamela Finney
Raymond Healy
Eleanor Hovda
Joseph P. Maceda
Kevin Mulligan
Laura Pawel

REPERTOIRE: "The Sphinx Suite: Sphinx, Sphinx's Night Out, Pawprints and Questions" (Hovda), "Hoof and Mouth," "Snort Too," and *PREMIERES* of "The No-Name Dance," "The Proteus Trio," and "The Big Band: I Think I Sea Anemone"

Kevin Mulligan, Eleanor Hovda, Joseph Maceda, Pamela Finney in "The Big Band. . . ."

Janet Goto Photo

EDEN'S EXPRESSWAY
February 13–17, 1975 (5 performances)
Dancers Studio Foundation presents Valerie Bettis' Theatre Dance Company in:

POEMS AND THE CORNER

By Arnold Meyer; Director, Valerie Bettis; Sets and Costumes, Annette Harper; Lighting, Suzanne Gothson; Sound, Gerald Kornbluth; Stage Manager, Sara Schrager; Music, Lou Rodgers; Piano, Kay C. Greene; Flute, Harriet Wohgelmuth; Violin, Jean Isenberg

COMPANY

David Beckman   Lou Rodgers
Laura Delano   Robin O. Smith
Carole Ann Lewis   Frank Wicks
Robert Petersen   Edmund Williams

PROGRAM: "Roses," "Solomon's Song," "Racer," "Night Fishing," "Lament," "By the River," "Colors," "From Wall Street," "Home," "Tripping," "Don't Take Drugs Get Married Young Man Part I," "The Corner"

Lou Rodgers, Laura Delano, Robert Petersen,
Carole Ann Lewis, Frank Wicks, David Beckman
in "Poems"

Natural History Improvisation Co.

ST. MARKS CHURCH
Tuesday, February 18, 1975
The Natural History Improvisation Company presents:

THE NATURAL HISTORY OF THE AMERICAN DANCER

performed by
Carmen Beuchat
Suzanne Harris
Cynthia Hedstrom
Rachel Lew
Mary Overlie
(No other details available)

CUNNINGHAM STUDIO
February 19, 20, 21, 1975*

DANCES BY ROSALIND NEWMAN

Director-Choreographer, Rosalind Newman; Lighting Designer, Nancy Golladay; Sound, Caryn Benjamin; Stage Manager, Morgan Muir

COMPANY

Livia Blankman, Tom Borek, Naomi Dworkin, Ken Fisher, Micki Geller, Susan Goldstein, Velerie Manner, Gretchen Henry, Jonathan Hollander, Kate Johnson, Robert Kahn, Clarice Marshall, Stormy Mullis, Rosalind Newman, Victoria Uris, Renee Wadleigh, Debra Wanner, Alyssa Nan Hess (harpist)

PROGRAM

"Orange Pieces" (Faust), "Chapter II," "Chapter III" (Sound of Frogs),"Third Watch" (Latin Mass), and *NY PREMIERE* of "Flakes" (Ceres Motion by Steve Drews)
* Program repeated at Universalist Arts Center on March 23, 1975

Tom Borek, Rosalind Newman in "Chapter III"
Lois Greenfield Photo

February 22–23, 1975*
The Cunningham Dance Foundation presents:

MERCE CUNNINGHAM & DANCE COMPANY

Director-Choreographer, Merce Cunningham; Lighting Designers, Mark Lancaster, Richard Nelson; Decor, Mark Lancaster; Costumes-Artistic Adviser, Jasper Johns; Musicians, David Behrman, John Cage, David Tudor; Music Coordinator, David Behrman; Administrator, Greg Tonning; Technical Director, Nancy Golladay; Stage Manager, Charles Atlas; President of Board, Calvin Tomkins

COMPANY

Merce Cunningham	Chris Komar
Karen Attix	Robert Kovich
Ellen Cornfield	Brynar Mehl
Meg Harper	Charles Moulton
Susana Hayman-Chaffey	Julie Roess-Smith
Cathy Kerr	Valda Setterfield

PROGRAM: "Events": complete dances, excerpts of dances from the repertoire, and often new sequences arranged for the particular performance and place, with the possibility of several separate activities happening at the same time.
* Repeated Apr. 26–27, May 3–4, 10–11, 17–18, 24–25, 31–June 1, 1975.

Top Left: Merce Cunningham (center back) and Dance Company

LARRY RICHARDSON DANCE GALLERY
Saturday, March 1, 1975

DIANE BOARDMAN and DIANE ELLIOTT

Choreography, Diane Boardman, Diane Elliot; Lighting Design-Production Manager, Jon Knudsen; Technician, Edward Marsan; Sound, Louise Wykell

PROGRAM

"Blind Date" (Thom Edlun, Elliot) danced by Diane Boardman, Rick Biles; "After-Image" (Leedy, Elliot) danced by Diane Elliot; "Phase Two, Three, Four" (Ives, Boardman) danced by Jeffrey Eichenwald, Patrice Evans, Kathleen Gaskin; "Whirlrim" (David Van Tiegham, Elliot) danced by Pam Buddner, Timothy Crafts, Mark Esposito, Carl Pellegrini, Karen Sing, Gail Stepanek; "Oolite" (Alfred Janson, Boardman) danced by Diane Boardman; "Baquette" (Handel, Boardman) danced by Donald Blumenfeld, Susan Creitz, Diane Elliot, Patrice Evans, Joan Gedney, Vic Stornant

Diane Boardman in her solo "Oolite"

WASHINGTON SQUARE METHODIST CHURCH
Wednesday & Thursday, March 5–6, 1975
Harry's Foundation presents:

HARRY

Choreography, Senta Driver; Lighting Design, Robin Kronstadt; Costumes, George Alspach; Production Supervisor, Penelope Curry; Stage Assistant, Catherine Samardza; Composer, Tom Johnson

COMPANY

Senta Driver	Andrea Stark
Vera Blaine	Marianne Bachmann
Tom Johnson	Timothy Driver

PROGRAM: "Melodrama" (Robbie Basho), "Two Steps Outside" (Lukas Foss, Vera Blaine), "Dances to This Music #1" (Robbie Basho), "The Star Game" (Tom Johnson), "Memorandum" (Senta Driver), "Comma," "From Here to There and Back Again" (James Lindholm), "Lecture with Singing" (Tom Johnson)

Senta Driver in "Harry"
Jessica Burstein Photo

SCHIMMEL CENTER FOR PERFORMING ARTS
March 5–8, 1975 (4 performances)

DAN WAGONER and DANCERS

Choreography, Dan Wagoner; General Manager, Frank Wicks; Lighting, Jennifer Tipton

COMPANY

Dan Wagoner, Christopher Banner, Robert Clifford, Emmy Devine, Sally Hess, Karen Levey, Judith Moss, George Montgomery, Melvin Berger

REPERTOIRE

"Meets and Bounds," "Brambles" (George Montgomery, Wagoner), "Duet" (Purcell), "Iron Mountain" (Hindemith), "Broken Hearted Rag Dance" (Scott Joplin), "Changing Your Mind" (Montgomery, Wagoner)
NY PREMIERES: "A Sad Pavane for These Distracted Times" (Tomkins), "Taxi Dances" (Popular)
WORLD PREMIERE: "Summer Rambo" (Bach, Wagoner; Costumes, Kae Yoshida)

**Left: Sally Hess, Karen Levey
in "Meets and Bounds"**

JAPAN HOUSE AUDITORIUM
Thursday, March 6, 1975
The Foundation for Ethnic Dance presents:

MATTEO ETHNOAMERICAN DANCE THEATER
in
IMAGES OF ASIA

Artistic Director-Choreographer, Matteo; Associate Director, Carola Goya; Assistant to Matteo, Terry Yorysh; Costume Director, Carola Goya; Stage Manager, Robin Schraft; Sound, Robert Walker

COMPANY

Matteo	Terry Yorysh
Socorro Santiago	Sandra Fernandez
Janet Krause	Ingrid Ross
Carolyn Deats	Homer Garza
Deborah Novotna	John Kirshy
Judith	Robert Chiarelli

PROGRAM: "Ajanta Rasa," "The Legend of Sita," "Ts'ing P'ing T'iao," "Pwe," "Djoged Alus," "Seraglio Story," "A Hilo Au," "Nippon Suite," "Vannamas," "Bharata Suite"

Terry Yorysh, Matteo in "Ts'ing P'ing T'iao"
V. Sladon Photo

Ching Valdes, Reynaldo Alejandro

LA MAMA
Wednesday, March 12, 1975
Third World Institute of Theatre Arts Studies presents:

REYNALDO ALEJANDRO & DANCERS

Director-Choreographer, Reynaldo Alejandro; Design and Staging, Cecile Guidote; Set Design, Bert Hechanova; Music Coordinator, Mutya Gener; Production Assistants, Linda Pichon, Jun Maeda; Lighting, Larry Steckman, Jean-Guy Lecut; Stage Manager, Luisa Reyes; Technical Director, Charles Jenulevich

COMPANY

Reynaldo Alejandro, Ching Valdes, Dulce Valdes, Melen Acaac, Kathy Serio, Vicky Tiangco, Luisito Marquez, Eugene Domingo, Ramon de Luna, Eddie Sese, Benny Felix, Cesar Villanueva

PROGRAM

"Sayaw Silangan" (A Philippine perspective through its indigenous dances)

105

WASHINGTON SQUARE METHODIST CHURCH
Thursday & Friday, March 13–14, 1975
Washington Square Methodist Church presents:

ROLANDO JORIF DANCE COMPANY

Director-Choreographer, Rolando Jorif

COMPANY

Karen Battell
Maria Bueno
Joan Doberman
David Lee
Rolando Jorif

PROGRAM: "Luxury I" (Ravel), and *PREMIERE* of "Luxury II"
(Songs recorded by Marlene Dietrich during World War II), "Solo"
(in silence)

ELEO POMARE VITAL ARTS CENTER
Saturday & Sunday, March 15–16, 1975

DANCES BY LINDA DIAMOND

Choreography, Linda Diamond; Lighting Designer-Stage Management, Richard Gottlieb, Orin Wechsberg; Costume Design, Linda Diamond, Nalla Wollen, Rudy Mishaan

DANCERS

Linda Diamond	Tim Koelikamp
David Corash	Elaine Shipman
Barbara Engelbrecht	Robyn Wishengrad

PROGRAM: "Duo" (John Cage), "Mandala" (H. Partch), "Dreamreel" (Oldfield-Cage-Penderecki), "Quetzal" (Gary Lynes), "A Propos" (William Lord)

CUNNINGHAM STUDIO
March 15–16, 1975

SARA SUGIHARA DANCING WITH THE FAMILY:

James Boyd	Laurie McKirahan
Mary Jo Buhl	Christopher Pilafian
Richard Caceres	Terry Plante
Carrie Klein	Linda Spriggs
Dana Luebke	Karen Wilson

Choreography, Sara Sugihara; Costumes, Mary Jo Buhl; Lighting Design, Nancy Golladay; Sound, Peter Matusewitch; Production Assistant, Christiana Glover

PROGRAM: "Ho" (Scarlatti), "Carrie Alone" (12th Century Organ Music), "CANADAdances" (Leo Kottke), "Dances for Nothing" (Messaien-Henderson-Bartok-Britten), "Road" (Paul Winter Consort)

THE ENERGY CENTER
Friday, March 21, 1975
The Energy Center presents:

THE LAURA VELDHUIS DANCE COMPANY

Director-Choreographer, Laura Veldhuis; Guest Choreographer, Gary Davis; Lighting Designer-Technical Consultant, Joop Veldhuis; Stage Manager, Civia Zoe; Costumes, Salvatore Guida, Joop Veldhuis

COMPANY

Alan D'Angerio	Tom Hackley
Gary Davis	Ellen Pundyk
Diana Gregory	Laura Veldhuis

PROGRAM: "March" (Charles Ives), "The Mind's Garden" (Benjamin Britten), "Green Mountain Suite" (Peter Isaacson-John Isaacson), "Scraffito" (Mozart, Gary Davis), "Scan" (Yoko Ono-John Lennon, Gary Davis), "Essence and Transcendence" (Alberto Ginastera)

Rolando Jorif, Maria Bueno

Dances by Linda Diamond
Peggo Cromer Photo

Sara Sugihara dancing "Ho"
Leslie Sanguinetti Photo

TERRA FIRMA STUDIOTHEATER
Fridays, March 21 and 28, 1975

SYNERGY COMPANY

Artistic Director-Choreographer, Katherine Liepe; Chairman of the Board, Martin Levinson; Associate Director, James Medalia; Technical Adviser, Philip Jackson; Musical and Technical Consultant, Dana McCurdy

COMPANY

Katherine Liepe	Rick Hood
Dianne Bryan	Tara Mitton
Freddick Bratcher	Elyssa Paternoster
Barbara Frasier	Paula Schapiro
Annabella Gonzalez	Debra Zalkind

"The Pacers" (Beethoven, Katherine Liepe), "Solution Scene" (Bach-Willson, Debra Zalkind), "In a Silent Way" (Dana McCurdy, Paula Schapiro), "Guitar Solo" (Villa-Lobos, Liepe), "Ballade" (Chopin, Dianne Bryan), "The Knot" (Balanese, Liepe), "Out of the Cradle Endlessly Rocking" (Bloch, Liepe), "The Numbered" (Zimmermann, Liepe)

Rick Hood, Katherine Liepe performing "Knot"

ARTISTS SPACE
Friday, March 28, 1975
Artists as Filmmakers Series 75 presents:

DOUGLAS TURNBAUGH AND COMPANY

Direction and Realizations, Douglas Turnbaugh; Cinematography, Arthur Whitfield; Designs, Eduardo Vicuna-McKenna; Poetry, Dennis Phillips, Rene Char; Cine-Choreography, Douglas Turnbaugh; Stage Choreography, Ben Dolphin

COMPANY

Ben Dolphin
Willi Kirkham
Douglas Turnbaugh

PROGRAM: "Surveillance" (Poulenc), "Monuments" (Frederick the Great), "La Mort d'Axel Baron Gouda" (Satie), "My Child," "Toward Soho" (Corelli), "Diaghilev/Nijinsky Apotheosis" (Sound Collage)

Ben Dolphin, Douglas Turnbaugh
in "Diaghilev/Nijinsky Apotheosis"

THEATRE OF THE RIVERSIDE CHURCH
April 2–6, 1975 (8 performances)

AMERICA HAS MANY FACES

Conceived, Choreographed and Coordinated by Matteo; Narrative Script, Walter Terry; Assistant to Matteo, Terry Yorysh; Costume Director, Carola Goya; Scenic Designer-Stage Manager, Robin Schraft; Sound, Robert A. Walker; Technical Assistants, Andy Tron, Terry Davis, Michael Brown; Management Consultant, Mark Jones; Narrator, Matteo

COMPANY

Matteo	Carola Goya
Terry Yorysh	Socorro Santiago
Carolyn Deats	Janet Krause
Sandra Fernandez	Judith Landon
Homer Garza	Ingrid Ross
Robert Chiarelli	Bonnie Campos
Deborah Novotna	John Kirshy
	David Cripps

PROGRAM: "Invocation," "Hoop Dance," "Zandunga," "Jarabe Tapatio," "Laendler mit Platl," "Osdansen," "Khorovod," "Minuette," "Can Can," "Le Ballet," "Yembela," "Cake Walk," "Land of the Shamrock," "The Sophisticated Clapper," "La Tertulia," "La Malaguena y El Torero," "Ole deLa Cura," "Los Panaderos," "El Fandango," "Ts'ing P'ing T'iao," "Havdalah Bukharian," "Okame to Gombei," "Juraku Mai," "Natanam Adinar," "Kaalbaisaikhi," "Ho o puka," "A Hilo Au," "Cigany Tanc Szatmar," "Hasapiko," "Mazur," "La Quadriglia Napolitana," "International Square Dance"

"International Square Dance" from
"America Has Many Faces" (V. Sladon Photo)

JAPAN HOUSE
Wednesday & Thursday, April 2–3, 1975

THE GREENHOUSE DANCE ENSEMBLE

Manager, Ron Reagan; Lighting, Paul Butler; Stage Manager, Eiko Levitch; Costume and Set Designers, Jim Pelletier, Ned Hallick, Judith Brusseau, Beth Burkhardt, Raya

COMPANY

Carol Conway	Lillo Way
Nada Reagan	Brian Webb
Natalie Richman	Robert Yohn

PROGRAM: "Blued Spaces" (David Whiteside, Nada Reagan), "Fifth Avenue Pigeon" (Charles Morrow, Natalie Richman), and *PREMIERES* of "Product of the Sides" (Sergio Cervetti, Carol Conway), "Prairie Bowl" (Bella Bartok, Brian Webb), "Untitled" (Gerard Schwarz, Lillo Way), "Untitled" (Roger Rundle, Robert Yohn)

Ron Reagan Photo

**Left: Nada Reagan, Cathy Ward
(Greenhouse Dance Ensemble)**

THEATRE OF THE RIVERSIDE CHURCH
April 9–12, 1975
The Committee for the Theatre of the Riverside Church presents:

THE RHODE ISLAND DANCE REPERTORY COMPANY

Founder-Artistic Director-Choreographer, Julie Strandberg; Co-Founder-Choreographer, Kathy Eberstadt; General Manager, J. Erik Hart; Scenic, Costume and Lighting Designer, Peter Anderson

COMPANY

Julie Strandberg	Carl Hardy
Kathy Eberstadt	Clifton Thompson
Cathy Bodner	Mary Reavey
Sharon Jenkins	Bill Finlay

REPERTOIRE: "Fantasies Lying in a Hammock" (Bach, Kathy Eberstadt), "Three Dreams the Night Clara Died" (Edward Elgar-William Walton, Drew Harris), "Six Bagatelles" (Anton Webern, Peter Sparling), "Pavane" (Gabriel Faure, David Briggs), "Trinity Square" (Norma Dalby), "Magical Oppositions" (Gerald Shapiro, Julie Strandberg), "Air Antique" (Lukas Foss, Don Redlich), "Last Exit" (Peter Sculthorpe, Mary Margaret Giannone), "Sweet Patchwork" (Bach-Pachelbel, Carolyn Adams), and *PREMIERE* of "Broken Glass: To My Father's Corpse" (Medieval, Eberstadt)

**Julie Strandberg, Cathy Bodner, Mary Reavey
in "Broken Glass . . ." (R. I. Dance Repertory Co.)**

Sybil Huskey in "Strung"

LARRY RICHARDSON DANCE GALLERY
Thursday & Friday, April 10–11, 1975
The Larry Richardson Dance Gallery in association with Dance Theater Workshop presents:

DANCES BY MICKIE GELLER SYBIL HUSKEY NANCY SALMON

Technical Director and Lighting Designer, Francis Roefaro; Stage Manager, Jill Coghlan; Costumes, Marilyn Geller, Leslie Innis

PROGRAM

"Strung" (Bach-McCutcheon-Saussy-Villa-Lobos, Sybil Huskey) danced by Sybil Huskey and Nancy Salmon; "Spells" (Prokofiev, Mickie Geller) danced by Mickie Geller; "Quartets" (Joan Baez-Judy Collins-Laura Nyro, Nancy Salmon) danced by Sybil Huskey, Judy Pisarro, Graciela Torino; "Musings" (Samuel Barber, Sybil Huskey) danced by Sybil Huskey; "Scraperace" (Choreographed by Mickie Geller) danced by Mickie Geller

BYRD HOFFMAN SCHOOL FOR BYRDS
April 11, 13, 18, 19, 1975

NANCY TOPF DANCE CONCERT

with
Heather Brown
Stephen Crawford
Marcia Weese

PROGRAM: "4 Corner Warm Up with Falls and Spirals, the Vertical and the Round," "Duet Form: Four Variations," "Spiral Solo," "Spiral Solo with Chalk Circles," "Patterns with Stephen's Story"

**Left: Heather Brown, Nancy Topf, Marcia Weese
in "Patterns with Story"**
Babette Mangolte Photo

BRANDEIS AUDITORIUM
Thursday & Friday, April 17–18, 1975
Circum-Arts presents:

THE RICHARD BILES DANCE COMPANY

Director-Choreographer, Richard Biles; Lighting Design-Stage Manager, Jon Garness; Technical Assistant, Mark Ammerman; Stage Manager, K. S. Tartt; Press, Phillip Weiner; Costumes, Richard Biles, Ann Segan

COMPANY

Richard Biles, Kathy Buchanan, Pamela Budner, Susan Creitz, Donna Evens, Kathy Kroll, Dianne Markham, Gale Ormiston, Carl Pellegrini, Sandra Seymour

PROGRAM

PREMIERES: "The Celebrants" (Albinoni-Badings-Korngold), "Fluxion" (Henze), "Pendulum" (Arranged Sounds-Berg-Floss-Macedonian-Folk-Bernstein-Bennett)

Richard Biles Dance Company in "The Celebrants"
Phillip Weiner Photo

TEARS
April 18, 19, 20, 1975
The Movement Work Centre presents:

MOVING ROAD SONG

Collectively Choreographed and Danced by Sheila Mason, Ruth Gould, Sheila Sobel; Guest Musician, Carol Rupert; Lighting Design, Craig Evans; Costumes, Monika Bjarnestam; Sound, David Fullemann

PROGRAM

"Middle-Eastern Music," "N.Y. Pro Musica," "Village Music of Bulgaria"

**Sheila Mason, Ruth Gould, Sheila Sobel
in "Moving Road Song"**

BROADWAY DANCE FESTIVAL
April 17–May 8, 1975

Executive Director, Martin Gregg; Executive Secretary, Frances Ford Seymour; Production Stage Manager, Charles Paul Gollnick; Props, James McDonough

ROBERT F. KENNEDY THEATRE
Thursday, April 17, 1975

CHAMBER DANCE GROUP

Artistic Director, Nanette Bearden; Company Manager, Hank Frazier; Lighting, Martin Shapiro; Costumes, William Hooks, Caroline deLone; Business Manager, Mary Hula

COMPANY

Christopher Corry, Richard Walton, Monica Diaz, Beth Kurtz, Sheila Nowosadko, Shelly Gunderman, Nina Valery, Daniel Taylor, Donald Byrd, Natch Taylor, Quinton Smith, Lois Silk, Joaquin La Habana, Justice Skae

PROGRAM: "Baroque" (Francoeur-Rameau-Nondonville, Marvin Gordon), "Pas de Deux" (Grieg, Charles Neal), "Harp Suite" (Nicanor Zabeleta, Gordon), "Pas de Trois" (Vitalli, Charles Neal), "Transients" (Rod Levitt, Gordon), "Journey" (Kryzysztof Penderecki, Gordon), "Solo" (Tribute to Billie Holliday), "Peace" (O'-Jas, Morton Winston-Otis Sallid)

Thursday, April 24, 1975

Chamber Dance Group in "Harp Suite"

THE NEW YORK DANCE ENSEMBLE

Artistic Directors, Oceola Bragg, Beteanne Terrell; Ballet Mistress, Oceola Bragg; Production Manager, Gary Flora; Lighting, Judy Rasmuson; Costumes, Irene Fedotowa; Choreographers, Julie Arenal, Gordon Edwards

COMPANY

Beteanne Terrell, Myron Curtis, Dale Muchmore, Susan Theobald, Alison Woodstock, Linda Griffin, Kelly Carrol, Lindsay Jones, Ellen Kulik

PROGRAM: "Prelude on Love—The Pardon," (Galt McDermot, Gordon Edwards), "Private Circus" (McDermot, Julie Arenal; Lighting, Judy Rasmuson; Decor, Charles B. Slackman; Costumes, Irene Fedotowa), "La Novela" (Julie Arenal)

Thursday, May 1, 1975

EDITH STEPHEN DANCE COMPANY

Artistic Director-Choreographer, Costumes, Edith Stephen; Manager, E. Kapel; Lighting, Martin Shapiro; Stage Managers, Richard Abrams, Beth Zakar; Administrative Assistants, Nancy Parent, Geoffrey Brown

COMPANY

Edith Stephen, Lark Alden, Ralph M. Thomas, Ben Dolphin, Diane Moore, Richard Moore, Jeanne Suggs, Ann Kohn

PROGRAM: "Love in Different Colors" (Michael Dreyfuss), "Paradise Revisited" (Om Kumar Joshee), "ContinuOM" (Scott Joplin), "The Peacock" (Switch on Bach), "Flight" (Tyrone Washington, Ralph M. Thomas), "Dream of the Wild Horse" (Jacque Lasri)

Thursday, May 8, 1975

ARGYR LEKAS SPANISH DANCE COMPANY

Director-Choreographer, Argyr Lekas; Costumes, Enrique Arteaga, Luis Rodriguez; Lighting, Martin Shapiro; Program Coordinator, Ruth Dresdner; Company Manager, Isidore Dresdner

COMPANY

Argyr Lekas, Melinda Bronson, Jorge Navarro, Ernesto Navarro, Christina Schonberger, Danie Keith, Carlotta, Laura Piedra, Rafael Beltran, Eugene Thomas, Bertilla (pianist), Domingo Alvarado (singer), Paco Juanas (guitarist), and special guest artists Manuel Arenas, Roberto Lorca

PROGRAM: "Ole Dela Curra," "Zapateado," "Farucca," Jota Valenciana," "Soleares," "Tarantos," "Guajiras," "Caracoles," "Peteneras-Sequiriyas," "Cuadro"

Maurice Seymour Photo

Manuel Arenas, Argyr Lekas in "Tarantos"
Above: Ralph M. Thomas of Edith Stephen Dance C[
in "Love in Different Colors"

AMERICAN THEATRE LAB
April 18–20, 1975 (4 performances)

JAN WODYNSKI DANCE COMPANY

Choreography and Costumes, Jan Wodynski; Technical Designs-Direction, Mike Wodynski; Technician, Jodi Strano

COMPANY
Jan Wodynski

Kathy Eaton	David Malamut
Joanne Edelmann	Julie Maloney
John Kelly	Madeleine Perrone
Robert Kosinski	Mike Wodynski

REPERTOIRE: "Farrago" (Vocal Improvisation), "Pit-stop" (Environmental Sound), "Tudo (for Charles)" (Partch), "Pashun Zone: Sekter Five" (Khatchaturian), "Freewensi" (M. Wodynski), "Contours" (Winter Consort), "Triad" (M. Wodynski), "Changeover" (M. Wodynski), "Interspace" (Collin Walcott), "Taktiks"

Jan Wodynski Dance Company in "Taktiks"
Chuck Saaf Photo

GRAMERCY ARTS THEATRE
Sunday, April 20, 1975
The Spanish Theatre Repertory Company (Gilberto Zaldivar, Producer; Rene Buch, Artistic Director; Robert Federico, Associate Producer) presents:

THE MARIANO PARRA SPANISH DANCE COMPANY

Director-Choreographer, Mariano Parra; Lighting Designer, Mark Goodman; Booking, Tornay Management, Ltd.

COMPANY

Mariano Parra	Marcia Martinez
Jerane Michel	Lillian Ramirez
Ines Parra	Emilio Prados, Guitarist
Mariana Parra	Luis Vargas, Vocalist
Diana Marcelo	Bruce Eberle, Pianist

PROGRAM: "Panaderos de la Flamenca," "Baile para Dos" (Granados), "Las Mujeres de Cadiz," "Farruca," "Goyescas" (Granados), "Jota Valenciana," "Romanza Gitana," "Zapateado," "La Cana," "Leyenda" (Albeniz), "Tablao Flamenco"

The Mariano Parra Spanish Dance Company
Mark Goodman Photo

AMERICAN MUSEUM OF NATURAL HISTORY
Sunday, April 20, 1975
The American Museum of Natural History presents a performance of Asian dances with:

WON-KYUNG CHO
MANJUSRI CHAKI-SIRCAR
HU YUNG-FANG
HU HUNG-YEN

PROGRAM: "The Dance of the Old Man," "The Mask Dance," "Invocation to Lord Shiva and Parvati," "Bharatnatyam," "Monkey Dance," "Double Sword Dance," "Ribbon Dance"

CHOREOGROUND
Friday, April 25, 1975
Wilson Morelli and the Morelli Ballet presents the World Premiere of:

TOM

PRINCIPALS: Wilson Morelli, Chris Stocker, Larry Leritz
(No other details available)

Chris Stocker, Larry Leritz in "Tom"

AERENA STUDIO
April 25–27, 1975*
The Multigravitational Experiment Group presents:

MULTIGRAVITATIONAL AERODANCE GROUP

Artistic Director-Choreographer, Stephanie Evanitsky; Manager, Catherine Farinon Smith; Filmmaker, Robert Fiala; Composers, Richard Cameron, Richard Hayman, David Rossiter

COMPANY

Stephanie Evanitsky	Catherine Farinon Smith
Suellen Epstein	Glenna Kay Gainer
Arthur-George Hurray	Donald Porteus
Barbara Salz	Bronya Weinberg
Robert Fiala	Richard Cameron
Richard Hayman	David Rossiter

REPERTOIRE
(1974–1975)

"Sure Was" (Thomas, Evanitsky), "Silver Scream Idols" (Collage, Evanitsky), "Splat" (Fiala, Evanitsky-Fiala), "Alien Connection" (Collage, Fiala), and *PREMIERE* of "Buff Her Blind—To Open the Light of the Body" (Hayman-Rossiter, Evanitsky)

*Repeated on weekends during May, 1975.

THEATRE OF THE RIVERSIDE CHURCH
April 25–27, May 2–4, 1975 (6 performances)

PHYLLIS LAMHUT DANCE COMPANY

Director-Choreographer, Phyllis Lamhut; Lighting Designer, Ruth Grauert; Technical Directors, Jon Garness, Lee A. Goldman; Sound, Suri Bieler; Technician, Craig Evans; Stage Manager, Ruth Grauert; Manager, Judith Scott; Costumes, Dennis Cady, Frank Garcia, Joan Gedney, Lou Uhlen

COMPANY

Phyllis Lamhut	Diane Elliot
Emery Hermans	Patrice Evans
Kent Baker	Thomas Evert
Donald Blumenfeld	Kathleen Gaskin
Diane Boardman	Joan Gedney
Jeffrey Eichenwald	Natasha Simon

REPERTOIRE: "Medium Coeli" (Thomas Mark Edlun), "Excerpts from Extended Voices," and *PREMIERES* of "Country Mozart" (Mozart-Traditional), "Solo with Company" (Czajkowski), "Conclave" (Sound Score, Thomas Mark Edlun; Designed by Dennis Cady; Costumes, Lou Uhlen)

Glenna Kay Gainer, Donald Porteous, Suellen Epstein in "Buff Her Blind. . . ." (Multigravitational Aerodance Co
Charles Dexter Photo

Phyllis Lamhut (L) and company in "Solo with Company"

Tony Nunziata in "Energy Changes"
Davidson Gigliotti Photo

BROOKLYN MUSEUM AUDITORIUM COURT
May 1–4, 1975
The Brooklyn Museum presents:

ELAINE SUMMERS DANCE AND FILM COMPANY

Director-Choreographer, Elaine Summers; Composer, Philip Corner

COMPANY

Tedrian Chizik
Roberta Escamilla
Robert Kushner
Tony Nunziata
Alexandra Ogsbury

PROGRAM: "Energy Changes," a continuous performance lasting four days, in which the dancer's responsiveness to inner life force becomes the dance.

AMERICAN THEATRE LAB
May 2–4, 1975

CONSORT DANCE ENSEMBLE

Administrative Director, Margaret O'Sullivan; Choreographers, Myra Hushansky, Donna Mondanaro; Costume Designe⁻, Sylvia Woods; Lighting Designer, Daniel Potucek

COMPANY

Selby Beebe, Myra Hushansky, Miriam Kenig, Donna Mondanaro, Margaret O'Sullivan, Bobbie Silvera, Guest Reader and Vocalist Rolando Policastro

PROGRAM

"Millenium" (Sound Collage, Mondanaro), "Games" (Improvisation, Mondanaro), and *Premieres* of "Pulses" (Luening-Ussachevsky, Husansky), "Portrait" (Poem, Mondanaro), "Paper Clowns" (Music and Choreography by Donna Mondanaro; Poem, Lawrence Ferlinghetti), "Unescorted" (Pete Seeger, Hushansky), "Encounter" (Iannis Xenakis), "Song" (Arnold Schoenberg, Mondanaro)

Consort Dance Ensemble in "Games"
Chuck Wilson Photo

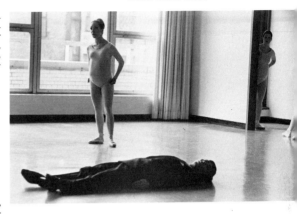

NEW DANCE GROUP STUDIO
Saturday, May 3, 1975*
The New Dance Group presents:

MOBILE UNITI
in
"Yok"

Choreography, Margot Colbert; Assistant to Choreographer, Marina Valenti; Poetry, Tape, Sets and Props, R. J. Colbert; Costumes, Marina; Assistant Set Designer, Sharon Shevell

COMPANY

R. J. Colbert	Holly Anne Lipton
Marina Valenti	Lottie Olcott
Margot Colbert	Michelle Beteta

*Program repeated May 10, 1975 at Terra Firma Studio Theater, and at the Joseph Jefferson Theatre May 11 and 18, 1975. (No photos available)

Right Center: Diane Drumet, Satoru Shimazaki, Judy Pisarro, Susan Whelan in "Signals"
Oleaga Photo

National Folk Ensemble of Peru
Satomeor Inc. Photo

THE NEW SCHOOL
May 3, 10, 17, 1975 (5 performances)

THE LAURA FOREMAN DANCE THEATRE

Director, Laura Foreman; Company Manager, Donna Moore; Booking Manager, Jane D. Schwartz; Associate Director-Rehearsal Mistress, Graciela Torino; Lighting Designer-Stage Manager, Raymond C. Recht; Sound, Paul Horenstein

COMPANY

Noel Chang	Judy Pisarro
Jeremy Dobrish	Nancy Salmon
Diane Grumet	Satoru Shimazaki
Leslie Innis	Carol Volanth
David Malamut	Susan Whelan
Hank O'Neal	Jeanne Hartman, Guest Artist

PROGRAM: "city of angels" (John Watts, Laura Foreman), "SIGNALS" (John Watts, Laura Foreman; Costumes, Raymond C. Recht, Alice Schwebke)

THE FELT FORUM
Sunday, May 4, 1975
Mel Howard in association with Madison Square Garden Productions presents:

THE NATIONAL FOLK ENSEMBLE OF PERU

Artistic Director, Victoria Santa Cruz; Assistant Director, Eduardo Gago Mago; Production Head, Marco Leclere; Scenery, Arturo Villacorta, Tula Espinoza; Costumes, Victoria Santa Cruz, Carmen Moore Morote, Atillo Lobo

PROGRAM

"Shapish," "Son de Los Diablos," "Kullawada," "Festejo," "K'ajelo," "Q'ara Chuncho," "Quena and Charango," "Carnival Limeno," "K'achampa," "Danza de Las Tijera," "Chonquinada," "Ya Yo Ta'Cansa," "Solischallay Solis," "El Mantequero," "Huaylars," "Zamacueca," "Diablada," Grand Finale

THEATRE OF THE RIVERSIDE CHURCH
Friday & Saturday, May 9–10, 1975

THE WETZIG DANCE COMPANY

Director-Choreographer, Betsy Wetzig; Lighting Designer, Robert McAndrew; Composer, Carl Michaelson; Sculptor, Richard Barnet; Sound, John Wetzig; Technical Directors, Robert McAndrew, Lee A. Goodman; Costumes, Carroll Bouman

COMPANY
Betsy Wetzig

Robert Chiarelli	Judy Lasko
Diana Fond	Evelyn Shepard
Meryl Green	Kathryn Woglom

PROGRAM: "Hello from Infinity" (Gunther Schuller), "Beginning" (Michaelson) "Soaring" (Schumann, Doris Humphrey), "Bring Your Child" (Wetzig), "A Woman's Jonah" (Michaelson)

David Lintner Photo

Right: Betsy Wetzig, Evelyn Shepard, Meryl Green in "Soaring"

Lee Connor, Nina Watt, Leif Wicklund in "Please Don't Stone the Clowns"

LARRY RICHARDSON DANCE GALLERY
May 15–17, 1975 (3 performances)
The Larry Richardson Dance Foundation presents:

CHOREOGRAPHY BY CARLA MAXWELL

Music Composed and Conducted by Stanley B. Sussman; Lighting Designs, Edward Effron; Production Stage Manager, David Rosenberg; Sound Coordinator, John Moore; Production Engineer, Mark Ammerman

COMPANY

Carla Maxwell, Nina Watt, Christopher Gillis, Debbie Carr, Susan Hogan, Penelope Hill, Marjorie Philpot, Tonia Shimin, Tryntje Shapli, Risa Steinberg, Lee Connor, Robyn Cutler, Penelope Garth, Kiki Lombardi, Peter Marsh, Gary Masters, Helen Snodgrass, Joe Pasternak, Louis Solino, Ed Notes, Leif "Knuckles" Wicklund, Facciana Bruta

PROGRAM

"aardvark brothers, swartz and columbo present Please Don't Stone the Clowns" (Couperin-Rameau-Scarlatti as arranged by Bob Wolinsky, pianist; Costumes, Carla Maxwell, Barbara Sexton), PREMIERES of "Place Spirit" (Sussman, Maxwell; Costumes, Allen Munch), "Blue Warrior" (Bach, Maxwell; Costumes, Allen Munch)

Emerson-Loew Photo

THEATRE OF THE RIVERSIDE CHURCH
May 15–18, 1975 (4 performances)

ZE'EVA COHEN
SOLO DANCE REPERTORY

Choreography, Ze'eva Cohen; Lighting Designer-Production Manager, Edward I. Byers; Pianist, Justin Blasdale; Technical Director, Lee Goldman; Costumes, Georgia Collins, Beth Burkhardt

PROGRAM

"Three Landscapes" (Alan Hovhaness-John Cage-Ali Akbar Kahn, Ze'eva Cohen), "Return" (Michael Czajkowski, Art Bauman), "Mothers of Israel" (Margalit Oved, Oved), and *World Premiere* of "Dreaming" (Alexander Scriabin, Anna Sokolow)

Ze'eva Cohen

EXCHANGE THEATER
May 15–19, 1975
Exchange Theater presents:

MIMI GARRARD DANCE THEATER

Director-Choreographer, Mimi Garrard; Lighting Designer-Stage Manager, Bill Campbell; Special Effects, James Seawright; Assistant Stage Manager, Jim McDonald; Technical Assistant, Ed Marsan; Technical Director, Keith Harewood; Costumes, Frank Garcia, Lou Uhlen; Press, Judith Scott

COMPANY

Mimi Garrard	Gary Davis
Gale Ormiston	Robert Kosinski
Irene Soler	Karen Levin
Janet Towner	Gloria McLean

PROGRAM: "Dualities" (Ghent), "Suite" (Brahms-Ghent), "Brazen" (Ghent), "Alla Marcia" (Popular), "Dreamspace" (Trimble)

Tom Caravaglia Photo

Karen Levin, Robert Kosinski, Mimi Garrard, Janet Towner, Gale Ormiston, Gary Davis, Irene Solen in "Dreamspace"

UNIVERSITY THEATRE
Friday, May 16, 1975
NYU Division of Art and Arts Education presents:

QUARTET OF DANCES

Lighting and Technical Director, Charles Miller; Technical Assistants, Darryl Brittain, Robin Graubard, Serelda Miller; Stage Managers, Rebecca Dinin, Jill Jacobs, Marybeth Gallant; Sound, Robert Sallier, Bonnie Robbins

PROGRAM

Kaleidoscope Dancers for Children (Judith G. Schwartz, Director) performing "Kaleidoscope," "Chairs," "Arhythmitix"; "Sagimusume" (Kichiji Fujita) danced by Sachiyo Ito; "Four Squares" (Robert Sallier, Kathy Duncan) danced by the Washington Square Repertory Dance Company (Laura Brittain, Director); "Nishimonai" (Traditional) danced by Shirly Botsford, Felice Dalgin, Sachiyo Ito, Rochelle S. Levine, Brenda Salter, Jonny Kyoko Sullivan; "The Edge" (Webern, Martha Rzasa) danced by Washington Square Repertory Dance Company; "Mourning Isis" and "Set'h" (Margalit Oved) choreographed and performed by Magda Saleh; "Ayako Mai" (Traditional, Ito) danced by Sachiyo Ito, Rochelle S. Levine, Brenda Salter; "Dance in Four Short Parts for Numerous Dancers" (Bach, Laura Brittain) performed by Washington Square Repertory Dance Company

Marylloyd Clayton, Sue Mandel, Marie Pintauro in "Four Squares" (Washington Square Repertory Dance Company)

THE HOUSE
Saturday & Sunday, May 17–18, 1975*
The House presents:

ANTHOLOGY and SMALL SCROLL

Conceived and Directed by Meredith Monk; Realized by The House; Music, Meredith Monk; Costume Consultant, Lanny Harrison; Lighting, Marie Gaines; Dedicated to C. S. Lewis

COMPANY

Meredith Monk	Daniel Ira Sverdlik
Tone Blevins	Lee Nagrin
Monica Moseley	Ping Chong

PROGRAM: "Anthology (The Queen's Entertainment): Mesa, Tablet, Lullaby, Tale, Soil, Do You Be," "Small Scroll"

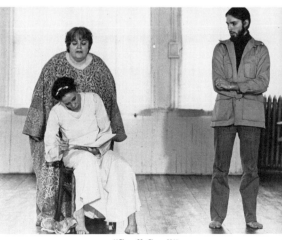

"Small Scroll"

HUNTER COLLEGE PLAYHOUSE
May 21–25, 1975 (5 performances)
Kazuko Hillyer in cooperation with the Foundation for the Vital Arts presents:

ELEO POMARE DANCE COMPANY

Artistic Director-Choreographer, Eleo Pomare; Managing Director, Michael E. Levy; General Manager, Virgil D. Akins; Lighting Designer, Gary Harris; Costumes, Eleo Pomare, Judy Dearing; Props and Sets, Michael Melitanov; Dance Captain, Frank Ashley; Lighting, David H. B. Drake

COMPANY

Eleo Pomare	Anita Littleman
Jennifer Barry	Strody Meekins
Charles Grant	Martial Roumain
Dyane Harvey	Rosalie Tracey
Joe Johnson	Mina Yoo
John Parks	Bill Chaison

POMARE II: Robin Becker, Irene Belk, Alistair Butler, Nan Imbesi, Pat Jones, John Juhl, June Segal, Tony Small

REPERTOIRE

"Radiance of the Dark" (Edward Hawkins Singers), "Passage" (Fellegara), "Serendipity" (Handel), "Roots" (American Folk-Billie Holiday-Nikki Giovanni), "Las Desenamoradas" (John Coltrane), "Narcissus Rising" (Collage by Michael E. Levy), "Movements II" (Morton Subotnick), "Transplant II" (Pointer Sisters-Graham Central Station), "Hushed Voices" (Ornette Coleman, Charles Mingus, Leon Thomas, Don Cherry, Chicago Art Ensemble), "Faces of Noon" (Varess), "Junkie" (Charles Mingus), and *WORLD PREMIERE* Wednesday, May 21, 1975 of "De La Tierra" (George Crumb-Walter Carlos-Harey Parten, Eleo Pomare; Costumes, Eleo Pomare) danced by the company.

New Beginnings company in "Rhythm"
Kenn Duncan Photo

TERRA FIRMA
Saturday & Sunday, May 17–18, 1975
Terra Firma Studio Theater presents:

WORKS BY ANNE WOODS & SYBIL HUSKEY

Lighting Design and Technical Direction by Nancy Kammer

PROGRAM

"A Dancey Dance" (Vivaldi, Choreographed and Performed by Sybil Huskey), "Surrounded" (Bach, Choreographed and Performed by Anne Woods), "Inflation" (Collage, Choreographed and Performed by Sybil Huskey), "Antique Roses" (Leonard Cohen, Choreographed and Performed by Anne Woods), "Memory Piece" (George Crumb, Choreographed and Performed by Anne Woods), "Strung" (Bach-McCutcheon-Saussy-Villa Lobos; Choreography, Sybil Huskey; Performed by Nancy Salmon, Sybil Huskey), "Camp" (Choreographed and Performed by Anne Woods)

Left: Anne Woods

Rosalie Tracey, Carl Paris, Mina Yoo, Carole Simpson, Charles Grant, Jennifer Barry, Henry Yu (Eleo Pomare Dance Co.) in "Serendipity" *(Jonathan B. Atkin Photo)*

THEATRE OF THE RIVERSIDE CHURCH
May 21–25, 1975
The Theatre of the Riverside Church presents:

NEW BEGINNINGS

Conceived and Choreographed by John Montgomery; Music Direction-Arrangements, Susan Romann; Costumes, Barbara Bec[...]; Stage Managers, Jack Timmers, Sandra Mande; Assistant Choreo[...]rapher, Leland Palmer; Technical Director, Lee A. Goldman; Ligh[...]ing Designer, Diana Banks

COMPANY

Gene Aguirre	Tony Pad[...]
Elly Barbour	Leland Palm[...]
Christine Barbour	Michael Perr[...]
Joan Bell	Paul Pizz[...]
Kyle Cittadin	Racine Romagu[...]
Wendy Lamoreaux	Susan Roma[...]
Frank Mastrocola	Connie Sha[...]

PROGRAM: "Rhythm," "Ease on down the Road," "Dream [...]bies," "Leroy Brown," "Wave," "Bluesette," "Dream for Tom[...]row," "Johnny Be Good," "Roll over Beethoven," "Vincen[...] "Malaguena," "Sail on Sweet Universe," "Come to the M[...]querade," "Masquerade Ballet," "Lady Marmalade," "MacArt[...] Park," "Be a Lion," "Gladiolus," "I Think I Like You," "Talk[...] Old Soldiers," "You're Nobody," "Walk Him Up"

QUEENS THEATRE-IN-THE-PARK
May 22–24, 1975
The Round House Company presents:

THE MARIA ALBA DANCE COMPANY

Director-Choreographer, Maria Alba; Lighting Designer, Beverly Emmons; Technical Advisers-Stage Managers, Maxine Fouros, Craig Miller; General Manager, Kermit Smith; Management, Artservices

COMPANY

Maria Alba
Roberto Cartagena
Paco Ortiz
Adonis Puertas

PROGRAM: "Mirabras," "Pinceladas," "Tarantos," "Encuentro," "Baile Para Dos," "Orgia," "Suite Colombiana"

Susan Cook Photo

Left: Maria Alba in "Tarantos"

SCHIMMEL CENTER FOR THE ARTS
May 22–25, 1975 (4 performances)
Pace University in New York presents:

DANCES WE DANCE

with
BETTY JONES & FRITZ LUDIN

REPERTOIRE: "Facets" (Nikolais, Murray Louis; Costumes, Frank Garcia), "The Warrior and The Widow" (Toru Takemitsu, Carl Wolz; Costumes, Carl Wolz), "On Dancing" (Josef Wittman, Martha Wittman; Costumes, Lenore Davis), "Duet" (Purcell, Dan Wagoner; Costumes, Dan Wagoner), "Pink Rocker" (Perrey Kingsley, Connie Jo Hepworth), "Play It as It Rings" (Sound Arranged, Shirley Ririe-Joan Woodbury; Costumes, Leo), "Journey #2: For an Angel and a Clown" (Josef Wittman, Martha Wittman; Costumes, Martha Wittman), "Journey to a Clear Place" (Henry-Schaeffer-Varese-Ussachevsky, Martha Wittman; Costumes, William Sherman), "Improv to Haydn" (Haydn, Fritz Ludin), "Untitled Solo" (Schumann, Martha Wittman), Lighting by Jennifer Tipton

Right: Betty Jones, Fritz Ludin in "Journey #2: For an Angel and a Clown"

HUNTER COLLEGE PLAYHOUSE
Tuesday, May 27, 1975
The Center for Inter-American Relations, The Hunter Arts Concert Bureau,, and The Embassy of Brazil present:

STAGIUM CHAMBER BALLET OF BRAZIL

Director-Choreographer, Decio Otero; Lighting and Sound, Herodino Loretto; Co-Director, Marika Gidali; Artistic Director, Ademar Guerra

COMPANY

Geralda Bezerra, Marika Gidali, Nadia Luz, Monica Mion, Beth Oliviera, Julia Ziviani, Milton Carneiro, Ademar Dornelles, Segastiao Freitas, Ricardo Gomes, Ricardo Ordonez, Decio Otero, Miguel Trezza

PROGRAM

"Jerusalem" (Almeida Prado, Decio Otero), "Diadorim" (Villa-Lobos-Violado-Folk Themes-Bird Songs, Otero), "Mary I, The Mad Queen" (Nobre-Santoro-Gomes-Lobo-Guerra-Vandre, Otero)

Stagium Chamber Ballet of Brazil in "Mary I, The Mad Queen"

117

WIND TUNNEL

(A Work in Progress)
with Nancy Topf, Heather Brown, Marcia Weese, Jon Gibson
(Sound), Terry O'Reilly (Construction)

PROGRAM

"Streams in the Tunnel," "Cloth Hanging off Triangles," "Arms
Filling the Space, Spreading," "Set Sequence," "Space Duet,"
"Pants Dance," "Patterns with Stops," "Cloth Dance"

Nancy Topf in "Wind Tunnel"
Babette Mangolte Photo

HIGH SCHOOL OF PRINTING
May 29, 30, 31, 1975
The School of Performing Arts presents:

DANCE CONCERT 1975

Producer, Lydia Joel; Assistants to the Producer, Crystal Smith,
Adrian Rosario; Technical Director, Thomas de Gaetani; Technical
Assistant, Elaine Gigueri; Stage Crew, Rhonda Edmonds, Sabrina
Davis, Roy Rodriguez, Tony Roldan; Ballet Mistress, Stephanie
Zimmerman; Conductor, Jonathan Strasser

COMPANY

Carol Beatty, Gregory Burge, Jane Burgman, Lori Cabrera, Leslie
Cirabisi, Charmaine Clarke, Anna Corchia, Nina Dostal, Robin
Estes, Judy Fairborne, Vicki Feller, Nicole Flender, Constance
Gerker, Daniela Goldman, Jeanne Hanrahan, Lisa Hernandez, Col-
lette Hiller, Susan Hobson, Cynthia Jackson, Linda Jefferson,
Cynthia Jones, Edward Jordan, Barbara Matthews, Angela McGre-
gory, Cary Regan, Sylvia Robinson, Jose Roldan, Venus Romero,
Adrian Rosario, Eric Sawyer, Crystal Smith, Kim Stroud, Janette
Tashiji, Darryl Tribble, Dwight Velasquez, Patricia Whaley

PROGRAM

"There Are Dreams" (Sarah Malament, Penny Frank), "Laurencia
Pas de Six" (Alexander Kraine, Dorothy Fiore after V. Chabukiani),
"Yaqui Indian Deer Dance" (Taped ritual performance, Jose
Coronado), "The Passing Parade" (Scott Joplin, Keith Lee), "Going
North, 1881" (Louisiana State Prisoners-Rev. Gary Davis-Sacred
Harp Singers-Fred McDowell, Dianne McIntyre), "Abstract Etch-
ings" (Hindemith, Keith Lee)

**Right Center: Adrian Rosario
in "Yaqui Indian Deer Dance"**
Martha Swope Photo

SYNOD HOUSE
May 29, 30, 31, 1975
The Church of St. John the Divine in association with Dance Theater
Workshop presents:

A TOWN IN THREE PARTS

Choreography, Mel Wong; Lighting Designer and Stage Manager,
Andy Tron; Assistant Stage Manager, Joan Certa; House Manager,
Susan Atran

COMPANY

Brigid Baker, Terese Capucilli, Susan Dibble, Reuben C. Edinger,
Susan Emery, Alan Good, Kristine Lindahl Hoffman, Gwyneth
Jones, Rosalind Newman, Grazia de la Terza, Renee Wadleigh,
Susanna Weiss, Leslie Wilson, Mel Wong

MARYMOUNT MANHATTAN COLLEGE
May 29, 30, 31, 1975
Marymount Manhattan College Theatre presents:

RUDY PEREZ DANCE THEATER

Direction, Choreography, Sound Collages, Rudy Perez; Production Manager-Lighting Designer, Chip Largman; Technical Assistants, Ken Merkel, Steve Lewis; Assistant to Mr. Perez, David
Varney; Company Manager, Sandy Fowkles; Audio, John Moore;
Composer, Noah Creshevsky

COMPANY

Karen Masaki
Rudy Perez
Jeffrey Urban
David Varney
Erin Martin, Guest Artist

PROGRAM: "Topload/Offprint," "Transit," *NY PREMIERE* of
"Daddy's Girl" (Duke Ellington, Erin Martin), Premieres of "Inter-
face," "Parallax"

**Mel Wong in "A Town
in Three Parts"**

CONSTRUCTION COMPANY DANCE STUDIO

May 29–June 1, 1975
Theater/Dance Associates presents:

GELMAN/PALIDOFSKY DANCE THEATRE

Artistic Directors, Linda Gelman, Meade Palidofsky; Business Manager, Paul Zuckerman; Designer, Margaret Sedgeman; Lights, Dave Gilbert; Sound, Paul Zuckerman; Masks, Dianne Austin

COMPANY

Anonymous Bacon	Sarah Martens
Doug Funt	Bettze McCoy
Linda Gelman	Meade Palidofsky
Karen Gelman	Margaret Sedgeman
Meg Gilbert	Eric Zuckerman
Martha Hirschman	Paul Zuckerman

PROGRAM: "3Dialogues for 2 Voices and 2 Bodies" (Written by Meade Palidofsky; Choreographed by Linda Gelman, Martha Hirschman, Sarah Martens), "To Philip" (Alan Gruskoff, Linda Gelman), "Six Impossible Things for Breakfast" (Written by Meade Palidofsky), "Cat's Cradle" (Conceived and Choreographed by Linda Gelman), "The Liturgy of the Mass according to Mary Magdalen" (Music, Jim Henja; Written by Meade Palidofsky; Choreography, Linda Gelman, Martha Hirschman)

Gelman/Palidofsky Dance Theatre in "Six Impossible Things before Breakfast"
E. Zuckerman Photo

THEATRE OF THE OPEN EYE

May 30–31, June 1, 1975
The Open Eye presents:

JAPANESE CLASSICAL DANCES

Choreography, Sachiyo Ito; Lighting Designer and Stage Manager, Mark Goodman

COMPANY
Sachiyo Ito

Esther Chaves	Felice Dalgin
Ari Darom	Dan Erkkila
John Genke	Teiji Ito
Andrea Stark	Cherel Winett

PROGRAM: "Wysteria Maiden," "Mitsumen Komori," "Melody of Akita Folk Song," "Nishimonai," "Ayako Mai," "Koku," "Sambaso"

Esther Chaves, Sachiyo Ito, Andrea Stark in "Ayako Mai" *(Japanese Classical Dance)*

CARNEGIE RECITAL HALL

Saturday, May 31, 1975

RITHA DEVI

in
Angana (Femina)

PROGRAM: "Eight Phases of the Eternal Eve," "Devi," "Devadasi," "Swadheena-Bhartrika," "Janani," "Mohini," "Virahotkanthita," "Kurathy," "Danavi"

TERRA FIRMA

Saturday & Sunday, May 31, June 1, 1975

RECENT WORKS TWO

Dances by Art Berger, Doris Ginsberg, and Holly Schiffer; Lighting Design, Tina Charney

PROGRAM

"Peggy's Room" (Sound Collage by Art Berger-Mason Klein; Choreography, Holly Schiffer; Performed by Art Berger-Holly Schiffer), "Broken Flight, In Ink" (Vivaldi, Choreographed and Performed by Doris Ginsberg), "Solo for Two Feet, Two Legs, Two Hands, Two Arms, One Torso, One Head, and Other Body Parts Too Numerous to Mention" (Conceived and Performed by Art Berger), "Untitled Solo" (Transman; Choreography, Art Berger; Performed by Holly Schiffer), "Her Dream" (Score Written and Directed by Stephen Samuels, Read by Stephanie Gallas; Choreography, Doris Ginsberg; Performed by Mickie Geller and Doris Ginsberg)

Ritha Devi

ANNUAL SUMMER DANCE FESTIVALS OF 1974

AMERICAN DANCE FESTIVAL
New London, Connecticut
June 26–August 3, 1974
Twenty-seventh Year

Director, Charles Reinhart; Dean, Martha Myers; Coordinator, Celia Halstead; Press, Jane Hughes Paulson, Mary Ann Doyle; Technical Director, Fred Grimsey, Lindsey Miller, Benjamin Howe, Mark Litvin

Wednesday, June 26, 1974

THE KATHRYN POSIN DANCE COMPANY: Kathryn Posin, Karen Attix, John Cwikala, Jennifer Douglas, Rosalind Newman, Christopher Pilafian, Lance Westergard, performing "Nuclear Energy I" (Nurock, Posin), "Nuclear Energy II" (Nurock, Posin), "Days" (Kirk Nurock, Posin), "Ghost Train" (Meredith Monk, Posin), "Bach Pieces" (Bach, Posin)

Friday & Saturday, June 28, 29, 1974

THE PAUL TAYLOR DANCE COMPANY (Artistic Director-Choreographer, Paul Taylor; General Manager, Judith Daykin; Administrator, Neil S. Fleckman; Musical Director, John Herbert McDowell; Company Manager, Perry Cline) with Paul Taylor, Carolyn Adams, Bettie DeJong, Eileen Cropley, Ruby Shang, Nicholas Gunn, Monica Morris, Elie Chaib, Lila York, Greg Reynolds, dancing "Party Mix" (Alexei Haieff, Taylor), "Untitled Quartet" (Stravinsky, Taylor), "3 Epitaphs" (American Folk, Taylor), "Post Meridian" (DeBoeck, Taylor), "So Long Eden" (Fahey, Taylor), "Duet" (Haydn, Taylor), "Big Bertha" (Band Machines, Taylor), "Public Domain" (McDowell, Taylor)

Sunday, June 30, 1974

TRISHA BROWN AND COMPANY: Carmen Beuchat, Trisha Brown, Carol Goodden, Sylvia Whitman, Jim Barth, Jed Bark performing "Skymap" "Group Primary Accumulation," "Pamplona Stones," "Accumulation"

Friday & Saturday, July 5 & 6, 1974

THE NIKOLAIS DANCE THEATRE (Sound, Choreography, Costumes, Lighting, Alwin Nikolais) with Lisbeth Bagnold, Rob Esposito, Bill Groves, Steven Iannacone, Janet Katzenberg, Lynn Levine, Suzanne McDermaid, Gerald Otte, Gladys Roman, Jessica Sayre, James Teeters, Fred Timm, performing "Suite from Sanctum," "Scenario," "Tent," "Divertissement," "Cross-Fade"

Wednesday, July 10, 1974

NORA GUTHRIE-TED ROTANTE DANCE COMPANY in "Corporate Images II" (Harvey Mandell, Ted Rotante), "Up 'n' Comin" (Work in progress; Jack Hansen, Nora Guthrie)

Thursday, July 11, 1974

SARA AND JERRY PEARSON with Kent Baker, Timothy Crafts, Tom Evert, Laura Fly, Fred Janis, Keats Johnson, Gary McKay, Harry Streep III, dancing "Vis-a-Vis" (Vivaldi, Gladys Bailin), "Auras" (Jerry Pearson-Dean Granros, Sara and Jerry Pearson), "Amnesia" (Takemitsu-Vivaldi, Sara Pearson), "A Mild Mannered Reporter" (Big Brother and the Holding Company, Jerry Pearson), "Magnetic Rag" (Scott Joplin, Sara and Jerry Pearson)

Thursday & Friday, July 11 & 12, 1974

MULTIGRAVITATIONAL EXPERIMENT GROUP (Artistic Director, Stephanie Evanitsky; Assistant Artistic Director, Robert Fiala; Lighting, Charles Dexter) with Suellen Epstein, Kay Gainer, Arthur-George Hurray, Donald Porteous, Barbara Salz, Bronya Wajnberg, Llewellyn Wheeler, premiering "Buff Her Blind—To Open the Light of the Body" (Sound, Richard Hayman, David Rossiter; Stephanie Evanitsky; Costumes, Nils Eklund)

Kathryn Posin Dance Company in "Nuclear Energy"
Johan Elbers Photo

Nikolais Dance Theatre in "Tent"

Nora Guthrie, Ted Rotante in "Corporate Images"
Lois Greenfield Photo

CONNECTICUT COLLEGE

Tuesday, July 16, 1974

DANIEL NAGRIN in "Changes: a retrospective of solo dances 1948–1974"

Wednesday & Thursday, July 17 & 18, 1974

CHUCK DAVIS DANCE COMPANY (Artistic Director-Choreographer, Chuck Davis; Musical Director, Yomo Awolowo; Lighting, Fred Grimsey) with Marilyn Banks, Sandra Burton, Monifa Olajorin, Milton Bowser, Chuck Davis, Charles Wynn, John Young, dancing "Dyembe and Chant," "Ibedi-Bedi," "Fofo," "N'Tore Dance," "Boot Dance," "Simple Prayer"

RITHA DEVI in "Bharatha Natyam," "Thillana," "Kuchipudi"

ANNA ARAGNO and GEORGE DE LA PENA in "Blue Bird Pas de Deux" (Tchaikovsky, Petipa)

LYNNE CHARLES and VICTOR BARBEE in "Flower Festival at Genzano Pas de Deux" (Paulli-Helsted-Gade, Bournonville)

Friday & Saturday, July 19 & 20, 1974

THE LOUIS FALCO DANCE COMPANY (Artistic Director, Louis Falco; Managing Director, Carl Hunt; Associate Directors, Jennifer Muller, Juan Antonio; Music Director, Burt Alcantara; Lighting, Richard Nelson; Stage Manager, Suzanne Egan) with Louis Falco, Jennifer Muller, Juan Antonio, Georgiana Holmes, Matthew Diamond, Mary Jane Eisenberg, Angeline Wolf, dancing "Twopenny Portrait" (Burt Alcantara, Falco), "Sleepers" (Falco), "Speeds" (Alcantara, Jennifer Muller), "Biography" (Alcantara, Muller), "Caviar" (Robert Cole, Falco)

Friday & Saturday, July 26 & 27, 1974

NANCY MEEHAN DANCE COMPANY: Nancy Meehan, Micki Goodman, Amy Horowitz, Trude Link, Sara Shelton, Mary Spalding, dancing "Yellow Point" (Rocco di Pietro, Meehan)

JENNIFER ... WITH FRIENDS: Jennifer Muller, Georgiana Holmes, Mary Jane Eisenberg, Angeline Wolf, Matthew Diamond, Lance Westergard, Carol-rae Kraus, dancing "Winter Pieces" (Curtis O. B. Curtis-Smith, Jennifer Muller)

MANUEL ALUM DANCE COMPANY: Manuel Alum, Felicia Norton, Joan Lombardi, Malou Airaudo, Dominique Mercy, Tony Constantine, dancing "Yemaya" (Ira Taxin, Manuel Alum)

BELLA LEWITZKY DANCE COMPANY: Lynda Davis, Sean Greene, Iris Pell, Bruce Taylor, Nora Reynolds, dancing "Five" (Max Lifchitz, Bella Lewitzky)

Sunday, July 28, 1974

PILOBOLUS DANCE THEATRE: Jonathan Wolken, Michael Tracy, Alison Chase, Moses Pendleton, Martha Clarke, Robby Barnett, performing "Ciona," "Triptych," "Pseudopodia," "Anaendrom," "Spyrogyra," "Dispretzled," "Monkshood's Delight"

Friday, August 2, 1974

LAURA DEAN AND DANCE COMPANY: Laura Dean, Grethe Holby, Diane Johnson, dancing "Changing" (John Smead, Laura Dean)

TRISHA BROWN AND COMPANY performing "Pamplona Stones"

PILOBOLUS DANCE THEATRE in "Monkshood's Delight"

Saturday, August 3, 1974

MULTIGRAVITATIONAL EXPERIMENT GROUP in "Buff Her Blind—To Open the Light of the Body"

NORA GUTHRIE and TED ROTANTE in "Learn To" (Charles Hansen—E. J. Miller, Nora Guthrie)

SARA and JERRY PEARSON in "Exposure" (Dennis Cochrane) choreographed and danced by Sara and Jerry Pearson

Top Right: Chuck Davis Dance Company and Drummers *(Irene Fertik Photo)*

Right Center: Louis Falco in "Twopenny Portrait"
Jack Mitchell Photo

Nancy Meehan
Dave Sagarin Photo

121

JACOB'S PILLOW DANCE FESTIVAL
Lee, Massachusetts
July 2–August 24, 1974
Forty-second Year

Founder, Ted Shawn (1891–1972); Acting Director, Charles Reinhart; Administrator, Grace Badorek; Policy Planning Committee, Donald Saddler, Stuart Hodes; Press, Nigel Redden, Linda Ossenfort

July 2–6, 1974

BOTTOM OF THE BUCKET BUT ... DANCE THEATRE: Ronald Baxter, Caren Calder, Mary Greely, Peggy Hewitt, Steve Humphrey, Nedia Padilla, Priscilla Scott, Roger Smith, Almeta Whitis, Diane Atkins, Daniel Ayette, Andre Barnes, Deidre Eli, Pat Howard, Tomasha Moore, Joanne Tulli, Ron White, performing "Roots" (Olatunji, Garth Fagan), "Liberation Suite" (Howard Roberts Chorale-Archie Shepp-Nina Simone-E. Rodney Jones-Pat Howard, Garth Fagan), "Thank You Jesus" (Billy Taylor-Don Shirley-Christian Tabernacle Choir, Garth Fagan)

RITHA DEVI in "Kuchipudi," "Tharangam," "Mahari Nritya," "Gati-Vilasa-Pallavi"

LISA BRADLEY and MICHAEL UTHOFF (July 2–3–4) dancing "Dusk" (Satie, Uthoff) and "Windsong" (Edward Elgar, Uthoff; Costumes, Alan Madsen)

GELSEY KIRKLAND and HELGI TOMASSON (July 5–6) dancing "Pas de Deux from The Nutcracker" (Tchaikovsky, Balanchine) and "Grand Pas de Deux from Don Quixote" (Minkus, Petipa)

July 9–13, 1974

DAN WAGONER AND DANCERS; Christopher Banner, Robert Clifford, Judith Moss, Emmy Devine, Sally Hess, Karen Levey, Anne Sahl performing "Brambles" (Written and Spoken by George Montgomery; Choreography, Dan Wagoner; Lighting, Jennifer Tipton), "Duet from Changing Your Mind" (Wagoner), "Taxi Dances" (Popular, Wagoner)

DENNIS WAYNE'S AMERICAN BALLET COMPANY: Robin Welch, James Dunne, Francesca Corkle, Donna Cowan, Dennis Wayne, dancing "Grand Pas de Deux from Don Quixote" (Minkus, Petipa), "Youth" (Samuel Barber, Richard Wagner), "A Sketch for Donna" (Bach, Paul Sanasardo; Costumes, Allen Madsen; *World Premiere*), and "Lazarus" (Fiser, Norman Walker)

July 15–16, 1974

MANUEL ALUM DANCE COMPANY: Malou Airaudo, Dominique Mercy, Kathleen Carlin, Tony Constantine, Joan Lombardi, Felicia Norton, Manuel Alum, performing "Deadlines" (Bach, Alum), "East - to Nijinsky" (Tal, Alum), and "Era" (Penderecki, Alum)

SANDRA JENNINGS and VICTOR BARBEE dancing "Flower Festival Pas de Deux" (Paulli-Helsted-Gade, Bournonville)

CARMEN deLAVALLADE and WESLEY FATA in "Portrait of Billie" (Holliday, Butler)

ANNA ARAGNO and GEORGE DE LA PENA dancing "Blue Bird Pas de Deux" (Tchaikovsky, Petipa)

CARMEN deLAVALLADE dancing "Creation" (Poem, James Waldon Johnson; Choreography and Costume, Geoffrey Holder)

July 17–20, 1974

NIKOLAIS DANCE THEATRE: Lisabeth Bagnold, Rob Esposito, Bill Groves, Steven Iannacone, Janet Katzenberg, Lynn Levine, Suzanne McDermaid, Gerald Otte, Gladys Roman, Jessica Sayre, James Teeters, Fred Timm, performing (All Choreography, Sound, Costumes, and Lighting by Alwin Nikolais), "Manits from Imago", "Foreplay," "Suite from Sanctum"

**Top Right: Bottom of the Bucket But ...
Dance Theatre** *(John Lindquist Photo)*

Right Center: Manuel Alum Dance Theatre
Oleaga Photo

Nala Najan

JACOB'S PILLOW

July 23–27, 1974

MIMI GARRARD DANCE COMPANY: Mimi Garrard, Gale Ormiston, Irene Soler, Karen Levin, Lynn Ruthenberg, Vic Stornant, Gloria McLean, Bill Setters, Janet Towner, performing "Phosphones" (Emmanuel Ghent, Garrard), "Video Variations" (Arnold Schoenberg, Garrard), "Dreamspace" (Lester Trimble, Garrard)

ELIOT FELD BALLET: Helen Douglas, Suzanne Erlon, Valerie Feit, Eliot Feld, Elizabeth Lee, George Montalbano, Christine Sarry, Jeff Satinoff, Naomi Sorkin, John Sowinski, dancing "Sephardic Song" (Traditional, Feld), "Cortege Parisien" (Chabrier, Feld)

July 30–August 3, 1974

JUDITH JAMISON and MIGUEL GODREAU in "Prodigal Prince" (Choreography and Music, Geoffrey Holder)
NALA NAJAN in "Pushpanjali," "Devaranama," "Krishna ni begane baro . . . ," "Trital or Jhaptal," "Kathak Court Dance of North India"
JOHN PARKS in "Just Me" (Kenny Baron, John Parks; Costume, Judy Dearing)
MIGUEL GODREAU dancing "Paz" (Ariel Ramirez, Godreau)
JUDITH JAMISON in "Nubian Lady" (Yuseff Lateef, John Parks)
JUDITH JAMISON, MIGUEL GODREAU, JOHN PARKS dancing "Icarus" (Matsushita, Lucas Hoving; Costumes, Larry LeGaspi)

August 6–10, 1974

CHUCK DAVIS DANCE COMPANY: Marilyn Banks, Sandra Burton, Monifa Olajorin, Milton Bowser, Chuck Davis, Charles Wynn, John Young, Yomi Awolowo, Babafemi, Philip Williamson, dancing "Dyembe and Chant," "Fofo," "Women's Dance," "Konkoba," "Post Initiation Dance," "Isicathula"

PEARL LANG AND DANCE COMPANY: Daniel Maloney, David Roche, Susan McLain, Bob Bowyer, Christine Dakin, Richard Arbach, Doborah Zalkind, Philip Grosser, Jacqulyn Buglisi, Jerome Sarnat, Alice Coughlin, Christopher Pilafian, Debra Arch, dancing "At This Point in Time or Place" (Lucas Foss-Charles Ives, Lang), "Shirah" (Hovhaness, Lang)

PILOBOLUS DANCE THEATRE: Jonathan Wolken, Michael Tracy, Alison Chase, Moses Pendleton, Martha Clarke, Robby Barnett, performing "Monkshood's Farewell"

JACOB'S PILLOW

August 13–17, 1974

MARIA ALBA SPANISH DANCE COMPANY: Maria Alba, Jose Antonio, Roberto Cartagena, Deardra Correa, Liliana Ramirez, Jorge Navarro, Ernesto Navarro, Luis Vargas (singer), Guillermo Rios (Guitarist), performing "Los Gitanos" (Vargas, Jose Antonio), "Tarantos" (Alba), "Taberna en Sevilla" (Choreography, Jose Antonio), "Yerma" (Guillermo Rios, Alba), "Pinturas Flamencas"

August 20–24, 1974

LOTTE GOSLAR'S PANTOMIME CIRCUS: Donna Baldwin, Bob Bowyer, Ray Collins, Gary Easterling, Daniel Giagni, Lotte Goslar, Jerri Lines, Clay Taliaferro, performing "Greetings," "For Feet Only," "All the King's Men," "Life of a Flower," "Splendor in the Grass," "A Dream," "Bird Fanciers," "The Come-on," "Collectors Items: 3 Music Boxes," "Grandma Always Danced," "Circus Scene" (All choreography and Costumes by Lotte Goslar)

JOSE LIMON DANCE COMPANY: Jennifer Scanlon, Carla Maxwell, Clay Taliaferro, Louis Solino, dancing "The Exiles, Movements 1 & 2" (Schoenberg, Limon), "The Moor's Pavane" (Purcell-Sadoff, Limon)

Chuck Davis Dance Company

Pearl Lang (R) and company in "Shirah" *(Fred Fehl Photo)*

Lotte Goslar's Pantomime Circus (Lotte Goslar (R))

123

NEW YORK DANCE FESTIVAL
Delacorte Theater, Central Park
New York, N.Y.

Producer, Joseph Papp; Associate Producer, Bernard Gersten; Executive Producer, Donald Saddler; Associate Producer, Stuart Hodes; Technical Coordinator, Rob Ingenthron; Stage Managers, Robert Kellogg, John Beven; Production Coordinator, Linda Rogers; Audio, Roger Jay, Michael Lawrence, Richard Nealy, Karen Kantor; Wardrobe Mistress, Alyce Gilbert; Stage Crew, Jason La-Padura, Pamela Allen, Mark Paquette; Presented by the New York Shakespeare Festival

PROGRAMS

Thursday, August 29, 1974

THE BLUE MOUNTAIN PAPER PARADE in "True Spirits" (Tape Collage, Chip Largman, Barbara Roan; Conceived by Barbara Roan; Choreographed and Directed by Irene Feigenheimer, Barbara Roan, Anthony LaGiglia; Additional Choreography, Annabelle Gamson, Jude Bartlett, and members of the company) performed by Nancy Scher, Jude Bartlett, Irene Feigenheimer, Laurie Gittleman, Dennis Florio, Laurie Uprichard, Amy Berkman, Suse Barnes Moore, Charles Madden, Genevieve Kapuler, Hollyce Yoken, Robert Marinaccio, Ellen Robbins, Barbara Roan, Avi Davis, Karen Chalom, John Moore, Ellen Jacob, Mary Benson, Joan Schwartz, Karla Wolfangle, Anthony LaGiglia

DIANNE McINTYRE'S SOUNDS IN MOTION in "Union" (Text, Langston Hughes, Margaret Walker; Choreography, Dianne McIntyre; Lighting, Sandra Ross) performed by Phillip Bond, William Donald, Lonnetta Gaines, Bernardine Jennings, Laurie Williams, and musicians Ahmed Abdullah, Babafumi Akunyun, Gwendolyn Nelson, Steven Solder "Jesus' Children of America" (*World Premiere:* Music, Stevie Wonder; Choreography, Quincy Edwards; Lighting, Sandra Ross) danced by Phillip Bond, William Donald, Linda Griffin, Carol Pennyfeather, Bernardine Jennings, Victor Braxton, Dianne McIntyre

MARIA ALBA SPANISH DANCE COMPANY in "Tarantos" danced by Maria Alba with Luis Vargas (Flamenco Singer), Guillermo Rios (Guitarist), "Taberna en Sevilla" (Choreographed by Jose Antonio) danced by Maria Alba, Jose Antonio, Deardra Correa, Liliana Ramirez, Jorge Navarro, Ernesto Navarro

ELIOT FELD BALLET in "The Gods Amused" (Claude Debussy, Eliot Feld; Lighting, Jennifer Tipton) danced by Lawrence Rhodes, Elizabeth Lee, Christine Sarry, "Cortege Parisien" (Emmanuel Chabrier, Eliot Feld; Costumes, Frank Thompson) danced by Christine Sarry, Helen Douglas, Naomi Sorkin, John Sowinski, George Montalbano, Jeff Satinoff

Friday, August 30, 1974

Same as Thursday's program but without Dianne McIntyre's Sounds in Motion, and the addition of CARMEN deLAVALLADE and WESLEY FATA in "Portrait of Billie" (Billie Holliday, John Butler)

Saturday, August 31, 1974

FRED BENJAMIN DANCE COMPANY in "Parallel Lines" (Hubert Laws-War, Fred Benjamin), and "Prey" (Alphonze Mouzon, Fred Benjamin; Costumes, Olon Godare) danced by Marilyn Banks, Milton Bowser, Ralph Farrington, Milton Myers, Keith Simmons, Jan Simons, Tina Steinway, Juanita Tyler, Terrin Miles, Karen Burke, Donald Griffith

PILOBOLUS DANCE THEATER in "Ciona" (Jon Appleton, Pilobolus Dance Theater), and "Anaendrom" (Jon Appleton, Pilobolus Dance Theater) performed by Jonathan Wolken, Michael Tracy, Alison Chase, Moses Pendleton, Martha Clarke, Robby Barnett

ELIOT FELD BALLET in "The Gods Amused" (Debussy Feld), and "Cortege Parisien" (Chabrier, Feld)

CARMEN deLAVALLADE and WESLEY FATA in "Portrait of Billie" (Holliday, Butler)

Top Right: Blue Mountain Paper Parade in "True Spirits" *(Bill Longcore Photo)*

Right Center: Elizabeth Lee, Lawrence Rhodes, Christine Sarry (Eliot Feld Ballet members) in "The Gods Amused" *(Tom Victor Photo)*

Pilobolus Dance Theater

NEW YORK DANCE FESTIVAL

BOTTOM OF THE BUCKET BUT ... in "Roots" (Olatunji, Garth Fagan), and "Liberation Suite" (Howard Roberts Chorale-Archie Shepp-Nina Simone-E. Rodney Jones, Garth Fagon)
PILOBOLUS DANCE THEATER in "Ciona" and "Anaendrom" (Jon Appleton, Pilobolus)
PEARL LANG AND DANCE COMPANY in "Shirah" (Alan Hovhaness, Pearl Lang) danced by Pearl Lang, David Roche, Bob Bowyer, Susan McLain, Christine Dakin, Doborah Zalkind, Jacqulyn Buglisi, Alice Coughlin, Debra Arch, Richard Arbach, Philip Grosser, Christopher Pilafian, Jerome Sarnat
Monday, September 2, 1974
PEARL LANG AND DANCE COMPANY in "At This Point in Time or Place" (Lucas Foss-Charles Ives, Pearl Lang), and "Shirah" (Hovhaness, Lang)
DENNIS WAYNE'S DANCE REPERTORY THEATRE in "Youth" (Samuel Barber, Richard Wagner; Costumes, Allen Madsen) danced by Bonnie Mathis, Dennis Wayne, "Sketch for Donna" (J. S. Bach, Paul Sanasardo; Costumes, Allen Madsen) danced by Donna Cowen, James Dunne, "Lazarus" (Fiser, Norman Walker; Costumes, David James) danced by Dennis Wayne
BOTTOM OF THE BUCKET BUT ... in "Liberation Suite," "Thank You Jesus" (Billy Taylor-Don Shirley-Christian Tabernacle Choir, Garth Fagan)
Tuesday, September 3, 1974
GEORGE FAISON UNIVERSAL DANCE EXPERIENCE in "Suite Otis" (Otis Redding, George Faison; Costumes, Will Rowe), and "Only the Righteous..." (Tape, Choreography and Costumes by George Faison) danced by Hope Clarke (guest artist), Vicky Baltimore, Veda Jackson, Christina Kimball, Claudia Lewis, Karen McDonald, Leah Randolph, Graciela Simpson, LeVon Campbell, Gary DeLoatch, George Faison, Keith Harris, Paul Hoskins
ZE'EVA COHEN in "Escape" (Kenyon Hopkins, Anna Sokolow), and "Countdown" (Songs of the Avergne, Rudy Perez)
KATHERINE LITZ in "The Fall of the Leaf" (Louis Gottschalk, Katherine Litz; Costumes, Remy Charlip)
DENNIS WAYNE'S DANCE REPERTORY THEATRE in "Lazarus" (Fiser, Walker) danced by Mr. Wayne, and "Sketch for Donna" (Bach, Sanasardo) danced by Donna Cowen, James Dunne
Wednesday, September 4, 1974
THE CLIFF KEUTER DANCE COMPANY in "Visit" (William Hellerman, Cliff Keuter; Lighting, Nicholas Lyndon) danced by Joan Finkelstein, Ellen Jacob, Elina Mooney, Karla Wolfangle
DENNIS WAYNE'S DANCE REPERTORY THEATRE in "Youth" (Barber, Wagner) danced by Bonnie Mathis, Dennis Wayne, and "Lazarus" (Fiser, Walker) danced by Dennis Wayne
KATHERINE LITZ in "The Fall of the Leaf" (Gottschalk, Litz)
GEORGE FAISON UNIVERSAL DANCE EXPERIENCE in "Reflections of a Lady" (Tape and Choreography, George Faison; Poetry, Norman Riley) danced by Hope Clarke (guest artist), and the company
Thursday, September 5, 1974
LAR LUBOVITCH in "Statement" (Stravinsky, Lubovitch)
ZE'EVA COHEN in "Escape" (Hopkins, Sokolow), and "Countdown" (Songs of the Avergne, Perez)
ROSE MARIE WRIGHT and KENNETH RINKER in "A Duet by Twyla Tharp" (Bach, Tharp)
ELEANOR D'ANTUONO and TED KIVITT in "Pas de Deux from Swan Lake Act II" (Tchaikovsky, Ivanov-Petipa), and "Don Quixote Grand Pas de Deux" (Minkus, Petipa)
LAR LUBOVITCH and SUSAN WEBER in "Eight Easy Pieces" (Stravinsky, Lubovitch)
GEORGE FAISON UNIVERSAL DANCE EXPERIENCE in "Reflections of a Lady" (Tape and Choreography, George Faison)

Top Right: Donna Cowen, James Dunne
Thomas Victor Photo

Right Center: Pearl Lang in "Shirah"
Fred Fehl Photo

Eleanor D'Antuono

THE YARD
Chilmark, Massachusetts
August 1–19, 1974

Director, Patricia N. Woolner; Assistant Director, Jack Moore

PROGRAMS

Thursday, August 1, 1974

"Broccoli" (Music, Ralph Towner, Mike Wodynski; Choreographed and performed by Bill Kirkpatrick), "Garden of Delights" (Sound, Evelyn DeBoeck; Choreography, Jack Moore; Performed by Sin Cha Hong, Diana Theodores, Jan Wodynski), "Ocydrome" (Choreography, David Malamut; Performed by Bill Bass, Sin Cha Hong, Bill Kirkpatrick, David Malamut), "Chamber" (Music, Mario Davidousky; Choreographed and performed by Sandra Genter), "Quonsethut" (Collaboration of Bill Bass, Bill Kirkpatrick, Jan Wodynski), "untitled solo" (Music, Meredith Monk; Choreographed and performed by Sin Cha Hong), "Pit Stop" (Music, Environmental; Choreographed by Jan Wodynski; Performed by David Malamut), "Crossroad" (Music, John Gates; Choreography, Sin Cha Hong; Performed by Bill Bass, Bill Kirkpatrick, David Malamut)

Thursday & Friday, August 15–16, 1974

"Ready" (Choreography, Irene O'Brian; Performed by Lisa Nalvin, Irene O'Brian, Francine Piggott, Diana Theodores), "Winds" (Music, Peter Neumann, Margot Page, Erin Martin, Mark Scally; Choreography, Patricia N. Woolner; Performed by Bill Bass, Bill Kirkpatrick, Saturo Shimazaki, Sandra Gener, Eva Vasques), "Belljar" (Sound Collection, Bill Bass, Jack Moore, Bill Kirkpatrick; Choreography, Bill Kirkpatrick; Performed by Lisa Nalvin), "Solo" (Choreographed and performed by Saturo Shimazaki), "Garden of Delights Part II" (Sound, Evelyn DeBoeck; Choreography, Jack Moore; Performed by Bill Bass, Bill Kirkpatrick, David Malamut), "bluedance" (Music, John Hagen; Choreography, Diana Theodores; Performed by Lisa Nalvin, Francine Piggott, Eva Vasquez, Diana Theodores)

Thursday, August 29, 1974

"Transformations" (Choreographed and danced by Micki Goodman), "Broccoli" (Music, Ralph Towner, Mike Wodynski; Choreographed and danced by Bill Kirkpatrick), "Poetry" (Read by Mildred Dunnock), "Daddy's Girl" (Music, Duke Ellington; Choreographed and Danced by Erin Martin with Bill Kirkpatrick)

Bill Bass, Reuben James Edinger, Bill Kirkpatrick, Morgan Muir, Patricia Woolner in "Dandelion Garden" *(Andrew B. Wile Photo)*

Sin Cha Hong in "Untitled Solo"
Michael Zide Photo

Erin Martin in "Daddy's Girl"
Michael Zide Photo

REGIONAL AND PROFESSIONAL DANCE COMPANIES
(Failure to meet deadline necessitated omission of several companies)

ALBERTA CONTEMPORARY DANCE THEATRE
Edmonton, Alberta, Canada

Artistic Directors-Choreographers, Jacqueline Ogg, Charlene Tarver; Managing Director, Ronald Holgerson; Guest Choreographers, Wallace Seibert, Marsha Padfield, Mary Moncrieff, Sherry Ogg; Stage Manager, Donald Bouzek.

COMPANY

Hamish Boyd, Gayle Fekete, Robert Fleming, Catherine Geddes, Maureen Herman, Ronald Holgerson, Joann Johnstone, Mary Moncrieff, Sherry Ogg, Oscar Riley, Lottie Schroen, and *Apprentices:* Blake Halwa, Geoffrey Hogan, Margo Kane, Jan Pezarro, Holly Pimm, David Wensel.

REPERTOIRE

"Saraband" (Visee, Ogg), "Alberta Suite" (Carlos-Schifrin-Copeland, Tarver), "Parmi Les Reves" (Lasry-Ouzounoff-Bashet, Ogg), "Haute Mer" (Ravel, Ogg)
PREMIERES: "Circles of Silence" (Revised-Archer-Forsyth, Ogg), "After the Judgment" (Copeland, Moncrieff), "The Canary" (Carlos, Sherry Ogg), "Reflections II" (John Scott, Marsha Padfield), "The Seagull and the Eagle," "The Hound and the Porcupine," "The Lion" (Albrecht-Coleman-Fields, Tarver; also titled "Gnash Nash" based on poems of Ogden Nash), "Pendulum of the Mind" (Shankar, Tarver), "Moods" (Jazz Medley, Siebert)

Forrest Bard Photos

**Alberta Contemporary Dance Theatre
in "Pendulum of the Mind"**

AMERICAN CHAMBER BALLET
New York, N.Y.

Director-Choreographer, Joel Benjamin; Assistant Director, Larry Line; Ballet Mistress Trutti Gasparinette; Technical Director, Betsy Tanner; Costumes, Gasparinetti; Audio, Acoustiguide; Management, Kazuko Hillyer International.

COMPANY

Melanie Adam, Joel Benjamin, Cheryl Carty, Trutti Gasparinetti, Ricardo Garcia, David Gleaton, Martha Goodman, Dana Greer, Gailanna Jensen, Richard Karsten, David Kottke, Larry Leritz, Larry Line, Audrey Ross, Rachel Verona

REPERTOIRE

"Nocturno" (Grieg, Charles Neal), "Spring Waters" (Rachmaninoff, Richard Holden), "Changing Time" (Toru Takemitsu-Lejaren Hiller, Trutti Gasparinetti), "The Ugly Girl of Uldergon" (Adam, Gasparinetti), "Le Pas de Quatre" (Pugni, Gasparinetti)

American Chamber Ballet

ANN ARBOR CIVIC BALLET
Ann Arbor, Michigan

Founder-Artistic Director, Sylvia Hamer; Co-Directors, TeDee A. Theofil, Mary Jane Williams; Musical Director, Georgia Bliss; Stage Craft, Alan Peterson; Stage Director, Jay King

COMPANY

PRINCIPALS: Donna Adams, Caroline Billings, Beverly Burck, Kathy Birchmeier, David Craig, Michael Eastman, Sherry Fisher, Steve Janick, Leslie Marich, Jeffrey Miller, Kathy Mull, TeDee A. Theofil, Mary Jane Williams
Tena Casey, Sarah Crane, Zerrin Crippen, Jan Nyquist, Patricia Parkis, Melanie Siebert, Beth Stoner, Gwen Werner, Jennifer Wilinson
Elaine Abbrecht, Cynthia Buchell, Renee Chung, Franz Harary, Lisa Kovanda, Carroll Oliva, Coleen Stackhouse, Wendy Walker, Susanne White

REPERTOIRE
(1974–75)

"Sleeping Beauty" (Tchaikovsky, Christine Dubouley), "Espana" Choreographed by Dom Orejudos), and *PREMIERES* of "Snow White and Seven Woodsmen," "Memento" (Choreographed by Dom Orejudos), "Eight to Eternity" (Choreographed by TeDee A. Theofil)

**Ann Arbor Civic Ballet
in "Memento"**

ANN ARBOR DANCE THEATRE
Ann Arbor, Michigan

Co-Presidents, Rusty Schumacher, Joan K. Woodward; Secretary, Nancy Adams Armendariz; Treasurer, Marti Reesman; Board Members, Mary Ann Daane, Alice Hinterman Hejna, Donna Jacobson
COMPANY: Names not submitted
PREMIERES: "Morning" (Oregon, Linda Reiff), "The Rime of the Ancient Mariner" (Choreographed by Donna Jacobson), "So You're a Wise Guy. . . . Eh?" (Sound Collage, Liz Colburn)
(No photos available)

ATLANTA BALLET
State Ballet of Georgia

Founder-Consultant, Dorothy Alexander; Director, Robert Barnett; Associate Directors, Merrilee Smith, Tom Pazik; Director of Apprentices, Joanne Lee; General Manager, Charles Fischl; Executive Secretary, Linda C. Fischl; Choreographers, Robert Barnett, Todd Bolender, Norbert Vesak, Duncan Noble, Tom Pazik, Ginger Prince Hall, Peggy Myers; Conductor, John Head; Lighting Designer, Charles Fischl; Costume Designer, Tom Pazik; Stage Managers, Lee Betts, Phil Hutcheson, Jeff Key; Press, Sally Way

COMPANY

Anne Burton, Rose Barile, Merry Clark, Amy Danis, Kathryn McBeth, Joanne McKenney, Ellen Richard, Steven Bradley, Ben Hazard, Ronald Jones, Tom Pazik
Candy Allen, Don Bailey, Wendy Crawford, Caitilin Driscoll, Mary Linn Durbin, David Hackney, Jaimie Kirk, Michele Lagoureur, James Lee, Susan Leslie, Caron Osborn, Heather Scupine, Alicia Stevenson
GUEST ARTIST: Burton Taylor

REPERTOIRE

"Gift to Be Simple" (Traditional, Vesak), "Concierto de Aranjuez" (Rodrigo, Barnett), "Lifeline" (Husa, Hall), "Pas de Trois" (Minkus, Balanchine), "Song of Love" (Suk, Noble), "Valse" (Strauss-Gungle, Barnett), "Glinkadances" (Glinka, Barnett), "Counterform" (John Fifter, Myers), "Just Two" (Varese, Hall), "Wedding Pas from Raymonda" (Glazounov, after Petipa), "Waltz Pas de Deux" (Nikode, Barnett), "Pas de Deux from Don Quixote" (Minkus, Traditional), "Flower Festival in Genzano" (Helsted, Bournonville), "Giselle" (Adam, Blair), "Nutcracker" (Tchaikovsky, Balanchine), "Serenade" (Tchaikovsky, Balanchine)
PREMIERES: "Good Morrow" (Mahler, Vesak), "Still Point" (Debussy, Bolender), "Great Scott" (Joplin, Pazik), "No Sunrise Finds Us" (Albanoni, Pazik), "Quatre Vignettes" (Britten, Barnett)

Paul Buckholdt Photos

**Left: Rose Barile, Tom Pazik, Ronald Jones
in "Lifeline" (Atlanta Ballet)**

Rose Barile in "Serenade" (Atlanta Ballet)

AUGUSTA BALLET COMPANY
Augusta, Georgia

Artistic Director, Ron Colton; Assistant Director, Zanne Beaufort; Lighting Designer-Production Manager, Jim Thomas; Stage Manager, Fran Simkins; Wardrobe, Dot Bowers; Press, Suzanne Beaufort

COMPANY

Zanne Beaufort, Kelly Bowers, Karen Carter, Lil Easterlin, Cammy Fisher, Laurie Hardman, Peggy Howard, Julie Jacobs, Julie Rece, Ann Weibel, Renee Williams, Bet Willingham
GUEST ARTISTS: Rose Barile, Steven Maynard, Tom Pazik

REPERTOIRE

"The Nutcracker" (Tchaikovsky, Barnett-Balanchine), "Les Sylphides" (Chopin, Merrilee Smith-Fokine), "The Rookery" (Xenakis-Husa, Ginger Prince), "A Brandenburg Movement" (Bach, Zompakos), "Gas" (Williams, Colton-Smotrel), and PREMIERE of "Bagatelles Op. 5" (Tcherepnin, Zompakos)

Augusta Ballet in "A Brandenburg Movement"

Austin Ballet in "Aurora's Wedding"
Bill Records Photo

BALLET DES JEUNES
Philadelphia, Pennsylvania
Merchantville, N.J.

Directress, Ursula Melita; Choreographers, Ursula Melita, Ruth Skaller, Carmencita Lopez; Sets, Tom Gallagher; Stage Manager, Janet Feldenkreis; Pianist, Irene Andrews; Production Manager, Pete Schussler; Wardrobe, Sherry Bazell, Marie Sinnott, Nancy Sterling Shomer, Teresa Angrisani Waugaman; Make-up, Angela Jenkins; Press, Fay Smelkinson

COMPANY

Cindy Alberts, Myra Bazell, Doris Bencic, Susan Berger, Ann Marie Bright, Sandy Bender, Torre Bressler, Karen Cebular, Esther Cohen, Claudia Collings, Miriam Cummings, Maria DeRosa, Amelia DeRosa, Joy Edelman, Eve Edelman, Andrea Elsner, Kim Forlini, Carolyn Franzen, Kathy Fuzer, Amanda Gamel, Marina Iossifides, Sally Jackson, Jennifer Jenkins, Leonard Jenkins, Sarah Jones, Sheila Jones, Caroline Krakower, Diane Landers, Debbie Lang, Jennifer Lockwood, Carol Maloney, Ginny Magee, Kathy Miller, Marylyn Morris, Connie O'Hara, Debbie O'Hara, Jeanne Papotto, Jackie Reisman, Amy Orloff, Lisa Robbins, Holly Ruckdeschel, Carol Rubin, Helene Sadler, Debbie Saldana, Karen Schussler, Maryann Sinnott, Wanessa Tillman, Donna Tambussi, Michele Triolo, Vicky Triolo, Marianne Trombetta, Dina Terry, Theresa Scott, Renee Vekkos, Chris Vlaskamp, Douglas Vlaskamp, Evelyn Wang, Lisa Weinstein, Amy Wilen, Michele Wood, Barbara Yeager

REPERTOIRE

"Sorcerer's Apprentice" (Dukas, Melita), "Snow Queen" (Mayer, Melita), "Pas de Quatre" (Pugni, Holgar Linden), "Hoe Down" (Copland, Melita), "Suite of Spanish Dances" (Folk, Lopez); "Rosin Box" (Padwa, Linden), "Hello World" (Mayer, Melita)
PREMIERES: "Excerpts from Carmen" (Bizet, Melita), "Tales of the Vienna Woods" (Strauss, Melita), "The Beauty of Dance and the Joy of Dance" (Chopin, Melita)

Dottie Jackson Photo

AUSTIN BALLET THEATRE
Austin, Texas

Artistic Director-Choreographer, Stanley Hall; Director, Judy Thompson; Sets and Costumes, Kathy Gee, Marguerite Wright; Lighting, Robe Dorris; Sound, Lee Thompson; Stage Manager, Mark Loeffler; Press, Jane Koock, Betty Adams

COMPANY

Jone Bergquist, Brantly Bright, Terri Lynn Wright, Steve Brule, Victor Culver, Ricardo Garcia, Byron Johnson, Ken Owens, George Stallings, Lisa Frantz, Shelley Schleier, Lisa Smith, Judy Thompson, Mary Claire Ziegler
Gina Adams, Tani Adams, Bonnie Bratton, Gail Brown, Nora Byrd, Arletta Howard, Lea Johnson, Eve Larson, Lynda Lindsay, Rosemary Thomas, Lucia Uhl, Michie Ward, Roberto Adams, Doug Becker, Anthony Chiu, Robert Ellis, Clint Fisher, Charles George, Jimmy Haile, Dave Larson, DeHart McMillan, Victor Shea, Russell Easley

REPERTOIRE

"Tchaikovsky Suite," "Le Combat" (Spartacus-Khatchaturian), "Napoli Pas de Trois" (Panlli-Helsted-Gade), "Tregonell" (Goldsmith-Ussachevsky), "Gemini" (Massenet), "Flickers," "Centennial Rag"
PREMIERES: "Aurora's Wedding" (Tchaikovsky, Hall), "Lark's Tongue in Aspic" (King Crimson, Hall), "Sylvia Suite" (Delibes, Hall)

Carolyn Franzen of Ballet des Jeunes

BALLET CONCERTANTES
San Juan, P.R.

Artistic Director and Choreographer, Lotti Tischer; Assistant Choreographer, Lotti Cordero

COMPANY

Lynette Anderson, Sandra Aresti, Rosamin Bennazar, Margie Cambian, Lily Fortuno, Cochita Miranda, Patricia Misner, Beatriz Morini, Vanessa Padilla, Conchita Schuck, Mary Ann Soto, Arlene Urrutia, Margarita Colon, Clarita Costa, Jorge Arce, Ivonne Cruz
GUEST ARTIST: Larry Leritz

REPERTOIRE

"The Sleeping Beauty," "Rapsodia Hungara," "Raices," "La Espera," "Las Pleydes," "Viva La Pepa," "La Carcajada," "El Sueno de Gloria," "Que Sera?"

BALLET JOYEUX
Lake Charles, Louisiana

Performing Company of Lake Charles Ballet Society; Artistic Director-Choreographer, Ida Winter Clarke; Assistant Director, Cissie Clarke; Designer, Emily Coleman; Technical Adviser, Ken W. Hine; Stage Manager, Lee Allured; President, Ruth K. White; Press, Della K. Thielen

COMPANY

Mari Ferguson, Polly Anderson, Kay Beatty, Barbara Berger, Phoebe Brian, Maureen Callahan, Bruce Campbell, Jesse Doty, Margaret Droddy, Beverly Facione, Catherine Hebert, Vicki Lanza, John Painter, Renee Plauche, Libby Tete
Jeannine Dolan, Lisa Fontenot, Lisa Greenlee, Marcia Hooper, Mary Kay Hudson, Lisa Khonke, Rebecca Pitre, Ashley Scott, Esther White, and apprentices
GUEST ARTISTS: Anna Argano, Leo Ahonen, Soili Arvola, Whit Haworth, Mary Margaret Holt, Edward Villella

REPERTOIRE

"Capriccio" (Mendelssohn, Richard Englund), "Fiddletunes" (Folk, Clarke), "Grand Tarantelle" (Gottschalk, Englund), "Gyre and Gambol" (Scarlatti-Albeniz-Weissberg-Villa-Lobos, James Clouser), "Les Patineurs" (Mayerbeer-Lambert, Clarke), "Papillons" (Shumann, Clarke), "Pas de Trois" (Adam, Ramon Segarra), "Nutcracker" (Tchaikovsky, Clarke)
PREMIERES: "A Song for Jose" (Bach, Marjorie Mussman), "Bouquets" (Adam, Clarke), "Ragtime Rhythms" (Scott Joplin, Cissie Clarke)

Jesse Doty, Mari Ferguson in "Song for Jose"
(Ballet Joyeux)

BALLET PACIFICA
Laguna Beach, California

Founder-Artistic Director-Choreographer, Lila Zali; General Director, Douglas Reeve; Press, Sally Reeve; Ballet Mistress, Kathy Jo Kahn; Technical Director, Carl Callaway; Wardrobe, Myrth Malaby; Choreographers, Kathy Jo Kahn, Carrie Kneubuhl, David Lichine, Victor Moreno, Michael Panaieff, Lisa Robertson, Benjamin Sperber, Nancy Sutton, Jill Sweet; Sets, Tania Barton, Anne Gordon, Sandra Winieski; Costumes, Tania Barton, Sandra Winieski, Lila Zali; Lights, Zachary Malaby, Darci Linke, Mike Modiano, Mark Vuille

COMPANY

Charles Colgan, Louise Frazer, Joan Ross Gair, Molly Lynch, David Panaieff, Caroll Stasney, Kristi Stephens
Randy Barnett, Julie Bradley, Barbara Byrnes, Louis Carver, Louisa Davis, Jennifer Engle, Roger Faubel, Kathy Jo Kahn, Carrie Kneubuhl, Robert Petel, Lisa Robertson, Belinda Smith, Glenn Smith, Elizabeth Snyder, Benjamin Sperber, Lisa Stolzy, Barbara Stuart, Nancy Sutton, Cynthia Tosh, Arabella Wibberley
ARTISTS IN RESIDENCE: Paul Maure, Victor Moreno

REPERTOIRE

"Black Swan Pas de Deux" (Tchaikovsky, Zali), "Boxed" (Various, Sweet), "Carmina Burana" (Orff, Zali), "Chopiniana" (Chopin, Carlson), "Fugitive Visions" (Prokofiev, Zali), "Graduation Ball" (Strauss, Lichine), "Illusion" (Ravel, Kahn), "Moldavian Dances" (Traditional, Moreno), "Moods of Ancient Russis" (Arensky, Zali), "Nutcracker" (Tchaikovsky, Zali), "Snow White" (Various, Kneubuhl), "Sunday in Vienna" (Strauss, Zali), "The Enchanted Toy Shop" (Bayer, Zali)
PREMIERES: "Be-Bop Beach" (Shak, Sperber), "Flutters and Creepers" (Shostakovich, Kahn), "La Dance et la Musique" (Chopin, Panaieff), "Papillons" (Schumann, Zali), "Space Race" (Preston, Kneubuhl), "Courtly Dances" (Britten, Kahn), "The Seasons" (Glazounov, Panaieff), "Things That Go Bump in the Night" (Shostakovich, Robertson-Sutton)

Sally Reeve Photo

Robert Petel, Roger Faubel, Kristi Stephens, Benjamin Sperber, Randy Barnett (Ballet Pacifica) in "Carmina Burana"

BALLET WEST
Salt Lake City, Utah

Artistic Director-Choreographer, Willam F. Christensen; Executive Vice President-General Manager, Robert V. Brickell; Company Manager, Steven H. Horton; Ballet Mistresses, Bene Arnold, Sondra Sugai; Production Manager, David K. Barber; Associate Production Manager-Lighting Director, Greg Geilmann; Costume Mistress, Sarah B. Price; Wardrobe, Linda Stasco; Press, Jo Ann Anton, Susan M. Gilbert; Conductor, Maurice Abravanel; Associate Conductor-Musical Director, Ardean Watts; Sets, Robert O'Hearn, Harry Callahan; Founder-Adviser, Mrs. John M. Wallace

COMPANY

PRINCIPALS: Bruce Caldwell, Suzanne Erlon, Charles Fuller, Philip Fuller, John Hiatt, Victoria Morgan, Michael Onstad, Tomm Ruud, Catherine Scott, Cynthia Young
SOLOISTS AND CORPS: Vivien Cockburn, Frank Hay, James Beaumont, Connie Burton, Catherine Buzard, Lynn Connolly, Kim Colosimo, Christopher Fair, Corey Farris, Sherri Finner, Donlin Foreman, Linda Gundmundson, Tauna Hunter, Diane Jenkins, Francine Kessler, Keith Kimmell, Richard Lohr, Leonore Maez, Elizabeth Nesi, Lesley Radoff, Carole Ann Ramme, Clark Reid, Tenley Taylor, Cary Tidyman, Cheryl Yeager, Derryl Yeager

REPERTOIRE
(1974–1975)

"Coppelia" (Delibes, W. F. Christensen), "The Nutcracker" (Tchaikovsky, W. F. Christensen), "Filling Station" (Virgil Thompson, Lew Christensen), "Irish Fantasy" (Saint-Saens, Jacques d'Amboise), "La Fille Mal Gardee" (Hertel, Jean Dauberval), PREMIERES: "Quintet" (Schubert, Tomm Ruud), "Echoes of Autumn" (Panufnik, Bill Evans), "Four Temperaments" (Hindemith, George Balanchine)   *James Kee, Robert Clayton Photos*

Right: Michael Onstad, Mary Bird, Frank Hay, Tenly Taylor, Derryl Yeager, Elizabeth Nesi in "Quintet"
Top: Mary Bird, Victoria Morgan, Tomm Ruud, Cheryl Yeager, Cynthia Young in "Echoes of Autumn"

**Cynthia Young, Michael Onstad
in "Quintet"**

**Suzanne Erlon, Tomm Ruud
in "Quintet"**

Raymond Serrano, Meg Elizabeth, Roman Jasinski,
Netta Blitman, Cynthia Gast (Ballet Repertory Co.)
in "Bournonville Divertissement"

BALLET REPERTORY COMPANY
New York, N.Y.

Presented by Ballet Theatre Foundation; Director-Choreographer, Richard Englund; Manager, Robert Yesselman; Ballet Mistress, Joysanne Sidimus; Rehearsal Coach, Gage Bush; Stage Manager, Rosemary Cunningham; Lighting, Tony Tucci; Wardrobe, Harriet Wallerstein; Accompanist-Musical Consultant, Dan Waite; Guest Coaches, Fiorella Keane, Eugene Tanner, Lorenzo Monreal

COMPANY

Sergio Cal, Fanchon Cordell, Meg Elizabeth, Ellen English, Cynthia Gast, Roman Jasinski, Linda Marx, Gregory Osborne, Richard Prewitt, Michelle Semler, Raymond Serrano, Christine Spizzo

REPERTOIRE
(1974–1975)

"Bournonville Divertissement" (Helsted-Gade-Paulli, Bournonville), "Combat" (de Banfield, Dollar), "Spring Waters" (Rachmaninoff, Messerer), "Annual" (Collage, Perez), "Don Quixote Pas de Deux" (Minkus, Petipa), "Black Swan Pas de Deux" (Tchaikovsky, Petipa), "Impressions" (Schuller, Sanders)
PREMIERES: "Variations Giocoso" (Gliere, Englund), "Spithre" (Pink Floyd, Englund), "Sets" (Ives, Englund), "Redbackrags" (Joplin, Englund), "Songs of the Auvergne" (Traditional, Bewley)

BALLET TACOMA
Tacoma, Washington

Formerly Concert Ballet Group of Tacoma; Director, Jan Collum; Assistant Director, David Hitchcock; Ballet Mistress, Leslie Jane; Costumes, Judy Loiland; Sound, Kearney Barton; Press, Lois Hampson

COMPANY

PRINCIPALS AND SOLOISTS: Erin Walk, Candy Crocker, Teresa Newton, Valli Hale, Jolene Chaney, Candi Joachim, Hunter Hale, Dale Petersen, David Hitchcock, Charles Talamantes
CORPS: Leslie Hall, Nannette Bales, Adelaide Talamantes, Monica Tarpenning, Janet Kinsman, Laurie Anderson, Patty Shippy, Deborah Ramsey, Robyn Jones, Maren Palmquist, Immaculada Dodd, Lorna Newton, Deidre Gimlett, Panchito Talamantes, Michael Crouch, Jim Williams

REPERTOIRE

"Technique with Joplin" (Joplin, Collum), "Earth Song" (John Cacavas, Collum), "Abraxas'. (Witold Lutoslawski, Leslie Jane), "Love Dawn" (Sibelius, Norbert Vesak), "Roanoke River 1865" (Buffy Sainte-Marie-Traditional, Charles Bennett), "Evanescence" (Bartok, Vesak)
PREMIERES: "City of Glass" (Robert Graittinger, Norbert Vesak), "Le Lac Quiet" (Debussy, Jan Collum), "Gramercy Park 1917" (Dvorak, Collum)

Right Center: Ballet Tacoma in
"Roanoke River 1865"

BALLET WESTERN RESERVE
Youngstown, Ohio

Director-Choreographer, Michael Falotico; Choreographers, Marilyn Jones, Marilyn Kocinsky, Suzanne Thomas, Edward Myers; Conductors, Franz Bibo, C. Watson, Michael Payne; Sets, Paul Kimpel, Robert Elden, Richard Gullickson, Galen Elser; Costumes, Robert Elden, Georgann Sherwood, Marilyn Jones, Bruce Mac, Roberta Johnson, Nancy Scott; Lighting, Kenneth Lowther; Stage Manager, Galen Elser; Press, Devie, Pershing, Bloomberg & Dory; Business Manager, Catherine McPhee; Company Manager, Roderic B. MacDonald; Executive Producers, Suzanne M. Frankle and Youngstown Symphony Ballet Guild

COMPANY

PRINCIPALS: Stephanie Dabney, Amy Taylor, Robert Terleck, Robert Tupper
SOLOISTS: Cathy Frankle, Jacqueline Melnick, Robin Miller, Karen Szauter
CORPS: Lisa Devine, Karen George, Amy Frick, Beth Rollinson, Susan Swan, Lenore Pershing, Nancy Tiberio
GUEST ARTISTS: Diana Byer, Brynar Mehl, Jean Anderson, Matthew Nash, Nicholas Cate, Arturo Azito, Robert Brassel

REPERTOIRE

(All choreography by Falotico, except where noted) "Prologus" (Donizetti), "End of Morning" (Contemporary, Marilyn Jones), "Rustic Variations" (Adam), "G & S for 8 + 2" (Sullivan), "Giselle Act II" (Adam, Myers), "The Nutcracker" (Tchaikovsky), "Pas de Cinq Classique" (Burgmuller)
PREMIERES: "Homage to Haydn" (Haydn), "Les Rendez-vous" (Glazounov), "Licorice Stick Frolic" (Weber), "Faschings Terzett" (Beethoven), "Mindscape" (Contemporary, Jones), "Rarae Aves" (Various), "Scott Joplin Gaieties" (Joplin), "Guitariana" (Giuliani), "Bolero 1830" (Traditional), "The Witching" (R. Moffatt), "Interludes" (Britten), "Grand Faux Pas de Deux" (Arranged Lanchbery)

Ballet Western Reserve
in "Homage to Haydn"

THE BOSTON BALLET
Boston, Massachusetts

Founder-Artistic Director, E. Virginia Williams; Executive Director, Ruth G. Harrington; Ballet Mistress, Sydney E. Leonard; Ballet Masters, James Capp, Lorenzo Monreal; Regisseuse, Ellen O'Reilly; Resident Choreographers, Ron Cunningham, Alfonso Figueroa, Lorenzo Monreal; Conductors, Arthur Fiedler, Michel Sasson; Lighting, Thomas Skelton; General Manager, Michael B. Judson; Production Manager, Aloysius Petruccelli; Press, Rosemary Polito, Brenn Stilley

COMPANY

PRINCIPALS: Elaine Bauer, David Brown, James Capp, Tony Catanzaro, Alfonso Figueroa, Woytek Lowski, Ellen O'Reilly, Anamarie Sarazin, Robert Steele, Edra Toth, Laura Young
SOLOISTS: Sanson Candelaria, David Drummond
Corps: Durine Alinova, Kathryn Anderson, Carinne Binda, Ron Cunningham, Kaethe Devlin, Leo Guerard, Mark Johnson, Shirley McMillan, Mark Mejia, Janet Moran, Stephanie Moy, Dierdre Myles, Gigi Nachtsheim, Clyde Nantais, Augustus Van Heerdens, Leslie Woodies

REPERTOIRE
(1974–1975)

"Allegro Brillante" (Tchiakovsky, Balanchine), "Adventures of Raggedy Ann 'n' Andy" (John Alden Carpenter, Ron Cunningham), "Concerto Barocco" (Bach, Balanchine), "The Gershwin Years" (Gershwin, Cunningham), "Graduation Ball" (Strauss, Lichine), "Le Corsaire Pas de Deux" (Drigo, Petipa), "The Nutcracker" (Tchaikovsky, E. Virginia Williams after Petipa-Ivanov), "Pas de Quatre" (Pugni, Dolin), "The Road of the Phoebe Snow" (Ellington-Strayhorn, Talley Beatty), "Serenade" (Tchaikovsky, Balanchine), "Symphony in C" (Bizet, Balanchine)
WORLD PREMIERES: "Hamlet" (Shostakovich, Lorenzo Monreal), "Summer" (Schubert, Agnes de Mille), "Tubby the Tuba" (Paul Tripp-George Kleinsinger, Ron Cunningham)
COMPANY PREMIERES: "The Abyss" (Marga Richter, Stuart Hodes), "Medea" (Bela Bartok, Brigit Cullberg), "Summerspace" (Morton Feldman, Merce Cunningham), "Winterbranch" (La Monte Young, Merce Cunningham)

**Top Right: Elaine Bauer, David Brown
Right Center: "The Road of the
Phoebe Snow"** *(Jack Mitchell Photo)*

Woytek Lowski, Deidre Myles in "Hamlet"
Donald Curran Photo

**David Brown, Robert Steele, Edra Toth, Walter
Kaiser in "Allegro Brillante"**
Michael Lemire Photo

133

THE BIRMINGHAM BALLET
Birmingham, Alabama

Artistic Director-Choreographer, Alfonso Figueroa; Associate Director, Suanne Ferguson; Ballet Mistress, Mira Popovic; Choreographers, Norman Walker, Jan Stripling, James Lewis; Costumes, Bob DeMorra, Alfonso Figueroa, Jan Stripling, Norman Walker, Sandro LaFerla, Vicki Vinson, Kristine Kaiser; Set Designers, Sandro LaFerla, Bob DeMorra, Alfonso Figueroa; Stage Managers, Aloysius Petruccelli, Walter Kaiser; General Manager, William P. Bond, Jr.; Business Manager, George P. Bergeron; Press, Cherie Woods

COMPANY

Janet Moran, Alfonso Figueroa, James Lewis, David Drummond, Jerilyn Dana, Jon Cristofori, Augustus vanHeerden, Thomas Richards, Kathryn Townsend, Mimi Ransley, Cynthia Gray, Marsha Hooks, Theresa Roach, Karen Simons, Vickey Vespaziani, Miguel Romero, Jane Randolph

REPERTIORE

"Prokofiev Concerto (Prokofiev, Figueroa), "In Corte Sia" (14th Century Madrigals, Stripling), "Terpsichoros" (Mozart, Figueroa), "Fantasy Dances" (Schumann, Lewis), "Primus" (Gassman, Figueroa), "Nutcracker Pas de Deux" (Tchaikovsky, Figueroa-Petipa), "Corsaire Pas de Deux" (Drigo, Lorenzo Monreal after Petipa), "Don Quixote Pas de Deux" (Minkus, Monreal after Petipa), PREMIERES: "Peter and the Wolf" (Prokofiev, Samuel Kurkjian), "Spring Waters" (Rachmaninoff, Messerer), "Graduation Ball" (Strauss, Ellen O'Reilly after Lichine), "Remember When?" (Traditional, Figueroa), "Autumn Dialogus" (Samuel Barber, Norman Walker)

Birmingham Ballet in "Remember When"
King Douglas Photo

Linda McMenamin, Yvonne Cook (Burlington Ballet) in "Little Women" *(Ron Williams Photo)*

Douglas Hevenor, Marlene Jones (California Ballet)

BURLINGTON BALLET COMPANY
Rancocas, N.J.

Director-Choreographer, Joan Kaletchitz Stebe; Lighting, Richard Walker; Costumes, A. Christina Giannine, Virginia McMenamin; Stage Manager, Richard Walker; Press, Arlene Innman, Peggy Morgan

COMPANY

PRINCIPALS: Thomas Candenzio, Yvonne Cook, Deborah Dutton, Mark Galante, Linda McMenamin, Dawn Tocci, Richard Walker
SOLOISTS: Steve Huber, Saundra Shaw, Kelly Shaw, Julie Stebe
CORPS: Susan Frantz, Beth Kuzy, Kathleen Nelboeck, Martha Jane Shannon, Marguarite Shumate, Suzanne Szepanski

REPERTOIRE

"Kinetic Anemone" (Gwendolyn Watson), "Waltz Bouquet" (Chopin), "Medley" (Popular), "Ballade" (Chopin), "Little Women" (Ives-Copland), "Loves' Dream" (Liszt)

CALIFORNIA BALLET COMPANY
San Diego, California

General Director, Robert G. Mahon; Artistic Director-Choreographer, Maxine Mahon; Administrative Assistant, Greg Smith; Conductor, David Hubler; Ballet Mistress, Sylvia Palmer; Wardrobe, Flora Jennings, Ruth Small; Technical Director, Nels Martin; Scenic Designer, Catherine Hand; Artistic Advisers, Charles Bennett John Hart, David Ward-Steinman, Elaine Thomas; Press, Robert Mahon Greg Smith

COMPANY

Marlene Jones, Douglas Hevenor, Frank Bays, Robin Briceno Linda Click, James Francis, Jeri Jones, Eugenia Keefer, Kevin Linker, Mike Melcher, Lydia Morales, Sylvia Palmer, Marcia Quigley, Steve Shirley, Uchi Sugiyama
David Chastain, Donna Cline, Arturo Fernandez, Adriel Frumin Cheryl Herrington, Amy Lovberg, Dennis Novak, Greg Smith Holly Ward
GUEST ARTISTS: Violette Verdy, Edward Villella

REPERTOIRE

"The Nutcracker" (Tchaikovsky, Maxine Mahon), "Coppelia (Delibes, Mahon), "Configurations on a Cloud" (Brahms, Mahon "Albinoni Pas de Deux" (Albinoni, Charles Bennett), "Raymond Variations" (Glazounov, Mahon)

CHICAGO BALLET
Chicago, Illinois

Director-Choreographer, Ruth Page; Artistic Director, Ben Stevenson; Company Manager, Peter H. Brown; Administrative Assistant, Stephanie Sormane; Press, Mildred Laemle; Ballet Master, Orrin Kayan; Technical Director, William Banks; Wardrobe Mistress, Zoe de Jong

COMPANY
PRINCIPALS: Carmen Mathe, Dennis Poole, Michelle Lees
SOLOISTS: Charlene Gehm, Dorio Perez
CORPS: Birute Barodicaite, Diedre Grohgan, Janis Harris, Jennifer Holmes, Suzanne Longley, Rosemary Miles, Cynthia Ann Roses, Michael Bjerknes, Thomas Boyd, Steven Cook, William Pizzuto, Kurt Putzig, William Sterner, Eric Weichardt
GUEST ARTISTS: Margot Fonteyn, Valery and Galina Panov, Ivan Nagy, Kirk Peterson, Neal Kayan (Conductor)

REPERTOIRE
(1974–1975)

"Bartok Concerto" (Bartok, Ben Stevenson), "Black Swan Pas de Deux" (Tchaikovsky, Petipa), "Catulli Carmina" (Orff, Ruth Page), "Courante" (Bach, Stevenson), "Danse Brilliante" (Glinka, Frederic Franklin), "Don Quixote Pas de Deux" (Minkus, Petipa), "Eaters of Darkness" (Britten, Walter Gore), "Esmeralda Pas de Deux" (Glazounov, Stevenson), "Grieg Pas de Deux" (Grieg, John Cranko), "Monotones" (Satie, Frederick Ashton), "One in Five" (Strauss, Ray Powell), "Peasant Pas de Deux from Giselle" (Adam, Traditional), "Peep Show" (Jean Francaix, Walter Gore), "Pi r2" (Edgar Varese, Lois Bewley), "The Prodigal Son" (Prokofieff, Balanchine), "Raymonda Pas de Dix" (Glazounov, Petipa), "Romeo and Juliet" (Tchaikovsky, Page), "Sleeping Beauty Pas de Deux" (Tchaikovsky, Petipa), "Three Preludes" (Rachmaninoff, Stevenson), "When Summoned" (Morton Subotnick, Bill Evans), and *PREMIERE* of "Mandala" (Nick Venden, Richard Arve)

Jack Mitchell Photos

Right: Thomas Boyd, Janis Harris, Rosemary Miles in "Bartok Concerto"

Dorio Perez, William Sterner, Carmen Mathe, Dennis Poole in "Romeo and Juliet"

Dennis Poole, Charlene Gehm in "Three Preludes"

135

CHARLESTON BALLET COMPANY
Charleston, S.C.

Directors, Choreographers, Scenic and Costume Designers, Don Cantwell and Robert Ivey; President of the Board of Directors, Anna Funderberg

COMPANY

Merran Funderburg, Grace Freeman, Kris Pierce, Justin Geilfuss, Louise Hall, Christine Cantwell, Mary McKeever, Vanessa Perot, Geormine Stanyard, Lisa Moseley, Debbie Horton, Evelyn Johnson, Chris Harrelson, Ann Osborne, Liza Nason, Helen Cannon, David North, Camilla Tezza, Robert Ivey, Don Cantwell
GUEST ARTISTS: Cathy Myers, Anita Lane, Cindy Huber, Terri Lawless, Patricia Strang, Rebecca Keating, Heidi Muller

REPERTOIRE
(1974–1975)

"The Nutcracker" (Tchaikovsky, after Ivanov), "Cinderella" (Prokofiev, Cantwell), "Hyperprism" (Varese, Cantwell)
PREMIERES: "Vivaldi Espanol" (Vivaldi, Cantwell), "1 + 7 MEC ATE" (S. Schwartz-Blood Sweat and Tears, Robert Ivey), "Swan Lake Act II" (Tchaikovsky, Cantwell-Ivey after Petipa), "Cry Witch" (Virgil Thompson, Ivey)

Bill Buggel Photo

Charleston Ballet Company

CHRYSLER CHAMBER BALLET
Norfolk, Virginia

Artistic Director-Choreographer, Randy Strawderman; Associate Director, Mary Marshall; Choreographers, Mary Marshall, Patricia Sorrell, Michael Lopuszanski; Ballet Mistress, Teresa Martinez; Designer, Ned Tyler; Sound, Bernie Melton, Leonard Horn, Robbie Creger; Wardrobe Mistress, Cathy Vastano; Press, Mal Vincent, Mary Dissen, Carol Cass, Don Harris; Production Adviser, W. H. Norrie Martin; Artistic Adviser, Gene Hammett

COMPANY

PRINCIPALS: Sandra Flader, Lorraine Graves, Lisa Hedley, Melissa Hoffer, Alexis Brown, Stacy Caddell, Deborah Dougherty, Kim Fielding, Ralph Hewitt, Jane Meredith, Marc Levy
SOLOISTS: Dave Mallard, Tom Luna, Sam Groover, Laurie Buckley, Michael Webster
CORPS: Maria ten Braak, Debbie Vastano, Anne Goldman, Denise Hernandez, Loretta Dodd, Paige Fillion, Mary Baker, Nancy Cantin, Ana Maria Martinez, Donna Sheppard, Terri Tompkins, Catherine Smith, Darryl Hickey, Lee Thompson
GUEST ARTISTS: Richard Prewitt, David Jackson

REPERTOIRE

"Don Quixote" (Minkus, Asaf Messerer), "Drums/hums/claps/-sticks/kicks" (Stebbing-Ford, Strawderman), "Interplay" (Gould, Robbins), "Homage to Bach" (Bach, Michael Lopuszanski), "Nutcracker Pas de Deux" (Tchaikovsky, Strawderman)
PREMIERES: "Gift of the Magi" (Tchaikovsky, Strawderman), "Scott Free" (Scott Joplin, Mary Marshall), "Pas Classique" (Auber, Marshall)

THE CHARLESTON BALLET
Charleston, West Va.

Director-Choreographer, Andre Van Damme; Stage Director, Strauss Wolfe; Lighting Director, William Lutman; President, Dr. Arnold C. Burke; Vice President, R. Elward Baker; Secretary-Treasurer, Mrs. Andre Van Damme; Costumes, Patrick Dawson, Maggy Van Damme; Sets, Patrick Dawson, Kozak

PRINCIPALS

Kim Pauley, Nor Brunschwyler, Jennifer Britton, Julianne Kemp, Ann Sergent, Herb Jones

REPERTOIRE
(1974–1975)

"Street Corner," "Storm," "Bouquet de Lilas," and *Premieres* of "Istar" (Rimsky-Korsakov, Van Damme), "Gypsy" (Folk, Van Damme), "The Rose" (Rachmaninoff, Van Damme), "Pavanne" (Rodrigo, Van Damme), "Motions" (Hartmann-Bartok, Van Damme)

Left Center: Kim Pauley, Nor Brunschwyler in "Istar"

**Lorraine Graves, Tom Luna
(Chrysler Chamber Ballet)**

"The Nutcracker"
Top Right: David Blackburn, Alyce Taylor
in "The Beloved"

CINCINNATI BALLET COMPANY
Cincinnati, Ohio

Artistic Director-Choreographer, David McLain; General Manager, Paul G. Wagner; Assistant Artistic Director, David Blackburn; Music Director, Carmon DeLeone; Production Coordinator-Resident Designer, Jay Depenbrock; Costumes and Scenery, Andreas Nomikos, Jay Depenbrock, Lester Horton, Ruth Hopper, Hugh Laing, Henry Heymann, Anne Warner, Karinska, Reuben Ter-Arutunian; Company Manager, Patricia C. Losey; Assistant to General Manager, Jeannine Kagan; Press, Valerie A. Lampe; Comptroller, Roma Sly; Wardrobe, Mildred Benzing; Sound, James C. Armstrong; Pianist, John Iden; Executive Secretary, Natalie Huston, Diane M. Barnhorst

COMPANY

Paula Davis, Diane Edwards, Colleen Giesting, Renee Hallman, Karen Karibo, Patricia Kelly, Carol Krajacic, Ellen Moritz, Merritt Robinson, Patricia Rozow, Claudia Rudolf, Susan Shtulman, Alyce Taylor, Katherine Turner, Deborah Wilson, John Ashton, Ian Barrett, David Blackburn, Michael Bradshaw, Karl Lindholm, Wayne Maurer, Michael Rozow, Roman Jasinski, Jr., Matthew Bridwell, James Truitte
APPRENTICES: Diane Barrett, Lynn Ferszt, Suzanne Haas, Coral Kordecki, Sheila McAulay, Marcia Sells, Pam Willingham, Martin Andrews, Patrick Hinson

REPERTOIRE

"Antiche Arie E Danze" (Respighi, McLain), "Aubade" (Poulenc, Sabline), "The Beloved" (Hamilton, Truitte-Horton), "Clouds" (Dvorak, McLain), "Concerto" (Poulenc, McLain), "Concerto Barocco" (Bach, Balanchine), "Divertissement Classique" (Burgmuller, Jasinski), "Et Cetera" (Palombo, Johnson), "Face of Violence" (Salome) (Horton-DeLeone, Horton-Truitte-DeLavallade), "Fandango" (Soler, Tudor), "Firebird" (Stravinsky, Jasinski-Larkin), "Frevo" (DeLeone, Truitte-Horton), "Guernica" (DeLeone, Truitte), "Guitar Concerto" (Castelnuovo-Tedesco, McLain), "Night Soliloquies" (Barlow-Rogers-Hanson, McLain), "Pas de Quatre" (Pugni, Dolin-Markova), "Les Patineurs" (Meyerbeer-Lambert, Martinez), "Serenade" (Tchaikovsky, Balanchine), "Tribute to Jose Clemente Orozco" (Klaus, Truitte-Horton), "The Unicorn, The Gorgon, The Manticore" (Menotti, Johnson), "Winter's Traces" (Verdi, McLain), and *PREMIERE* of full length "The Nutcracker" (Tchaikovsky, Franklin-Jasinski-Larkin)

Sandy Underwood Photos

Colleen Giesting, Wayne Maurer
in "Tribute to Jose Clemente Orozco"

COBB MARIETTA BALLET
Marietta, Georgia

Director-Choreographer, Iris Hensley; Ballet Master, Terrell Paulke; Stage Manager, Don Kordecki; Staff, Sheila Hart, Donna Rizzo, Bobby Archard, Sharon Long

COMPANY
Joy Bray, Cindy Chavis, Melanie Furst, Katie Groves, Sheila Hart, Nancy Jo Hays, Kathy Johnson, Kathy Kelley, Suzanne MacIntyre, Elizabeth Ramsden, Leah Sabiston, Beth Sproat, Pam Schutz, Sharon Story, Lynne Taylor, Diana Whipkey, Dawn McBrayer, Nancy Tolbert

REPERTOIRE
"The Seven Last Words of Christ" (Theodore DuBois, Hensley), "Swings 'N' Things," "Ode to Joy" (Beethoven, Sheila Hart), "Symphony for Strings" (Beethoven, Hensley), "Fantasy Variations" PREMIERE: "Graduation Ball" (Johann Strauss, David Lichine; Staged by Vivian Phillips; Directed by Iris Hensley)

Top Right: Members of Cobb Marietta Ballet in "Fantasy Variations"

Colorado Concert Ballet in "Cinderella" *(Ken Victor Photo)*

COLORADO CONCERT BALLET
Denver, Colorado

Artistic Directors, Lillian Covillo, Friedann Parker; Business Manager, Norma Olssen; Press, Gary Berman, Mary Lou Zimmerman; Designers, Henry Lowenstein, Bruce Jackson; Stage Manager, Timothy Kelly; Choreographers, Lillian Covillo, Friedann Parker, Richard Denny

COMPANY
PRINCIPALS: Laura Walker, Nancy Shadwell, Keith Kimmel, Karlya Shelton, Lisi Gotaas
SOLOISTS: Theresa Nieto, Charles Rowbotham, David Taylor
CORPS: of 20 (names not submitted)
GUEST ARTIST: Dan Conover

REPERTOIRE
"Giselle" (Adam), "Firebird" (Stravinsky, Lillian Covillo-Freidann Parker), "Romeo and Juliet" (Berlioz, Parker), "Concerto for 10" (Prokofiev, Richard Denny), "Straw Hats in the Park" (Poulenc, Denny)
PREMIERE: "Pyramid" (Debussy, Deidre Nepa)

DALLAS CIVIC BALLET
Dallas, Texas

Artistic Director-Choreographer, George Skibine; Associate Director, Marjorie Tallchief; General Manager, Mary Heller Sasser; Conductors, Louis Lane, Dr. Michael Semanitsky; Sets and Costumes Designer, Peter Hall; Lighting Designer, Allan Gibson; Stage Manager, Jeannine Stegen; Press, Sarah Birge

COMPANY
SOLOISTS: Kevin Brown, Jeff Geise, Cindy Jones, Deanne Tomlinson, Karen Travis
CORPS: Jan Absolom, Nanette Ambroze, Shannon Baker, Amy Bergquist, Doris Boettigheimer, Michele Goldstein, Susan Gibbs, Cathy Hansen, Karen Legere, Susan Legere, Gail Pennington, Josette Radelat, Andrea Riley, Vicki Rutschman, Janyce Scott, Judi Spinella, Jean Morscheck, Melissa Kirk, Myra Oujesky, Marla Bartos, Thomas Clower
GUEST ARTISTS: Edward Villella, Magdalena Popa, Stefan Banica

REPERTOIRE
(1974–1975)
"Firebird," "Bolero," "Le Corsaire," "Daphnis and Chloe," "La Peri," "The Nutcracker," "Sketches," "Idylle," "Design for Strings," "Gaite Parisienne," "Gloria," "Concerto Barrocco," "Anabel Lee," "Cantata Profana," "Nutcracker Suite," "Giselle," "Tempo Vivo," "Graffitti," "Suite de Danses"

Dallas Civic Ballet

DALLAS METROPOLITAN BALLET
Dallas, Texas

Artistic Directors-Choreographers, Ann Etgen, Bill Atkinson; Technical Director, Jeannine Stegin; Costumes, S. Rozelle; Press, Melba Whatley

COMPANY

King Douglas, Suzette Mariaux, Scott Chapman, Mitzi Smith, Richard Condon, Jacquie Kessler, Sam Lopez, Christy Dunham, Mark Kessler, Trish Muller, Fred Bailey, Tracey Forsyth, Carol MacInnes, Karen Stevens, Jerry Kelley, Mark Tatum, Trudi Perrin, Suzanne Wagner, Dale E. Smith, Roger Malone, Mary Hall, Megan Ready, Martha Mullen, Mary Kay Douglas, Sheryl Halt
GUEST ARTISTS: Helgi Tomasson, Kay Mazzo, Ruth Page (Choreographer)

REPERTOIRE

"Carmina Burana" (Orff, Page), "Three G's" (Glazounov-Gounod-Fliere), "Christina's World" (Collage, Norbert Vesak), "Wand of Youth" (Elgar), "Graduation Ball" (Strauss, Carrow after Lichine), "La Valse" (Ravel, Marc Wilde), "The Night before Christmas" (Burgmuller, Adams)," "Roundrock" (Collage), "Country Garden" (Grainger)
PREMIERE: "Rags" (Scott Joplin)

Jacquie Kessler, Richard Condon, Christy Dunham, Sam Lopez, Mitzi Smith, Scott Chapman of Dallas Metropolitan Ballet

DANCE GUILD OF VIRGINIA
Virginia Beach, Virginia

Producer, Nancy A. McClees; Director, Vija M. Cunningham; Business Manager-Stage Manager-Lighting Designer, Beth Hudson; Costumes and Sets, Gail Sedel, Arlene Cohen, Bob Weaver; Narrator, Sunday Abbott

COMPANY

PRINCIPALS: Vija Cunningham, Ann John, Heidi Robitshek, Maggie Schmidt
CORPS: Gail Sedel, Karen Bocher, Susan Bates, Debra Kasmauski, Charles Lipka, Kathy McDonald, Chuck Foster, Ann Watkins, John Medlin, Beth Heaton, Sharon Stepnick

REPERTOIRE

(All choreography by Vija Cunningham except where noted) "Swingcussion" (Dodds), "Lunarian Rites" (Jungle Odyssey, Ann John), "Two Five Strut" (Joplin, Judith Hatcher), "Idyl" (Walter-Olnick-Schaeffer), "Line, Dot and Squiggle" (Diercks), "Dripsody" (LeCaine), "Bees" (Rice), "Child's Spring" (Conger-Lohoefer), "Suite in Three Movements" (Miller, Gail Sedel), "Abstractions" (Sauter & Finnegan), "Peter and the Wolf" (Arranged by Oliver Nelson) "Danse" (Stravinsky), "Impressions of Degas" (Chopin), "Mysterious Mountain" (Hovhaness)
PREMIERES: "Snow" (Debussy, Hans Van Manen), "Variation and Coda from Le Corsaire" (Drigo, Petipa), "Flower Festival Pas de Deux" (Helsted, Bournonville), "The Ragtime Dance" (Joplin, Heidi Robitshek), "Hoe Down" (Copland, Major Burchfield), "H & R" (Percussion, I. H. Robitshek, Jr; Hans Van Mannen; Re-staged by Heidi Robitshek), "Composition X: (Erb), "Blues P. M." (Debussy), "Interlude" (Gregorian Chants, Ann John), "The Elephant's Child" (Jungle Odyssey-Stravinsky-Tribal Music-Varese-Lehman)

DANCE COLLECTIVE/MASS MOVEMENT
Boston, Massachusetts

Managing Director, Janet Spencer; Directors-Choreographers, Martha Armstrong Gray, Beth Soll, Ruth Wheeler

COMPANY

Martha Armstrong Gray
Beth Soll
Ruth Wheeler
REPERTOIRE (1974–1975): "Renaissance Suite" (Dieuport, Wheeler) "Mourning Dance" (None, Soll), "Winter Dance I" (Stockhausen, Soll), "Spell" (Coltrane, Soll), "Piano Rolls" (Blake, Wheeler), "The Flying Leap of the Flea" (Kay-Schuller, Wheeler), "Flowering into New Battles" (Yamash'ta, Gray), "Little Diversion" (Moderne & Holland-Dozier, Gray), "Canon in D Major" (Pachelbel, Gray)

Left Center: Dawn Kramer, Martha Armstrong Gray, Susan Dowling in "Mourning Dance"
Howe Derbyshire Photo

John Medlin, Maggie Schmidt
(Dance Guild of Virginia) 139

Dayton Ballet in "Trimorphous"
Walt Kleine Photo

DELAWARE REGIONAL BALLET
Dover, Delaware

Formerly Delaware State Ballet Company; Artistic Director-Artist-in-Residence, Cherie Noble; President, Marion Tracy; Resident Choreographer, Bill Comer; Lighting, Judith Haynes; Costumes, Betty Mathews, Joan Fels; Stage Manager, Sharyn Lewis; Press, Ellie Boone; Guest Choreographers, John Mineo, Istvan Rabovsky

COMPANY

Renee Breault, Mary Lu Bruner, Bill Comer, Elizabeth Fels, Susan Foster, Laurie LeBlanc, Carol Mathews, Susie Mathews, Sven Osmuandson, Tana Parker, Beth Anne Riggi, Mike Shortell, Nena Todd, Donna Wilkinson
GUEST ARTISTS: Roger Bigelow, Gregory Drotar, Linda Giancaspro, Edward Myers, Ginny Portz, John Prinz, Istvan Rabovsky, Zhandra Rodriguez, 5 by 2 Dance Company, Theatre Dance Collection

REPERTOIRE

"Free to Dream" (Shirley, Comer), "Pas de Quatre" (Pughi, Asmus), "Peter and the Wolf" (Prokofiev, Asmus), "Nutcracker" (Tchaikovsky, Asmus), "Rodrigo Suite" (Rodrigo, Asmus)
PREMIERES: "Fractions and Refractions" (Pachebel-Noble), "Interpretations on Edd Kalehoff" (Kalehoff, Mineo), "Sleeping Beauty Excerpts" (Tchaikovsky, Noble after Petipa), "The Gypsy" (Traditional, Rabovsky)

Lida Moser Photo

**Valentine Boving, Jay Fullinwider
(Discovery Dance Group)**

DAYTON BALLET COMPANY
Dayton, Ohio

Artistic Director-Choreographer, Josephine Schwarz; Associate Directors, Jon Rodriguez, Bess Saylor; Costumes, Hermene Schwarz, Barbara Trick; Technical Director, John Rensel; Audio Director, Tom Conway

COMPANY

Gretchen Albrecht, Ebony Barkley, Laura Beavers, Beth Berdes, Cara Bolling, Cynthia Bowden, Teri Breh, Gregory Clough, Jimmy Daniel, Judy Denman, Amy Duell, DeAnn Duteil, Jeff Gribler, Timothy Graves, Rachel Hobart, Charles Hoffman, Daniel Jamison, Stewart Jarrett, Robin Kohn, Mechelle Meredith, Meggin Rose, Earl Roosa, Camille Ross, Jennifer Sprowl, Diane Stapp, Mary Stewart, Randy Styron, Constance Wirth, Betsy Tolley
GUEST ARTIST: Dan Duell

REPERTOIRE

"Concertino" (Pergolesi, Koner), "Die Linie" (Keats, Saylor), "Periphrastic" (Denisov, Saylor), "Concerto Barocco" (Bach, Balanchine), "Dulce et Decorum Est" (Penderecki, Rodriguez), "Homage to Georg Frederich" (Handel, Rodriguez), "Amahl and the Night Visitors" (Menotti, Schwarz), "Fliessende Tanzschrifte" (Hindemith, Saylor), "Pas de Trois" (Tchaikovsky, Rodriguez), "Ophelia" (Stravinsky, Saylor), "Nutcracker Act II" (Tchaikovsky, Rodriguez), "Willoughby" (Prokofiev, Sebastian), "Crucifixion" (Hindemith-Shostakovich, Saylor), "Ruth" (Jacobi, Schwarz), "Papillon" (Schumann, Schwarz), "Trimorphous" (Bach, Rodriguez)
PREMIERES: "Chopin's Revenge" (Chopin, Clough), "Tarantella" (Gottschalk, Balanchine), "At Half Past Six in the Afternoon" (Schuman, Rodriguez), "Schubertiad" (Schubert, Rodriguez), "Raggae On" (J. Winter, Saylor), "Lincoln Portrait" (Copland, Saylor), "Annabelle Lee" (Franklin-Foote-Ives, Clough)

Delaware Regional Ballet
Lida Moser Photo

DISCOVERY DANCE GROUP
Houston, Texas

Director-Choreographer, Camille Long Hill; Choreographers, Pam Stockman, Lynn Reynolds; Booking, Valentine Boving; Press, Lee Hickle

COMPANY

Valentine Boving, Cathy Buck, Linda Castillon, Paul Clements, Rick Durapou, Jay Fullinwider, Kathy Guinn, Gary Hardy, Kathleen Parker, Lynn Reynolds, Leticia Rodriguez, Pam Stockman, Pat Williams, Lisa Trussel

REPERTOIRE

(All choreography by Camille Long Hill except where noted) "Inhibitions" (Mingus), "Night Is for Dreaming" (E. Bernstein), "Sea Visions" (M. Garson), "Yesterday, Today and Tomorrow" (Fripp-Sinfield-McDonald), "A Time Remembered" (Ravel, Ron Sequoio), "Web of Decision" (Fischer), "Prelude" (Villa-Lobos, Sequoio), "The Families" (Gaure, Lynn Reynolds), "Etude" (Mauriat)
PREMIERES: "The I of Me" (Mingus), "Jazz Bit #3" (Franklin), "Rhapsody" (Debussy), "Unholy Trinity" (Lord, Pam Stockman)

Horace F. Oleson Photo

Billy Siegenfeld, Wanda Pruska, Don Redlich,
Barbara Roan, Irene Feigenheimer in "Patina"

DON REDLICH DANCE COMPANY
New York, N. Y.

Director-Choreographer, Don Redlich; Lighting Design, Jennifer Tipton, Nicholas Wolff Lyndon; Stage Manager, Mark Litvin; Costumes, Doreen Ackerman, Margaret Tobin; Masks, Ralph Lee; Sheldon Soffer Management

COMPANY
Irene Feigenheimer
Wanda Pruska
Don Redlich
Barbara Roan
Billy Siegenfeld
REPERTOIRE: "Jibe" (Norma Dalby), "Earthling" (Debussy), "Cahoots," "Passin' Through" (Traditional), "Estrange," "Three Bagatelles" (Lukas Foss), "Patina" (Besard-Caroso-Galilei-Gianancelli)

EGLEVSKY BALLET COMPANY
Massapequa, N. Y.

Director-Choreographer, Andre Eglevsky; Assistant Director, Jane Miller; Conductors, Claude Monteux, Carl Porter, Martin Dreiwitz; Sets, Tom Shanton; Costumes, Dosi Sorokin, John Raczynski; Stage Manager, Edward Cucurello

COMPANY
PRINCIPALS AND SOLOISTS: Jane Miller, Dermot Burke, Michelle Semler, Sally Silliman, Suzanne Nadeau, Natasha Obarovitch, Robert Peterson, Fred Mann, Valerie Feit, Roberto Medina
CORPS: Mary Reichenbach, Emanelle Davis, Allison Morgan, Christine Wright, Adrian James, Patrick Madden, Robin Lyon

REPERTOIRE
(1974–1975)
PREMIERES: "Cinderella" (Prokofiev, Eglevsky; in three acts), "The Nutcracker" Tchaikovsky, Eglevsky assisted by Jane Miller and Dermot Burke), "Les Patineurs" (Meyerbeer, Eglevsky)

Susan Cook Photos

Eglevsky Ballet in "Les Patineurs"

ELMIRA-CORNING BALLET
Elmira, N.Y.

Founder-Artistic Director-Choreographer, Madame Halina; Conductor, David Einfeld; Technical Director, Floyd Lutomski; Guest Choreographers, Henry Danton, Rochelle Zide, Val Deakin, James DeBolt, Michael Falotico, Paschal Guzman

COMPANY
Stephanie Schmid, Elizabeth Howell, Carla Chamberlain, Karen Minch, Jeanine Clate, Dorothy Lindsay, Wendy Tuller, Darlene Errett, Kathryn Smith Gaye, Lin Horton, Mary Lemark, Betsy Buch, Kirsten Winsor, Sally Updyke, Maureen Dooley, Margaret Thompson, Mary Ellen Hagy, Lindsay O'Connor, Cathy Curran, Margaret Kornuszko, Cathy Fascetti, Lorreine Gile, Jackie Meckes, Deborah Gerstel, Wavelyn Aronson, Mathew Smith, Mark Smith
GUEST ARTISTS: William George, Diana Bayer, Carmen Mathe, Martin Fredman, Eleanor D'Antuono, Ramon Segarra, James DeBolt, Seija Simonen, Rochelle Zide, William Glassman, Ellen Everett, Veronique Laroce, Richard Gradus, Paschal Guzman

REPERTOIRE
"Masquerade" (Khatchaturian, Halina), "Hat Trick" (Buhlme, Deakin), "Red, White and Blue" (Soussa, Halina), "Coppelia" (Delibes, Ashton-Deakin), "La Fille Mal Gardee" (Lanchberry, Deakin), "Sleeping Beauty" (Tchaikovsky, Petipa), "Bayadere" (Adam, Denton), "Capriccio Italien" (Tchaikovsky, Denton), "Sortie et Entre" (Mozart, Halina), "Mozartiana" (Mozart, Halina), "Karnival" (Arranged, Halina)
PREMIERES: "Sylvia" (Delibes, Falotico-Halina), "Wooden Prince" (Bartok, Falotico), "La Comedia" (Arranged, Falotico), "Circus" (Shostakovich, Halina)

Debra Salmirs, William Hagh in "Sylvia"
(Elmira-Corning Ballet)

ERICK HAWKINS DANCE COMPANY
New York, N.Y.

Director-Choreographer, Erick Hawkins; Music Director, Lucia Dlugoszewski; Conductor, Joel Thome; Guest Conductor, David Gilbert; General Manager, Mark Z. Alpert; Lighting Designer-Stage Manager, Daniel Koetting

COMPANY
Erick Hawkins

Cathy Ward
Robert Yohn
Kristen Peterson
Cori Terry
Kevin Tobiason

John Wiatt
Nada Reagan
Natalie Richman
Alan Lynes
Victor Lukas

REPERTOIRE
(1974–1975)

"Early Floating" (Dlugoszewski), "Cantilever" (Dlugoszewski), "Black Lake" (Dlugoszewski), "Angels of the Inmost Heaven" (Dlugoszewski), "Dawn Dazzled Door" (Takemitsu), "Classic Kite Tails" (Diamond), "Greek Dreams, with Flute" (Matsudaira), "Meditation on Orpheus" (Hovhaness)

David Hoff Photos

Right: Erick Hawkins in "Meditation on Orpheus"
Below: "Dawn Dazzled Door"

Beverly Brown, Carol Conway, Natalie Richman, Nada Reagan, Robert Yohn, Erick Hawkins in "Greek Dreams, with Flute"

EMPIRE STATE BALLET THEATRE
Buffalo, N.Y.

Artistic Director-Choreographer, Barbara Striegel; Executive Director, Thomas Banasiak

COMPANY

Michelle Becker, Carolyn Pulk, Moira Murphy, Lisa Mast, Ruth Ann Jaworski, Jean Bacon, Leslie Rice, Sandy Rice, Thomas Banasiak, Randy Banasiak, Judy Van Order, Jan Vukson, Norm Clerc, Harris Ferris

REPERTOIRE

"Petrouchka" (Stravinsky), "Firebird" (Stravinsky), "Hip & Straight" (Focus), "Ravel Pas de Deux," "Apollo—Leader of the Muses" (Ravel), "Gluck Ballet Suite" (Gluck), "Pas de Quatre" (Pugni, Perrot), "Butterfly Lovers" (Shen Yuen), "Nights in the Garden of Spain" (deFalla)
PREMIERES: "The Nutcracker" (Tchaikovsky, Striegel), "Coppelia" (Delibes, Striegel)

Michelle Becker, Thomas Banasiak
(Empire State Ballet)

FIRST CHAMBER DANCE COMPANY
Seattle, Washington

Artistic Director, Charles Bennett; Business Manager, David Fagerstrom; Ballet Master, Petty Brunson; Musical Director, Harriet Cavalli; Costume Designer-Wardrobe Master, Alan Madsen; Stage Managers, Richard Weil, Tom Durnell; Press, Ruth Brinton; Administrative Assistant, Darlene Green

COMPANY

Charles Bennett	Alex Hoff
Rita Agnese	Marlene Jones
Frank Bays	Sara de Luis
Flemming Halby	Dana Sapiro
Douglas Hevenor	Donna Silva

GUEST ARTISTS: Ray Bussey, William Carter, Agnes de Mille, Diane Germaine, Yurek Lazowski, Cruz Luna, Teodoro Morca, Jay Norman, Jacques Patarozzi, Mimi Paul, Dini Roman, Frank Schaufuss

REPERTOIRE

"Nagare" (Traditional, Bennett), "Under Green Leaves" (Telemann, Bennett), "Recollection of an Age" (Boieldieu, Bennett), "Largo" (Beethoven, Bennett), "By Candlelight" (Buffy Ste-Marie, Bennett), "Where . . . to?" (Baird, Sokolow), "Judgment of Paris" (Weill, Tudor), "Contrasts" (Lewis, Norman), "La Chasse" (Massenet, Lotte Goslar), "The Myth" (Kodaly, Sanasardo), "Pas de Quatre" (Pugni, Dolin), "Flower Festival Pas de Six and Pas de Deux" (Helsted, Bournonville-Bennett), "The Exiles" (Schoenberg, Jose Limon), "Leyenda" (Albeniz, Morca), "La Monja Gitana" (Agama, Manolo Vargas), "Les Demoiselles Militantes" (Lumbye, Bennett) "Take 7 Roll 'Em" (Sound Score, Bennett)
PREMIERES: "Albinoni Adagio Pas de Deux (Albinoni, Bennett), "Don Quixote Pas de Deux" (Minkus, Petipa-Bennett), "Three Virgins and a Devil" (Respighi, Agnes deMille), "Football Players" (James Sellars, Bennett), "Spring Waters" (Rachmaninoff, Messerer), "Suite Espanola" (Albeniz-Bach-deFalla, Teodora Morca), "Carmina Burana" (Orff, Bennett), "Chopiniana" (Chopin, Fokine-Bennett)

THE FINE ARTS DANCE THEATRE
Milwaukee, Wisconsin

Director-Choreographer, Myron Howard Nadel; General Manager, Barbara Banasikowski Smith; Music Director-Conductor, Richard Cameron; Production Director-Designer, Ronald A. Castleman; Stage Manager, Sally Ann Mesich; Choreographers, Susie Bauer, Carla Graham-White, Barbara Banasikowski Smith, Susan Spalding

COMPANY

Susie Bauer
Carla Graham-White
Myron Howard Nadel
Barbara Banasikowski Smith
Susan Spalding
Katherine Zavada

REPERTOIRE: "Summer Sequence" (Mozart, Graham-White), "Me Dance" (Poulenc, Graham-White), "Triptych" (Kodaly, Smith), "Lotus Land" (Kreisler-Scott, Bauer), "The Loser" (Harrison, Nadel), "The Day They Whitewashed the Buzzards" (Smith-Zavada), "Earthsong" (Cameron, Spalding), "Chaconne" (Busoni-Bach, Nadel-Limon)

Left Center: Barbara Banasikowski Smith, Myron Howard Nadel, Carla Graham-White, Susie Bauer in "Chaconne"

Douglas Hevenor, Donna Silva
(First Chamber Dance Company)

143

Georgia Dance Theatre Company
Nelson Danish Photo

FLORIDA BALLET THEATRE
Tampa, Florida

Chairman, Richard Rader; Associate Chairman, Betty Lee Rey; Ballet Mistress, Charlotte Addington; Choreographer-in-residence, Frank Rey; Stage Manager, Arthur Spanton; Lighting Designer, Sydne Morris

COMPANY
Julie Beronda, Sheri Brockmeier, Debi Gallo, Dawn Kersey, Teil Rey, Cathy Miller Smith, Suzanne Spanton, Cathy Wood, Jinkey Gleaton, Debra Fasting, Beverly Tennille, Renee Roos, Sandi Wargo, Laura Fernandez, Judi Hall, Florence Harmon, Mary Frances Leto, Josette Manougian, Diana Melon, Lili Morris, Michelle Morrison, April Pozzi, Sandy Ramsey, Tami Webb, Debbie White, Cricket Willis, Debra Acosta, Andrea Boss, Teri Boynton, Kelly Clements, Lona Coonradt, Cheryl Diaz, Beth Dretzka, Karla Ledoux, Bonnie Lowrie, Mike Manougian, Margie Meitin, Mikki McDowal, Jackie Page, Tammy Pridgen, Victoria Reynolds, Desiree Rutkin, Cathy Smith, Missy Swanson, Peggy Taylor, Jennifer Woehlk, Shay Yanger, Angela Zummo

REPERTOIRE
"Les Sylphides" (Chopin, Fokine), "Elevenseventeen" (Miles, Rey), "The Nutcracker" (Tchaikovsky, Rey),
PREMIERES: "Souvenirs" (Villa-Lobos, Rader-Addington), "Please Ma" (Joplin, Rader), Variations on America" (Ives, Rey), "Simon Suite" (Simon, Addington), "The Renaissance" (Bachrach, Rey)

**Bruce Becker, Jane Kosminsky (5 X 2 Company)
in "There Is a Time"**
Zachary Freyman Photo

144

GEORGIA DANCE THEATRE COMPANY
Augusta, Georgia

Artistic Director-Choreographer, Frankie Levy; Ballet Mistress, Suzanne Denning; Assistant to Director, Ann-Toni Estroff; Costume and Set Designers, Claude Astin, Keith Cowling, Ann-Toni Estroff, Frankie Levy; Lighting Designers, Ann-Toni Estroff, Frankie Levy; Sound, Bernard Chambers, Claude Astin; Press, Nelson Danish

COMPANY
PRINCIPALS: Bebe Graham, Suzanne Denning, Dede Shiver, Tina Hagler, Martha Simkins, Cathy Adams
CORPS: Lynn Harp, Ann-Marie Schweers, Wanda McIntyre, Melissa Pierce, Alexander Gibson, Keith Hendrix, Martha Teets, Andrea Lum
WORKSHOP: Suzanne Taylor, Amy Barksdale, Kim Hale, Deborah Berlin, Dana Patchen, Laura Hensley, Jennifer Botnick, Laura Botnick, Eileen Schweers, Kim Kortick, Velvie Ketch
APPRENTICES: Joy Shapiro, Charlene Linder, Sharon Palmer, Heidi Ableman, Cindy Jacobsen, Christie Cliatt, Dana Rollins
GUEST ARTISTS: Edward Villella, Violette Verdy, Allegra Kent, Bonnie Mathis, Dennis Wayne, Frank Ohman, Nolan T'sani, Linda Yourth, Polly Shelton, Susan Hendl, Richard Rein

REPERTOIRE
(All premieres, and choreographed by Frankie Levy) "The Little Match Girl (Mahler), "Chopin Today" (Chopin), "Garden Dances" (Chopin), "Danzas Espanoles" (Moszkowski), "Pas de Trois" (Glinka, after Eglevsky), "Holy Hopping, Hallelujah" (Geld-Udel, Giordano)

**Charlotte Addington, Richard Rader
(Florida Ballet Theatre) in "Souvenirs"**

5 BY 2 DANCE COMPANY
New York, N.Y.

Artistic Directors, Jane Kosminsky, Bruce Becker; Administrator, Rena Shagan; Stage Manager, James Harrison; Lighting Designer, F. Mitchell Dana

COMPANY
Jane Kosminsky
Bruce Becker

REPERTOIRE: "There Is a Time" (Dello Joio, Jose Limon), "Negro Spirituals" (Traditional, Helen Tamiris), "Meditations of Orpheus" (Hovhaness, Norman Walker), "Cold Sunday Afternoon" (Donald Erb, Cliff Keuter), "Sola" (Penn-Oldham, Mario Delamo) PREMIERES: "Gallopade" (Joseph Lanner, James Waring), "Indeterminate Figure" (Robert Starer, Daniel Nagrin)

HARTFORD BALLET
Hartford, Connecticut

Artistic Director-Choreographer, Michael Uthoff; Executive Director, Enid Lynn; Managing Director, Ellsworth Davis; Tour Manager, Gary Lindsey; Assistant to the Director, Lisa Bradley; Administrative Assistant, Michael Simson; Technical Director, Gus Pollek; Production Manager, David Owen; Costumer, Mary Wolfson; Wardrobe Mistress, Beulah Cole; Costumes, Carl Michell, David James, Pauline Lawrence, Alan Madsen, Larry King, Michael P. Duffy, Lotte Goslar, The Boyd Works; Sets, James Steere, Morton Fishman, Anni Albers, Carl Michell; Lighting, Jennifer Tipton, Tony Marques, David Owen, Joel Grynheim; Conductors, Robert Cole, Efrain Guigui, Edward Simons, Meir Weisel

COMPANY

Jack Anderson, Kevin Aydelotte, Noble Barker, Lisa Bradley, Robert Buntzen, Leslie Craig, Thomas Giroir, Judith Gosnell, Karen Kelly, Debra McLaughlin, Joan Merrill, John Perpener, Sandra Ray, Roland Roux, John Simone, Jeanne Tears

REPERTOIRE
(1974–1975)

"Brahms Variations" (Brahms, Uthoff), "Cantata" (Ginastera, Uthoff), "ChiaraScuro" (Parris, Mary Staton), "Concerto Grosso" (Vivaldi, Uthoff), "Day on Earth" (Copland, Doris Humphrey), "Dusk" (Satie, Uthoff), "F. Jasmine's Quiet Space" (Wakeman, Katherine Gallagher), "History of America" (Compiled, Enid Lynn), "La Malinche" (Lloyd, Limon), "Marosszek Dances" (Kodaly, Uthoff), "Nutcracker" (Tchaikovsky, Uthoff-Lynn), "Peter and the Wolf" (Prokofiev, Uthoff), "Quartet in D Minor" (Schubert, Lois Bewley), "Windsong" (Elgar, Uthoff)
PREMIERES: "Come, Come Travel with Dreams" (Scriabin, Anna Sokolow), "Duo" (Clark, Uthoff), "Leggerios" (Beethoven, Lotte Goslar), "Pastorale" (Handel, Uthoff) "White" (Traditional Japanese, Jennifer Mullen)

HARTFORD BALLET CHAMBER ENSEMBLE
Hartford, Connecticut

Directors-Choreographers, Michael Uthoff, Enid Lynn; Managing Director, Ellsworth Davis; Tour Manager, Gary Lindsey; Administrative Assistant, Michael Simson; Technical Director, Phil Darrell; Costumes, Mary Wolfson; Rehearsal Assistants, Dianne Fleming, Scott Channing, Robyne Watkin, Katherine Gallagher

COMPANY

Brian Adams, Allyson Barker, David Curwen, Debbie Evens, Elisabeth Fisk, Melissa Klein, Robert Kowalski, Christel Meyer, June Rosenfeld, Susan Ross, Bradford Roth, Jeffrey Schweizer, Rebecca Wood

REPERTOIRE
(1974–1975)

"Concerto Grosso" (Vivaldi, Uthoff), "Dusk" (Satie, Uthoff), "Florestan Pas de Trois" (Tchaikovsky, Robyn Watkin), "Giselle Peasant Pas de Deux" (Adam, Watkin), "Meatwaves" (Miller, Enid Lynn), "Peter and the Wolf" (Prokofiev, Uthoff), and *PREMIERE* of "Something Happened" (Laws, Perpener)

Left Center: Bob Kowalski, Melissa Klein, Jeffrey Schweizer, Allyson Barker in "Meatwaves" Top Right: Kevin Aydelotte, Sandra Ray in "Leggerios"

Lisa Bradley, Michael Uthoff Above: John Perpener, Jack Anderson, Thomas Giroir, Noble Barker in "Cantata"

GUS GIORDANO JAZZ DANCE COMPANY
Wilmette, Illinois

Director-Choreographer, Gus Giordano; Dance Coordinator, Lea Darwin; Manager, Libby Beyer; Lighting Designer-Stage Manager, David Miller

COMPANY

Gus Giordano	Erik Geier
Pattie Obey	James Homan
Julie Walder	Jeffery Mildenstein
Meribeth Kisner	Clarence Teeters

REPERTOIRE: "The Matriarch" (Ingle, Giordano), "Solstice" (Subotnick, Bill Evans), "Judy" (Songs of Judy Garland, Giordano), "Pas de Trois" (Tchaikovsky, Bruce Merrill after Petipa), "Glitzville, U.S.A." (Songs of the 1950's, Debbie Hallek), "Fluctuation" (Bernstein, Jim Kolb), "The Rehearsal" (Stevens, Jim Kolb), "Solar Wind" (Pointer Sisters, Ernest Morgan), "Bach to Bach" (Bach, Julie Walder), "Slaughter on 10th Avenue" (Rodgers, Giordano), "Tribute" (Hayes, Giordano), "American Heritage" (Mann, Giordano), "Ragtime to Rock," "N.Y. Export: Opus Jazz" (Prince, Giordano), "Holy Hoppin' Hallelujah" (Geld-Udell, Giordano), and *PREMIERE* of "Fancy Free" (Bernstein, Walder-Giordano)

Left: Gus Giordano Company
EPS Studios Photo

HAMPTON ROADS CIVIC BALLET
Hampton, Virginia

Directors, Edgerton B. Evans, Muriel Shelley Evans; Choreographers, Joan Ashlyn, Lisa Shaw, Edgerton B. Evans, Muriel Shelley Evans; Sets, Mary Beaven; Lighting, Tim Van Noy; Stage Manager, C. O. Seaman, Stephanie Messick; Press, Marika Anthony, Susan McAllister

COMPANY

SOLOISTS: Lisa Shaw, Darcy Evans, Michele Lequeux, Danny Gunter, Susan McAlister
CORPS: Joanne Crum, Cathy Welsh, Michelle Cawthorn, Vicki Church, Kari Buttles, Kathy Johnson, Teresa Adams, Carolyn Wilson
APPRENTICES: Mary Vinosky, Kathryn Blevins, Sidney Sale, Jane White, Joanna Walberg, Margaret Zehmer, Kim Hastings, Connie Alvis, Kyra White, Mary Anna Durkovich, Corinne Jantz, Sophia Jantz
GUEST ARTIST: Leo Schmidt

REPERTOIRE

"The Nutcracker" (Tchaikovsky, Petipa-Ivanov), "Trois Encore" (Shostakovitch, Joan Ashlyn), "Les Patineurs" (Meyerbeer, Muriel Shelley Evans), "Festival" (Folk Music, Traditional), and *PREMIERE* of "The City Mouse and Country Mouse" (Beethoven, M. S. Evans)

Left: Kari Buttles, Michelle Cawthorn in "The City Mouse and the Country Mouse"

I.D.E.A. COMPANY
Santa Monica, California

Director-Choreographer, Claudia Chapline

COMPANY

Claudia Chapline
Lisa Wolford
Kate Zundell
Beth Markowitz
Harold Schwarm
Robert Grauch
Don Bondi

REPERTOIRE:"Light Drawing" (George Belle), "Perimeters" (Poetry and Choreography, Claudia Chapline), "Egg Play" (Collage), "My Grandmother Went to the Moon," "Mantra" (Collage), "Lumen" (George Belle), "The Telephone Book" (Sound Collage), "The Grand Tour and Raggedy Ann," "Seasons of Love"

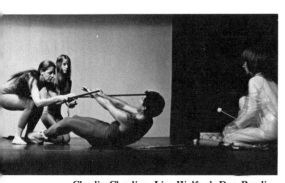

Claudia Chapline, Lisa Wolford, Don Bondi, Sharon Shore in "Perimeter" *(Lyn Smith Photo)*

HOUSTON BALLET
Houston, Texas

Acting Artistic Director, James Clouser; Ballet Master, Nicholas Polajenko; Conductors, Charles Rosenkrans, Hugo Fiorato; Lighting Designer, Jennifer Tipton; Company Manager, Jane V. Hayes; Stage Manager, Patrick Ballard; Orchestra Manager, Ralph Liese; Pianist-Librarian, Michael McGraw; Costumer, Brauna Ben-Shane; Props, Kenneth Trammell; Wardrobe Mistress, Ray Delle Robbins; General Director, Henry Holth; Press, Ron Christopher

COMPANY

PRINCIPALS: Leo Ahonen, Soila Arvola, Barbara Pontecorvo, Andrea Vodehnal
SOLOISTS: Brian Andrew, Whit Haworth, Mary Margaret Holt, Nancy Onizuka, Robert Raimondo, Denise Smokoski, Bruce Steivel
CORPS: Lauren Bowman, Lisa Chalmers, Mary Jane Doornbos, Gloria de Santo, Viorica Ene, Rodwic Fukino, Jory Hancock, Deidre Kawolics, Leath Nunn, Natasha Lewczuk, Melissa Lowe, Mark McLaughlin, Tommy Newby, Kenneth Oberly, Stephen Baranovics, Carole Valleskey, Kathleen Vander Velde, Michele White
GUEST ARTISTS: Edward Villella, Violette Verdy, Natalia Makarova, Ivan Nagy, Frederic Franklin

REPERTOIRE

"Constantia" (Chopin, William Dollar), "Black Swan Pas de Deux" (Tchaikovsky, Petipa), "Through a Glass Lightly" (Collage by Sonja Zarek, James Clouser), "Nutcracker" (Tchaikovsky, Frederick Franklin), "Prodigal Son" (Prokofiev, Balanchine), "Coppelia" (Delibes, Franklin), "Pas de Quatre" (Pugni, Dolin), "Carmina Burana" (Orff, Clouser), "Swan Lake Act II" (Tchaikovsky, Petipa), "Napoli Act III" (Helsted-Gade-Paulli, Bournonville), "Caprichos" (Bartok, Herbert Ross), "Don Quixote Pas de Deux" (Minkus, Petipa), "Danse Brillante" (Glinka, Franklin), "Pas de Dix" (Glazounov, Balanchine), "Homage" (Gounod, Franklin), "Suspension" (Ray Green, May O'Donnell), "Design with Strings" (Tchaikovsky, John Taras)
PREMIERES: "Allen's Landing" (Fisher Tull, Clouser), "Con Spirito" (Smetana, Clouser), "Gershwin Songbook" (Gershwin, Clouser), "Three Trios" (Bartok, Clouser), "Water Music" (Handel, John Taras)

Bill Records, Galloway Photos

Right Center: "Carmina Burana"

**Andrea Vodehnal, Frederic Franklin
in "Coppelia"**

**Andrea Vodehnal, Edward Villella
in "Prodigal Son"**

"Con Spirito"

147

THE ITHACA DANCEMAKERS
Ithaca, N. Y.

Artistic Directors-Choreographers, Helen Alexander, Saga Ambegaokar, Stephen Buck, Barbara Dickinson, Janice Kovar, Peggy Lawler; Administrative Director, Sorrel Fisher; Production Manager, Rosemary Harms; Lighting Designer, Bill Owen

COMPANY

Helen Alexander, Saga Ambegaokar, Stephen Buck, Barbara Dickinson, Janice Kovar, Peggy Lawler, Karen Bell, Sam Costa, Charles Bruner, Kristin Draudt, Alix Keast, Jill Lerner, Carl Thomsen

REPERTOIRE

"Linnunrata" (Borden, Ambegaokar), "Triangle" (Stephen Buck), "Solo Solo" (Buck), "The Unanswered Question" (Ives, Dickinson), "Venus in Capricorn" (Scott-Yuze, Janice Kovar), "Circuit" (Peggy Lawler)
PREMIERES: "No. 14 for Ellen" (Drews, Helen Alexander), "Glitz" (Alexander), "Tapestries" (Borden, Ambegaokar), "Thanks for the Lift" (Saga Ambegaokar), "Aurora Borealis" (Ambegaokar), "You and I" (Ruether, Barbara Dickinson), "Lento" (Dvorak, Janice Kovar), "Rhythms" (Dvorak, Kovar), "Concert" (Peggy Lawler)

Right Center: The Ithaca Dancemakers in "Tapestries I & II"

INNER CITY REPERTORY DANCE COMPANY
Los Angeles, California

Administrative Director, Luther James; Choreographers, Donald McKayle, William Couser, Ruby Millsap, Carolyn Dyer; Production Manager, William Grant III; Costumes, Darlene Naylor; Rehearsal Director, Carolyn Dyer; Executive Director, C. Bernard Jackson

COMPANY

Harvey Cohen	Carolyn Dyer
Regina Bell	Ruby Millsap
Cliff De Reita	Ron Bush
Geronne	Leslie Hardesty Sisson
Keith Harris	Linda Slocum
Stanley Perryman	Linda Young

Guest Artist: Jose Lorenzo
REPERTOIRE: "Migrations," "M.S.G." (Borodin, Carolyn Dyer), "Because My Feet Are Dancing" (Ruby Millsap-W.H. Grant III, Ruby Millsap), "Orozco" (Kenneth Klaus, Lester Horton), "Aguere de Ogum" (Zak Diouf, Jose Lorenzo), "G.S.M." (Wayne Peterson, Dyer), "Songs of the Disinherited" (Arranged by Phillip Moore III, Donald McKayle), "I'm on My Way" (Phillip Moore III), "Upon the Mountain" "Angelitos Negros" (Roberta Flack, McKayle), "Shaker Life"

Top Left: Leslie Hardesty Sisson, Linda Young, Ruby Millsap, Geronne, Linda Slocum

THE JACKSON BALLET
Jackson, Mississippi

Director-Choreographer, Gayle Parmelee; Conductor, Lewis Dalvit; Costume Designers, Franklin Adams, Karlen Bain; Lighting, James McGahey; Stage Manager, Peter Jones; Chairman of the Board, Walter E. Lydick; President, Mrs. John E. Miller

COMPANY

Adrienne Bass, Joanna Bass, Theresa Campbell, Angela Clark, Katherine Denton, Ann Hester, Elizabeth Ann Humphries, Linda Kirby, Tracy Knight, Tami Miller, Melinda Robinson, Terri Rogers, Sharon Sanders, Elizabeth Townsend, Beth Ware, Anita Whitley, David Keary, John Leach, Richard Rector
APPRENTICES: Patricia Benefield, Ginger Buzhardt, Denise Coker, Marion Enochs
GUEST ARTISTS: Natalia Makarova, Ivan Nagy

REPERTOIRE

"Reverence" (Bach), "All Rights Reserved—Even on the Moon" (Satie), and *PREMIERES* of "Birthday Contribution" (Haydn), "Irish Folk Tale" (Anderson)

David Keary, Katherine Denton in "Birthday Contribution"
David Sandberg Photo

JACOBS LADDER DANCE COMPANY
New York, N.Y.

Artistic Director-Choreographer, Judith Jacobs; Company Manager, Henry D. Weiss

COMPANY
Christopher Clark
Judith Huffman
Judith Jacobs
Lorna Lable
Fred McKitrick
Deborah Novak
Cathy Smardza
Alejandro Wang

REPERTOIRE: "Yankee Doodling" (Collage), "Superdupersoupermarket" (Collage), and *PREMIERE* of "Nostalgia to N. O. W."

Top Left: Judith Jacobs in "Nostalgia to N.O.W."

JACKSONVILLE BALLET THEATRE
Jacksonville, Florida

Founder-Artistic Director-Choreographer, Dulce Anaya; President, Tom Schifanella; Designers, Robin Shepherd, Andrew Liliskis; Costumes, Phil Phillips, Memphis Wood, Allison Miraglia, Lydia Roberts, Maurice Geoffrey; Sound, Rush Bulloch; Lighting-Stage Manager, Nick Ciccarello

COMPANY
PRIMABALLERINA: Dulce Anaya
SOLOISTS: Harriet Webb, Elaine Pennywitt
CORPS: Anne Brown, Patricia Chipman, Charmion Clark, Richard Coleman, Cindy Crombie, Katherine Fisher, Mary Bouchnour, Mary C. Haut, Wendy James, Kenley Jones, Billye Kay Kersey, Meme Menard, Charles Nowlin, Emilie Olsen, Lisa Permenter, Mike Ryan, Debbie Sidbury, Leslie Snow, Betty Vogl, Randy Allen
APPRENTICES: Laurie Hammers, Kathy Mattair, Jane Mauney, Jill Neppl, Angela Schifanella, Becky Steele, Gwen Wade, Lynn Van Hynning, Jennifer Childers, Dorothy Gorospe
GUEST ARTISTS: Adolfo Andrade, Miguel Campaneria, Stanley Pincus, Alexander Filipov, Barbara Sandonato, Haydee Gutierrez, Art Hutchinson, Alexei Yudenich, Ted Kivitt, Edward Villella

REPERTOIRE
(All choreography by Dulce Anaya except where noted) "Nutcracker" (Tchaikovsky), "Swan Lake" (Tchaikovsky, after Mary Skeaping version), "Giselle" (Adam, after Anton Dolin version), "Le Grand Pas de Quatre" (Pugni, Lester), "Raggedy Ann Rag" (Oleg Briansky), "Aria" (Stravinsky, Haydee Gutierrez), "Overture" (Schubert), "Vida Efimera" (Sibelius), "Firebird" (Stravinsky), "Concerto" (Grieg), "Quartet" (Shostakovich), "Les Sylphides" (Chopin, Fokine), "Polovetsian Dances from Prince Igor" (Borodin, Fokine), "Aurora's Wedding" (Tchaikovsky, Petipa), "The Statue" (Richard Coleman), "Rhapsody in Blue" (Gershwin), "Serious Ballet or Fun?" (Ponchielli), "Perspectives" (Prokofiev, Betty Balfour Marks)
PREMIERE: "Sleeping Beauty" in 4 acts (Tchaikovsky, Anaya after Beriosoff's version)

Dulce Anaya, Ted Kivitt in "Swan Lake"
Al Inclan Photo

Jan Van Dyke in "Waltz"
Jo Tartt, Jr. Photo

JAN VAN DYKE & DANCERS
Washington, D.C.

Artistic Director-Choreographer, Jan Van Dyke; Lighting Designer-Technical Director, Jack Halstead

COMPANY
Jan Van Dyke	Carlo Perlo
Amoret Barbee	Ruth Rivin
Elly Canterbury	Diane Shaffer
Sandy Eisenberg	Valerie Shanks
Jean Jones	Rosemary Wells

GUEST ARTISTS: Virginia Freeman, Marcia Sakamoto

REPERTOIRE
"Waltz" (Strauss), "Big Show" (Sousa), "Beauty and the Beast" (Bob Labaree, Sally Nash), "Rain Dance" (Sally Nash)
PREMIERES: "Ella" (Sylvia Fine, Jan Van Dyke), "Paradise Castle" (George Crumb-Irving Berlin, Van Dyke), "Ceremony" (Leo Sayer-Dave Courtney-Hank Williams, Van Dyke)

THE JOSE GRECO COMPANY
New York, N.Y.

Artistic Director, Jose Greco; Choreography, Nana Lorca; Musical Director and Pianist, Roger Machado; Special Tour Director, Robert Lopas; Managing Director, Carlton S. Sedgeley; Tour Direction, Kolmar-Luth Entertainment, Royce Carlton Inc., and under the auspices of The Jose Greco Foundation for Hispanic Dance; Production conceived and created by Jose Greco and Nana Lorca

COMPANY

Jose Greco*	Nana Lorca
Teo Santelmo	Alessandra Greco
Jose Luis Greco	Patricia Santana
Jose Ramos	Paco Alonso

Luis Rivera, Guest Artist

Flamenco Singer, Jose Silva "El Moro"; guitarists: Ricardo Modrego, Gino Dauri

PROGRAM

"Introduction," "Farruca," "El Vito," "Seguidillas Reales," "Alegrias," "Nobleza Andaluza," "Solea," "Escenas Madrilenas," "Bolero," "Romance Gitano," "Zapateado de Camperos," "Castellana," "Jota," "Andalucia Flamenca"

* The 1974–1975 season included Mr. Greco's farewell world tour. He will continue as artistic director of the company, and perform occasionally.

Right: Nana Lorca, Jose Greco

The Jose Greco Company of Spanish Dancers

JOHN PASQUALETTI'S PACIFIC BALLET
San Francisco, California

Artistic Director-Choreographer, John Pasqualetti; General Manager, Laurie Wakefield; Costumer, Mary Ann Seymour; Stage Manager, John O'Neil; Lighting Designer, Bill Deavenport

COMPANY

John Loschmann, Susan Alleluia, Deborah Frates, Jeffrey Sherwood, Carolyn Goto, Carolyn Meyerhoffer, Jackie Tertrou, Kahz Zmuda, Allen Gebhardt, Alex Nibley, Peter Reed, Rose Brotherton, Ann Butler, Nancy Henderson, Fred Johnston, Peter Hempel, Allyson Way, Cathy Prior

REPERTOIRE

(all choreography by John Pasqualetti except where noted) "Basha Bella" (Berberian, Nancy Henderson), "Textures" (Takemitsu), "Candide" (Constant), "Murder in the Cathedral" (Holst, Allen Gebhardt), "Sonata" (Copland, Ann Butler), "Pas de Deux" (Tchaikovsky, David Lopes), "Illuminations" (Britten), "Six Wives of Henry VIII" (Wakeman), "Walk to Paradise Garden" (Delius, John Loschmann), "Hymn of the Seventh Galaxy" (Corea, Nancy Henderson), "Fifth Position" (Prokofiev, Ann Butler), "Seasons" (Takemitsu), "Daphne of the Dunes" (Partchi), "Songs of Celebration" (William Russo), "Symphony for a Man Alone" (Pierre Schaffer-Pierre Henry), "Eighth Symphony" (Mahler), "Streetcar Named Desire" (North), "Scheherazade" (Ravel), "Song of the Nightingale" (Stravinsky), "Hermit Songs" (Barber), "Bolero" (Ravel, Marc Wilde), "Brujo" (Barber, Nancy Henderson), "Romeo and Juliet" (Tchaikovsky), "Apollo" (Stravinsky), "Rhapsody in Blue" (Gershwin), "Duo Concertant" (Stravinsky), "Coral Island" (Takemitsu), "Peter Pan" (Stravinsky)

Carolyn Meyerhoffer, John Pasqualetti, Peter Reed in "Illuminations"

KANSAS CITY BALLET
Kansas City, Missouri

Artistic Director-Choreographer, Tatiana Dokoudovska; Conductor, Glenn Block; Guest Pianist, Sofia Levinson; Ballet Mistress, Vicki Allen Reid; Designers, Kansas City Art Institute Theatre Design Class; Costumes by choreographers; Stage Manager, Carlton Carroll; President, Mrs. Paul Hunt, Jr., Press, Mrs. Harry Athan; Business Manager, Barbara Scanlon

COMPANY

Dolly Allard, Sandie Balot, Kim Bean, Toinette Biggins, Joel Czarlinsky, Steve Eads, Cathy Eberhart, Hal Epstein, Carol Feiock, Flora Hall, Michele Hamlett, Melissa Kelly, Donna King, Ernest Mavis, Lisa Merrill, Linda Van Osdol, Richard Orton, Dawn Parrish, Peggy Ply, Anita Porte, Jeannine Price, Jean Quick, Debra Shore, Melinda Suske, Mike Tankersley, Carl Welander, Francis Wardle
GUEST ARTISTS: Fernando Bujones, Naomi Sorkin

REPERTOIRE

"Ruse d'Amour" (Liadov, Dokoudovska), "La Bayadere Pas de Deux," "La Fille Mal Gardee Pas de Deux," "The Nutcracker" (Tchaikovsky, Dokoudovska), and *PREMIERES* of "Traversal Tapestry" (Schubert, Vicki Allen Reid), "The Sisters" (Schoenberg, Patrick Crommett)

Left Center: Joel Czarlinsky, Dolly Allard in "The Sisters"
Bill Batson Photo

KUNI DANCE THEATRE COMPANY
Los Angeles, California

Artistic Director-Choreographer, Masami Kuni; Choreographers, Paul Edwards, Jo Ann Mayeda, Henrietta Soloff, Miriam Tait; Electronic Music, Ken Heller, Masami Kuni; Lighting, Larry Wiemer, Jerry McColgan; Costumes, Masami Kuni, Henrietta Soloff; Stage Manager, Fred Sutton; Press, Paul Edwards

COMPANY

Stephanie Romeo, Tomiyo Nagahashi, Jo Ann Mayeda, Valerie Sied, Miriam Tait, Linda Wojcik, Becky Wiemer, Susan Deppipo, Henrietta Soloff, Chris Drath, Janey McCoy, Lois Greyston, Paul Edwards, Chris Yamaga, George Jane
GUEST ARTISTS: Jundy Jarvis, Kazuo Kamizawa, Chie Murata

REPERTOIRE

"Room" (Masami Kuni)' "Song of Chain" (Kuni), "Circle without Circumference" (Kuni), and *PREMIERE* of "The Sea" (Kuni)

Kuni Dance Theatre Company in "Circle without Circumference"

151

LES GRANDS BALLETS CANADIENS
Montreal, Canada

Founder-Director, Ludmilla Chiriaeff; Artistic Director, Brian Macdonald; Executive Director, Richard d'Anjou; Manager-Director of Productions, Colin McIntyre; Musical Director-Conductor, Vladimir Jelinek; Resident Choreographer, Fernand Nault; Ballet Masters, Linda Stearns, Brydon Paige; Reptiteur-Production Assistant, Daniel Jackson; Lighting Designer, Nicholas Cernovitch; Assistant to Artistic Director, Alain Pauzé; Press, Yves Dupré; Company Coordinator, Eileen Heath; Technical Director, Tex Pinsonneault; Stage Manager, Maxine Glorsky Fouros; Wardrobe, Nicole Martinet; Sets, Claude Berthiaume

COMPANY

Annette av Paul, Maniya Barredo, James Bates, Alexandre Belin, Lillian Bertolino, Anthony Bouchard, Richard Bouchard, Cathy Buchanan, Patti Caplette, Lucie Desnoyers, Robert Dicello, Louise Doré, Leslie-May Downs, Heather Farquarson, Richard Foose, Guillermo Gonzalez, David Graniero, Trudi Hirsch, Barbara Jacobs, Judith Karstens, Ondine Kozlov, David LaHay, Margery Lambert, Maurice Lemay, Candace Loubert, Cathy Laurent, Shirley New, Rafael Reyes, Mannie Rowe, Dwight Shelton, Anne Sprincis, John Stanzel, Christopher Tabor, Laszlo Tamasik, Susan Toumine, Sonia Vartanian, Michael Vrooman, Shauna Wagner, Vincent Warren, Wendy Wright

REPERTOIRE
(1974–1975)

"Four Temperaments" (Paul Hindemith, George Balanchine), "The Lottery" (Stravinsky, Brian Macdonald), "Tam Ti Delam" (Gilles Vigneault, Macdonald), "The Nutcracker" (Tchaikovsky, Balanchine), "Serenade" (Tchaikovsky, Balanchine), "Romeo and Juliet" (Harry Freedman, Macdonald)

Alexandre Belin, Maniya Barredo in "Tam Ti Delam'
Arnott Rogers Photo

Alexandre Belin, Annette av Paul in "Romeo and Juliet"
Robert Ragsdale Photo

Vincent Warren, Helene Heineman in "The Lotter
Pierre Gaudard Photo

DANCES AFFIRMING LIFE
Southport, Connecticut

Direction, Choreography, Costumes and Lighting by Louise Mattlage
COMPANY: (names not submitted)

REPERTOIRE

"Antigoen" (Bach), "The Witches from Shakespeare" (Parsch), "The Sailor" (Spellman), "Celebration," "Yes!" (Iron Butterfly), "100th Psalm" (Bach), "13th Psalm" (Bach), "Kaddish" (Traditional), "Job" (Greenlea), "Thank You, God" (Messaien), "Pythagorian Prayer" (Bach), "Shalom" (Traditional)
PREMIERES: "Alananita Nana" (Traditional), "In This Awsome Moment" (Alan Brogh), "Frozen Tears" (Dorothy Joslin), "What Is It About?" (May Swenson), "Rejoice" (Merle Good)

Right: Louise Mattlage

LOUISVILLE BALLET COMPANY
Louisville, Kentucky

Artistic Directors-Choreographers, Richard and Cristina Munro; Costume Designer, Doug Watts; Lighting Designers, Michael Watson, Geoffrey Cunningham, James Stephens; Conductors, George Marriner Maule, James Livingston

COMPANY

Pam Baird, Carla Black, Lisa Campbell, Pam Childress, Karen Lea Connelly, Judy Eckman, Donna Hoess, Lisa Hayes, Anabel Ishkanian, Chris Karibo, Cindy Lewis, Janet McSweeney, Mary Means, Lynn Melillo, Kay Nickens, Colleen O'Callaghan, Lisa Patrick, Gail Peterson, Mary Kay Quarles, Janet Shaffner, Jan Tabacheck, Janine Whitfill, Therese Whitfill, Stan Bobo, Lee Brunner, Vincent Falardo, David Guffy, Peter McGrath, Larry Ponzi, David Thurmond, Doug Watts, Steve Monroe

REPERTOIRE

"Shakers" (Traditional, Doris Humphrey), "Peter and the Wolf" (Prokofiev, Mary Munro), "The Nutcracker" (Tchaikovsky, Richard and Cristina Munro), "Pas de Trois" (Tchaikovsky, Richard and Cristina Munro), "Polovetsian Dances" (Borodin, Richard and Cristina Munro), "Don Quixote Pas de Deux" (Minkus, Petipa), "Sleeping Beauty Act III" (Tchaikovsky, Petipa), "Pas de Quatre" (Pugni, Richard and Cristina Munro), "Swan Lake Act II" (Tchaikovsky, Vladimir Bourmeister), "Jeux de Mer" (Ravel, Richard Munro), "Les Sylphides" (Chopin, Fokine), "Brahms Fantasy" (Brahms, Richard Munro)
PREMIERES: "Invitation to Madness" (George Crumb, Stan Bobo), "Spirituals" (Morton Gould, Richard Munro), "Dance Divertimento" (Shostakovitch, Richard and Cristina Munro), "Carmina Burana" (Carl Orff, Richard and Cristina Munro)

Center Right: Louisville Ballet
James M. Yuhr Photo

LOYOLA UNIVERSITY BALLET
New Orleans, Louisiana

Director-Choreographer, Lelia Haller; Artistic Director, Joseph Hebert; Sets, Costumes, Lighting, Rene J. Toups; Stage Manager, Bill Murphy

COMPANY

SOLOISTS: Rene Toups, Janet Comer, Willis Tassain, Joel Laciura, Dawn Capdepon, Mary Ann Fisher, Barbara Fitzgerald, Lynn Berry
CORPS: Lynn Berry, Pam Casey, Andrea Canale, Lisa Derchin, Olga Hayward, Cathy Hackett, Juanita Gandy, Julie Medina, Celeste Ford, Mary Meade Murphy, Mary Emma Pierson, Ann Plamondon, Betsy Read, Melanie Sicard, Claudia Vasilovik, Linda Upton, Pam Vidal, Joan Wolf, Dianne Eustis, Debby Mialaret, Carol Fitzwilliams, Patti Larse, Georgie Lees, Tracey Lynch, Louanne King, Ark Nelson, Victorino Chen, Everett Lundsford, James Meyers, Joe Ampolo

REPERTOIRE

(All choreography by Lelia Haller) "The Snow Maiden" (Balalaika Orchestra), "Peter and the Wolf" (Prokofiev), "Sacre du Printemps" (Stravinsky), "Petrouchka" (Stravinsky, after Fokine), "Firebird" (Stravinsky, after Fokine), "Les Deux Pigeons" (Messenger, after Merante), "Dance Macabre" (Saint-Saens)

Rene Toups, Joel Laciura
(Loyola University Ballet)

MACON BALLET GUILD
Macon, Georgia

Artistic Director-Choreographer, Gladys Lasky; President, Binks Solomon Hart; Lighting and Sound, E. C. McMillan; Stage Managers, Louis Friedel, B. R. Catherwood; Press, Elizabeth Drinnon

COMPANY

PRINCIPALS: Leslie Bowen, Mary Holliday, Mary O'Shaughnessey (Names of other members of company not submitted)

REPERTOIRE
(1974–1975)

"Peter and the Wolf" (Prokofiev, Lasky), "Strauss Suite" (Strauss, Lasky), "Clair de Lune" (Debussy, Lasky), and divertissements from classical repertoire

Top Left: Members of Macon Ballet Guild in "Strauss Suite" *(Danny Gilleland Photo)*

MARIN CIVIC BALLET
San Rafael, California

Director, Leona Norman; Associate Director, Grace Doty; Ballet Master, Howard Sayette; Lighting Designer-Technical Director, Robert G. Finley, Jr.; Costumes, Nancy Gallenson; Stage Manager, Jayme Gallenson; Press, Joel Wolfson; Conductor, Hugo Rinaldi; Choreographers, Ruthanna Boris, Thor Sutowski, Ramon Segarra

COMPANY

Colleen Caudill, Laurie Davis, Katie Dougherty, Kathy Gould, Rachel Hay, Mindy Jonas, Lucette Katerndahl, Alison Leidel, Ann Little, Laura Przetak, Lynn Rothman, Michelle Savage, Cindy Shatz, Robin Sicard, Nell Stewart, John Tucker, Carolen Weisenburg

GUEST ARTISTS: Kay Mazzo, Helgi Tomasson

REPERTOIRE

"Brahm's Waltzes-Opus 39" (Brahms, Charles Weidman), "Trois Gymnopedies" (Satie, Ronn Guidi), "Divertissement d'Adam" (Adam, Ramon Segarra), "Paquita" (Minkus), "Peasant Pas de Deux from Giselle" (Burgmuller, Petipa), "Scorpio" (Marvin Gaye, Jim Piersall)
PREMIERES: "Concerto in C" (Francois-Adrien Boieldieu, Thor Sutowski), "Tape Suite" (Hub Miller, Ruthanna Boris)

Marin Civic Ballet members
Michael E. Bry Photo

Adrienne Subotnik, Michael Kessler (Metropolitan Ballet) in "Death of Actaeon"

METROPOLITAN BALLET COMPANY
Bethesda, Maryland

Director-Choreographer, Charles Dickson; Assistant Director-Choreographer, Alan Woodard; President, Mary Ellen Irey; Set and Lighting Designer, Richard Carleton Hankins; Costumes, E. Raye LeValley; Wardrobe Mistress, Gladys Fuller; Stage Manager, Richard Carleton Hankins; Sound, Everett Fuller; Guest Teachers: Patricia Wilde, Sallie Wilson, Royes Fernandez, Ronald Emblen, Vassilie Trunoff

COMPANY

PRINCIPALS: Elaine Browning, Adrienne Subotnik, Cathy Caplin, Michael Kessler

SOLOISTS: Anne Berry, Christine Philion, Jacqueline Reed

CORPS: Elizabeth Spicer, Lili Petrov, Athena Smith Ann Stanley, Demetra Karousatos, Connie Oxford, Georgina Slavoff, Wendy Carpenter, Valerie Striar, Jane Madle, Nancy Szabo, Donna Beam, Katharine Feulner, James Parsons, Miles Everett

REPERTOIRE

"Snow Maiden" in 3 acts (Tchaikovsky, Dickson-Woodard), "Sylvia" in 3 acts (Delibes, Dickson-Woodard), "Britten Variations" (Britten, Woodard), "Tarantella" (Rossini-Respighi, Dickson), "Ballet Romantique" (Helsted, Woodard), "Waltz" (Tchaikovsky, Dickson)
PREMIERES: "Sestetto" (Marcello, Dickson), "The Death of Actaeon" (Poulenc, Dickson), "Anticipation" (Glazounov, Dickson)

METROPOLITAN BALLET OF ST. LOUIS
St. Louis, Missouri

President, Diane Duckworth; Aristic Director-Choreographer, Nathalie LeVine; Associate Director, Gary Hubler; Directors, Ralph Dellinger, Wendy Eckart, Judy Halbert; Stage Manager, Bernie Corn; Costumes, Judy Halbert; Wardrobe Mistress, Sella Koblick; Press, Maureen Sutton

COMPANY

Lisa Armantrout, Patty Barry, Paul Cavin, Dina Duckworth, Beth Eckart, Janet Ferguson, Kim Gavin, Anna Marie Harris, Patty Kelsten, Karen Kemp, Melinda Koblick, Valerie Ratts, Laura Reynolds, Mary Lou Sinnott, Kathy Sutton, Melanie Winner, Jane Barry, Cindy Butler, Halli Cohn, Lisa Dellinger, Anita DeMarco, Amy Eckart, Scott Eckart, Richard Fischer, Elizabeth Guller, Laura Halbert, Denise Harris, Beth Katz, Angela Liao, Nancy Liaw, Nikki LeVine, Kelly McGinnis, Kendra Pahl, Fred Reifsteck, Martin Schmidt, Laurie Stream, Karen Van Meter, Kathleen Webber
GUEST ARTISTS: Gary Hubler, Mark Krupinski

REPERTOIRE

"The Nutcracker" (Tchaikovsky, Ruth Page), "Swan Lake Act II" (Tchaikovsky, after Ivanov), "Pas de Quatre" (Pugni, after Dolin), "Gymnopedie" (Satie, LeVine), "Rag" (Joplin, Marian Levin), "Love Set" (Rossini-Britten, LeVine), "Bluebird" (Tchaikovsky, after Petipa), "Don Quixote" (Minkus, Michael Maule), "Air on 6 Strings" (Bach, Gary Hubler), "Pas de Trois" (Tchaikovsky, after Petipa)
PREMIERES: "The Skaters" (Meyerbeer-Lambert, LeVine), "Foyer de la Danse" (Schumann, LeVine), "Back to Bach" (Bach, Hubler), "Contradanses" (Beethoven, LeVine)

Miami Ballet in "Cinderella"
Michael Hoban Photo

MATTI LASCOE DANCE THEATRE COMPANY
Huntington Beach, California

Artistic Director-Choreographer, Matti Lascoe; Executive Director, Jerry Lascoe; Directors, Anita Metz Grossman, Sonya Newberg, Phyllis Wapner; Musical Adviser, Anita Metz Grossman; Lighting Desigher, Tom Ruzika; Sound, John Williams; Stage Managers, Tom Grond, Renee Stoddard

COMPANY: Names not submitted

REPERTOIRE

"Jubilatore" (Pachelbel-Corelli-Ricciotti), "Synaptic Junction" (Tape by Don Dittmer), "Thursday between 3 and 5" (Dick Hyman), "Marion's Garden" (Roger Kellaway), "Exit" (Morton Subotnick), "hemidemisemiquaver" (Subotnick), "Quasi" (Pachelbel), "Ellipsis," "Fiveforoctoberfive" (Darius Milhaud), "Little Green Box on Modale" (Ramsey Lewis), "Deja Vu" (Jelly Roll Morton)

Top Left: Matti Lascoe Dance Company in "hemidemisemiquaver" *(Lyn Smith Photo)*

Gary Hubler, Melinda Koblick in "Don Quixote"
Michael D. Eastman Photo

MIAMI BALLET COMPANY
Miami, Florida

Artistic Director-Choreographer, Thomas Armour; Co-Directors, Robert Pike, Renee Zintgraff, Martha Mahr; Conductor, Akira Endo; Designers, Francois Cloutier, Richard Mix, Patricia Strauss, Renee Zintgraff, Allan Madsen; Stage Manager, Demetrio Menendez; Ballet Mistress, Martha Mahr

COMPANY

SOLOISTS: Mark Goldweber, Renee Zintgraff, Robert Pike, Richard Schill, Nanette DiLorenzo, Cathy Contillo, Annemarie Amanzio, Rio Cordy, Lynn Huck, Marlene Monsour, Marcia Sussman, Julie Smith, Grace Suarez, Ann England
CORPS: Elizabeth De La Torre, Sheri Franzen, Rebecca Granda, Kathy Krawczyk, Lynn Lardizabal, Anne Parshall, Denise Peterson, Lenore Redmond, Allison Rosen, Andrea Tiger, Nancy Undt, Jayne Ziska, Julia Hickey, Diane Lee, Kate Prahl, Lorna Prentiss, Susan Willig, Vicki Eidenire, Marianne Gordon, Edward Bilanchone, Roy Duncan, Steven Undt, Samuel Velazquez, Charlie Watkins, Randy Parrott
GUEST ARTISTS: Natalia Makarova, Violette Verdy, Karena Brock, Charlene Gehm, Patricia Strauss, Lourdes Lopez, Betty Chamberlin, Carol Roca, Ivan Nagy, Ted Kivitt, Edward Villella, Peter Martins, David Coll, Larry Long, Dennis Poole, Ben Stevenson, Hiller Huhn, Vicente Nebrada, Roman Jasinski, Greg Osborne, Manuel Molina, Joel Robertson, Jerome Swigart

REPERTOIRE

"Swan Lake" in 4 acts (Tchaikovsky, Petipa-Ivanov), "Paquita" (Minkus, Jean Paul Comelin), "Prelude" (Rachmanioff, Ben Stevenson), "Black Swan Pas de Deux" (Tchaikovsky, Petipa), "Tchaikovsky Pas de Deux" (Tchaikovsky, George Balanchine), "Pas de Quatre" (Pugni, Stevenson)
PREMIERES: "Why" (Charles Ives, Patricia Strauss), "Daphnis and Chloe" (Ravel, Thomas Armour), "Waltz" (Gliere, Violette Verdy), "Ballet Suite" (Shostakovitch, Robert Pike)

MID-HUDSON BALLET COMPANY
Poughkeepsie, N.Y.

President, Joseph Towers; Artistic Directors-Choreographers, Estelle & Alfonso; Costumes, Olive Pearson; Company Manager, Mrs. Louis Sedare; Production Manager, Mrs. Clifton Woodard; Ballet Mistress, Karen Cassetta; Sets, Lloyd Waldon, Ruth Waldon; Press, Eileen Bellizzi

COMPANY

Cynthia Bonnett, Cathy Cassetta, Karen Cassetta, Mary Anne Fiorillo, Colleen Holt, Betty Jean Theysohn, Tracey Vita, Taryn Noel Weinlein

REPERTOIRE

"Origins in Geometric Progressions," "Oh Happy Day," "Spectrum," "Pan," "El Victorio Luis Alonso" "The Line, "Everyman," "The Waltz," "The Holiday Ballet," "Little Match Girl," "Pollution," "Variations to Concerto," "Etudes," "High"

Right: Members of Mid-Hudson Ballet Company

MINNESOTA DANCE THEATRE
Minneapolis, Minnesota

Artistic Director-Choreographer, Loyce Houlton; Technical Director, John Linnerson; Resident Designer, Judith Cooper

COMPANY

Jon Benson, Michael Brown, Nancy Duncan, Tish Fonda, Cheryl Gomes, Marianne Greven, Michael Hackett, Peter Hauschild, Ronald Holbrook, Sara Jay, Siri Kommedahl, Erin Luebke, Chris Lyman, Michael Rist, Carey Starr, Roberta Stiehm, Andrew Thompson, Susan Thompson, Wendy Wright, David Voss

REPERTOIRE

"Billy the Kid" (Copland, Loring), "Circles" (Stravinsky, Houlton), "Flower Festival Pas de Deux" (Helsted, Bournonville), "Earthsong" (Copland, Houlton), "La Malinche" (Lloyd, Houlton), "Minkus Mix" (Minkus, Petipa), "Nutcracker Fantasy" (Tchaikovsky, Houlton), "Pas de Quatre" (Pugni, Dolin), "Riders of the Earth Together" (Penderecki, Koons), "Sleeping Beauty Act III" (Tchaikovsky, Petipa), "Wingborne" (Vivaldi, Houlton) PREMIERES: "Five" (Xenakis, Voss), "Encounters" (Henze, Houlton), "Primavera" (Rossini, Uthoff), "Seedless Stonemoons" (Crumb Houlton), "Yellow Variations for Mirror Dancers" (Vivaldi, Houlton)

Left: Peter Hauschild, Susan Thompson
in "Seedless Stonemoons"
Ike Austin Photo

MISSISSIPPI COAST BALLET
Gulfport, Mississippi

Artistic Director-Choreographer, Delia Weddington Stewart; President, Margaret Booth; Manager, Bennie Stewart; Lighting, Jerry Wilson, Bennie Stewart; Conductor, James Shannon; Stage Manager, Bennie Stewart; Press, Jerry Kinser

COMPANY

PRINCIPALS: Delia Stewart, Molly Pisarich Johnson, Hazle Shaw, Merrily Carter, Julie Stewart, Jill Wilson, Ellen Booth, Christina Backstrom, Donna Martin, Audie Smith, Mark Hamilton

REPERTOIRE
(1974–1975)

"Invitation to the Dance" (Weber, Hazle White Shaw), "No U Turn" (Henry Cowell, Merrily Bertucci Carter), "Woman's Suite" (War, Christina Backstrom), "Pat-Terns" (Don Ellis, Delia Stewart) PREMIERES: "The Light" (Mark Hamilton, Delia Weddington Stewart), "Charades" (Debussy, Stewart), "Pendulous" (John Cage-Lou Harrison, Hazle White Shaw)

Molly Pisarich Johnson, Mark Hamilton, Jill Wilton
(Mississippi Coast Ballet)

NANCY SPANIER DANCE THEATRE
Boulder, Colorado

Artistic Director-Choreographer, Nancy Spanier; Lighting Designer, Michael Watson; Costume Designer, Barbara B. Wilson; Technical Director, Russell Haney; Press, Judith Marx

COMPANY
Nancy Spanier

Paul Oertel
Alma La Wrentz
Jeri McAndrews

Bob Kallus
Allen Nause
Doug Jessop

GUEST ARTISTS: Gary Cowan, Clarice Marshall, Jane Hoffner, Debra Wanner, Rebecca Perces, Peter Jackson

REPERTOIRE
"Swine Luck," "Mauvais Jeu," "Glass Camellias," "Time Wounds All Heals"
PREMIERES: "Phase Twone," "Deja Vu," "A Peep Show: For Women Only"

Right: Nancy Spanier, Alma LaWrentz in "Phase Twone"
Tom Byers Photo

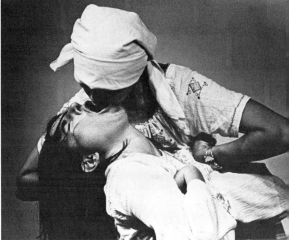

NEW JERSEY DANCE THEATRE GUILD
Edison, N.J.

Artistic Director-Choreographer, Alfredo Corvino; Ballet Mistress, Andra Corvino; Ballet Chairman, Patricia McCusker; Business Director, Helen Bechtold; Administration and Production Consultant, Yvett Cohen; President, Gertrude Weinberg; Costumes, Gail Rae, Marcella Corvino; Sets, Norman Cohen; Stage Managers, Vern Fowler, Jackie Lynn

COMPANY
Linda Acker, Laura Baldante, Felicia Battista, Judy Bolanowski, Margaret Bonis, Nancy Butchko, Eileen Byrne, Ruth Capaldo, Cecily Douglas, Kathy Gatto, Gina Greco, Beth Hnat, Joanne Long, Karen Lowande, Nelly Macys, Michelle Massa, Claire Miller, Mary Beth Nollstadt, Jean Raison, Lori Richardson, Linda Rooney, Patricia Scarangello, Janice Sorrentino, Maryellen Stickles, Mary Stoltenberg, Debbie Strauss, Lisa Torcicollo
GUEST ARTISTS: Eleanor D'Antuono, David Coll, Joseph Fernandez, Edilio Ferraro, Mercie Hinton, Dana Luebke, Michael Rivera, Jay Seaman, Victor Vargas
REPERTOIRE: "The Nutcracker" (Tchaikovsky, Corvino-Ivanov), "Pas de Quatre" (Pugni, Dolin), "Don Quixote Pas de Deux" (Minkus, Pepita), "Dance of the Hours" (Ponchielli, Dobrovinskaya), "On the Pond" (Meyerbeer, Kelley), "Mission Accomplished" (Primrose, Kelley), "Roda-Roda" (Album for the Young-Pinto, Asmus), "Jazz Today" (Scorpio-Coffey, Kelley), "Far Out" (Taurus-Coffey, Kelley), "Beauty and the Beast" (Prokofiev, Patrelle)

NEW ENGLAND DINOSAUR
Boston, Massachusetts

Director-Choreographer, Toby Armour; Guest Artistic Director, James Waring; Company Manager, Janet Spencer; Musical Director, Ezra Sims; Lighting Designer-Stage Manager, Robert Seder; Associate Director, Lois Ginandes

COMPANY
Sara Brummel
Jean Churchill
Willard Hall
Elizabeth Mallinckrodt
Michael Mao

REPERTOIRE: "Temptation" (Classic Tangos, Lois Ginandes), "Black Breakfast" (Popular, Armour) "Elliptic Spring" Mark Kazanoff, Armour), and *PREMIERES* of "Arena" (Stravinsky, Waring), "Artifices de L'Air" (Mozart, Waring), "A New Kind of Love" (Varied, Waring), "Adagio" (Mozart, Armour), "Scene I: Fragments of a Garden" (Ezra Sims, Armour), "Night Colors" (Liapunov, Waring)

Bradford Herzog Photo

Left Center: Jean Churchill, Elizabeth Mallinckrodt, Michael Mao in "Black Breakfast"

New Jersey Dance Theatre Guild's "Nutcracker"

NEW YORK DANCE THEATRE
New York, N.Y.

Frank Ohman, Artistic Director

David Brown
Elaine Bauer
Christine Spizzo
Wilfred Schuman
Kathleen Smith

Lynda Yourth
Robert Maiorano
Judith Shoaff
Stephen Rockford

REPERTOIRE: (all choreography by Frank Ohman except where noted) "Preludes" (Gershwin), "Rococo Variations" (Tchaikovsky), "Trio in C Minor" (Brahms), "Illusions" (Ives), "Bacharach Medley" (Bacharach), "Melodie" (Tchaikovsky), "Night Song" (Tchaikovsky), "Winter Dreams" (Tchaikovsky), "Stars and Stripes" (Sousa, Balanchine), "Sextet for Strings" (Tchaikovsky), "Concerto in F" (Gershwin), "Deliverance" (Britten)

Satomeor Photo

Top Left: New York Dance Theatre

NORTH CAROLINA DANCE THEATRE
Winston-Salem, N.C.

Director, Robert Lindgren; General Manager, Rod J. Rubbo; Ballet Mistress, Sandra Williams; Press, Louise A. Bahnson; Stage Manager, Bruce Tyrrell; Wardrobe Mistress, Pat Hanlon

COMPANY

Leslie Cook, Judy Crump, Larry Harper, Carey Homme, Jan Horne, Julie Jordan, Liz Kuethe, Richard Lane, Melinda Lawrence, Steve Majewicz, Mike Michael, Gwen Spear, Katie Straubel, Rodney Winfield

REPERTOIRE

"A Time of Windbells" (Norbert Vesak), "Bach: Brandenburg Three" (Charles Czarny), "Fugitive Visions" (Job Sanders), "La Malinche" (Jose Limon), "Mudai" (Kazuko Hirabayashi), "Myth" (Alvin Ailey), "Peter and the Wolf" (Nelle Fisher), "Raymonda Divertissements" (Balanchine-Danilova), "Screen Play" (Job Sanders), "Symphony 13" (Duncan Noble), "The Grey Goose of Silence" (Norbert Vesak), "The Tempest" (Duncan Noble), "Vis-a-Vis" (Charles Czarny), and *PREMIERE* of "Nocturnal Sun" (Michael Colina, Richard Kuch)

Katie Straubel, Steve Majewicz, Mike Michael in "Nocturnal Sun" (N.C. Dance Theatre)

Nina Bataller, Christopher Monks in "En Espana"

ORLANDO BALLET COMPANY
Huntington, N.Y.

Artistic Director-Choreographer, Vincent Orlando; Producer, Sara Dean Orlando; Financial Adviser, John Pancake; Representative, Virginia Page; Lighting, Marc Schlackman; Bernard Scherer, Andrew Nitolli; Sets, Vincent Orlando; Costumes, Betty Orlando; Wardrobe Mistress, Judy Brennan; Stage Manager, Joseph Straccia; Technicians, Steve Suarez, Jeff Rigby, Gene Zagorsky, Stephanie Zagorsky, Steven Plotzger

COMPANY

PRINCIPALS: Nina Bataller, Anita Jorgensen, Christopher Monks, Vincent Orlando, Leslie Perrell, George Stewart
SOLOISTS: Deborah Brennan, Lori Darley, Jamie Diton, Lorna Glick, Kate Keating
CORPS: Julianne Brennan, Valery Diliberto, Julie Josephson, Morna O'Riordan, Ann Papoulis, Pamela Plotsgerova, Jacqueline Riley, Steven Suarez, Jessica Teich
GUEST ARTIST: David Ewing

REPERTOIRE

(All choreography by Vincent Orlando except where noted) "Frogs" (Satie, James Pendill), "En Espana" (Granados), "Red Riding Hood," "Acquiesce" (Deutsch), "Mozart Variations" (Mozart)
PREMIERES: "Pas de Quatre" (Pugni, Dolin), "To Laura" (Liszt) "Misa Criolla" (Ramirez)

OLYMPIA BALLET COMPANY
Olympia, Washington

Artistic Director, Virginia Woods; Art Director, Ray Gilliland; Costume Director, Clarice Campbell; Music Director, Ken Olendorf; President, Charles M. Foster

COMPANY

Debbi Haverlock, Debi Campbell, Gail Tveden, Kathy Minnitti, Nancy Isely, Sue Foster, Eric Foster, Kendra Olendorf, Jade Yehle, Shirley Owens, Leigh Ann Bell, Dan Heitzmann, Stephen Burke, Vicki Ross, Gene Gylys, Mary Ann Murphy, Denise Egan, Karen Ward, Krystal Shoop

REPERTOIRE

In celebration of twentieth anniversary for the company, "Nostalgia '74" was premiered. It included excerpts from the most popular works during the past 20 years, and two one-act ballets: "Entrance to Hades" (Hindemith, Virginia Woods), and "Frankie and Johnny" (Gershwin, Virginia Woods).
PREMIERES: "The Old West" (Traditional-Copland, Woods), "Bicentennial of Dance" covering 200 years of dance in America.

Olympia Ballet in "Bicentennial of Dance"
Ray Gilliland Photo

PENINSULA BALLET THEATRE
San Mateo, California

Director-Choreographer, Anne Bena; Set Designer, Lila Vulty; Costumes, Lorraine Lehre, Alice Weiner; Lighting Designer, David Arrow; Manager, Edward Bena; Sound, Ken Rebman; Props, Stuart Harman; Wardrobe, Jeannette Owlette

COMPANY

Rosine Bena, Urs Frey, Sam Weber, Jeanne Harriss, Linda Triplett, and Misses Amarillo, Bartlett, Brayer, Crosby, Gaumer, Kish, Kueffer, Laak, Manzon, C. McCarthy, L. McCarthy, Myers, Riola, Rosenberg, Stephansen, Walsh, Messers McCoy, Simmers, Williams
GUEST ARTIST: Robert Gladstein

REPERTOIRE

"The Class" (Delibes, Rosine Bena), "Entre Cinq" (Faure, Antony Valdor), "Holberg Suite" (Greig, John Cranko), "Nutcracker" (Tchaikovsky, Anne Bena), "Paradox" (Kylian, Jiri Kylian), "Roundabout" (Arnold, Martin Buckner), "Valse" (Nicode, Robert Barnett)
PREMIERES: "Carnival Tu Tu" (Milhaud, Dick Ford), "Swan Lake" (Tchaikovsky, Rosine Bena)

**Right Center: Rosine Bena, Urs Frey
in "Holberg Suite"**

Pepsi Bethel (C) and company

PEPSI BETHEL AUTHENTIC JAZZ DANCE THEATRE
New York, N.Y.

Artistic Director-Choreographer, Pepsi Bethel; Costumes, Maria Contessa; Sets, Pepsi Bethel; Lighting, Peter Matusewitch; Technical Assistants, Eric Kohlman, Bruce Jayson-Lazarus; Stage Manager, Richard Allert

COMPANY

Pepsi Bethel, Theresa Ross, Alfred Gallman, Louisa Harris, Beau Parker, Amneris Rodriguez, Clarkston A. McPhee, Gregory B. Hinton, Pat Falcon, Antoinette Young, Bethschivba Bacchus

REPERTOIRE

"Tabernacle," "New Orleans," "Caribbean Rythms," "The Blues," "Jazz Suite"
PREMIERES: "Misty" (Errol Garner-Joe Crocker), "Family" (Morgana King), "Flirtation" (Tommy Dorsey)

PITTSBURGH BALLET THEATRE
Pittsburgh, Pennsylvania

Founder-Artistic Director-Choreographer, Nicolas Petrov; Artistic Director, Frederick Franklin; General Manager, Dr. S. Joseph Nassif; Music Director-Conductor, Phyllis Conner; Scenery and Costume Designers, Henry Heymann, Frank Childs, Rouben Ter-Arutunian, Stephen F. Petipas; Lighting Designer, Pat Simmons; Company Manager, E. F. West; Stage Manager, Alan Forino; Technical Director, Loudon Seth; Costume Coordinator, Stephen F. Petipas; Costume Mistress, Janet Groom; Press, Christine Hurst; Executive Assistant, Susan Prescott; Assistant to Mr. Petrov, Barbara Guterl

COMPANY

PRINCIPALS: Dagmar Kessler, Alexander Filipov, Jordeen Ivanov, JoAnn McCarthy, Thierry Dorado
SOLOISTS: Suzanne Davis, Jeanne Loomis, Susan Perry, Gernot Petzold, Rudolf Sellers
CORPS: Sharon Bowditch, Susan Degnan, Lucia Filipov, Patricia Frost, Ellen Glickman, Barbara LeGault, Nola Nolen, Eileen Peterson, Deborah Pleak, Kay Prud-homme, Deidre Salyer, Laurie Savarino, Cynthia Schowalter, Susan Stone, Karen Strawson, Patricia Triplett, Carol Wade, Michael Abbitt, Bruce Abjornson, Gregory Begley, Thomas Christopher, Peter Degnan, George Giraldo, Michael Hall, Paul McRae, Roland Morisette, Paul Plesh, David Roeger, Mark Schneider, Roger Triplett
GUEST CHOREOGRAPHERS: Milenko Banovitch, Vitale Fokine, Leonide Massine, Ruth Page, Stuart Sebastian, John Taras

REPERTOIRE

"Cinderella" (Prokofiev, Petrov), "Coppelia" (Delibes, Jelincic), "Giselle" (Adam, Coralli-Franklin), "La Sylphide" (Lovenskjold, Bournonville/Franklin), "Nutcracker" (Tchaikovsky, Ivanov), "Romeo and Juliet" (Prokofiev, Petrov), "Swan Lake" (Tchaikovsky, Petrov-Franklin), "Carmina Catulli" (Orff, Page), "Contrasts" (Fetler, Banovitch), "Dohnanyi Suite" (Dohnanyi, Taras), "Gaite Parisienne" (Offenbach, Massine), "Gopak" (Khatchaturian, Petrov), "Les Sylphides", "Pas de Dix" (Glazounov, Balanchine), "Pas de Quatre" (Pugni, Dolin-Franklin), "Peter and the Wolf" (Prokofiev, Petrov), "Petrouchka" (Stravinsky, Fokine), "Rite of Spring" (Stravinsky, Petrov), "Scenes de Ballet" (Stravinsky, Petrov), "Soiree Musicale" (Britten, Petrov), "Spectre de la Rose" (Maria von Weber, Fokine), "Suite de Danses Moldaves" (Golperin, Petrov), "Corsaire" (Drigo, Petipa), "Don Quixote" (Minkus, Gorsky), "Spring Waters" (Rachmaninoff, Jelincic), and *PREMIERE* of "Steel Symphony" (Balada, Petrov)

Michael Friedlander Photos

Thierry Dorado, Jo Ann McCarthy in "Dohnanyi Suite"
Top Right: Dagmar Kessler, Nicolas Petrov in "Coppelia"

Alexander Filipov, Jordeen Ivanov in "Romeo and Juli
Above: Dagmar Kessler in "Giselle"

PILOBOLUS DANCE THEATER
Norwich, Vermont

Founders-Directors, Moses Pendleton, Jonathan Wolken; Choreographers, The Company; General Manager, Chris Ashe; Booking Manager, Shaw Concerts

COMPANY

Alison Chase
Martha Clarke
Robert Morgan Barnett

Moses Pendleton
Michael Tracy
Jonathan Wolken

REPERTOIRE: "Walklyndon," "Anaendrom" (Jon Appleton), "Ocellus" (Pendleton-Wolken), "Aubade," "Ciona" (Appleton), "Pilea" (Steve Radecke, Alison Chase), "Pseudopodia" (Jonathan Wolken), "Terra-cotta" (Peter Schickele, Clarke-Barnett), "Monkshood's," "Farewell" (Traditional), "Alraune" (Jon Appleton)

Top Right: Pilobolus Company

Premiere Dance Arts members in "Funky Stuff"

PRINCETON REGIONAL BALLET
Princeton, N.J.

Artistic Director-Choreographer, Audree Estey; Ballet Mistress, Judith Leviton; General Manager, L. Wendell Estey; Press, Jean Brunner Pariso; Costume Coordinators, Ruth Pettit, Gloria Woodside

COMPANY

PRINCIPAL: Dodie Pettit
SOLOISTS: Diana Zeydel, Diane Partington, Sherry Alban, Linda Edwards, Susan Olson, Pat McDonald, Bebe Neuwirth, Christina Klotz, Robin Tantum
CORPS: Mary Lou Barber, Jane Billington, Ann Lynn Chianese, Susannah Cohen, Lynne Dennis, Bernadette Dockry, Jeffery Ferguson, Michelle Fisher, Holly Friedman, Terri Greenwald, Catherine Guerin, DeNeece Gurney, Anne Herzog, Abigail Kaplan, Penny Kingan, Lorri Lee, Evelyn Richmond, Julio E. Rivera, Libby Shifman, Pat Sliwinski, Marjorie Tansey, Suzanne Vaucher, Gale Wilson, Julie Winterbottom, Pamela Worley, Kasia Worrell
GUEST ARTISTS: David Anderson, Larry Hunt, Carol Bryant, Maxine Lampert

REPERTOIRE

"The Nutcracker" (Tchaikovsky, Audree Estey-Lila Brunner), "Coppelia" (Delibes, Judith Leviton-Frederic Franklin), "Peter and the Wolf" (Prokofiev, Estey), and *PREMIERES* of "Cinderella" (Prokofiev, Judith Leviton), "Cadences" (Henry Cowell, Ruth Langridge)

PREMIERE DANCE ARTS COMPANY
Denver, Colorado

Artistic Director-Choreographer, Gwen Bowen; Conductor, Gordon Parks; Sets, Gwen Bowen, Mark Schneider; Costume Mistress, Joan Cope; Lighting, Kathleen Caldwell; Props, Joyce Rider, Gerri Cacciatore; Press, Charles Kelly

COMPANY

SOLOISTS: Daniel Greenwald, Elaine Lenhart, Debra Norbloom, Valerie Pearson, Mark Schneider, Dixie Turnquist
CORPS: Deb Andres, Douglas Bair, Kristine Breed, Jayne Cacciatore, Suzanne Cacciatore, Crystal Chapman, Carla Close, Holly Cope, Vickie Field, Gina Grey, Tuffy Hardy, Linda Jacoby, Rise Kelly, Nikki Killian, Karin Kimmel, Irene Kropwiansky, Katherine Kuhlman, Carol March, Kathy Maurer, Cecilia Patkowsky, Collette Porter, Joyce Rider, Beth Shafer, Steven Snyder, Carrie Taylor, Valerie Thornburg, Debra Totten, Christina Zinn

REPERTOIRE

"Moldavian Suite" (Traditional, John Landovsky), "Coppelia Act II" (Delibes, Alexandra Danilova), "Variations from Sleeping Beauty" (Tchaikovsky, Petipa), "It's a Small, Small World" (Sherman, Bowen), "Not So Classical Ballet" (Shostakovich, Mark Schneider), "Funky Stuff" (Selected, Debra Norbloom), "Fogelberg Variations" (Dan Fogelberg, Schneider), "Raymonda Pas de Deux" (Glazounov, Balanchine), "Firebird" (Stravinsky, Schneider), "Paraszt" (Brahms, Bowen), "A Very Special Angel" (Goldmark, Bowen)

David Anderson, Dodie Pettit in "Coppelia"
(Princeton Regional Ballet)

161

RICHARD ARVE TRIO
RICHARD ARVE DANCE TROUPE
Chicago, Illinois

Founder-Director-Choreographer, Richard Arve; Composer-Conductor, Doris Conrad; Lighting, Tom Hagglund, Tern Bowman; Press, William Raffeld

COMPANY

Richard Arve, Violetta Karosas, Mimi Rozak (Trio), Debbie Barko, Margaret Lynne DiCianni, Dawn Marie Guch, Karen Zehme, Larry Ippel, Jerry James, Russell Lome, Ric Moyano

REPERTOIRE

"Pandemonium Shadow Show," "Number 9," "Fulfill a Dream," "In Memoriam," "Railrider," "Primate," "Introspection," "Argemedon," "Beyond the Gate of Ishtar," "Three in One," "Bloodrush," "The Engulfed Cathedral"

RIO GRANDE VALLEY CIVIC BALLET
McAllen, Texas

Artistic Director-Choreographer, Doria Avila; Administrative Director, Alfred J. Gallagher; Conductor, Vasilios Priakos; Executive Secretary, Jeanne Ross; Ballet Master, Ben Ortiz; Sets, Peter Wolf Associates; Costumes, Barbara Woodall, Jeanne Ross, Michelle Ross; Light Design, Stage Manager, Maurine Rockhill; Props, Severa Zambrano

COMPANY

PRINCIPALS: Ben Ortiz, Colette Ross, Homer Garza, Bonnie Bazar
SOLOISTS: Rosemary Cavazos, Michelle Nichols, Carlos Cantu, Gary Rochell
CORPS: Lori Anderson, Linda Acevedo, Teresa Blue, Cindy Gonzales, Machelle Goodenough, Michael Guerra, Debbie Hinjosa, Lezlie Hollister, Aide Lugo, Yvette Martinez, Donna Patrick, Leslie Stone, Sheryl Uhlaender, Ascension Almanza, Herman Cepeda, Willie Shives, Mark Wilder, Douglas Woodall, Melissa Barrera, Rangel Cavazos, Stephen Lyssy
GUEST ARTISTS: Judith Aaen, Anthony Sellers

REPERTOIRE
(1974–1975)

(All choreography by Doria Avila except where noted)
"The Nutcracker" (Tchaikovsky, William Martin-Viscount-Doria Avila after Ivanov), "Flower Festival at Genzano" (Helsted-Paulli, Bournonville), "Don Quixote Grand Pas de Deux" (Minkus, Petipa), "Sylvia Ballet Suite" (Delibes), "Montmartre" (Offenbach), "Fiesta Mexicana!" (Traditional), "Carmen Suite" (Bizet)
PREMIERES: "Feria en Espana" (Massanet), "Fiesta de Huapango" (Moncayo), "Carnival of Death" (Menotti), "Celebration in the Sun" (Ginastera)

Top Left: Mimi Rozak, Richard Arve, Violetta Karosas in "Primate"

Gary Rochell, Rosemary Cavazos, Carlos Cantu, Colette Ross in "Feria en Espana" *(Jacqueline K. Guerra Photo)*

RONDO DANCE THEATER
Bedford, N.Y.

Director-Choreographer, Elizabeth Rockwell; Manager-Booking Agent, Claire Miller; Lighting, Cyclops, Ira Landau; Financial Assistant, Rosetta Newton; Press, Jean George

COMPANY

Randall Faxon	Stephen Rockford
Kate Johnson	Anthony Small
Hannah Kahn	Catherine Sullivan
Jane Lowe	Edward Zawacki

REPERTOIRE

"The Execution" (Purcell, Elizabeth Rockwell), "Creatures All" (Elizabethan, R. Newton and Company), "Three" (Yusef Lateef Milton Myers), "Three Pieces for Clarinet" (Stravinsky, Myers), "Rink" (Haydn, Sandra Genter), "Sunday Go to Meeting" (Beverly Glenn, Myers), "Randdance" (Elton John, Gus Solomons, Jr.) "Holy Moses" (John & Taupin, Myers), "Afro Duo" (Iron Butterfly, Joseph Holmes), "Tout de Suite" (Miles Davis, Marianne Folin) "Triptych" (Villa-Lobos, Rockwell), "Duo" (Copland, Rockwell) "Scorpio" (Coffey, D. Griffith), "Genesis" (Collage, Rockwell) "Take Five" (Desmond, Rockwell), "Palomas" (Oliveros, Manuel Alum)
PREMIERES: "Line Drawings" (Silence and Voice, Elizabeth Keen), "Spill/Quell" (Hall-Evans, Hannah Kahn), "Poison Variations" (Watson-Press, Elizabeth Keen)

Debbie Zalkind, Stephen Rockford, Kate Johnson, Edward Zawacki (Rondo Dance Theater) in "Mary, Queen of Scots"

ROYAL WINNIPEG BALLET
Winnipeg, Canada

Artistic Director, Arnold Spohr; Associate Director, Vernon Lusby; Ballet Master, Frank Bourman; Production Coordinator, Richard Rutherford; Music Director, Neal Kayan; Choreographers, John Neumeier, Norbert Vesak; Wardrobe, Doreen Macdonald; Stage Manager, Bill Riske; Technical Director, David Nelson; Regisseurs, Terry Thomas, Sheila Mackinnon; Pianist, Barbara Malcolm Riske; Concertmaster, Charles Dobias; General Manager, Jim Cameron; Assistant General Manager-Company Manager, Peter Hawkins; Business Manager, Gloria Samoluk; Press, Maggie Morris, Margery Poggi, Woodrow Bennett, Gail Galagan

COMPANY

PRINCIPALS: Ana Maria de Gorriz, Louise Naughton, Bonnie Wyckoff, Sylvester Campbell, Craig Sterling, Terry Thomas, Anthony Williams
SOLOISTS: Kathleen Duffy, Kimberly Graves, Trish Wilson, William Starrett
CORPS: Betsy Carson, Katherine Collingwood, Sheri Cook, Arleen Dewell, Pattianne Douglas, Peter Garrick, Frank Garoutte, David Herriott, Eric Horenstein, David Hough, Bill Lark, Cynthia McCollum, Roger Shim, Margaret Slota, Harry Williams
GUEST ARTISTS: Mikhail Baryshnikov, Gelsey Kirkland, David Moroni, Sheila Mackinnon, Richard Rutherford

REPERTOIRE
(1974–1975)

"Fall River Legend" (Morton Gould, Agnes de Mille), "Pas de Deux Romantique" (G. Rossini, Jack Carter), "Grand Pas Espagnol" (M. Moszkowski, Benjamin Harkarvy), "Donizettiana Grad Pas de Deux" (Donizetti, Todd Bolender), "What to Do till the Messiah Comes" (Chilliwack-Syrinx-Phillip Werren, Norbert Vesak), "Nutcracker" (Tchaikovsky, John Neumeier), "Moments" (A. Dvorak, Larry Hayden), "Etude: Printemps" (Krein-Yarulin-Minkus-Hertel, David Moroni), "Rodeo" (Aaron Copland, Agnes de Mille), "Pictures—A Ballet Trilogy" (Scriabin-Cornyshe-Bark-Rabe-Mahler-Mortenson-Simon & Garfunkel-Moussorgski, John Neumeier)
PREMIERES: "Adagietto 1971" (Gustav Mahler, Oscar Araiz), "The Green Table" (F. A. Cohen, Kurt Jooss), "Rigodon" (Michael Perrault, Brydon Paige), "Inquest of the Sun" (Gregory Martindale, Norbert Vesak)

Sheri Cook, James Mercer, Louise Naughton, Anthony Williams, Bonnie Wyckoff, Craig Sterling in "Grand Pas Espagnol" Above: "Pictures—The Game" Top: "The Nutcracker"

163

SACRAMENTO BALLET
Sacramento, California

Artistic Director-Choreographer, Barbara Crockett; Associate Director-Choreographer in Residence, Jean-Paul Comelin; Conductor, Daniel Kingman; Guest Conductor, Daniel Forlano; Costume and Scenic Designer, Don Ransom; Scenic Designer, Linda Stanfill; Lighting Designer-Stage Manager, Bruce Kelley; Stage Manager, Larry Stanfill

COMPANY

Mary Anderson, Mary Atmore, Madeline Baenen, Stuart Carroll, McGarry Caven, Marc Diamond, Jody Downes, Cheryl Gomes, Charles Haack, Holly Hanson, Maria Holtz, Gary Jader, Lynn Kitade, Valorie Kondos, William Lawler, Margaret Luther, Diane Mark, Julia Marszalkoviski, Leslie McBeth, Charron McCalman, Kathy Moriarty, Ann Moser, Lark Pipes, Robyn Renollet, Andrew Rist, Richard Rock, Teresa Stadler, Georgeanna Supple, Heather Werby, Kimberly Willett
GUEST ARTISTS: Susan Magno, Jonas Kage, Deborah Dobson, John Hiatt

REPERTOIRE
(1974–1975)

"Pas de Quatre" (Pugni, Anton Dolin), "The Shakers" (Traditional, Doris Humphrey), "Paquita" (Minkus, Jean-Paul Comelin after Petipa), "A La Foire" (Shostakovich, Dom Orejudos), "Swan Lake Act II" (Tchaikovsky, Comelin after Ivanov), "Coppelia" (Delibes, Margarita DeSaa after Alicia Alonso), "La Ronde" (Rossini, Barbara Crockett), "Nutcracker" (Tchaikovsky, Lew Christensen-Barbara Crockett)
PREMIERES: "In the Mists" (Leon Janacek, Jean-Paul Comelin), "Earthsong" (Aaron Copland, Loyce Houlton), "Diversions" (Benjamin Britten, Jean-Paul Comelin)

Theresa Daniels, Jim Shipley in "Megatherium"
(St. Louis Civic Ballet)

Alba Calzada, Jerry Schwender and Sacramento Ballet in "Coppelia" *(Ronald B. Johnson Photo)*

ST. LOUIS CIVIC BALLET
St. Louis, Missouri

Artistic Director-Choreographer, Stanley Herbertt; Directors, LaVerne Meyering, Betty McRoberts; Conductor, Gerhard Zimmerman; Designers, Stanley Herbertt, June Morris; Stage Manager, John Holman; Press, Mary Breyer, Barbara Rosenthal; Repetiteur, Kyle Wehmueller; Wardrobe, Marion Wehmueller, Mary Ann Grothe; Props, Celia Hantz; President, Barbara Corday

COMPANY

Jim Akman, Monica Albers, Laurie Bartram, Ginny Burt, Amy Corday, Karen Cracchiola, Theresa Daniels, John Dement, Michelle Jarrett, Linda Grimme, Mary Heidbreder, Stephanie Kretow, Gus Licare, Tiffany Maierhoffer, Kathy Massot, Tony Parise, Tena Polukewich, Kim Reitz, Jim Shipley, Patty Smith, Kyle Wehmueller
GUEST ARTISTS: Linda Kintz, Daryl Gray, Mark Trares

REPERTOIRE
(1974–1975)

(All choreography by Stanley Herbertt except where noted) "While Paris Sleeps" (Offenbach), "The History of Dance from Jig to Jet" (Selected), and *PREMIERES* of "Megatherium" (Baroque), "Romantique" (Traditional), "Magyar" (Glazounov, June Morris), "Crea-ta-Dance" (Selected)

SOMERSET REGIONAL BALLET
COMPANY
Somerset, N.J.

Director-Choreographer, Mme. Eleonora Stein; Technical Supervisor, S. V. G. Troyanoff; Guest Choreographer, Larry Leritz; Lighting Design, Paul Thomas; Wardrobe Mistress, Arlene Maltz

COMPANY

Denise Barrood, Robin Bloink, Suzanne Briedermier, Ghislaine Darden, Natalie Darden, Gay Dempsey, Peggy Donovan, Shelagh Duval, Margaret Kuhn, Hedy Levine, Rose Marie Norton, Elizabeth Schrum, Jennifer Statile, Pat Tamasy, Renee Brodbar, Fred Lesniak, Josianne Darden, Linda Silverman

REPERTOIRE

"Borero 1830" (James O'Turner), "Karate Kapers" (Strauss), "Naila" (Delibes), "The Croud" (Grieg), "Baba Yaga" (Lliadow), "The Nutcracker" (Tchaikovsky), "Ole South America" (Traditional)

Larry Leritz, Shelagh Duval
(Somerset Regional Ballet)

THE SANASARDO DANCE COMPANY
New York, N.Y.

Director-Choreographer, Paul Sanasardo; Associate Director-Choreographer, Diane Germaine; Designers, Robert Natkin, Robert Baley; Stage Manager, Judy Kayser; Press, John Udry; Exclusive Agents, H. I. Enterprises; Executive Director, William Weaver

COMPANY
Diane Germaine, Joan Lombardi (Principals), Michele Rebeaud, Willa Kahn (Soloists), Janet Panetta, Anne-Marie Hackett, Elyssa Paternoster, Jeri McAndrews, Robin Shimel, Douglas Nielsen, Harry Laird, Alex Dolcemascolo, Jose Meier (Corps)
GUEST ARTISTS: Bonnie Mathis, Dennis Wayne, Miguel Godreau, Bert Terborgh

REPERTOIRE
(All choreography by Paul Sanasardo except where noted) "Shadows" (Satie-Scarlatti-Bach), "Footnotes" (Lester), "The Path" (Drews), "Stop-over" (Erb, Diane Germaine), "Fatal Birds" (Ginastera), "Metallics" (Cowell-Badings)
PREMIERES: "The Platform" (Bach) "Ecuatorial" (Varese, Anna Sokolow), "The Amazing Graces" (Dvorak), "A Consort for Dancers" (Watson)

Right: "Footnotes"

**Michele Rebeaud, Paul Sanasardo
in "The Path"**

**Joan Lombardi, Michele Rebeaud
in "Shadows"**

SAN FRANCISCO BALLET
San Francisco, California

Artistic Director-Choreographer, Lew Christensen; Associate Artistic Director, Michael Smuin; President-General Manager, Richard E. LeBlond, Jr.; Company Manager, Philip Semark; Press, Penelope McTaggart; Production Manager, Parker Young; Conductor, Earl Bernard Murray; Associate Conductor, Denis deCoteau; Costume Designers, Robert O'Hearn, Robert Fletcher, Seppo Nurmima, Jose Varona, Marcos Paredes, Paul Cadmus, Tony Duquette, Russell Hartley, Rouben Ter-Arutunian, Cal Anderson, Tony Walton, Willa Kim, William Pitkin; Sets, Robert Fletcher, Ming Cho Lee, Paul Cadmus, Seppo Nurmima, Tony Walton, Tony Duquette, Russell Hartley, Rouben Ter-Arutunian; Lighting, Jennifer Tipton; Props, Robert Kirby; Regisseurs, Richard Cammack, Virginia Johnson

COMPANY

Damara Bennett, Maureen Broderick, Madeleine Bouchard, Val Caniparoli, Gardner Carlson, Laurie Cowden, Allyson Deane, Nancy Dickson, Michael Dwyer, Betsy Erickson, Attila Ficzere, Alexander Filipov, Robert Gladstein, Michael Graham, Victoria Gyorfi, John McFall, Lynda Meyer, Cynthia Meyers, Anton Ness, Gina Ness, Anita Paciotti, Roberta Pfeil, Laurie Ritter, Tina Santos, Daniell Simmons, Jim Sohm, Michael Thomas, Elizabeth Tienken, Paula Tracy, Vane Vest, Gary Wahl, Diana Weber, Jerome Weiss, Deborah Zdobinski
GUEST ARTISTS: Cynthia Gregory, Judith Jamison, Galin and Valery Panov

REPERTOIRE

"Airs de Ballet" (Gretry, Christensen), "Beauty and the Beast" (Tchaikovsky, Christensen), "Beloved" (Anderson, Horton), "Black Swan Pas de Deux" (Tchaikovsky, Petipa), "Celebration" (Luigini, Gladstein), "Cinderella" (Prokofiev, Christensen-Smuin), "Con Amore" (Rossini, Christensen), "Cry" (Coltrane-Nyro-Voices of Harlem, Ailey), "Divertissement d'Auber" (Auber, Christensen), "Don Juan" (Rodrigo, Christensen), "Don Quixote Pas de Deux" (Minkus, Petipa), "Dying Swan" (Saint-Saens, Fokine), "Eternal Idol" (Chopin, Smuin), "Fantasma," "Filling Station" (Thomason, Christensen), "Flower Festival Pas de Deux" (Helstead-Paulli, Bournonville), "For Valery Panov" (Rachmaninoff, Smuin), "Four Temperaments" (Hindemith, Balanchine), "Harlequinade" (Drigo, Rachmaninoff), "Harp Concerto" (Reinecke, Smuin), "Jest of Cards" (Krenek, Christensen), "Jinx" (Britten, Christensen), "La Sonnambula" (Bellini Reiti, Balanchine), "Les Sylphides" (Chopin, Fokine), "Mother Blues" (Russo, Smuin), "NRA" (Jepson, Gladstein), "Nutcracker" (Tchaikovsky, Christensen), "Pas de Quatre" (Pugni, Lester-Dolin), "Pulcinella Variations" (Stravinsky, Smuin), "Schubertiade" (Schubert, Smuin), "Serenade" (Tchaikovsky, Balanchine) "Shakers" (Humphrey, Humphrey), "Symphony in C" (Bizet, Balanchine), "Tealia" (Holst, McFall), "Variations de Ballet" (Glazounov, Christensen-Balanchine)

Stephanie Maze, Arne Folkedal Photos

Vane Vest, Diana Weber in "Harp Concerto"
Above: Alexander Filipov in "Don Juan"

166 Top: (L) Madelein Bouchard, Attila Ficzere in "Eternal Idol"
(R) Vane Vest, Lynda Meyer in "Romeo and Juliet"

SOUTHERN REPERTORY DANCE THEATER
Carbondale, Illinois

Artistic Director-Choreographer, Lonny Joseph Gordon; Production Coordinator, Holly Catchings; Designers, C. James Wright, Ruth K. Bauman, Russell Lascelles, Maura Junius; Technical Director, Karen Johns; Stage Manager, Liz Grossman; Props, Hilary Bloom; Sound, Glen Sabatka; Press, Robert Pocklington

COMPANY

Linda Albaugh, Roy Broersma, Steven Budas, Douglas Bush, Holly Catchings, Diana Cushway, Belinda Engram, Salvatori Geraci, Susan Ghent, Lonny Gordon, Chequette Hanko, Maura Junius, Mieko Kanazawa, Moira Logan, Susan McGrath, Robin Miles, Michael Murray, Joseph Novak, Melissa Nunn, Cindy Pierce, Marliss Rossiter, Andrew Skalko, Morgan Smith, Janet Stoecker, Patti Tedrow, Lisa Thompson, Jaris Waide, Rosalind Zeisler
GUEST ARTISTS: Daniel Nagrin, Viola Farber Mildred Dickenson, Carroll Russell, Shirley Mordine, Audrey Zellan, Melissa Nunn

REPERTOIRE

"Black Zinnia" (Bryce Robbley, Lonny Joseph Gordon), "Spirit" (Gary White, Gordon), "Paper Women" (Bette Midler, Gordon), "Bach Suite" (Bach, Holly Catchings-Andrew Skalko), "Sparkle Plenty" (Henri Bouchet, Moira Logan), "Holy Figures in the Playground" (Ives-Central China Philharmonic-Todd Dockstader, Gordon), "When Things Come Quick and Clear" (Lonny Joseph Gordon, Andrew Skalko), "Early Flight" (David Riddles, Moira Logan), "The Yellow Roses Etudes" (Scriabin, Gordon), "Hybrid Spaces" (Scriabin, Gordon), "Sabbath" (Choreography by Lisa Thompson), "Phrases for Louise" (Gordon)

Southern Repertory Dance Theater
in "The Yellow Roses Etudes"
Elliot Mendelson Photo

SOUTHERN THEATRE BALLET COMPANY
Jacksonville, Florida

Founder-Artistic Director-Choreographer, Marta Jackson; Guest Choreographer, Gayle Parmelee; Technical Director-Lighting and Set Designer, Nick Ciccarello; Costumes, Mary Lovelace; Ballet Mistress, Virginia Pelegrin; Press, Leonardo Favela

COMPANY

Mary Allen, Nancy Bock, Sharon Booth, Donna Cohan, Pam Davis, Susan Donziger, Staci Deane, Carrie Klett, Joy Farris, Bonnie Fumo, Cindy Goldsmith, Sara Howell, Gentry Linville, Coroline Lovelace, Dulcie Lanier, Joan Frazier, Cheryl Nobles, Virginia Pelegrin, Isabel Pelegrin, Tracy Ryan, Susu Saltmarsh, Mary Saltmarsh, Pamela Huelster, Ellic Edelson, Randy Wood, Neyda Castells, Annie Coroalles, Terri Deane, Elizabeth Howell, Martha Lopez, Nery Llorente, Gigi Morales, Lourdes Palomino, Ceci Mari Perez, Dane Smith, Elaine Underwood, Barbara Spraggins, Theresa Thweatt

REPERTOIRE

"Nutcracker" (Tchaikovsky, Parmelee), "Swan Lake Act II" (Tchaikovsky, Jackson after Petipa), "Grand Pas de Quatre" (Pugni, Jackson), "Aurora's Wedding" (Tchaikovsky, Jackson after Petipa), "El Amor Brujo" (DeFalla, Jackson), "Rochene" (Glazounov, Jackson), "Esprit" (Britten, Parmelee), "Ballet School," "Carmina Burana," "Sleeping Beauty"

Southern Theatre Ballet Company
Belton S. Wall Photo

STANZE PETERSON DANCE THEATRE
San Francisco, California

Director-Choreographer, Stanze Peterson; Lighting Design, Richard Farr; Representative, Fred Clark; Costumes, Stanze Peterson

COMPANY

Janet Ross	Mimi Platner
Virginia Kester	Vernon DeVerney
Frances Parham	Stanze Peterson

REPERTOIRE: (All choreography by Stanze Peterson except where noted) "Preludes Intimes" (Carlos Salzedo), "Cortege" (John Lewis), "Interim" (Steven Chambers-Quincy Jones-Fleetwood Mac-retha Franklin), "The Sameness Wheel" (Quincy Jones-Mal Walron-Laura Nyro), "Women's Song" (Pierre Baynes), "Untitled Work #4" (Traditional), "Scars" (Weather Report-News Broadcasts)
PREMIERES: "Ships" (Ollie Wilson), "Come Dambala" (McKay-Nina Simone), "Quartet" (Byrd & Gerald-Millie Jackson, Janet Ross), "Gone Forgot Unfamed" (Black Poetry), "Chains and Things" (B. B. King)

Stanze Peterson Dance Theatre Company

TANCE AND COMPANY
San Francisco, California

Artistic Director-Choreographer, Tance Johnson; Musical Director-Lighting Designer, Carl Sitton; Costumes, Connie Iwerson; Stage Manager, Carol McIntyre; Press, Marcia Hill

COMPANY

Evelyn Ante, Gina Bonati, Ercilia Santos, Rosa Wang, Claire Dixon, Yvonne Murray, Estella Sisneros, Laura Valdez, Nora Martinson, Terry Valdez, Dennis Parlato, Gerry Luckham, Aaron Wesley, Lannie Costello
GUEST ARTISTS: Susan Williams, Bruce Bain

REPERTOIRE

"Pavanne" (Faure, Tance Johnson), "Surrender" (Contemporary, Johnson), "Structures" (Bartok, Bruce Bain), "Bailecito de Luces" (Los Calchakis, Johnson), "Celebrate" (Rock, Deborah Quanain), "The Chase" (Rock, Evelyn Ante)
PREMIERES: "Encounter" (Benson, Tance Johnson), "Canticle" (Chopin, Johnson), "Ceremony of the Cords" (Xenakis, Johnson), "Duo" (Sitton, Johnson)

Rosa Wang, Gerry Luckham (Tance and Company)
in "Canticle"

Susan Smallwood of Thelma Olaker Youth Ballet
Mort Fryman Photo

THELMA OLAKER YOUTH CIVIC BALLET COMPANY
Southside, Virginia

Artistic Director-Choreographer, Christin Parks; Artistic Adviser, Gene Hammett; Business Manager, Nancy J. Seavy; Costumer, Hattie McMillan; Technical Director, Ben Keys; Stage Manager, Eugene Corrigan
COMPANY: Names not submitted

REPERTOIRE

"Ecole de Ballet" (Offenbach, Gene Hammett), "Graduation Ball" (Strauss, Christin Parks), "Excerpts from Gilbert and Sullivan" (Choreographed by Christin Parks)

TOLEDO BALLET COMPANY
Toledo, Ohio

Founder-Artistic Director-Choreographer, Marie Bollinger Vogt; Conductors, Serge Fournier, Harold Hanson, Jr.; Designer, Bill Smith; Costumer, Rosalind Gonia; Production Coordinator, Evelyn Brandman; President, Carol Van Sickle

COMPANY

Craig Barrow, Rick Bauer, Polly Brandman, Kathy Carter, Sue Carter, Ed Drill, Nancy Gigliotti, Beth Glasser, Laurie Hansen, Rebecca Hawkins, Hollis Hibscher, Ernst Hillenbrand, Karin Jacobson, Judith Nasatir, Kim Parquette, Jean Peterson, Cris Phillips, Jill Putnam, Debbie Roshe, Liz Skalski, Mara Steinberg, Jo Anne Ullman, Tracy Van Sickle, Ron Von Westernhagen, Laura Wade, Donna Wolf
GUEST ARTISTS: Marianna Tcherkassky, Terry Orr, Soili Arvola, Leo Ahonen

REPERTOIRE

"The Nutcracker" (Tchaikovsky), "Giselle" (Adam), "Water Music Suite" (Handel), "Swan Lake" (Tchaikovsky), "Symphony for Fun" (Gillis), "Capriccio Espagnole" (Rimsky-Korsakov), "Les Patineurs" (Meyerbeer), "Italian Symphony" (Mendelssohn), "Graduation Ball" (Strauss) "Les Sylphides" (Chopin), "Old King Cole," "American Dance Suite" (Julia Smith), "Red Pony" (Copland)

Carolyn Jo Smith, Ann Sanderson in "The Nutcracker"
(Toledo Ballet)

UTAH REPERTORY DANCE THEATRE
Salt Lake City, Utah

General Manager, Bruce A. Beers; Press, Susan Landes; Company Manager, Sherryn C. Barrell; Designer-Production Manager—M. Kay Barrell; Stage Manager-Technical Director, Gary Justesen; Designer-Costumer, Ron Hodge; Secretary, Ellen C. Bayas.

COMPANY

Ellen Bromberg, Michael Bruce, Rich Burrows, Kay Clark, Michael Dean, Martin Kravitz, Gregg Lizenbery, Ruth Jean Post, Ron Ruhey, Linda C. Smith, Karen Steele, Lynne Wimmer

REPERTOIRE

For Betty" (Vivaldi, Evans), "5 Songs in August" (Sussman, Evans), "Hard Times" (Traditional, Evans), "Jukebox" (Glenn Miller, Evans), "Tin-Tal" (Misra, Evans), "Passengers" (None, Vila Farber), "The Brood" (Henry, Richard Kuch), "There Is a Time" (Dello Joio, Limon), "Between Me and Other People There Is Always a Table and a Few Empty Chairs" (Alcantara, Jennifer Muller), "Suite of Psalms" (Getman, Carla Maxwell), "Filigree in Parts" (Harris, Ruth Jean Post), "Tricycle" (Harrison, Ruth Jean Post), "Fatal Words" (Ginastera, Sanasardo), "Synapse" (Nature Sounds, Karen Steele), "Chant" (Shostakovich, Tim Wengerd), "From a Branch Nothing Cried From" (Bortz, Lynne Wimmer)

Ross Terry Photos

Bill Evans, Lynne Wimmer, Linda C. Smith, Gregg Lizenberry in "The Brood"
Top Right: Utah Repertory Dance Theatre Company

**Jerri Kummery and Tulsa Civic Ballet
in "Il Favorito"**

TULSA CIVIC BALLET
Tulsa, Oklahoma

Artistic Directors-Choreographers, Roman Jasinski, Moscelyne Larkin; Conductor, Franco Autori; Manager, Charles Ellis; Set Designers, Jerry Harrison, Albert Martin, Kathryn Phelps; Costumes, Moscelyne Larkin, Mrs. L. E. Maines; Lighting Designer, M. M. Donnelly; President, Eugene A. Pelizzoni

COMPANY
PRINCIPALS: Gail Gregory, Donna Grisez
SOLOISTS: Matthew Bridwell, Jerri Kummery, Mary Beth Minor, Cinda Potter, Gail White
CORPS: Cynthia Ball, Diane Bembenek, Bonnie Boswell, Dorothy Bridwell, Lisa Collins, Lynn Collins, Duncan Emanuel, Peyton Foster, Timothy Fox, Kimmy Jin, Tracy Lockwood, Carolyn Paddock, Emily Palik, Allison Reid, Kimberly Smiley, Hope Theodoras, Annette Wean, Susan West, Cheryl Willis
APPRENTICES: Amy Bechtel, Lisa Bethell, Mary Beth Bigbie, Kim Dooley, Mary Ellen Evans, Sharon Goodwin, Julie Harris, Cindy Hood, Joni Meyers, Lucy Tuttle, Emily Worrall
GUEST ARTISTS: Charles Ellis, Bob Barnes, Cynthia Gregory, Peter Martins, Violette Verdy, John Clifford, Colleen Geisting, Roman L. Jasinski, Edward Tuell, Magdalena Popa, Stefan Banica

REPERTOIRE
(All choreography by Roman Jasinski) "Divertissement Classique" (Burgmuller-McDermott) "Il Favorito" (Vivaldi), "The Nutcracker" (Tchaikovsky), "Swan Lake Act II" (Tchaikovsky), "Khachaturiana" (Khachaturian), "Tchaikovsky Divertissement" (Tchaikovsky-McDermott), "Bach for a Hep Margrave" (Bach)

Valentina Oumansky in "Zen Zen"
Garo Photo

VALENTINA OUMANSKY DRAMATIC DANCE ENSEMBLE
Hollywood, California

Valentina Oumansky	Dellamaria Marino
Marilyn Carter	Robin Stever
Michael Johnson	Tarumi Takagi
Marni Mahaffay	Beth Gage

REPERTOIRE: (All works choreographed by Valentina Oumansky) "A Bow Is a Bow Is a Bow" (Bach-Purcel), "Adoration" (Hovhaness), "Afro-American Jazz Legend" (Jazz 1926–1971), "Cortez, the Conqueror" (Ginastera), "Conversations in Silence and Sound" (Klauss), "El Popol Vuh" (Elisabeth Waldo), "Facade" (Sitwell-Walton), "Ghazals" (Hovhaness), "God in a Box" (Berio), "Homage to the Southwest Indian" (Herman Stein), "In the Hills" (Hovhaness), "With Apologies to Aesop the Horse" (Herman Stein), "Who Is Hieronymus?" (Bruce Groughton), "Zen Zen", "Rin Tin Tin Superstar" (Hovhaness)

VIRGINIA BEACH COMMUNITY BALLET COMPANY
Virginia Beach, Virginia

Artistic Adviser, Meredith Baylis; Artistic Director, Virginia L. Biggs; Ballet Mistresses, Betty Jean Walker, Janet S. Smith; Wardrobe, Kim Crosby; Sets and Costumes, Mike Bell

COMPANY
PRINCIPALS: Janet S. Smith, Karen Peacock, Melinda Sullivan, Shelia Francis, Dana Snead, Jody Norris
CORPS: Mary Korbett, Debbie Stevens, Terri Early, Tawni Cullen, Jennifer Scott, Jill Clair, Dolly Mannis, Tiffany Biggs, Lisa Biggs, Cynthia Breslau, Kimberly Griffin, Leslie Fudala, Maria Griffith, Deborah Lusty

REPERTOIRE
"Dance Romantique" (Schumann, Betty Jean Walker), "Reflection" (Satie, Betty Jean Walker), "The Enchanted Ogre" (Shostakovich, Janet S. Smith)

**Shelia Francis, Dana Snead, Karen Peacock,
Jody Norris (Virginia Beach Ballet) in "Dance
Romantique"**

Ronald R. Young Photo

WESTCHESTER BALLET COMPANY
Ossining, N.Y.

Artistic Director-Choreographer, Iris Merrick; Set and Lighting Designers, Hallie Flanagan, John Knudson, David Auslander; Costumes, Janet Crapanzano, Jacqueline Stoner; Press, Dorothy Meinel, Mary Anne Rodino

COMPANY

PRINCIPALS: Sue Crapanzano, Lenore Meinel, Vivian Crapanzano, Elizabeth Wedge, Paula Wandzilak, Iris Merrick
SOLOISTS: Heather Behling, Patricia Morrissy, Jill Robie, Phyliss Crowder, Jane Brayton, Iromie Weeramantry
CORPS: Nell Compo, Elizabeth Grusky, Laurie Beckett, Elaine Seravalli, Erica Cargill, Karin Berzins, Molly Jackson, Julie Wilde, Jill Offenberg, Carolyn Ellis, Robin Wild, Abigail Santiago, Elizabeth Terzian, Tiffany Behling, Sue Cargill, Laurie Offenberg, Lori Zaykowski, Priscilla Wright, Laura Hubler, Aleza Firat, Michelle Brucellaria, Sue Cancro, Linda Joenk, Kathleen Doran, Martha Materazo, Dawn Timmons, Karen Kurkjy, Eileen Condreaut, Vivian Smith, Lori Matthews, Mary Ellen Morris, Camille Cordes, Diane Duva, Laura Pogano, Sue Kenny, Maureen Moriarty, Nancy Wellman, Jane Levin
GUEST ARTISTS: Charles Brideau, Daryl Gray, Peter Fonesca, Gary Cordial, Paul Boos, Jean Pierre Frohlich, David Otto, William Otto, Harlan Crowder

REPERTOIRE

(All choreography by Iris Merrick except where noted) "Suite of Schubert Dances of Isadora Duncan" (Schubert, Julia Levien), "Romeo and Juliet" (Tchaikovsky), "Cinderella" (Prokofiev), "Holliday" (Anderson), "Le Retour" (Kabalevsky), "Sleeping Beauty" (Tchaikovsky), "Caprice" (Shostakovich), "Emperor Valse" (Strauss), "Peter and the Wolf" (Prokofiev), "Nutcracker" (Tchaikovsky), "Cry Baby Dolls" (Kabelevsky), "East of the Sun" (Grieg), "Seasons" (Chausson), "Come What May" (Reissager), "Star Maiden" (McDowell), "Swan Lake Act II" (Tchaikovsky), "Dream Toy Shop" (Rossini-Britten), "Secret River" (Leyden), "Summer Day" (Prokofiev), "Giselle" (Adam, Barry Edson-Iris Merrick), "Tarkus" (Emerson-Lake-Palmer, Edward Roll), "The Tailor and the Doll" (Britten)

Susanna Organek, Mark Franko (Zsedenyi Ballet) in "Coppelia" *(Lily Franko Photo)*

WASHINGTON DANCE THEATRE
Washington, D.C.

Artistic Director-Choreographer, Erika Thimey; Stage and Light Directors, Bill DeMull, Guy LeValley; Costume Designers, Hertha Woltersdorf, Dagmar Wilson; Narrators, Lee Reynolds, Carolyn Stewart

COMPANY

Sharon Bodul, Margaret Chinn, Miriam Cramer, Sally Crowell, Julie Houghton, Lorraine Johnson, Stephen Johnson, E. Raye LeValley, Karen Murden, Bonnie Notes, Carol O'Toole, Diana Parson, Sandra Walker

REPERTOIRE

(All choreography by Erika Thimey except where noted) "Ceremony of Carols" (Britten), "A Fear Not of One" (Lohoefer), "Psalm" (Ott), "Trapped" (None, Stephen Johnson), "Predictions" (Weather Reports, Sally Crowell), "Playthings of the Wind" (Gassman-Sala), "Noisy Hello" (Butler), "Elephant's Child" (Lohoefer), "Big and Little" (Audrey Vincent Biase)
PREMIERES: "Superstition" (Audrey Vincent Biase, Erika Thimey), "Santa Maria de Iquique" (Luis Advis, Thimey)

Top Left: Sharon Bodul, Sandra Walker, Stephen Johnson in "Superstition" *(Howard Millard Photo)*

Vivian Crapanzano, Daryl Gray (Westchester Ballet) in "Cinderella" *(Curt R. Meinel Photo)*

ZSEDENYI BALLET
New York, N.Y.

Formerly Romantic Ballet Repertory Company; Director-Choreographer, Karoly Zsedenyi; Set Designer, Charles Barnes; Stage and Company Manager, Anke June

COMPANY

SOLOISTS: Susanna Organek, Elizabeth Kim, Silvia Palumbo, Linda Sloboda, Mark Franko, Angel Betancourt, Robert Chipok, Annelis Meyer
CORPS: Fern McBride, Debbie Marx, Stephan Isaacson, Neil Applebaum, Stewart Pimsler

REPERTOIRE

"Coppelia" (Delibes, Karoly Zsedenyi), "The Hungarian Peasant Wedding" (Zoltan Kodaly, Zsedenyi), "The Wooden Prince" (Bela Bartok, Zsedenyi), "Four Fragments from Petrouchka" (Stravinsky, Zsedenyi)

Leo Ahonen

Frances Alenikoff

Manuel Alum

Gerd Andersson

Reid Anderson

BIOGRAPHIES OF DANCERS AND CHOREOGRAPHERS

ABARCA, LYDIA. Born Jan. 8, 1951 in NYC. Studied at Fordham U., Harkness House. Debut 1968 with Dance Theatre of Harlem.

ADAIR, TOM. Born in Venus, Tex. Joined American Ballet Theatre in 1963, elevated to soloist in 1966.

ADAMS, CAROLYN. Born in N.Y.C. Aug. 16, 1943. Graduate Sarah Lawrence Col. Studied with Schonberg, Karin Waehner, Henry Danton, Wishmary Hunt, Don Farnworth. Member of Paul Taylor Co. since 1965. Director of Harlem Dance Studio.

ADAMS, DIANA. Born in Stanton, Va. Studied with Edward Caton, Agnes de Mille. Made professional debut in 1943 in "Oklahoma!" Joined Ballet Theatre in 1944. N.Y.C. Ballet 1950. Now ballet mistress-teacher at School of American Ballet. N.Y.C.

AHONEN, LEO. Born June 19, 1939 in Helsinki, Finland. Studied at Kirov Theatre. Scandinavian School of Ballet. Joined company and rose to principal. Appeared with Bolshoi Ballet. Joined National Ballet of Holland as dancer and ballet master; Royal Winnipeg Ballet 1966; San Francisco Ballet 1968. Since 1972 principal and teacher with Houston Ballet.

AIELLO, SALVATORE. Born Feb. 26, 1944 in N.Y. Attended Boston Cons. Studied with Danielian, Stanley Williams. Rosella Hightower. Professional debut with Joffrey Co. in 1964, subsequently with Donald McKayle, Pearl Lang, Patricia Wilde, Alvin Ailey, Harkness Ballet, and in Bdwy musicals. Joined Royal Winnipeg Ballet 1971. Promoted to principal 1972.

AILEY, ALVIN. Born Jan. 5, 1931 in Rogers, Tex. Attended UCLA. Studied with Lester Horton, Hanya Holm, Martha Graham, Anna Sokolow, Karel Shook, and Charles Wiedman. Debut 1950 with Lester Horton Dance Theatre, and became choreographer for company in 1953. Formed own company in 1958 and has toured U.S. and abroad. Now N.Y. City Center based.

AITKEN, GORDON. Born in Scotland in 1928. Joined Saddler's Wells Ballet in 1954. Soloist with Royal Ballet.

ALBA, MARIA. Born in China of Spanish-Irish parentage. Began studies in Russian School of Ballet, Peking. Moved to Spain, studied with Regla-Ortega, and La Quica. After professional debut in teens, became one of world's foremost Spanish dancers at 21. Toured with Iglesias Co., and Ballet Espagnol. With Ramon de los Reyes, formed company in 1964 that has toured U.S., S. America and Europe.

ALBANO, JOSEPH. Born Dec. 29, 1939 in New London, Conn. Studied with Vilzak, Legat, Bartholin, Hightower, Danielian, Graham, Weidman, and Limon. Performed with Charles Wiedman Co., Ballet Russe, Martha Graham, Joos-Leeder, N.Y.C. Ballet. Founder-artistic director-choreographer of Hartford Ballet Co., Established Albano Ballet 1971. First dancer to serve as Commissioner for Conn. Commission for the Arts.

ALBRECHT, ANGELE. Born Dec. 12, 1942 in Frieburg, Ger. Studied at Royal Ballet, and with Lula von Sachnowsky, Tatjanti Granzeva, Rosella Hightower. Debut 1960 with Ntl. Theater Mannheim; Hamburg Staatsoper 1961–7; Ballet of 20th Century from 1967.

ALDOUS, LUCETTE. Born Sept. 26, 1938 in Auckland, N.Z. Studied at Royal Ballet School. Joined Rambert, London's Festival Ballet (1963), Royal Ballet (1966), Australian Ballet (1971).

ALENIKOFF, FRANCES. Born in N.Y.C.; graduate Bklyn Col. Studied with Graham, Limon, Horton, Anthony, Sanasardo, Humphrey, Sokolow, Barashkova, Dunham, Fort, Flores. Debut 1957. Since 1959 toured with own company, and as soloist. Has choreographed Bdwy musicals.

ALEXANDER, ROD. Born Jan. 23, 1922 in Colo. Studied with Cole, Holm, Maracci, Riabouchinska, Horton, Castle. Debut with Jack Cole Dancers, then in Bdwy musicals before forming own company and becoming choreographer for Bdwy and TV.

ALLEN, JESSICA. Born Apr. 24, 1946 in Bryn Mawr, Pa. Graduate UCol., NYU. Debut 1970 with Jean Erdman Dance Theatre. Also appeared with Gus Solomons, Matt Maddox.

ALLENBY, JEAN. Born Apr. 29, 1946 in Bulawayo, Rhodesia and began training there. Debut 1966 with Cape Ballet. Joined Stuttgart in 1971 and promoted to principal.

ALONSO, ALICIA. Born Alicia Martinez, Dec. 21 in Havana; married Fernando Alonso. Studied with Federova, and Volkova, and at School of American Ballet. Made debut in musicals. Soloist with Ballet Caravan 1939–40. Ballet Theatre 1941. In 1948 formed own company in Havana. One of world's greatest ballerinas.

ALUM, MANUEL. Born in Puerto Rico in 1944. Studied with Neville Black, Sybil Shearer, Martha Graham, Mia Slavenska. Joined Paul Sanasardo Company in 1962, and is its assistant artistic director. Has appeared with The First Chamber Dance Quartet, and American Dance Theatre Co. Also teaches and choreographs, and formed own company 1972.

ALVAREZ, ANITA. Born in Tyrone, Pa. in 1920. Studied with Martha Graham, and appeared with her company 1936–41. Since 1941 has appeared in Bdwy musicals.

AMOCIO, AMEDEO. Born in 1942 in Milan, Italy. Studied at LaScala, and joined company, rising to soloist. Has created many ballets and choreographed musicals and films.

AMMANN, DIETER. Born Feb. 5, 1942 in Passau, Ger. Attended Essen Folkway School. Joined Stuttgart Ballet in 1965; promoted to principal.

ANAYA, DULCE. Born in Cuba; studied with Alonso, at School of Am. Ballet: joined Ballet Theatre at 15, Ballet de Cuba where she became soloist. In 1957 was prima ballerina of Stuttgart Opera before joining Munich State Opera Ballet for 5 years, Hamburg Opera for 3. Returned to U.S. and joined Michael Maule's Dance Variations, Ballet Concerto. Founder-Director of Jacksonville (Fla.) Ballet Theatre since 1970.

ANDERSON, CAROLYN. Born Apr. 28, 1946 in Salt Lake City. Graduate Univ. Utah. Studied with Willam Christensen, Patricia Wilde, Peryoslavic, Cayton, Weisburger, Danilova, Vladimiroff. Principal dancer with Ballet West before joining Pa. Ballet as soloist.

ANDERSON, REID. Born Apr. 1, 1949 in New Westminster, BC, Can. Studied with Dolores Kirkwood, and Royal Ballet School. Appeared in musicals before joining London's Royal Opera Ballet 1967, Stuttgart Ballet 1969; promoted to principal.

ANDERSSON, GERD. Born in Stockholm June 11, 1932. Pupil of Royal Swedish Ballet, and Lilian Karina. Joined company in 1948; became ballerina in 1958.

ANDROS, DICK. Born in Oklahoma City, March 4, 1926. Trained with San Francisco Ballet, American Theatre Wing, Ballet Arts, Met Ballet, Ballet Theatre, Ballet Russe. Has appeared with San Francisco Ballet, Irene Hawthorne, Marian Lawrence, John Beggs, Eve Gentry, Greenwich Ballet, Lehigh Valley Ballet, and Dance Originals. Now choreographs and teaches. Artistic director Batsheva Co. 1974.

ANTONIO. Born Antonio Ruiz Soler Nov. 4, 1922 in Seville, Spain. Studied with Realito, Pericet, and Otero. Made professional debut at 7. Became internationally famous with cousin Rosario as "The Kids From Seville." Formed separate companies in 1950's, his becoming Ballets de Madrid. Made N.Y. debut in 1955 and has returned periodically.

ANTONIO, JUAN. Born May 4, 1945 in Mexico City. Studied with Xavier Francis. Am. Ballet Center, Ballet Theatre School. Made debut 1963 in Mexico with Bellas Artes, N.Y. debut 1964 with Ballet Folklorico, subsequently danced with Glen Tetley, Louis Falco, Pearl Lang, Gloria Contreras, and Jose Limon. Now associate director of Falco Co., and teaches.

ANTUNEZ, OSKAR. Born Apr. 17, 1949 in Juarez, Mex. Studied with Ingeborg Heuser, and at Harkness School. Made debut with Les Grands Ballets Canadians in 1968. Joined Harkness Ballet in 1968.

APINEE, IRENE. Born in Riga, Latvia where she began training at 11. Moved to Canada; founded school in Halifax. Became leading dancer with National Ballet of Canada, and in 1956 became member of Les Ballets Chiriaeff, now Les Grands Ballets Canadiens. Soloist with Ballet Theatre in 1959. Rejoined Les Grands Ballets in 1965.

Charthel Arthur	Dick Andros	Annette av Paul	Richard Arve	Gladys Bailin

APONTE, CHRISTOPHER. Born May 4, 1950 in NYC. Studied at Harkness House, and made debut in 1970 with the Harkness company. Joined Alvin Ailey 1975.

ARMIN, JEANNE. Born in Milwaukee. Aug. 4, 1943. Studied with Ann Barzel, Stone and Camryn, Ballet Russe, and in Paris with Mme. Nora. Made debut with Chicago Opera Ballet in 1958, joined Ballet Russe (1959) American Ballet Theatre (1965). Has appeared on Bdwy.

ARMOUR, THOMAS. Born Mar. 7, 1909 in Tarpon Springs, Fla. Studied with Ines Noel Armour. Preobrajenska, Egorova. Debut with Ida Rubenstein, followed by Nijinska's company, Ballet Russe, Ballet Russe de Monte Carlo. Founder-Artistic Director Miami Ballet.

ARNOLD, BENE. Born in 1935 in Big Springs, Tex. Graduate UUtah. Trained with Willam, Harold, and Lew Christensen at San Francisco Ballet. Joined company in 1950, becoming soloist in 1952, Ballet Mistress 1960–63. Joined Ballet West as Ballet Mistress 1963.

AROVA, SONIA. Born June 20, 1927 in Sofia. Bulgaria. Studied with Preobrajenska; debut 1942 with International Ballet, subsequently appearing with Ballet Rambert, Met Opera Ballet, Petit's Ballet, Tokyo-Kamaski Ballet, Ballet Theatre, Ruth Page Ballet Co., Norwegian State Opera Ballet. Co-Director San Diego Ballet from 1971.

ARPINO, GERALD. Born on Staten Island, N.Y. Studied with Mary Ann Wells. May O'Donnell, Gertrude Shurr, and at School of American Ballet. Made debut on Bdwy in "Annie Get Your Gun." Toured with Nana Gollner, Paul Petroff Ballet Russe; became leading male dancer with Joffrey Ballet, and NYC Opera. Currently choreographer and assistant director of Joffrey Ballet and co-director of American Ballet Center.

ARTHUR, CHARTHEL. Born in Los Angeles. Oct. 8, 1946. Studied with Eva Lorraine, and at American Ballet Center. Became member of Joffrey Ballet in 1965.

ARVE, RICHARD. Born in Clemson, S.C. Studied with Graham, Cunningham, Joffrey, Hayden; soloist with Ruth Page Ballet, Chicago Opera Ballet, Flower Hujer, Phyllis Sabold, Erica Tamar, Maggie Kast. Now teaches, and director of Richard Arve Dance Trio.

ARVOLA, SOILI. Born in Finland; began ballet studies at 8; joined Finnish Ballet at 18; San Francisco Ballet 1968–72; Houston Ballet 1972–. Also choreographs and appears with Ballet Spectacular.

ASAKAWA, HITOMI. Born Oct. 13, 1938 in Kochi, Japan. Studied and made professional debut in Nishino Ballet 1957. Joined Ballet of 20th Century 1967.

ASAKAWA, TAKAKO. Born in Tokyo, Japan, Feb. 23, 1938. Studied in Japan and with Martha Graham. Has appeared with Graham Co., and with Alvin Ailey, Donald McKayle, and Pearl Lang, and in revival of "The King and I." Now permanent member of Graham company.

ASENSIO, MANOLA. Born May 7, 1946 in Lausanne, Switz. Studied at LaScala in Milan. Danced with Grand Theatre de Geneve (1963–4), Het Nationale Ballet (1964–6), NYC Ballet (1966–8), Harkness Ballet 1969–.

ASHLEY, FRANK. Born Apr. 10, 1941 in Kingston, Jamaica. Studied with Ivy Baxter, Eddy Thomas, Neville Black, Martha Graham. Has appeared with National Dance Theatre of Jamacia, Helen McGehee, Pearl Lang, Marth Graham, Yuriko, Eleo Pomare. Also choreographs.

ASHTON, FREDERICK. Born in Guayaquil, Ecuador, Sept. 17, 1906. Studied with Massine and Marie Rambert. Joined Ida Rubinstein Co. in Paris in 1927, but soon left to join Rambert's Ballet Club for which he choreographed many works, and danced. Charles Cochran engaged him to choreograph for his cabarets. In 1933 was invited to create works for the newly formed Vic Wells Co. and in 1935 joined as dancer and choreographer. Moved with company to Covent Garden, and continued creating some of world's great ballets. Was knighted in 1962; first man so honored for services to ballet. After serving as associate director of Royal Ballet, became its director with the retirement of Dame Ninette de Valois in 1963. Retired in 1970.

ASTAIRE, FRED. Born Frederick Austerlitz in Omaha, Neb. May 10, 1899. Began studying at 5; was in vaudeville with sister Adele at 7; Bdwy debut in 1916 in "Over The Top." Appeared in many musicals and films.

ATWELL, RICK. Born July 29, 1949 in St. Louis, Mo. Studied with Dokoudovsky, Mattox, Krassovska, and Wilde. Joined Harkness Ballet in 1967 after appearing in several musicals.

AUGUSTYN, FRANK. Born 1953 in Hamilton, Ont., Can. Studied at Ballet School of Canada. Joined Natl. Ballet of Canada in 1970, rising to principal in 1972.

av PAUL, ANNETTE. (Wiedersheim-Paul). Born Feb. 11, 1944 in Stockholm. Studied at Royal Ballet School, and made debut at 7; Royal Opera House Ballet. Appeared with Royal Winnipeg Ballet before joining Harkness Ballet in 1966.

AYAKO. (See Uchiyama. Ayako)

BABILEE, JEAN. Born Jean Gutman Feb. 2, 1923 in Paris. Studied at School of Paris Opera. In 1945 became premier danseur in Les Ballets des Champs-Élysees. Toured with own company. Guest artist with ABT.

BAGNOLD, LISBETH. Born Oct. 10, 1947 in Bronxville, N.Y. UCLA graduate. Studied with Gloria Newman, Limon, Nikolais, Murray Louis. Joined Nikolais Dance Theatre in 1971.

BAILIN, GLADYS. Born in N.Y.C. Feb. 11, 1930. Graduate Hunter Col. Studied with Nikolais and joined his company in 1955. Has also appeared with Murray Louis and Don Redlich.

BAKER-SCOTT, SHAWNEEQUA. Born in Bronx; attended Hunter Col., CCNY. Studied with Holm, Humphrey-Wiedman, NDG, Ailey, Beatty, Holder, Clarke, Graham. Began 1952 with Donald McKayle, subsequently with Destine, New Dance Group, Ailey, Marchant, Dancers Theatre Co., Eleo Pomare.

BALANCHINE, GEORGE. Born Georges Malitonovitch Balanchivadze in St. Petersburg, Russia on Jan. 9, 1904. Graduate Imperial School of Ballet. Debut 1915 in "Sleeping Beauty." Began choreographing while still in school. Left Russia in 1924 to tour with own company. Became associated with Diaghilev in Paris where he choreographed more than 10 works. Thence to Copenhagen as Ballet Master of Royal Dutch Ballet, then joined newly formed Russes de Monte Carlo. Formed Les Ballets in 1933 and toured Europe. Invited to establish school in N.Y., and in 1934 opened School of American Ballet, followed by American Ballet Co. Choreographed for Met (1935–8). Bdwy musicals, and for such companies as Original Ballet Russe, Sadler's Wells Theatre Ballet, Ballet Russe de Monte Carlo, Ballet Theatre, and Ballet Society. Formed NYC Ballet which premiered in 1948, and won international acclaim under his direction and with his brilliant choreography.

BALLARD, MICHAEL. Born July 17, 1942 in Denver, Colo. Studied with Nikolais and Louis at Henry Street Playhouse, and made professional debut with Alwin Nikolais Co. in 1966. Joined Murray Louis Co. in 1968.

BALOUGH, BUDDY. Born in 1953 in Seattle, Wash. where he began studying at 9. Trained at ABT School, and in 1970 joined Am. Ballet Theatre, rising to soloist in 1973. Also joined Ballet of Contemporary Art in 1973, for which he choreographs.

BANKS, GERALD. Born Feb. 4 in NYC. Attended CCNY, American Ballet Center. Joined Dance Theatre of Harlem 1969.

BARANOVA, IRINA. Born in Petrograd, Russia in 1919. Studied with Olga Preobrajenska. Soloist with Opera; Ballet Russe 1932–40; ballerina with Ballet Theatre 1941–2. More recently has been appearing in plays and musicals, and teaching at Royal Academy.

BARI, TANIA. (formerly Bartha Treure). Born July 5, 1936 in Rotterdam. Studied with Netty Van Der Valk, Nora Kiss, Asaf Messerer. Joined Bejart's Ballet in 1955; principal from 1959.

BARKER, JOHN. Born in Oak Park, Ill., Nov. 20, 1929. Studied at Chicago U., and with Bentley Stone, Walter Camryn, Margaret Craske, Antony Tudor, Pierre Vladimiroff, Anatole Oboukoff, Valentina Perevaslavic, and Maria Nevelska. Made professional debut with Page-Stone Camryn Co. in 1951. Has appeared with Chicago Opera Ballet, Juilliard Dance Theatre, and Jose Limon Co.

BARNARD, SCOTT. Born Oct. 17, 1945 in Indianapolis, Ind. Graduate Butler U. Studied with Perry Bronson, Robert Joffrey, Gerald Arpino, Richard Englund, Hector Zaraspy. Debut 1963 with St. Louis Opera. Joined Joffrey Ballet in 1968.

BARNES, NERISSA. Born Feb. 2, 1952 in Columbus, Ga. Attended UIll. Debut 1969 with Julian Swain Inner City Dance Co. Joined Alvin Ailey company in 1972.

BARNETT, DARRELL. Born Sept. 24, 1949 in Miami, Okla. Attended Okla U. Studied with Mary Price, Ethel Winter, Betty Jones, Martha Graham. Debut in 1970 with Ethel Winter, subsequently with Yuriko, Mary Anthony, Pearl Lang, Erick Hawkins, Richard Gain, Kazuko Hirabayashi. Joined Harkness Ballet in 1971. Made soloist 1973.

BARNETT, ROBERT. Born May 6, 1925 in Okanogan, Wash. Studied with Nijinska, Egoroba, Preobrajinska, and at School of American Ballet. Made debut with Original Ballet Russe; joined NYC Ballet in 1950; Atlanta Ballet in 1958, and its director from 1963. Choreographs, and operates own school.

BARREDO, MANIYA. Born Nov. 19, 1952 in Manila, PI. Attended St. Paul Col., American Ballet Center. Debut 1965 with Philippine Harivaya Dance Co. Joined Joffrey Ballet 1972.

BARTA, KAROLY. Born Aug. 5, 1936 in Bekescsaba, Hungary. Debut there at 11 with folk ensemble. Studied at Hungarian State Ballet Inst.; performed with Budapest opera and ballet. First choreographic work at 15. Joined Hungarian National Folk Ensemble before emigrating to U.S. in 1957. Attended Met Opera Ballet, and Stone-Camryn School. Joined Chicago Opera Ballet, and continued to choreograph for various groups. Co-founder of Hungarian Ballets Bihari for which he dances and choreographs, and was teacher-director for Birmingham Civic Ballet for 5 years.

BARYSHNIKOV, MIKHAIL. Born Jan. 27, 1948 in Riga, Latvia. Began training at Latvian Opera Ballet School. Moved to Kirov school and joined company at 18 as soloist. Was guest artist with Bolshoi Ballet in Toronto, Can., when he defected in 1974. Has appeared with ABT, Australian Ballet, Hamburg and Paris Opera Ballets.

BATES, JAMES. Born Feb. 8, 1949 in Dallas, Tex. Studied with Moreno, Nault, Danilova, Fallis, and Harkarvy. Joined Les Grands Ballets Canadiens in 1968.

BAUMAN, ART. Born in Washington, D.C. Studied at Juilliard, Met, and Martha Graham schools. Has danced with Lucas Hoving, Paul Sanasardo, Charles Weidman. Has choreographed numerous works and teaches. Is asst. director of DTW.

BAYS, FRANK. Born June 6, 1943 in Bristol, Va. Attended King Col. Studied with Perry Brunson, and at Am. Ballet Center. Debut with American Festival Ballet 1964; joined Joffrey Ballet 1965; First Chamber Dance Co. 1972.

BEALS, MARGARET. Born Mar. 5, 1943 in Boston. Studied with Mattox, Graham, Sanasardo, Slavenska. Has appeared in musicals, and with Valerie Bettis, Jean Erdman, Pearl Lang, Jose Limon, and Paul Sanasardo. Also choreographs, and performs in concert.

BEATTY, TALLEY. Made professional debut in Bdwy musicals. Joined Ballet Society in 1947. Has more recently toured, given solo performances, formed own company for which he choreographs, and teaches.

BECKER, BRUCE. Born May 28, 1944 in NYC. Graduate Utah State U. Studied at O'Donnell-Shurr, Graham, and Don Farnworth studios. Debut 1961 with Norman Walker, subsequently on Bdwy, with Tamiris-Nagrin, Limon, O'Donnell; joined Batsheva in 1969. Now dances with own company.

BECKLEY, CHRISTINE. Born Mar. 16, 1939 in Stanmore, Eng. Studied at Royal Ballet School, joined company and advanced to solo artist.

BEJART, MAURICE. Born Jan. 1, 1927 in Marseilles, France. Studied at Opera Ballet School, and with Leo Staats. Danced with Opera Ballet until 1945; Ballets de Roland Petit (1947–49); International Ballet (1949–50); Royal Swedish Ballet (1951–2). In 1954 organized Les Ballets de l'Etoile and debuted as choreographer. Company became Ballet Theatre de Maurice Bejart. In 1959 appointed director of Theatre Royale de la Monnaie, Brussels, and its name was changed to Ballet of the 20th Century.

BELHUMEUR, CHANTAL. Born Mar. 20, 1949 in Montreal, Can. Studied with Graham, Les Grands Ballets Canadiens and became member 1965; joined Eleo Pomare in 1971.

BELIN, ALEXANDRE. Born Apr. 3, 1948 in Mulhouse, France. Made debut in 1966 with Les Grands Ballets Canadiens.

BENJAMIN, FRED. Born Sept. 8, 1944 in Boston. Studied with Elma Lewis, ABT, Claude Thompson, Talley Beatty. Has danced in musicals, with Boston Ballet, and Talley Beatty Co. Also teaches and choreographs.

BENJAMIN, JOEL. Born Feb. 21, 1949 in NYC. Attended Juilliard, Columbia; studied with Alwin Nikolais, Martha Graham, and at American Ballet Center. Made debut in Paris in 1963. Formed own company in 1963. Director American Chamber Ballet.

BENNETT, CHARLES. Born in Wheaton, Ill. Studied with Bentley Stone, made debut with Ruth Page's before joining American Ballet Theatre. Member of NYC Ballet before formation of First Chamber Dance Quartet, now First Chamber Dance Co.

BENTLEY, MURIEL. Born in NYC. Studied with Tomaroff, Tarasoff, Swoboda, Fokine, Ruth St. Denis, Dolin and at Met Opera School. Made debut with Ruth St. Denis in 1931. Has appeared with Jose Greco 1936–7, at Met 1938–9; joined Ballet Theatre in 1940. Has since danced with Jerome Robbins' Ballets: U.S.A.

BERG, BERND. Born Nov. 20, 1943 in East Prussia. Began training at 11 in Leipzig. Joined Stuttgart Ballet in 1964; became soloist in 1967.

BERG, HENRY. Born in Chicago, Apr. 4, 1938. Studied with DeRea, Morrelli, Lew Christensen. Made professional debut with Ballet Alicia Alonso in 1958, subsequently joining San Francisco Ballet (1962), and Joffrey Ballet (1967).

BERGSMA, DEANNE. Born Apr. 16, 1941 in South Africa. Studied with Royal Ballet and joined company in 1958. Became soloist in 1962, principal in 1967.

BERIOSOVA, SVETLANA. Born Sept. 24, 1932 in Lithuania. Came to U.S. in 1940; studied at Vilzak-Shollar School. Debut with Ottawa Ballet Co. in 1947. Appeared with Grand Ballet de Monte Carlo 1947; Met Opera 1948; Sadler's Wells 1950, and became ballerina in 1954 with Royal Ballet.

BESWICK, BOB. Born Nov. 11, 1945 in San Francisco. Studied with Cunningham, Sokolow, Waring, Louis, Bailin, Nikolais. Made debut in 1967 with Utah Repertory Dance Theatre, subsequently with Nikolais Co. Choreographer and teacher.

BETHEL, PEPSI. Born in Greensboro, NC. Attended Adelphi Col. Toured Africa and performed during 1969–70. Since 1971 has been artistic director-choreographer for Pepsi Bethel Authentic Jazz Dance Theatre.

BETTIS, VALERIE. Born in 1920 in Houston, Tex. Studied with Hanya Holm. Debut with Miss Holm's company in 1937, and as a choreographer in 1941. Subsequently appeared as dancer-choreographer for several Bdwy productions, and own company that toured U.S. and abroad. Teaches in own studio in NYC.

BEWLEY, LOIS. Born in Louisville, Ky. Studied with Lilias Courtney. Made debut with Ballet Russe de Monte Carlo; subsequently with ABT, Ballets U.S.A., NYC Ballet.

BHASKAR. Born Bhaskar Roy Chowdhury in Madras, India, Feb. 11, 1930. Studied with G. Ellappa. Made debut in Madras in 1950 as concert dancer with own company which he brought to NYC in 1956. As dancer and/or choreographer, has appeared on Bdwy, and internationally; teaches.

BIEVER, KATHRYN. Born May 9, 1942 in Bryn Mawr, Pa. Studied in Ballet Russe School, Pa. Ballet School. Made debut in 1964 with American Festival Ballet before joining Pennsylvania Ballet. Joined Les Grands Ballets Canadiens 1972.

BILES, RICHARD. Born in Salem, Ore. Attended Ill. Inst. of Tech., UWisc. Joined Dance Repertory Theater 1970–71. With Nikolais Dance Theatre 1970–71. Formed own company with which he tours. Also teaches.

BIRCH, PATRICIA. Born in Englewood, N.J. Studied at School of Am. Ballet, Cunningham, and Graham schools. Made debut with Graham company. Has appeared in concert, on Bdwy, and with Donald Saddler, Valerie Bettis. Also choreographs.

BJORNSSON, FREDBJORN. Born in Copenhagen in 1926. Entered Royal Danish Ballet school 1935; graduated into company and became soloist in 1949; became one of great leading mimes and exponent of Bournonville style.

BLACKSTONE, JUDITH. Born May 10, 1947 in Iowa City, Iowa. Studied with Donya Feuer, Paul Sanasardo, Mia Slavenska, Karoly Zsedenyi. Debut with Sanasardo Co. in 1958.

BLAIR, DAVID. Born in Yorkshire, Eng. July 27, 1932. Trained at Royal Ballet School. Subsequently joined its company, rising to principal dancer in 1955. Honored by Queen Elizabeth with title Commander of the Order of the British Empire.

BLANKSHINE, ROBERT. Born Dec. 22, 1948 in Syracuse, N.Y. Studied at American School of Ballet. Professional debut in 1965 with Joffrey Ballet which he left in 1968. Joined Berlin Opera Ballet in 1970; Frankfort Ballet 1972.

BOARDMAN, DIANE. Born Jan. 17, 1949 in NYC. Bklyn. Col. graduate. Began training at 6, studying with Murray Louis, James Truitte, Wilson Morelli, and John Medicros. Has appeared with Murray Louis, Alwin Nikolais, Phyllis Lamhut companies. Also teaches and choreographs.

BOLENDER, TODD. Born in Canton, O. in 1919. Studied with Chester Hale, Vilzak, and at School of American Ballet. Soloist with Ballet Caravan in 1937, Littlefield Ballet in 1941; founder-director of American Concert Ballet in 1943; joined Ballet Theatre in 1944, Ballet Russe de Monte Carlo in 1945. First choreography in 1943. Became dancer-choreographer for Ballet Society, and has continued to choreograph for various companies; was director of Cologne and Frankfurt Opera Ballets.

BONNEFOUS, JEAN-PIERRE. Born Apr. 25, 1943 in Paris. Attended Paris Opera School of Dance. Made debut in 1964 with Opera Ballet and became premier danseur. Appeared with companies in Frankfort, Moscow, Milan, Berlin, Oslo, Toronto before joining NYC Ballet in 1970 as a principal.

| Bhaskar | Lisa Bradley | Bruce Caldwell | Jilise Bushling | Steven Caras |

BORIS, RUTHANNA. Born in 1918 in Brooklyn. Studied at Met Opera School, with Helene Veola, and Fokine. Member of American Ballet in 1935, Met soloist in 1936, and premiere danseuse 1939–43. Joined Ballet Russe de Monte Carlo in 1943. Has choreographed a number of works. Now teaches.

BORTOLUZZI, PAOLO. Born May 17, 1938 in Genoa, Italy. Debut 1958 with Italian Ballet. Joined Bejart Ballet in 1960, rising to principal dancer. Joined ABT in 1972 as principal.

BOUTILIER, JOY. Born in Chicago, Sept. 30, 1939. Graduate of U. Chicago. Studied at Henry St. Playhouse, and with Angelina Romett. Debut with Nikolais in 1964, subsequently with Mimi Garrard, Phyllis Lamhut, and Murray Louis. Has choreographed and appeared in own concerts.

BOWMAN, PATRICIA. Born in Washington, D.C. Studied with Fokine, Mordkin, Legat, Egorova, and Wallman. Ballerina at Roxy and Radio City Music Hall, with Mordkin Ballet in 1939, Ballet Theatre in 1940, and appeared with Chicago Opera, Fokine Ballet, and in musicals and operettas. Now teaches.

BRADLEY, LISA. Born in Elizabeth, N.J. in 1941. Studied at Newark Ballet Academy, American Ballet Center, and with Joyce Trisler. Appeared with Garden State Ballet before joining Joffrey Ballet in 1961. Invited to study classic roles with Ulanova. Joined First Chamber Dance Co. in 1969; Hartford Ballet 1972 where she also teaches.

BRASSEL, ROBERT. Born Nov. 3, in Chicago. Attended Ind. U., American Ballet Center. Trained with Robert Joffrey, Hector Zaraspe, Lillian Morre. Joined Joffrey Ballet in 1965, ABT in 1968.

BRIANSKY, OLEG. Born in Brussels Nov. 9, 1929. Studied with Katchourovsky, Gsovsky, Volkova. Joined Les Ballets des Champs-Elysees; became lead dancer in 1946. Subsequently with Ballets de Paris, London Festival Ballet, Chicago Opera Ballet. Formed own company, and teaches.

BRIANT, ROGER. Born May 4, 1944 in Yonkers, N.Y. Studied at Joffrey Center, Martha Graham Studio, O'Donnell-Shurr Studio. Has appeared on Bdwy, and with Martha Graham, Glen Tetley, Donald McKayle, Norman Walker companies.

BROCK, KARENA. Born Sept. 21, 1942 in Los Angeles. Studied with Lanova, Lichine, Riabouchinska, DuBoulay, and Branitzska. Danced with Natl. Ballet of Netherlands before joining American Ballet Theatre in 1963. Became soloist in 1968, principal 1973. Has appeared in musicals and films.

BROOKS, ROMAN. Born July 5, 1950 in Millington, Tenn. Attended Harbor-Compton Jr. Col. Studied with Eugene Loring. Joined Dance Theatre of Harlem 1973.

BROWN, CAROLYN. Born in Fitchburg, Mass. in 1927. Graduate of Wheaton College. Studied with Marion Rice, Margaret Craske, Antony Tudor and Merce Cunningham. Professional debut with Cunningham in 1953 and appeared in almost entire repertoire of company in roles she created. Left company in 1973 to choreograph.

BROWN, KELLY. Born Sept. 24, 1928 in Jackson, Miss. Studied with Bentley Stone, Walter Camryn. Made professional debut with Chicago Civic Opera Ballet in 1946; soloist with Ballet Theatre (1949–1953). Has since appeared in films, musicals, and on TV.

BROWN, LAURA. Born Sept. 1, 1955 in San Francisco, Cal. Studied at Ballet Celeste, San Francisco Ballet. Joined Dance Theatre of Harlem 1972.

BROWN, SANDRA. Born Jan. 6, 1946 in Ft. Wayne, Ind. Studied with Tudor, Craske, Graham, Limon. Made debut in Juilliard concert in 1967, subsequently dancing with DTW, James Clouser, James Waring, and Lucus Hoving.

BRUHN, ERIK. Born Oct. 3, 1928 in Copenhagen. Attended Academie of Royal Danish Theatre, and Royal Danish Ballet with which he made his debut in 1947. Became its leading male dancer, and has appeared as guest soloist with all leading companies throughout the world. For brief period was a principal dancer with American Ballet Theatre, and a permanent guest artist. Is considered one of world's greatest classical dancers. Appointed Director of Ballet of Royal Swedish Opera in 1967. Retired in 1972. Resident producer National Ballet of Canada 1973. Resumed dancing career 1974.

BRYANT, HOMER. Born Mar. 29, 1951 in St. Thomas, VI. Attended Adelphi U. Debut 1970 with Manhattan Festival Ballet; Joined Dance Theatre of Harlem 1973.

BUCHTRUP, BJARNE. Born Aug. 11, 1942 in Copenhagen. Studied with Birger Bartholin, Leon Danielian. Appeared in musicals before joining West Berlin Ballet Co. in 1963. Danced with Manhattan Festival Ballet (1965–66) and joined American Ballet Theatre in 1967.

BUIRGE, SUSAN. Born in Minneapolis, June 19, 1940. Graduate of U. Minn. Studied at Juilliard, Henry St. Playhouse, Conn. College. Made professional debut with Nikolais Co. in 1964. Has also appeared with Murray Louis, Mimi Garrard, Bill Frank, Juilliard Dance Ensemble, and Jose Limon. Also choreographs, and teaches.

BUJONES, FERNANDO. Born Mar. 9, 1955 in Miami, Fla. Attended Cuban Ntl. Ballet School, School of American Ballet, Juilliard. Debut 1970 with Eglevsky Ballet, followed by Ballet Spectacular 1971–2, American Ballet Theatre 1972. Raised to soloist 1973, principal 1974.

BURKE, DERMOT. Born Jan. 8, 1948 in Dublin, Ire. Studied at Royal School of Dance. Appeared with Royal Concert Group before joining Joffrey Company in 1966, National Ballet 1972; Joffrey 1975.

BURR, MARILYN. Born Nov. 20, 1933 in New South Wales. Studied at Australian Ballet School; made debut with Ntl. Ballet Co. in 1948. Joined London Festival Ballet in 1953 as soloist; became ballerina in 1955. Joined Hamburg State Opera Co. in 1963. Had danced with Natl. Ballet of Wash.

BUSHLING, JILISE. Born in 1957 in Santa Monica, Ca. Studied at American Ballet Theatre School, Sch. of Am. Ballet. Made debut in 1972 with Joffrey II Co. Joined NYCB in 1974.

BUSSEY, RAYMOND. Born Mar. 8, 1946 in Pawtucket, R. I. Studied with Perry Brunson, Tupine, and at Joffrey School. Made professional debut with American Festival Ballet in 1962. Joined Joffrey Company in 1964.

BUSTILLO, ZELMA. Born in Cartagena, Columbia, but came to N.Y.C. at 6. Graduate HS Performing Arts. Appeared with Thalia Mara's Ballet Repertory, at Radio City Music Hall, with American Festival Ballet, Joffrey Ballet Co. (1965), National Ballet (1970).

BUTLER, JOHN. Born in Memphis, Tenn., Sept. 29, 1920. Studied with Martha Graham and at American School of Ballet. Made debut with Graham company in 1947. Appeared in Bdwy musicals before becoming choreographer. Formed own company with which he toured.

CALDWELL, BRUCE. Born Aug. 25, 1950 in Salt Lake City, U. Studied with Bene Arnold, Willam Christensen at UUtah. Joined Ballet West in 1967; became principal in 1973.

CALZADA, ALBA. Born Jan. 28, 1947 in Puerto Rico. UPR graduate. Studied in San Juan and made debut with San Juan Ballet in 1964. Was guest with Eglevsky and Miami Ballets before joining Pa. Ballet. in 1968. Now a principal.

CAMMACK, RICHARD L. Born Oct. 24, 1945 in Knoxville, Tenn. Graduate Butler U. Studied at Harkness House, American Ballet Theatre School. Joined ABT in 1969.

CAMPANERIA, MIGUEL. Born Feb. 5, 1951 in Havana, Cuba. Studied at Ntl. Ballet of Cuba, and made debut with company in 1968. Joined Harkness Ballet and became soloist in 1973.

CAMPBELL, SYLVESTER. Born in Oklahoma. Joined NY Negro Ballet 1956, and subsequently Het Netherlands Ballet 1960, Ballet of 20th Century, Royal Winnipeg Ballet 1972.

CAMRYN, WALTER. Born in Helena, Mont., in 1903. Studied with Bolm, Maximova, Swoboda, Novikoff, and Muriel Stuart. Appeared with Chicago Civic Opera Ballet. Page-Stone Ballet, and Federal Theatre as premier danseur and choreographer. Teacher at Stone-Camryn School, Chicago. Has choreographed more than 20 ballets.

CANDELARIA, SANSON. Born July 13, 1947 in Albuquerque, NMex. Joined Les Grands Ballets Canadiens 1965, Lisbon's Gulbenkian Ballet 1969, American Classical Ballet 1971, Boston Ballet 1972.

CARAS, STEPHEN. Born Oct. 25, 1950 in Englewood, N.J. Studied at American Ballet Center, School of American Ballet. Made debut in 1967 with Irene Fokine Co. Joined N.Y.C. Ballet in 1969.

CARLSON, CAROLYN. Born in Oakland, Calif., Mar. 7, 1943. Graduate of U. Utah. Studied at San Francisco Ballet School, and Henry St. Playhouse. Professional debut in 1965 with Nikolais Co. Has also appeared with Murray Louis, and in New Choreographers Concert.

CARROLL, ELISABETH. Born Jan. 19, 1937 in Paris. Studied with Sedova, Besobrasova. Made debut in 1952 with Monte Carol Opera Ballet; joined Ballet Theatre in 1954, Joffrey Ballet in 1962, and Harkness Ballet in 1964.

CARTER, RICHARD. Became principal male dancer of San Francisco Ballet in 1958. With Nancy Johnson, performed in more than fifty countries around the world. Was director and premier danseur of the San Diego Ballet Co. for which he created 14 ballets. Now with San Francisco Ballet.

CARTER, WILLIAM. Born in 1936 in Durant, Okla. Studied with Coralane Duane, Carmalita Maracci. Joined American Ballet Theatre in 1957, N.Y.C. Ballet in 1959. Helped to organize and appeared since 1961 with First Chamber Dance Co. Joined Martha Graham Co. 1972, ABT 1972.

CARTIER, DIANA. Born July 23, 1939 in Philadelphia, Pa. Studied with Tudor, Doubrouska, Balanchine, Joffrey, Griffith, and Brunson, Debut 1960 with Met Opera Ballet, subsequently with John Butler, N.Y.C. Opera Ballet, Zachary Solov, and Joffrey Ballet since 1961.

CASEY, SUSAN. Born in April 1949 in Buffalo, N.Y. Studied at Ballet Russe, and Harkness Schools, and with Kravina, Danielian, Shollar, Vilzak, and Volkova. Joined American Ballet Theatre in 1965; became its youngest soloist in 1969.

CASTELLI, VICTOR. Born Oct. 9, 1952 in Montclair, N.J. Studied at Newark Ballet Acad., School of American Ballet. Appeared with Garden State Ballet, and Eglevsky Ballet before joining NYC Ballet in 1971.

CATANZARO, TONY. Born Nov. 10, 1946 in Bklyn. Studied with Norman Walker, Sanasardo, Danielian, Lillian Moore, Lang, Joffrey, Jaime Rogers. Debut 1968 in musicals, subsequently appearing with Norman Walker, Harkness Youth Ballet, N.J. Ballet, Boston Ballet; joined Joffrey in 1971. Returned to Boston Ballet 1973.

CATON, EDWARD. Born in St. Petersburg, Russia. Apr. 3, 1900 Studied at Melidova's Ballet School, Moscow, and made professional debut in 1914. Joined Max Terptzt Co. (1918), Ourkransky-Pavley Co. (1919), Pavlova (1924), Chicago Opera Ballet (1926), American Ballet (1934), Catherine Littlefield (1935), Mikhail Mordkin (1938), Ballet Theatre (1940), retired in 1942 to become teacher and choreographer.

CAVRELL, HOLLY. Born Sept. 2, 1955 in NYC. Attended Hunter Col., studied with Pearl Lang, Patsy Birch, Rod Rodgers, Alwin Nikolais, American Dance Center, Debut 1972 with Ballet Players; Joined Martha Graham Co. 1973.

CEBRON, JEAN. Born in Paris in 1938. Made debut in 1956 in London. Joined Joos Folkwangballet. Tours world in concert.

CESBRON, JACQUES. Born May 10, 1940 in Angers, France. Studied at Paris Opera Ballet School, and joined company in 1958. Member of Harkness Ballet before becoming soloist with Pennsylvania Ballet in 1966. Left in 1969.

CHAIB, ELIE. Born July 18, 1950 in Beirut, Lebanon. Began studies in Beirut in 1966. Made debut 1969 as soloist with Beirut Dance Ensemble. Came to U.S. in 1970; appeared in Joffrey's "Petrouchka," Chamber Dance Ensemble before joining Paul Taylor Co. 1973.

CHAMBERLIN, BETTY. Born Nov. 10, 1949 in Madison, Wisc. Studied with Armour, LaVerne, Nault, Skibine, and at ABT. Joined American Ballet Theatre in 1969; Eliot Feld 1974.

CHAMPION, GOWER. Born in Geneva, Ill., June 22, 1920. After appearing in vaudeville, night clubs, and on Bdwy, made debut as choreographer for "Lend An Ear" in 1946. Is now in great demand as choreographer and director of musicals, and films.

CHAPLINE, CLAUDIA. Born May 23, 1930 in Oak Park, Ill. Graduate George Washington U. Studied with Davis, Weidman, Hoving, Humphrey, Horst, Nikolais, Deitz, Limon, Graham, Cassan, Maracci, Rousellat. Debut 1948 with Evelyn Davis Co.; subsequently with Doris Humphrey, Gloria Newman, Instant Theatre, and in 1973 formed IDEA Co. for which she directs and choreographs.

CHARLIP, REMY. Born Jan. 10, 1929 in Brooklyn, NY. Attended Cooper Union, Reed Col. Studied at New Dance Group, with Merce Cunningham, Jean Erdman. Appeared with Cunningham for 11 years. Now choreographs.

CHASE, DAVID. Born June 18, 1948 in Mill Valley, Cal. Graduate URochester. Studied with Walter Nicks, Karl Shook, Graham School, Joffrey School, Nadia Potts, Norbert Vesak. Debut 1971 with Norbert Vesak, subsequently with Walter Nicks Co., Kazuko Hirabayashi; joined Martha Graham Co. 1972.

CHASE, LUCIA. Born March 24, 1907 in Waterbury, Conn. Studied at Theatre Guild School, and with Mikhail Mordkin. Became member of his company and danced title role in "Giselle" in 1937. Was principal dancer with Ballet Theatre when it was founded in 1939. In 1945 became co-director with Oliver Smith of American Ballet Theatre. In recent years has appeared only with her company in "Fall River Legend," "Swan Lake," and "Las Hermanas."

CHAUVIRE, YVETTE. Born Apr. 22, 1917 in Paris. Studied at Paris Opera School. Appeared with Paris Opera Ballet, London Festival Ballet, Royal Ballet (1959). In 1963 appointed director of Paris Opera Ballet School.

CHING, CHIANG. Born Jan. 26, 1946 in Peking, China. Graduate Peking School of Dance. Producer-Director of Great Wall Dancers of San Francisco. Also teaches and choreographs.

CHIRIAEFF, LUDMILLA. Born in 1924 in Latvia. Began training at early age in Berlin with Alexandra Nicolaieva. Joined de Basil's Ballets Russe, was soloist with Berlin Opera Ballet, and prima ballerina at Lausanne Municipal Theatre. Opened own academy in Geneva and choreographed for Ballet des Arts, Geneva. Moved to Canada in 1952 and organized own company, ultimately leading to her being founder and artistic director of Les Grands Ballets Canadiens.

CHOUTEAU, YVONNE. Born in Ft. Worth, Tex. in 1929. Studied with Asher, Perkins, Vestoff, Belcher, Bolm, at Vilzak-Shollar School of American Ballet. Made debut as child in American Indian dance company at Chicago's 1933 Fair. Joined Ballet Russe de Monte Carlo in 1943. Now teaches, makes guest appearances, and is Co-Director of Okla. Civic Ballet.

CHRISTENSEN, HAROLD. Born Dec. 24 in Brigham City, Utah. Studied with Balanchine. Appeared with Met Opera Ballet (1934), Ballet Caravan, San Francisco Opera Ballet, San Francisco Ballet. Retired to teach and direct San Francisco Ballet School.

CHRISTENSEN, LEW. Born May 9, 1906 in Brigham City, Utah. Studied with uncle Lars Christensen at American School of Ballet. Performer and choreographer since 1934, on Bdwy for Met Opera, Ballet Caravan, American Ballet Co., and N.Y.C. Ballet. In 1938, with brothers Harold and William, founded San Francisco Ballet; has been general director since 1951.

CHRISTENSEN, WILLAM. Born Aug. 27, 1902 in Brigham City, Utah. Studied with uncle Lars Christensen, Nescagno, Novikoff, and Fokine. Made debut with Small Ballet Quartet in 1927, subsequently becoming choreographer, ballet master, director and teacher. With brothers Harold and Lew, formed San Francisco Ballet which he directed until 1951 when he established School of Ballet at U. of Utah. Is director-choreographer for Utah Civic Ballet which he organized in 1952, now Ballet West.

CHRISTOPHER, ROBERT. (formerly Robert Hall). Born Mar. 22, 1942 in Marion, Md. Studied with Harry Asmus, Vincenzo Celli, Celo Quitman. Made debut in 1960 with National Ballet of Venezuela; subsequently with Stuttgart Ballet, ABT, Anne Wilson, Valerie Bettis, Sophie Maslow; soloist and ballet master for Garden State Ballet, and appears with Downtown Ballet.

CHRYST, GARY. Born in LaJolla, Calif. Studied with Walker, Hoving, Limon, Jaime Rogers, Nina Popova, ABC. Debute at 16 with Norman Walker, subsequently with McKayle, Washington Ballet, N.Y.C. Opera, before joining Joffrey Ballet in 1968.

CLARE, NATALIA. Born in Hollywood, Calif. Studied with Nijinska, Egorova; joined de Basil's Ballet Russe, then Markova-Dolin Co., Ballet Russe de Monte Carlo. In 1956, established school in North Hollywood, and founded Ballet Jeunesse for which she is artistic director and choreographer.

CLARKE, THATCHER. Born Apr. 1, 1937 in Springfield, Ohio. Made professional debut with Met Opera Ballet in 1954, subsequently joined Ballet de Cuba, Ballet Russe de Monte Carlo, San Francisco Ballet, and American Ballet Theatre. Has appeared in several musicals.

CLAUSS, HEINZ. Born Feb. 17, 1935 in Stuttgart. Studied at Stuttgart Ballet School, and with Balanchine. Joined Stuttgart Ballet in 1967 after appearing with Zurich Opera Ballet, and in Hamburg; promoted to principal.

CLEAR, IVY. Born in Camden, Maine, Mar. 11, 1948. Studied at Professional Children's School of Dance and School of American Ballet. Made professional debut in 1963 with N.Y.C. Ballet. Soloist with Joffrey Ballet from 1965 to 1969.

CLIFFORD, JOHN. Born June 12, 1947 in Hollywood. Studied at American School of Dance and School of American Ballet. Appeared with Ballet of Guatemala and Western Ballet before joining N.Y. City Ballet in 1966. Soloist since 1969. Has choreographed 7 works for the company, in addition to works for other companies. Left in 1974 to become artistic director-choreographer for Los Angeles Ballet.

CLOUSER, JAMES. Born in 1935 in Rochester, N.Y. Studied at Eastman School of Music, Ballet Theatre School. Joined ABT in 1957, Royal Winnipeg Ballet in 1958, rising to leading dancer in 1959, subsequently choreographed, composed and designed for it, and became ballet master and assistant director. Has appeared in concert, taught, and tours with wife Sonja Zarek. Ballet master for Houston Ballet.

| Tina Croll | John Clifford | Eileen Cropley | Alfredo Corvino | Jerilyn Dana |

COCKERILLE, LILI. Born in Washington, D.C. Studied at Fokine School. Wash. School of Ballet and School of American Ballet. Made professional debut with N.Y.C. Ballet in 1963, joined Harkness Ballet in 1964, Joffrey Co. in 1969.

COFFMAN, VERNON. Born Dec. 5, 1947 in Tucson, Ariz. Studied with Lew and Harold Christensen. Made professional debut with San Francisco Ballet in 1964. Joined Joffrey Ballet in 1966, and American Ballet Theatre in 1967.

COHAN, ROBERT. Born in N.Y.C. in 1925. Soloist with Martha Graham Co. Opened own school in Boston, joined faculty of Harvard's Drama Center, made solo tours here and abroad, taught in Israel and choreographed for Batsheva Co. Now director of London Contemporary Dance Theatre.

COHEN, ZE'EVA. Born Aug. 15, 1940 in Israel. Studied at Juilliard, and appeared with its Dance Ensemble. Joined Anna Sokolow Co. 1961, subsequently with Pearl Lang, and in solo concerts. Choreographs and teaches.

COLEMAN, LILLIAN. Born Nov. 21, 1949 in N.Y.C. Attended SUNY, Harkness School. Made debut with New Dance Group.

COLL, DAVID. Born Mar. 20, 1947 in Chelsea, Mass. Studied with Vilzak, Nerden, Van Muyden, Fallis, Christensen. Made debut in 1965 with San Francisco Ballet. Joined American Ballet Co. in 1969. ABT in 1970. Became soloist in 1972.

COLLIER, LESLEY. Born Mar. 13, 1947 in Kent, Eng. Studied at Royal Academy of Dancing, Royal Ballet School. Joined Royal Ballet in 1965.

COLLINS, JANET. Born in New Orleans in 1917. Studied with Carmalita Maracci, Bolm, Lester Horton, Slavenska and Craske. Appeared in solo concerts before becoming premiere danseuse of the Met Opera Ballet (1951–54). Now teaches.

COLTON, RICHARD. Born Oct. 4, 1951 in N.Y.C. Attended Hunter Col., ABT School, American Ballet Center. Debut 1966 with James Waring Co.; joined Joffrey Ballet 1972.

COMELIN, JEAN-PAUL. Born Sept. 10, 1936 in Vannes, France. Studied at Cons. of Music and Art; made debut with Paris Opera Ballet in 1957. Soloist for London Festival Ballet in 1961, principal in 1962. Joined National Ballet for 1967, Pa. Ballet in 1970; Left in 1972. Associate director Sacramento Ballet.

CONDODINA, ALICE. Born in Phildelphia; graduate of Temple U. Studied with Tudor, Zaraspe, Danielian, and at Met Opera Ballet, Ballet Theatre, and American Ballet Schools. Danced with Ruth Currier, Lucas Hoving, Sophie Maslow, Jack Moore, and Jose Limon Companies. Director-choreographer for own company since 1967.

CONOVER, WARREN. Born Feb. 5, 1948 in Philadelphia, Pa. Studied with Peter Conlow, Harkness House. Debut 1966 with Pa. Ballet. Subsequently with Harkness Ballet, Eglevsky Ballet, Niagara Ballet, Richmond Ballet; joined ABT 1971, soloist 1973.

CONRAD, KAREN. Born in 1919 in Philadelphia. Made debut with Littlefield Ballet (1935–7), subsequently with Mordkin Ballet, and Ballet Theatre. Retired in 1946 and opened school in Atlanta.

COREY, WINTHROP. Born in 1947 in Washington, D.C. Studied with Ntl. Ballet and appeared with company. Joined Royal Winnipeg Ballet in 1966; Ntl. Ballet of Canada 1972; principal 1973.

CORKLE, FRANCESCA. Born Aug. 2, 1952 in Seattle, Wash. Studied with Virginia Ryan, Perry Brunson, Robert Joffrey. Joined Joffrey Ballet in 1967.

CORKRE, COLLEEN. Born in Seattle, Wash. and began training at 4. Debut with Chicago Opera Ballet. Dancer and choreographer for several musicals. Formed own company that tours every season.

CORVINO, ALFREDO. Born in Montevideo, Uruguay, where he studied with Alberto Poujanne. Also studied with Margaret Craske, Antony Tudor. Was premier danseur, assistant ballet master, and choreographer for Municipal Theatre, Montevideo. Appeared with Jooss Ballet, Ballet Russe de Monte Carlo, Metropolitan Opera Ballet. Juilliard dance faculty since 1952.

COSI, LILIANA. Born in Milan, and entered LaScala School in 1950. Was exchange artist with Bolshoi; made debut as prima ballerina in 1965 in "Swan Lake" with Bolshoi. Named prima ballerina of LaScala in 1968, and Assoluta in 1970. Has appeared as guest artist with many companies.

COWEN, DONNA. Born May 2, 1949 in Birmingham, Ala. Studied with Gage Bush, Richard Englund, School of American Ballet, Joffrey. Made debut in 1968 with Huntington Dance Ensemble; joined Joffrey Ballet in 1969.

CRAGUN, RICHARD. Born in 1945 in Sacramento, Cal. Studied in London's Royal Ballet School and in Denmark. Joined Stuttgart Ballet in 1962 and quickly emerged as principal.

CRANE, DEAN. Born Jan. 5, 1932 in Logan, Iowa. Made professional debut at 14 as aerialist with Pollock Circus. Studied with Nimura, Dokoudovsky, Tudor and Petroff. Became first dancer and choreographer with Ballet Arts Co. Has also appeared on Bdwy and in clubs. Teaches.

CRASKE, MARGARET. Born in England. Studied with Cecchetti. Appeared with Diaghilev Ballets Russe, de Valois group. Became Ballet Mistress for Ballet Theatre in 1946, subsequently joined Met Opera Ballet School staff and became its assistant director. Currently with Manhattan School of Dance.

CRAVEY, CLARA. Born July 1, 1950 in West Palm Beach, Fla. Trained at Harkness School, and made debut with company in 1968.

CRISTOFORI, JON. Born in Buzzard's Bay, Mass., and began training at 15. Became lead student dancer in National Ballet of Wash., and toured with it until joining Joffrey Ballet. Left in 1969.

CROLL, TINA. Born Aug. 27, 1943 in N.Y.C. Bennington Col. graduate. Studied with Cunningham, Fonaroff. Debut 1964 in Kaufmann Hall. Has danced and choreographed for DTW since 1965. Formed own company in 1970 for which she choreographs.

CROPLEY, EILEEN. Born Aug. 25, 1932 in London. Studied with Sigurd Leeder, Maria Fay, Martha Graham, Don Farnworth. Made debut in 1966 with Paul Taylor Co.

CUNNINGHAM, JAMES. Born Apr. 1, 1938 in Toronto, Can. Graduate UToronto, London Academy Dramatic Arts. Studied at Martha Graham School. Choreographed for and performed with own company from 1967.

CUNNINGHAM, MERCE. Born Apr. 16 in Centralia, Wash. Studied at American School of Ballet. Professional debut as soloist with Martha Graham in 1940; with company through 1945. Began choreographing in 1946; in 1952 formed own company that has toured extensively every year. Teaches in his N.Y.C. studio.

CUNNINGHAM, RON. Born in Chicago; graduate Roosevelt U. Studied with Robert Lunnon, Eric Braun, Wigman, Cunningham, Humphrey, Weidman. Debut 1965 with Allegro American Ballet. Subsequently with Lucas Hoving, Kazuko Hirabayashi, Daniel Nagrin, Lotte Goslar, Zena Bethune, Ballet Concepts, Boston Ballet 1972.

CURRIER, RUTH. Born in 1926 in Ashland, Ohio. Studied with Doris Humphrey and Elsa Kahl. Made debut in 1949 with American Dance Festival. Soloist with Jose Limon Co. 1949–63. Since 1956 has been director-choreographer for own company which has toured U.S. Also teaches. Now director of Jose Limon Co.

CUTLER, ROBYN. Born May 25, 1948 in Atlanta, Ga. Attended Juilliard. Made debut 1972 with Jose Limon Co.

d'AMBOISE, JACQUES. Born July 28, 1934 in Dedham, Mass. Joined N.Y.C. Ballet at 15 after 7 years at School of American Ballet; rapidly rose to premier danseur in 1953. Has appeared in films and on TV and choreographed.

DANA, JERILYN. Born in Portland, Me., where she began dancing at 6. Studied with Boston Ballet, and graduated into company. Became soloist in 1969.

DANIAS, STARR. Born Mar. 18, 1949 in N.Y.C. Studied at School of Am. Ballet. Debut 1968 with London Festival Ballet, subsequently joined Joffrey Ballet in 1970.

DANIELIAN, LEON. Born Oct. 31, 1920 in N.Y.C. Studied with Mordkin and Fokine. Debut with Mordkin Ballet in 1937. Appeared with Original Ballet Russe, Ballet Russe de Monte Carlo, Ballet Theatre, Ballet des Champs Elysees, and San Francisco Ballet. Was choreographer-director of Ballet de Monte Carlo. Now with American Ballet Theatre School.

Eleanor D'Antuono

Jeff Duncan

Laura Dean

Michael Denard

Bettie de Jong

DANIELS, DANNY. Born in 1924 in Albany, N.Y. Studied with Thomas Sternfield, Jack Potteiger, Vincenzo Celli, Elisabeth Anderson-Ivantzova, Anatole Vilzak. Appeared in musicals, as soloist with orchestras, and Agnes de Mille Dance Theatre before becoming choreographer for TV and Bdwy musicals.

DANILOVA, ALEXANDRA. Born Nov. 20, 1906 in Peterhof, Russia. Graduate of Imperial School of Ballet, and became member of company. Subsequently with Balanchine's company, Les Ballets Russes de Diaghilev, Ballet Russe de Monte Carlo (both de Basil's and Massine's). Made N.Y.C. debut in 1948 at Met with Massine's company. Has appeared with and choreographed for N.Y.C. Ballet. In 1954 formed and toured with own company, The Concert Dance Group; choreographer for Met 1961–62. Now teaches.

DANTE, SHARON. Born Jan. 8, 1945 in Torrington, Conn. Graduate UHartford. Studied with Graham, Limon, Weidman, ABT School. Appeared with Charles Weidman, Larry Richardson, Rudy Perez, Jose Limon. Founder-Director of Nutmeg Ballet.

D'ANTUONO, ELEANOR. Born in 1939 in Cambridge, Mass. Danced with Ballet Russe de Monte Carlo for 6 years before joining Joffrey Ballet in 1960. Became member of American Ballet Theatre in 1961; principal since 1963.

DAVIDSON, ANDREA. Born in 1955 in Montreal, Can. Studied at Ntl. Ballet School, and joined company in 1971; Promoted to soloist in 1972.

DAVIS, MARTHA HILL. Born in East Palestine, O. Graduate Columbia, NYU. Debut with Martha Graham (1929–31). Director of Dance, Bennington (1934–42), NYU (1930–51), Juilliard since 1951. Founder Conn. Col. School of Dance and American Dance Festival.

DAVIS, ROBERT. Born March 13, 1934 in Durham, N.C. Studied at Wash. School of Ballet, and with Fokine, Franklin, and Joffrey. Debut in 1960 and has appeared as principal dancer with Washington Ballet, National Ballet of Canada, and Joffrey Ballet. Is also director and choreographer.

DEAN, LAURA. Born Dec. 3, 1945 on Staten Island, NY. Studied with Lucas Hoving, Muriel Stuart, Matt Mattox, Martha Graham, American Ballet Center, Mia Slavenska. Appeared with Paul Taylor, Paul Sanasardo. Formed own company in 1971.

DEANE, MICHAEL. Born Nov. 4, 1950 in NYC. Graduate UColo. Studied with Larry Boyette, Robert Christopher, Dan Wagoner, Joffrey School. Debut 1974 with Paul Taylor Co. Member Repertory Dance Theatre 1974–75.

DeANGELO, ANN MARIE. Born Oct. 1, 1952 in Pittston, Pa. Trained at San Francisco Ballet School and made debut with its company in 1970. Joined Joffrey 1972.

DE BOLT, JAMES. Born in Seattle, Wash. Studied with Marian and Illaria Ladre, and at U. Utah. Debut with Seattle's Aqua Theatre. Joined Joffrey Ballet in 1959, subsequently with N.Y.C. Opera Ballet, N.Y.C. Ballet 1961, Manhattan Festival Ballet 1965. Is also a costume designer and choreographer. Re-joined Joffrey Co. in 1968. Currently premier danseur with Oslo's Den Norske Opera.

DE GANGE, ANN. Born Sept. 22, 1952 in New London, Conn. Juilliard graduate. Studied with Corvino, Tudor, McGehee, Winters. Debut 1971 with Kazuko Hirabayashi, subsequently with Martha Graham Co. from 1972.

DE JONG, BETTIE. Born in Sumatra, and moved to Holland in 1947. Made debut with Netherlands Pantomime Co. Studied with Martha Graham and joined company; subsequently with Pearl Lang and Lucas Hoving. Joined Paul Taylor in 1962.

DELAMO, MARIO. Born during January 1946 in Havana, Cuba. Studied with May O'Donnell, Gertrude Shurr, Norman Walker. Debut 1966 with Norman Walker Co.; Glenn Tetley 1969; Alvin Ailey 1970; Martha Graham Co. 1972.

DELANGHE, GAY. Born Aug. 21, 1940 in Mt. Clemens, Mich. Studied at Severo School. Professional debut in 1960 and toured with "The Dancemakers." Choreographer, performer and teacher since 1965. Joined Lucas Hoving Co. in 1967.

de LAPPE, GEMZE. Born Feb. 28, 1922 in Woodhaven, Va. Attended Hunter Coll. and Ballet Arts School. Studied with Duncan, Fokine, Nimura, Caton, and Nemtchinova. Has appeared with Ballet Theatre and Agnes de Mille Dance Theatre and in Bdwy productions.

de LAVALLADE, CARMEN. Born March 6, 1931 in Los Angeles. Attended LACC, and studied with Lester Horton. Professional debut with Horton Dance Theatre. Bdwy debut in 1954. Has appeared with John Butler, Met Opera, de Lavallade-Ailey, Donald McKayle, and Ballet Theatre.

DELZA, SOPHIA. Born in N.Y.C. Studied in China. Professional debut 1953 in program of Chinese dances. Has toured world in concert, and been choreographic consultant for Met Opera, LCRep. Theatre, and Bdwy musicals.

de MAYO, FRED DOUGLASS. Studied at Abbey Theatre, and with Fokine, Youskevitch, Pereyaslavec, and in Paris with Preabrajenska. Appeared with National Ballet, Met. Opera Ballet. Founder of Newburgh Ballet. Now Director of Dance at West Point, and teaches at New Paltz SUNY.

de MILLE, AGNES. Born in N.Y.C. in 1909. Graduate of UCLA. Studied with Kosloff, Rambert, Karsavina, Tudor, Sokolova, Caton, Craske, Stroganova, and Dolmetsch. Debut in 1928 in own dance compositions and toured with them in Europe. Became leading choreographer for Bdwy. Created first ballet "Black Ritual" for Ballet Theatre in 1940. In 1953 organized Agnes de Mille Dance Theatre which toured U.S. Has also choreographed for Ballet Russe de Monte Carlo, and Royal Winnipeg Ballet. In 1973 organized and choreographs for Heritage Dance Theatre.

DENARD, MICHAEL. Born Nov. 5, 1944 in Dresden, Germany. Studied in Toulouse and Paris. Has appeared with Berlin Opera, and Paris Opera Ballets, with Bejart, and joined ABT (1971) as principal.

DENVERS, ROBERT. Born Mar. 9, 1942 in Antwerp. Studied with Nora Kiss, Tania Grantzeva, Peretti; joined Bejart's Ballet in 1963; Ntl. Ballet of Canada.

De SOTO, EDWARD. Born Apr. 20, 1939 in The Bronx. Attended Juilliard, AADA, New Dance Group Studio. Danced with Gloria Contreras, Judith Willis, Sophie Maslow, Art Bauman, Valerie Bettis, before joining Limon Co. in 1966.

DESTINE, JEAN-LEON. Born in Haiti, March 26, 1928. Attended Howard U. Made professional debut at Jacob's Pillow in 1949. Formed own company and has toured U.S., Europe, and Japan. Also teaches.

DIAMOND, MATTHEW. Born Nov. 26, 1951 in N.Y.C. Attended CCNY. Debut 1967 with Matteo and the Indo-American Dance Co. Subsequently with Norman Walker, N.Y.C. Opera, Louis Falco, Jose Limon 1975.

DI BONA, LINDA. Born July 21, 1946 in Quincy, Mass. Studied at Boston Ballet School and made debut with company in 1965. Joined Harkness Ballet 1972.

DICKSON, CHARLES. Born June 30, 1921 in Bellwood, Pa. Studied with Fokine, Massine, Dolin, Tudor, Volkova, Preobrajenska, Egorova, Balanchine, Volkova, Markova, Loring, Nijinska. Debut 1938 with Ballet Russe de Monte Carlo; AmBalTh 1940–42; Alicia Alonso Ballet 1952–55; Borovansky Ballet of Australia 1955–58; ballet master London Festival Ballet 1958–61; artistic director-ballet master Ballet Municipal de Santiago 1963–76; from 1971 director Metropolitan Academy, and Metropolitan Ballet Co.

DISHONG, ZOLA. Born Aug. 4, 1945 in Albany, Cal. Studied with Lew Christensen, Anatole Vilzak, Michael Lland, Patricia Wilde. Debut 1962 with San Francisco Ballet; subsequently ABT 1967.

DOBRIEVICH, LOUBA. Born Feb. 9, 1934 in Bajina Basta, Yugoslavia. Studied at Belgrade Academy of Dance. Debut 1954 with Opera Zagreb; subsequently with Paris Theatre Ballet 1958, Maurice Bejart Co. from 1959.

DOBRIEVICH, PIERRE. Born Dec. 27, 1931 in Veles, Yugoslavia. Studied at Etudes de Droit. Debut 1955 with Opera Zagreb; subsequently with Paris Theatre Ballet 1957, Ludmila Cherina 1958, Les Etoiles de Paris 1959, Maurice Bejart from 1960.

DOBSON, DEBORAH. Born June 23, 1950 in Sacramento, Ca. Studied at San Francisco Ballet Sch., Sch. of Am. Ballet. Debut 1968 with Andre Eglevsky Co., joined ABT in 1969; promoted to soloist in 1973; joined Stuttgart 1975.

Fred de Mayo   Carmen de Lavallade   James Dunne   Deborah Dobson   Richard Englund

DOKOUDOVSKY, VLADIMIR. Born in 1922 in Monte Carlo. Studied with Preobrajenska; made debut at 13; became soloist with Ballet Russe de Monte Carlo, Mordkin Ballet, Ballet Theatre. Premier danseur with Original Ballet Russe (1942–52). Has choreographed several ballets. Now teaches.

DOLIN, ANTON. Born Sydney Francis Patrick Chippendall Healey-Kay in Slinfold, Sussex, Eng. July 27, 1904. Studied with Astafieva, Nijinska. With Diaghileff Company 1921–9, principal dancer with Sadler's Wells 1931–5. Ballet Russe 1939, 1946–8. Founder, director, and dancer with Markova-Dolin Co. 1935–8, 1945, 1947–8. Danced, restaged, and choreographed for Ballet Theatre from inception to 1946. 1949 organized and danced with London Festival Ballet until 1961. Currently artistic adviser of Les Grands Ballets Canadiens.

DOLLAR, WILLIAM. Born Apr. 20, 1907 in East St. Louis, Mo. Studied with Fokine, Mordkin, Balanchine, Vladimiroff, and Volinine. Lead dancer with Philadelphia Opera, American Ballet 1936–7, Ballet Caravan 1936–8, Ballet Theatre 1940, American Ballet Caravan 1941, New Opera Co. 1942, Ballet International 1944, ballet master for American Concert Ballet 1943, Ballet Society 1946, Grand Ballet de Monte Carlo 1948, N.Y.C. Ballet. Has choreographed many works, and teaches.

DONN, JORGE. Born Feb. 28, 1947 in Buenos Aires. Attended School of Teatro de Colon. Appeared in musicals before joining Bejart Ballet in 1963, rising to leading male dancer.

DORADO, THIERRY. Born in 1950 in Paris, France. Studied with Nina Tikanova, Paris Opera School. Debut with Paris Opera Ballet; appeared with Nice Opera Ballet, Ballets de Roland Petit, Stuttgart (1969–70). Joined Ballet West as principal 1973.

DOUGLAS, HELEN. Studied with Maggie Black, Karoly Zsedenyi, Vincenzo Celli, Margaret Craske. Debut 1966 with Met Opera Ballet. Joined Joffrey 1966–68; ABT 1968–71, Eliot Feld 1973. Also lecturer.

DOUGLAS, SCOTT. Born June 16, 1927 in El Paso, Tex. Studied with Lester Horton and Ruth St. Denis. Appeared with San Francisco Ballet, Ballets U.S.A., John Butler, Ballet Theatre, Nederlands National Ballet, Glen Tetley Co. Ballet Master for ABT.

DOWELL, ANTHONY. Born in London Feb. 16, 1943. Studied with June Hampshire, entered Royal Ballet School at 10. Debut as hunter in "Swan Lake" at Covent Garden Opera House. Joined Sadler's Wells Opera Ballet, and Royal Ballet in 1961. Is now a principal.

DOYLE, DESMOND. Born June 16, 1932 in South Africa. Joined Royal Ballet in 1951. Became soloist in 1953; is now a principal and teacher.

DRAPER, PAUL. Born 1909 in Florence, Italy. Began studies at early age, and became tap soloist, elevating it to ballet-tap concert form. Made debut in 1932 in London. Continues to give solo performances, teaches, and is photographer.

DRIVER, SENTA. Born Sept. 5, 1942 in Greenwich, Conn. Graduate Bryn Mawr, Ohio State U. Studied with Maggie Black, Don Farnworth, and at O'Donnell-Shur Studio. Joined Paul Taylor Company in 1967, left in 1973 to choreograph.

DU BOULAY, CHRISTINE. Born in 1923 in Ealing, Eng. Trained in Sadler's Wells Ballet School. Soloist with International Ballet before joining Sadler's Wells. Settled in U.S. in 1950, and with husband, Richard Ellis, became founders and directors of Illinois Ballet Co.

DUBREUIL, ALAIN. Born in Monte Carlo, Mar. 4, 1944. Studied at mother's ballet school until awarded scholarship at Arts Educational School (1960). Joined London Festival Ballet in 1962 and became soloist in 1964.

DUDLEY, JANE. Dancer-choreographer. Born in N.Y.C. in 1912. Studied with Martha Graham, Hanya Holm, Louis Horst. Leading dancer with Graham Co. (1937–44). With Sophie Maslow and William Bales, formed concert Dance Trio. Retired in 1954 to teach.

DUELL, DANIEL. Born Aug. 17, 1952 in Rochester, NY. Attended Fordham U., School of American Ballet. Debut 1971 with Edward Villella, subsequently with Eglevsky Ballet, Dayton Ballet, Lincoln Center Repertory Dancers, NYCB 1974.

DUFFY, DIANE. Born in Philadelphia, Pa. Studied at Pa. Ballet Sch., Harkness House. Debut at 15 with Pennsylvania Ballet; joined Harkness, National, Eliot Feld Ballet (1973).

DUNCAN, JEFF. Born Feb. 4, 1930 in Cisco, Tex. Attended N. State Tex. U., studied with Holm, Nikolais, Limon, Cunningham, Schwetzoff, Tomkins, Joffrey. Assistant to Doris Humphrey and Anna Sokolow. Debut 1952 at Henry St. Playhouse. Has appeared with New Dance Group, Juilliard Dance Theatre, Anna Sokolow, Jeff Duncan Dance Co., and is founder-director of Dance Theatre Workshop. Has also appeared in Bdwy musicals.

DUNHAM, KATHERINE. Born June 22, 1912, in Chicago. Debut with Chicago Opera Co. in 1933. Bdwy debut 1940 in "Cabin In The Sky." Formed own company for which she choreographed; toured with it in 1943, and subsequently in 57 other countries. Founded Katherine Dunham School of Cultural Arts in N.Y.C. in 1943.

DUNNE, JAMES. Born in Waldwick, N.J. Studied with Irene Fokine, and at School of American Ballet, Harkness House. Joined Harkness Ballet for 4 years, then Joffrey Ballet.

EBBELAAR, HAN. Born Apr. 16, 1943 in Hoorn, Holland. Studied with Max Dooyes and Benjamin Harkarvy. Danced with Nederlans Dans Theater before joining American Ballet Theatre in 1968 as soloist; promoted to principal in 1969, Dutch Natl. Ballet (1970).

EBBIN, MICHAEL. Born June 5, 1945 in Bermuda. Studied at Patricia Gray's, National Ballet, American Ballet, American Ballet Center, and Harkness Schools. Has danced with Eleo Pomare, Cleo Quitman, Australian Dance Theatre, Anna Sokolow, Talley Beatty, and Rod Rodgers companies, and appeared on Bdwy. Joined Ailey company 1972.

EDWARDS, LESLIE. Born Aug. 7, 1916 in Teddington, Eng. Studied with Marie Rambert at Sadler's Wells School. Debut 1933 with Vic-Wells Ballet, subsequently joined Ballet Rambert, Royal Ballet. Now teaches and makes guest appearances.

EGLEVSKY, ANDRE. Born in Moscow Dec. 21, 1917. Received training in France. At 19 joined Rene Blum's Ballet de Monte Carlo. Came to U.S. in 1937, and after appearing with all major companies, joined Ballet Theatre. In 1947 appeared with Grand Ballet du Marquis de Cuevas. In 1950 joined N.Y.C. Ballet and danced leading male roles until 1958, also created "Scotch Symphony" and other ballets for the company. In 1955, with his wife, prima ballerina Leda Anchutina, opened school in Massapequa, L.I., and in 1960 formed local classical ballet company which he directs.

EISENBERG, MARY JANE. Born Mar. 28, 1951 in Erie, Pa. Attended Hunter, New School. Studied with Graham, ABT, Harkness schools. Debut 1969 with Glen Tetley, subsequently with Keith Lee, Contemporary Dance Ensemble, Louis Falco.

ELLIS, RICHARD. Born 1918 in London. At 15 joined Vic-Wells Ballet which became Sadler's Wells Ballet. Important member of company until 1952. After touring U.S. with company in 1949–50, settled in Chicago. With wife, Christine Du Boulay, became founders and co-directors of Illinois Ballet Co.

ENCKELL, THOMAS. Born in Helsinki, Finland, Oct. 14, 1942. Studied with Margaret Craske. Professional debut with Met Opera Ballet in 1962. Joined Finnish Natl. Opera Ballet 1965. Manhattan Festival Ballet 1966.

ENGLUND, RICHARD. Born in Seattle, Wash. Attended Harvard, Juilliard. Studied with Tudor, Graham, Volkova. Appeared with Limon, Met Opera, Natl. Ballet of Canada, ABT, and in musicals. Currently teaches and choreographs.

ENTERS, ANGNA. Dancer, choreographer, and mime was born in 1907 in N.Y.C. Created own style of dance and pantomime that she has performed all over the world. Is also a writer and painter.

ERDMAN, JEAN. Born in Honolulu, Hawaii. Graduate of Sarah Lawrence College (1938). Studied at Bennington, American School of Ballet, Hisamatsu, Martha Graham, Pukui and Huapala Hawaiian Dance Schools. Professional debut 1938 with Martha Graham, and as a choreographer in 1942. Organized own company in 1950, and made annual tours through 1960. World tour 1963–5 with "The Coach With The Six Insides" which she conceived and staged. Head of NYU Dance Dept. for 5 yrs.

ERICKSON, BETSY. Born in Oakland, Cal. Attended Cal. State U., San Francisco Ballet School. Debut with San Francisco Ballet. Joined American Ballet Theatre 1967; returned to SF Ballet 1973.

ESTELLE & ALFONSO. Born in N.Y.: trained with Haakon, Mattox, Juarez, LaSylphe, Nettles, Chileno, Wills, Thomas. Toured widely as team. Currently operate school in Poughkeepsie, N.Y., and artistic directors for Mid-Hudson Regional Ballet.

ESTNER, ROBERT. Born in North Hollywood, Calif. Attended Los Angeles City Valley Jr. Col. Studied with Robert Rossalatt, Natalie Clare, Andre Tremaine, Carmalita Maracci, and at ABC. Appeared with Ballet Concerto, Pacific Ballet, Ballet La Jeunesse, before joining Joffrey Co.

EVANS, BILL. Born Apr. 11, 1946 in Lehi, Utah. Graduate Univ. Utah. Studied at Harkness House, American Dance Center, ABT School. Made debut in 1966 with Ruth Page Ballet. Joined Repertory Dance Theatre in 1967 as dancer and choreographer.

EVERETT, ELLEN. Born in Springfield, Ill. June 19, 1942. Studied in Chicago and School of American Ballet. Professional debut 1958 with Ruth Page's Chicago Opera Ballet. Soloist with American Ballet Theatre from 1967. Raised to principal 1973. Has also appeared on Bdwy.

FADEYECHEV, NICOLAI. Born in Moscow in 1933. Studied at Bolshoi School and joined company in 1952; became soloist in 1953, and subsequently premier danseur.

FAISON, GEORGE. Born Dec. 21, 1945 in Washington, D.C. Attended Howard U. Studied with Louis Johnson, Claude Thompson, Alvin Ailey, Dudley Williams, Elizabeth Hodes. Appeared on Bdwy and with Universal Dance Experience (1971).

FALCO, LOUIS. Born in N.Y.C.; studied with Limon, Weidman, Graham, and at American Ballet Theatre School. Danced, choreographed, and toured with Jose Limon, Co., as principal dancer for 10 years, choreographed for other groups, and own company which he formed in 1967.

FALLET, GENEVIEVE. Born Aug. 2, 1943 in Switzerland. Studied at Royal Ballet, and with Yuriko, Cunningham, Wagoner, DTW. Has danced with London and Paris companies, with Frances Alenikoff, and solo.

FALLIS, BARBARA. Born in 1924 in Denver, Colo. Moved to London in 1929. Studied at Mona Clague School. Vic-Wells and Vilzak-Shollar Schools. Debut 1938 in London. Danced with Vic-Wells Ballet 1938–40; Ballet Theatre in 1941; Ballet Alicia Alonso (1948–52), N.Y.C. Ballet (1953–58). Now teaches.

FARBER, VIOLA. Born in Heidelberg. Ger., Feb. 25, 1931. Attended American U. and Black Mt. College. Studied with Katherine Litz, Merce Cunningham, Alfredo Corvino, and Margaret Craske. Debut 1952 with Merce Cunningham, subsequently with Paul Taylor, and Katherine Litz. More recently, choreographing, and guest artist with Merce Cunningham.

FARRELL, SUZANNE. Born Roberta Sue Ficker Aug. 16, 1945 in Cincinnati. Began ballet studies in Cincinnati, subsequently attending School of American Ballet. After 15 months joined N.Y.C. Ballet, and became a principal dancer in 1965. Joined National Ballet of Canada in 1970, Bejart (1970), returned to NYCB in 1975.

FAXON, RANDALL. Born Sept. 26, 1950 in Harrisburg. Pa. Studied with Elizabeth Rockwell. Martha Graham, Paul Sanasardo, Alfredo Corvin, and at Juilliard. Debut 1969 with Ethel Winter; joined Lucas Hoving in 1970.

FEDICHEVA, KALERIYA. Born in Leningrad in July 1937. Attended Kirov School; joined company in 1956; Resigned in 1974 and came to U.S. in 1975. Appeared with Terpsichore Co.

FEDOROVA, NINA. Born Apr. 24, 1958 in Philadelphia, Pa. Studied at Pa. Ballet School, Sch. of Am. Ballet. Made Debut with NYC Ballet in 1974.

FEIGENHEIMER, IRENE. Born June 16, 1946 in N.Y.C. Attended Hunter Col. Studied with Holm, Graham, Cunningham, ABC. Debut 1965 with Met Opera Ballet, subsequently danced with Merry-Go-Rounders, Ruth Currier, Anna Sokolow, Cliff Keuter, Don Redlich.

FELD, ELIOT. Born 1943 in Brooklyn. Studied with Richard Thomas and at School of American Ballet. Appeared with N.Y.C. Ballet, and on Bdwy before joining American Ballet Theatre in 1963. Co-founder (1969), director, dancer, and choreographer for American Ballet Co. Rejoined ABT in 1971. Debuted Eliot Feld Ballet 1974.

FERNANDEZ, ROYES. Born July 15, 1929 in New Orleans. Studied with Lelia Hallers and Vincenzo Celli. Appeared with Ballet Russe, Markova-Dolin, Ballet Alicia Alonso, de Cuevas' Ballet, before joining Ballet Theatre. Premier danseur since 1957. Retired in 1973 to teach. Has appeared with several companies as guest artist.

FIBICH, FELIX. Born May 8, 1917 in Warsaw, Poland; attended dance and theatre schools, and made professional debut there in 1936. Became dancer-choreographer in 1939. Formed own company that has toured widely with Israeli and Chassidic dancers. Also teaches.

FIFIELD, ELAINE. Born in Sydney, Aust. Studied at Sadler's Wells, RAD. Debut 1948 with Sadler's Wells Co., subsequently appeared with Royal Ballet, Australian Ballet.

FIGUEROA, ALFONSO. Born May 24, 1947 in N.Y.C. Graduate Boston Cons. Studied with Virginia Williams, Thomas-Fallis, Pearl Lang. Debut 1967 with Boston Ballet; subsequently Pearl Lang, American Ballet 1968, Alvin Ailey 1970, Boston Ballet 1971.

FILIPOV, ALEXANDER. Born Mar. 19, 1947 in Moscow. Studied at Leningrad Kirov School. Debut with Moiseyev Ballet, defected and appeared with Pa. Ballet, Eglevsky Ballet, ABT (1970), Pittsburgh Ballet 1971, San Francisco Ballet 1974.

FISHER, NELLE. Born Dec. 10, 1920 in Berkeley, Cal. Appeared with Martha Graham Co., in Bdwy musicals; choreographs and teaches.

FITZGERALD, HESTER. Born Oct. 1, 1939 in Cleveland, O. Trained with Nedjedin, Levinoff, and at Ballet Russe, American, and Ballet Theatre schools. Debut with Ballet Russe 1956; subsequently with N.Y.C. Ballet, ABT, and Harkness Ballet.

FLINDT, FLEMMING. Born Sept. 30, 1936 in Copenhagen. Entered Danish Royal Ballet School at 10; became member at 18. Invited by Harald Lander to appear in London; returned to Danish Ballet and became leading dancer before joining Paris Opera as danseur etoile, and choreographing. Ranks among world's greatest male dancers, and has achieved recognition as choreographer. Became director of Royal Danish Ballet in 1966.

FONAROFF, NINA. Born in N.Y.C. in 1914. Studied with Martha Graham, at School of American Ballet. Danced with Graham (1937–46) before forming own company in 1945. Is now teacher-choreographer.

FONTEYN, MARGOT. Born May 18, 1919 in Surrey, Eng. Began training at 14 with Astafieva, and a few months later entered Sadler's Wells School. Solo debut with company in 1934 in "The Haunted Ballroom." In 1935, succeeded to ballerina roles of Markova. Unrivaled in roles of Aurora and Chloe. Made Dame of British Empire by Queen Elizabeth. Guest star of Royal Ballet, and considered Prima Ballerina Assoluta of the world.

FOREMAN, LAURA. Born in Los Angeles. U. Wisc. graduate. Danced with Tamiris-Nagrin, Marion Scott, Harriet Anne Gray, Ann Halprin. Director of Laura Foreman Dance Company; Founder/Director of Choreographers Theatre/ChoreoConcerts; director New School Dance Dept.

FOSSE, BOB. Born in Chicago June 23, 1927. Appeared in musicals and clubs before becoming outstanding choreographer for Bdwy, films, and TV.

FOSTER, RORY. Born Feb. 3, 1947 in Chicago, Ill. Attended Ill. Benedictine Col. Studied with Robert Lunnon, Doreen Tempest, Vincenzo Celli. Debut 1962 with Allegro American Ballet; joined American Ballet Theatre 1970.

FOWLER, TOM. Born Feb. 18, 1949 in Long Beach, Cal. Graduate U. Cin. Studied with David Howard, Claudia Corday, David McLean, Margaret Black, Richard Thomas, Harkness House. Debut 1971 with American Ballet Company. Joined Joffrey 1974.

FRACCI, CARLA. Born Aug. 20, 1936 in Milan, Italy. Began training at 8 at La Scala with Edda Martignoni, Vera Volkova, and Esmee Bulnes. Became prima ballerina of La Scala in 1958; joined London Festival Ballet as guest artist. Now permanent guest artist with American Ballet Theatre.

FRALEY, INGRID. Born Nov. 1, 1949 in Paris, France. Studied at San Francisco Ballet, and made debut with company in 1964. Subsequently with Kiel-Lubeck Opera Ballet, Fokine Ballet, Eglevsky Ballet, joined American Ballet Theatre 1969; Joffrey 1975.

FRANKEL, EMILY. Born in N.Y.C. Studied with Weidman, Holm, Graham, Craske, Tudor, and Daganova. Professional debut 1950. Founder, director, choreographer, and dancer with Dance Drama Co. since 1955. Has made 8 transcontinental tours, a State Dept. sponsored tour of Europe, and British Arts Council tour of England and Scotland.

FRANKLIN, FREDERIC. Born in Liverpool, Eng. in 1914. Studied with Legat, Kyasht, and Pruzina. Made debut as child dancer; went to London at 17; appeared in music halls, night clubs, and musicals before joining Markova-Dolin Co. 1935–7. Premier danseur with Ballet Russe de Monte Carlo from 1938; became its ballet master in 1944. Artistic adviser ABT (1961). Director National Ballet (1962–74); Artistic director Pittsburgh Ballet Theatre from 1974.

FRAZER, SUSAN. Born in NYC. Studied at Sch. of Am. Ballet, and with Jean Hamilton, Vladimir Dokoudovsky. Joined National Ballet 1968; promoted to soloist 1972. Joined ABT 1974.

FREDERICK, JULIA. Born in Boston. Studied and performed with Boston Ballet, Harkness Ballet, N.Y.C. Ballet. Also danced with Penn. Ballet, Garden State Ballet, and N.Y.C. Opera Co. Resident soloist with Hartford Ballet.

FREEDMAN, LAURIE. Born July 7, 1945 in N.Y.C. Graduate Bennington Col. Studied with Graham, Cunningham, Zena Rommett. Debut 1967 with Merry-Go-Rounders, subsequently with Batsheva Dance Co. (1968).

FREEMAN, FRANK. Born July 16, 1945 in Bangalore, India. Studied at Royal Ballet School. Joined company in 1963. Joined London Festival Ballet as soloist in 1971.

Robert Estner	Nina Fedorova	Royes Fernandez	Mimi Garrard	Lonny Joseph Gordon

FUENTE, LUIS. Born in 1944 in Madrid where he began studies at early age. Joined Antonio's Ballets de Madrid in 1963; Joffrey Ballet 1964–1970. National Ballet (1970) as principal; London Festival Ballet 1972.

FUERSTNER, FIONA. Born Apr. 24, 1936 in Rio de Janeiro. Attended San Francisco State College. Studied at San Francisco Ballet School (debut with company 1952). School of American Ballet, Ballet Rambert, Royal Ballet, Ballet Theatre schools. Has danced with Les Grands Ballets Canadiens, San Francisco, N.Y.C. Center, and Philadelphia Opera ballet companies. Principal dancer with Pennsylvania Ballet. Became Ballet Mistress in 1974.

GABLE, CHRISTOPHER. Born 1940 in London, began studies at Royal Ballet School. At 16 joined Sadler's Wells Opera Ballet, and next year Covent Garden Opera Ballet. In 1957 became member of Royal Ballet and at 19 advanced to soloist. Retired in 1967 to act.

GAIN, RICHARD. Born in Belleville, Ill. Jan. 24, 1939. Studied with Lalla Baumann, and Martha Graham. Professional debut with St. Louis Municipal Opera, followed by musicals. Became member of Graham Co. in 1961, also danced with Jazz Ballet Theatre, Lotte Goslar, Sophie Maslow, and Pearl Lang, and formed concert group "Triad" that performed in N.Y. and on tour. Joined Joffrey Co. in 1964; ABT in 1967. Teaches at N.C. School of Arts.

GARDNER, BARBARA. Born June 7, 1940 in Lynbrook, NY. Graduate Stanford U. Studied with Wigman, Sanasardo, Cunningham. Has appeared with Nikolais, Marion Scott, Phoebe Neville, Elina Mooney, and her own company. Also teaches.

GARRARD, MIMI. Born in Gastonia, N.C. Attended Sweet Briar College. Studied at Henry St. Playhouse, with Julia Barashkova. Angelina Romet. Has appeared with Alwin Nikolais and Murray Louis companies, and own company for which she choreographs.

GARTH, MIDI. Born in N.Y.C. Studied with Francesca de Cotelet, Sybil Shearer, Louis Horst. Has choreographed and performed solo concerts in N.Y. and on tour. Also teaches.

GARY, M'LISS. Born Nov. 8, 1951 in Lisbon, Port. Graduate Natl. Ballet Academy. Studied with Oleg Tupine, Richard Thomas, Barbara Fallis. Debut 1969 with National Ballet, joined American Ballet Co. in 1971.

GAYLE, DAVID. Born July 10, 1942 in Yorkshire, Eng. Appeared in Covent Garden opera ballets before joining Royal Ballet. Left in 1970 to teach in Buffalo.

GENNARO, PETER. Born 1924 in Metairie, La. Studied at American Theatre Wing. Debut with Chicago San Carlo Opera 1948, and Bdwy bow same year. After several musicals and TV, choreographed "Seventh Heaven" in 1955. Is much in demand as dancer and choreographer on television.

GENTRY, EVE. Born Aug. 20, in Los Angeles. Used own name Henrietta Greenhood until 1945. Studied with Holm, Graham, Humphrey, Weidman, Tamiris, Barashkova, at Ballet Arts Studio, and American Ballet Center. Debut with Hanya Holm. Since 1949, director-choreographer-soloist with own company.

GERMAINE, DIANE. Born July 5, 1944 in N.Y.C. Studied with Martha Graham. May O'Donnell, Norman Walker, Paul Sanasardo. Debut with Sanasardo in 1963. Has appeared in concert with Norman Walker, and teaches.

GEVA, TAMARA. Born 1908 in St. Petersburg, Russia. Studied at Maryinsky Theatre. Joined Diaghilev. Came to U.S., signed by Ziegfeld, subsequently appeared in musicals and films and with American Can Ballet.

GIELGUD, MAINA. Born Jan. 14, 1945 in London. Studied with Karsavina, Idzikovski, Egorova, Gsovsky, Hightower. Debut 1961 with Petit Ballet, subsequently with Ballet De Marquis de Cuevas, Miskovitch, Grand Ballet Classique, joined Bejart Ballet in 1967.

GILPIN, JOHN. Born in 1930 in Southsea, Eng. Was child actor; joined Ballet Rambert 1945, London's Festival ballet 1950, becoming artistic director and principal dancer. Guest artist with ABT and Royal Ballet. Resigned as artistic director Festival Ballet but remains premier danseur.

GIORDANO, GUS. Born July 10, 1930 in St. Louis. Graduate U. Mo. Debut at Roxy N.Y.C., 1948, subsequently appeared in musicals on TV before becoming choreographer. Currently director of Giordano Dance Studio in Evanston, Ill., and his own company.

GLADSTEIN, ROBERT. Born Jan. 16, 1943 in Berkeley, Calif. Attended San Francisco State College, and studied at San Francisco Ballet School. Became member of San Francisco Ballet in 1960 and choreographed 13 ballets. Joined American Ballet Theatre in 1967, became soloist in 1969. Rejoined S.F. Ballet 1970.

GLASSMAN, WILLIAM. Born 1945 in Boston and began dance studies at 7. Scholarship to School of American Ballet. Studied with Alfredo Corvino and Margaret Craske. Appeared in musicals, with N.Y.C. Opera, and on TV, before joining American Ballet Theatre in 1963. Promoted to soloist 1965. Now with Niagara Frontier Ballet.

GLENN, LAURA. Born Aug. 25, 1945 in N.Y.C. Graduate Juilliard. Joined Limon Co. in 1964. Has also performed with Ruth Currier, Sophie Maslow, Valerie Bettis, and Contemporary Dance Sextet. Joined Jose Limon Co. 1975.

GLUCK, RENA. Born Jan. 14, 1933. Juilliard graduate. Studied with Graham, Tudor, Horst, Blanche Evans. Founding member of Batsheva Dance Co. in 1963. Also choreographs.

GLUSHAK, NANETTE. Born Dec. 31, 1951 in NYC. Studied at School of Am. Ballet. Made debut with American Ballet Theatre in 1967. Promoted to soloist 1973.

GODREAU, MIGUEL. Born Oct. 17, 1946 in Ponce, P.R. Studied at Joffrey Ballet Center, School of American Ballet, Ballet Russe, and with Martha Graham. Debut 1964 with First American Dance Co., subsequently with Ailey, McKayle, and Harkness Ballet. After appearing on Bdwy, organized and danced with own company in 1969. Returned to Ailey Co. in 1970. Left to appear in London, and as principal with Birgit Cullberg Co. in Sweden.

GODUNOV, ALEKSANDR. Born in 1950 on the island of Sakhalin, north of Japan. Began training in Riga, Latvia. Debut at 17 with Igor Moiseyev's Young Classical Ballet. Made debut with Bolshoi in 1970 as principal.

GOLLNER, NANA. Born 1920 in El Paso, Texas. Studied with Kosloff. Soloist with American Ballet 1935, de Basil's Ballet Russe 1935–6. Blum's Ballet Russe 1936–7. Ballet Theatre 1939–48. Only American to achieve rank of ballerina in foreign country.

GOODMAN, ERIKA. Born Oct. 9 in Philadelphia. Trained at School of American Ballet, and American Ballet Center. Debut with N.Y.C. Ballet 1965. Appeared with Pa. Ballet, and Boston Ballet before joining Joffrey Ballet in 1967.

GOPAL, RAM. Born Nov. 20. Hindu dancer, came to U.S. in 1938, and with own company has toured world as its soloist. Operates own school.

GORDON, LONNY JOSEPH. Born in Edinburg, Tex. Graduate of U.Tex. and U.Wisc. Studied at Grand Kabuki Theatre in Tokyo, and with Koisaburo Nishikawa, Richo Nishikawa. Has given solo performances throughout Japan and U.S. Director Southern Repertory Dance Theater.

GORDON, MARVIN. Born in N.Y.C. Graduate Queens Col. Studied with New Dance Group, Met Opera School, Graham, Humphrey, and Weidman. Appeared on Bdwy and TV, in concert with Doris Humphrey, and Pearl Lang. Choreographed before becoming founder-director of Ballet Concerts, that has appeared in N.Y. and on tour throughout U.S.

GOSLAR, LOTTIE. Born in Dresden, Ger. Studied at Mary Wigman School. Toured Europe as dance mime before coming to U.S. in 1937. Formed own pantomime company for tours of U.S. and Europe. Also teaches.

GOTSHALKS, JURY. Born in Riga, Latvia. Studied at Latvian Natl. Ballet School. Appeared with National Ballet of Canada, Les Grands Ballets Canadiens, N.Y.C. Opera. Since 1968, teacher at U.Wisc., and director of Milwaukee Ballet.

GOVRIN, GLORIA. Born Sept. 10, 1942 in Newark, N.J. Studied at Tarassof School, American Ballet Academy, School of American Ballet. Joined N.Y.C. Ballet in 1957. Promoted to soloist at 19.

GOYA, CAROLA. Born in N.Y.C. Studied with Fokine, Otero, LaQuica, Maria Esparsa. Danced with Met Opera before solo debut as Spanish dancer in 1927. Appeared with Greco before partnership with Matteo in 1954.

181

GRAHAM, MARTHA. Born May 11, 1893 in Pittsburgh. Studied at Denishawn School of Dance; made debut with its company in 1919, and danced with them until 1923. First choreographed and appeared in N.Y.C. in a program of 18 original works in 1926, followed by annual concerts until 1938. A founder of Bennington (Vt.) Dance Festival where she staged several premieres of her works. Formed own company with which she has made numerous successful tours throughout world. Founded Martha Graham School of Contemporary Dance in 1927, and remains its director. Has created over 100 dances.

GRANT, ALEXANDER. Born Feb. 22, 1925 in Wellington. New Zealand. Entered Sadler's Wells School in 1946, and five months later joined company. Has created more major roles than any other male dancer with Royal Ballet.

GRAY, DIANE. Born May 29, 1944 in Painesville, Ohio. Attended Juilliard. Studied with Graham, Tudor, Youskevitch, Schwezoff, Melikova, Hinkson, Winter, McGehee, Ross. Debut 1964 with Martha Graham Co. Has also appeared with Helen McGehee, Yuriko, Pearl Lang, Sophie Maslow, Jeff Duncan.

GRECO, JOSE. Born Dec. 23, 1919 in Montorio-Nei-Frentani, Compobasso, Italy. Studied with Mme. Veola in N.Y.C., Argentinita and La Quica in Madrid. Debut as soloist 1935 with Salmaggi Opera Co. Partner with La Argentinita 1943–4. Pilar Lopez 1946–8, before organizing own company in 1949, with which he has become internationally famous.

GREENFIELD, AMY. Born July 8, 1940 in Boston. Studied with Graham, Cunningham, Fonaroff, Robert Cohan, American Ballet Center. Made debut in 1965. Has appeared in concert and with DTW.

GREGORY, CYNTHIA. Born July 8 in Los Angeles where she studied with Lorraine, Maracci, Panaieff, and Rossellat. Danced with Santa Monica Civic Ballet, L.A. Civic Light Opera in 1961 joined San Francisco Ballet, subsequently S.F. Opera Ballet, and American Ballet Theatre in 1965, became principal in 1968.

GREY, BERYL. Born in Highgate, England, June 11, 1927. Began studies at Sadler's Wells Ballet School, and at 15 danced "Swan Lake" with its company. Left in 1957 but returned for guest appearances. Appointed in 1966 to head Arts Education School, London. Director London Festival Ballet, made Commander British Empire in 1973.

GRIFFITHS, LEIGH-ANN. Born Dec. 5, 1948 in Johannesburg, S.A. Studied at Royal Ballet School. Joined Stuttgart Ballet in 1968.

GRIGOROVICH, YURI. Born in Leningrad Jan. 2, 1927. Graduated from Leningrad Ballet School and became one of leading soloists with Kirov Co. In 1964 became choreographer for Moscow Bolshoi Ballet Co.

GROMAN, JANICE. Born in New Britain, Conn. Joined N.Y.C. Ballet at 16. Later with ABT, and First Chamber Dance Quartet.

GUERARD, LEO. Born Jan. 18, 1937 in Boston, Mass. Studied at School of American Ballet. Debut 1952 with ABT; subsequently with Grand Ballet de Cuevas 1957, Skandinavian Ballet 1960, Royal Winnipeg Ballet 1963, Western Theatre Ballet 1964, Intl. Ballet Caravan 1968, Boston Ballet 1968.

GUNN, NICHOLAS. Born Aug. 28, 1947 in Bklyn. Studied with Ellen Segal, Helen McGehee, June Lewis, Don Farnworth. Appeared with Stuart Hodes Co. Joined Paul Taylor Co. in 1969.

GUTELIUS, PHYLLIS. Born in Wilmington, Del. Studied with Schwetzoff, Tudor, Graham. Joined Graham Company in 1962. Has appeared on Bdwy, with Glen Tetley, Yuriko, Sophie Maslow, John Butler.

GUTHRIE, NORA. Born Jan. 2, 1950 in N.Y.C. Studied with Marjorie Mazia, Martha Graham, and at NYU. Debut 1970 with Jean Erdman Co.

GUZMAN, PASCHAL. Born in Arecibo, P.R. Attended Harkness, National Ballet, Graham, Dalcroze schools. Debut 1964 with National Ballet, subsequently with Baltimore Ballet, Washington Dance Repertory, Penn. Ballet, New America Ballet, Ballet Concerto, Downtown Ballet.

GYORFI, VICTORIA. Born in Wenatchee, Wash. Studied at San Francisco Ballet, and made debut with its company. Appeared with Munich Ballet, Bayerische Staats Oper, and returned to SF Ballet.

HAAKON, PAUL. Born in Denmark in 1914 Studied at Royal Danish Ballet School, with Fokine, Mordkin, and at School of American Ballet. Debut with Fokine in 1927. Danced and toured with Anna Pavlova. Became premier danseur with American Ballet in 1935. Appeared in musicals and nightclubs. In 1963 became ballet master and instructor of Jose Greco Co.

HACKNEY, PEGGY. Born Dec. 28, 1944 in Miami, Fla. Graduate Duke U., Sarah Lawrence Col. Has performed with Deborah Jowitt, Micki Goodman, Jose Limon Co., Tina Croll, and Jeff Duncan. Teaches extensively.

HAISMA, RICHARD. Born Aug. 6, 1945 in Grand Rapids, Mich. Studied with Nancy Hauser and appeared with her company before joining Murray Louis Co.

HALL, YVONNE. Born Mar. 30, 1956 in Jamaica, WI. Studied at Dance Theatre of Harlem and made debut with company in 1969.

HAMILTON, PETER. Born in Trenton, N.J. Sept. 12, 1915. Attended Rutgers. Danced in Broadway musicals before becoming choreographer and teacher.

HAMMONS, SUZANNE. Born Aug. 26, 1938 in Oklahoma City. Attended San Francisco Ballet, American Ballet Center, and Harkness schools. Debut in 1958 with San Francisco Ballet; subsequently joined Harkness, and Joffrey Ballet companies.

HANITCHAK, LEONARD R., JR. Born July 24, 1944 in Oklahoma City. Studied with Ethel Butler, Graham, and Cunningham. Has danced with DTW, and Rudy Perez Co.

HANKE, SUSANNE. Born in 1948 near Berlin. Studied with Anneliese Morike, Anne Woolliams, and at Royal Ballet School. Debut 1963 in Wuerttemberg State Theatre Ballet. Joined Stuttgart Ballet in 1966.

HARKAVY, BENJAMIN. Born in N.Y.C. in 1930. Studied with Chaffee, Caton, Preobrajenska, and at School of Am. Ballet. Made debut with Bklyn. Lyric Opera, for which he also choreographed. Opened school in 1955 and formed concert group. Ballet master for Royal Winnepeg, and Nederlands Ballet. Artistic Director of Pa. Ballet 1972.

HARKNESS, REBEKAH. Born in St. Louis, Mo. Promoted American dancers for several years before establishing Harkness Ballet in 1965, and Harkness Ballet School.

HARPER, LEE. Born Nov. 10, 1946 in Hickory, N.C. Juilliard graduate. Studied with Tudor, Limon, Koner, Lindgren, Cunningham, Alvin Ailey.

HARPER, MEG. Born Feb. 16, 1944 in Evanston, Ill. Graduate of U. Ill. Studied with Merce Cunningham and made professional debut with his company in 1968.

HARRIS, RANDAL. Born in Spokane, Wash. Attended Pacific Lutheran U. Studied with Joffrey, Edna McRae, Jonathan Watts ABC. Joined Joffrey Ballet in 1970.

HART, DIANA. Born Apr. 21, 1952 in Lansing, Mich. Attended Juilliard, and Martha Graham schools. Made debut 1973 with Graham Company. Has also appeared with Saeko Ichinohe Co.

HART, JOHN. Born in London in 1921. Studied with Judith Espinosa, and at Royal Acad. Joined Sadler's Wells in 1938, and rose to principal. Became ballet master in 1951, asst. director in 1962.

HARVEY, DYANE. Born Nov. 16, 1951 in Schenectady, N.Y. Studied with Marilyn Ramsey, Paul Sanasardo. Appeared with Schenectady Ballet, Dance Uptown, Miguel Godreau, Eleo Pomare, Movements Black, Story Time Dance Theatre.

HARWOOD, VANESSA. Born June 14, 1947 in Cheltenham, Eng. Studied with Betty Oliphant, Ntl. Ballet School, Rosella Hightower. Debut 1965 with National Ballet of Canada; became principal in 1970.

HASH, CLAIRE RISA. Born May 18, 1946 in Norwich, Conn. Studied at U. Colo. and NYU. Debut 1970 with Jean Erdman Co.

HAUBERT, ALAINE. Born in N.Y.C. Attended U. Utah. Studied with Helen Averell, Raoul Pause, Kira Ivanovsky, Dorothy Dean, Alan Howard, William Griffith. Debut with Monterey Peninsula Ballet, subsequently with Pacific Ballet, ABT, Joffrey Ballet.

HAUPERT, LYNN. Born Aug. 16, 1954 in Syracuse, NY. Studied with Paul Sanasardo, Dance Theatre of Harlem. Debut 1972 with Paul Sanasardo Dance Co.

HAWKINS, ERICK. Born in Trinidad, Colo. Studied at School of American Ballet. Appeared with American Ballet 1934–7, Ballet Caravan 1936–9, and with Martha Graham, before becoming choreographer, teacher, and director of his own company.

HAYDEE, MARCIA. Born April 18, 1940 in Rio de Janeiro. Studied at Royal Ballet School, London. Debut with Marquis de Cuevas Ballet. Joined Stuttgart Ballet in 1961, becoming its prima ballerina.

HAYDEN, MELISSA. Born in Toronto, Can. April 25, 1923, where she received early training before becoming charter member of N.Y.C. Ballet in 1949. Has appeared with Natl. Ballet of Canada, Ballet Theatre, and Royal Ballet. In great demand as educator and lecture-demonstrator. Has also appeared on Bdwy. Director "Ballet Festival." Retired 1973 to teach.

HAYMAN-CHAFFEY, SUSANA. Born Jan. 31, 1948 in Tenterden, England, Studied at Sadler's Wells School, and with Lepeshinskaya, Graham, Cunningham. Made debut in 1968 with Merce Cunningham.

HAYWARD, CHARLES SUMNER. Born May 2, 1949 in Providence, R.I. Attended Juilliard. Debut in 1968 with Jose Limon Company.

HEINEMAN, HELEN. Born Aug. 13, 1947 in Highland Park, Ill. Attended Hunter Col. Studied with Sybil Shearer, Mme. Swoboda Debut 1963 with National Ballet; became soloist before leaving in 1966. Ballet Russe 1967; Nederlands Dans Theater 1968–9; Harkness Ballet 1970.

HELPMANN, ROBERT. Born April 9, 1909 in Mt. Gambier Austl. Attended King Alfred Col.; studied with Laurent Novikov Debut in Austl. musicals; in 1933 joined Sadler's Wells (now Royal Ballet), and rose to soloist from 1933–50. Became choreographer and created ballet "Hamlet" in 1942. Recently has devoted time to acting, guest performances, and directing Australian Ballet. Made Commander of British Empire in 1964.

HERBERTT, STANLEY. Born in Chicago in 1919. Studied with Tudor, Caton, Ivantzova. Member of Polish Ballet, Littlefield, Chicago and San Carlo Opera Ballets before joining Ballet Theatre in 1943. Founder-Director of St. Louis Ballet. Also teaches and choreographs.

Melissa Hayden   **Paschal Guzman**   **Lone Isaksen**   **Al Huang**   **Denise Jackson**

HERMANS, EMERY. Born June 25, 1931, in Seattle. Studied with Vaunda Carter, and at Henry St. Playhouse. Debut 1968 with Nikolais Co. Has danced with Carolyn Carlson, Al Wunder, and in own works.

HIATT, JOHN. Born Oct. 5, 1939 in St. George, U. Studied at UUtah, and became charter member and principal of Ballet West in 1963.

HIGHTOWER, ROSELLA. Born Jan. 30, 1920 in Ardmore, Okla. Studied at Perkins School. Appeared with Ballet Russe de Monte Carlo 1938–41. Ballet Theatre 1941–5. Markova-Dolin 1946. Original Ballet Russe 1946–7. Teaches in Cannes and makes guest appearances.

HILL, CAROLE. Born Jan. 5, 1945 in Cambridge, Eng. Studied at Royal Ballet School and made debut with Royal Ballet Co. in 1962.

HILL, MARTHA. (see DAVIS, MARTHA HILL)

HINKSON, MARY. Born in Philadelphia, March 16, 1930. Graduate of U. Wisc. Studied with Graham, Horst, Shook, June Taylor, Schwezoff. Debut with Graham Co. in 1952. Also danced with John Butler, N.Y.C. Opera, and N.Y.C. Ballet.

HOCTOR, HARRIET. Born in Hoosick Falls, N.Y. Studied with Tarasov, Chalif, Dolin, Legat. Danced in vaudeville, theater, and films before opening own school in Boston in 1941, where she teaches.

HODES, STUART. Born in 1924. Studied with Graham, Lew Christensen, Ella Daganova, and at School of American Ballet. Leading dancer with Graham (1947–58), appeared in Bdway musicals, and as soloist in own works. Choreographer and instructor with Harkness Ballet. Now teaches, and heads NYU Dance Dept.

HOFF, ALEXIS. Born Aug. 31, 1947 in Chicago. Studied with Melba Cordes, Betty Gour, Edna MacRae and at Stone-Camryn School. Made debut with Chicago Lyric Opera Ballet in 1961. Joined Harkness Ballet in 1965, becoming soloist in 1968.

HOFF, STEVEN-JAN. Born June 24, 1943, in Hilversum, Holland. Studied at Amsterdam Academie of Dance. Appeared in musicals before joining American Ballet Theatre in 1966. Became soloist in 1969. Joined Garden State Ballet 1970. Formed own "Film and Dance Theatre" in 1971.

HOFFMAN, PHILLIP. Born in Rochester, N.Y. Attended Miami Dade Jr. Col. Studied with Thomas Armour, and at Harkness House, ABC. Joined Joffrey Ballet in 1969.

HOGAN, JUDITH. Born Mar. 14, 1940 in Lincoln. Neb. Studied with Martha Graham. Made debut with Bertram Ross in 1964. Danced with Glen Tetley before joining Graham Co. in 1967.

HOLDEN, RICHARD. Born Aug. 8 in Braintree, Mass. Graduate of London Inst. of Choreology. Appeared with George Chaffee Ballet, Met Opera, Ballets Minerva. Choreologist for Harkness Ballet, and director of Tucson Civic Ballet.

HOLDEN, STANLEY. Born in London, Jan. 27, 1928. Studied with Marjorie Davies Romford. Made professional debut in 1944 with Royal Ballet and remained until 1969. Now teaches, and makes guest appearances.

HOLDER, CHRISTIAN. Born in Trinidad. Studied in London, and with Martha Graham, Bella Malinka, ABC, Joined Joffrey Ballet.

HOLDER, GEOFFREY. Born in Port-of-Spain, Trinidad, Aug. 1, 1930. Attended Queens Royal College. With brother's dance company in Trinidad, later its director. With own company, made first U.S. appearance in 1953. Besides touring, and giving annual concerts with his group, has appeared on Bdwy, with Met opera, and John Butler Co., also choreographs and designs.

HOLM, HANYA. Born in 1898 in Worms-am-Rhine, Germany. Attended Hoch Conserv., Dalcroze Inst., Wigman School. U.S. debut with own company in 1936, followed by annual performances and transcontinental tours. Came to U.S. in 1931 to found N.Y. Wigman School of Dance which became her school in 1936. Has choreographed musicals and operas in U.S. and London.

HOLMES, GEORGIANA. Born Jan. 5, 1950 in Vermont. Studied with Pauline Koner, Duncan Noble, Job Sanders, Boston School of Ballet. Debut 1969 with Norman Walker; subsequently with Pearl Lang, Louis Falco, Paul Sanasardo, Manual Alum. Also teaches.

HONDA, CHARLOTTE. Born June 2, 1940 in San Jose, Calif. Graduate Ohio State U. Studied with Cunningham, Graham, Hoving, Limon, Sanasardo, Farnworth. Debut in 1967 with Larry Richardson; subsequently with Katherine Litz, ChoreoConcerts, and Laura Foreman.

HORNE, KATHRYN. Born in Ft. Worth, Tex., June 20, 1932. Studied with Margaret Craske, Antony Tudor. Debut 1948 with Ft. Worth Opera Ballet. Appeared with American Ballet Theatre as Catherine Horn (1951–56), a principal dancer Met Opera Ballet (1957–65), Manhattan Festival Ballet (1963–8), also ballet mistress and teacher for MFB.

HORVATH, IAN. Born in Cleveland, O., June 3, 1945. Studied with Danielian, Joffrey. Appeared in musicals, and on TV before joining Joffrey Ballet. With ABT from 1967, soloist in 1969.

HOSKINS, PAUL. Born Sept. 5, 1952 in Collinsville, Ill. Attended Southern Ill. U. Studied with Katherine Dunham. Joined Alvin Ailey Co. 1972.

HOVING, LUCAS. Born in Groningen, Holland. Attended Dartington Hall, and Kurt Jooss School. Professional debut with Kurt Jooss Ballet in 1942. Has appeared with Graham, Limon, and his own company. Has also appeared in Bdwy musicals.

HOWARD, ALAN. Born in Chicago. Studied with Edna MacRae and in Europe. Joined Ballet Russe de Monte Carlo in 1949 and became premier danseur. Appeared with N.Y.C., and Met Opera Ballets before being appointed director of Academy of Ballet in San Francisco. Founded and is artistic director of Pacific Ballet.

HOWELL, JAMES. Born in Yakima, Wash. Attended U. Wash. Studied with Else Geissmar, Martha Graham, Doris Humphrey, Mary Wigman, Margaret Craske, Alfredo Corvino, Robert Joffrey. Original member of Joffrey Ballet.

HUANG, AL. Born in Shanghai, came to U.S. in 1955. Attended Oregon State U., Perry-Mansfield School, graduate UCLA and Bennington. Studied with Carmelita Maracci. Appeared with Lotte Goslar before forming own co., with which he tours when not teaching.

HUGHES, KENNETH. Born in Virginia; attended NC School of Arts, School of Am. Ballet. Debut 1969 with American Ballet; subsequently with Lar Lubovitch, American Classical Ballet, Les Grands Ballets Canadien, ABT 1972.

HUGHES, MICHAELA. Born Mar. 31, 1955 in Morristown, NJ. Made debut 1973 with Houston Ballet. Joined Eliot Feld Co. in 1974.

HUJER, FLOWER. Born in Hollywood, Calif. Studied with Theodore Kosloff, Charles Weidman. Has toured in solo concerts and choreographs.

HUNTER, JENNY. Born Aug. 20, 1929 in Modesto, Calif. Studied with Merce Cunningham, Charles Weidman, Marjorie Sheridan. Debut 1951 with Halprin-Lathrop Co. With Dancers' Workshop Co. until 1958 when she left to found, direct, and choreograph for own company, Dance West.

HYND, RONALD. Born in London, April 22, 1931. Studied with Marie Rambert, Angela Ellis, Volkova Idzikowski, and Pereyaslavee. Professional debut 1949 with Ballet Rambert. Joined Royal Ballet in 1951, and graduated from corps to principal dancer.

INDRANI. Born in Madras, India. Studied with Pandanallur Chokkalingam Pillai, Sikkil Ramaswami Pillai, Devas Prasad Das, Narasimha. First dancer to present Orissi classic dance outside India. Tours extensively in solo and with company.

ISAKSEN, LONE. Born Nov. 20 in Copenhagen where she studied with Edithe Feifere Frandson. Accepted in Royal Danish Ballet School at 13. In 1959 joined group organized by Elsa Marianne Von Rosen and shortly elevated to soloist. In 1961 studied at Joffrey's American Ballet Center, and appeared with his company. In 1965 joined Harkness Ballet, and became one of its principal dancers until 1970, when she joined Netherlands Natl. Ballet.

ISRAEL, GAIL. Born in Paterson, N.J. Studied with Alexandra Fedorova. Rose to soloist with Ballet Russe before joining American Ballet Theatre in 1962.

JACKSON, DENISE. Born in N.Y.C.: attended ABC. Danced with N.Y.C. Opera Ballet, joined Joffrey Ballet in 1969.

JAGO, MARY. Born in 1946 in Henfield, Eng. Trained at Royal Ballet School. Joined Covent Garden Opera Ballet in 1965; Natl. Ballet of Canada 1966; now a principal.

JAMES, JANICE. Born Feb. 14, 1942 in Salt Lake City, U. Studied with Willam and Lew Christensen; Joined NYC Ballet in 1963; joined Ballet West 1965, and is now a principal, and teacher.

JAMISON, JUDITH. Born in 1944 in Philadelphia. Studied at Judimar School, Phila. Dance Acad., Joan Kerr's School, Harkness School, and with Paul Sanasardo. Debut 1965 with ABT. Joined Ailey Co. in 1965, Harkness Ballet 1966, and rejoined Ailey in 1967.

JAYNE, ERICA. Born Aug. 8, 1945 in Amersham, Eng. Studied at Royal Ballet School, RAD. Debut 1962 with Royal Opera Ballet. Currently principal with Les Grands Ballets Canadiens.

JEANMAIRE, RENEE ZIZI. Born Apr. 29, 1924 in Paris. Studied at L'Opera de Paris with Volinine, and with Boris Kniaserf. Debut with Ballet de Monte Carlo in 1944. Joined Ballet Russe de Colonel de Basil (1945–47), Petit's Ballets de Paris in 1948. Has appeard in musicals and films.

JENNER, ANN. Born March 8, 1944 in Ewell, Eng. Began studies at 10 with Royal Ballet School. Debut with Royal Ballet in 1962. Became soloist in 1966, principal in 1970.

JENSEN, CHRIS. Born Jan. 24, 1952 in Los Angeles, Cal. Studied with Albert Ruiz, Harriet DeRea, Carmelita Maracci, and at School of Am. Ballet. Debut 1970 with Ballet du Grand Theatre de Geneve; joined Harkness Ballet 1972.

JERELL, EDITH. Studied with Antony Tudor, Margaret Craske, Dokoudovsky, Brenna, Pereyaslavee, Joffrey, Popova, Gentry, Norman Walker, Nona Schurman, Nancy Lang. Lazowski, Dunham, and Nimura. Appeared with Met Opera Ballet as principal or solo dancer for 10 years. Is now teacher, concert and guest artist.

JHUNG, FINIS. Born May 28, 1937 in Honolulu where he began training. Gradute of U. Utah. Appeared on Bdwy before joining San Francisco Ballet in 1960. Advanced to soloist when joined Joffrey Ballet in 1962. Joined Harkness Ballet as soloist in 1964. Now teaches.

JILLANA. Born Oct 11, 1936 in Hackensack. N.J. After studying from childhood at School of American Ballet, joined N.Y.C. Ballet in teens, rising rapidly to ballerina. With ABT (1957–8) returned to NYCB (1959). Retired in 1966. Is active in teaching and touring U.S. Artistic Adviser for San Diego Ballet.

JOFFREY, ROBERT. Born Dec. 24, 1930 in Seattle, Wash. Began studies with Mary Ann Wells, later attended School of American Ballet, and studied with May O'Donnell and Gertrude Shurr. Debut as soloist with Petit's Ballets de Paris. Appeared with O'Donnell company, and taught at HS Performing Arts and Ballet Theatre School before starting his own American Ballet Center in 1950. Formed first company in 1952 that was resident co. of N.Y. Opera, and made tours in his own works in the U.S. and abroad. Reorganized group appeared in 1965 and has been internationally acclaimed. Is now City Center company.

JOHNSON, BOBBY. Born Oct. 26, 1946 in San Francisco. Studied at Harkness House and with Joffrey, Mattox, Jack Cole, Fokine. Has appeared on Bdwy and with Fred Benjamin Co.

JOHNSON, LOUIS. Born in Statesville, N.C. Studied with Doris Jones, Clara Haywood, and at School of American Ballet. Debut with N.Y.C. Ballet in 1952. Appeared in musicals before forming, choreographing for, and dancing with own group. Teaches, and on staff of Negro Ensemble Co.

JOHNSON, NANCY. Born in 1934 in San Francisco. Studied with Harold and Lew Christensen at San Francisco Ballet School, eventually becoming principal dancer of S.F. Ballet Co. With Richard Carter, toured world, appearing in fifty nations. Was prima ballerina with San Diego Ballet Co.

JOHNSON, PAMELA. Born in Chicago where she studied with Richard Ellis and Christine Du Boulay. Made debut with their Illinois Ballet Co. Joined Joffrey Ballet in 1966, American Ballet Theatre 1972.

JOHNSON, RAYMOND. Born Sept. 9, 1946 in N.Y.C. Graduate Queens Col. Studied with Alwin Nikolais, Murray Louis, Gladys Bailin, Phyllis Lamhut. Debut 1963 with Nikolais, joined Murray Louis in 1968; subsequently with Rod Rodgers, Joy Boutilier, Rudy Perez. Also teaches and choreographs.

JOHNSON, VIRGINIA. Born Jan. 25, 1950 in Washington, DC. Attended NYU, Washington School of Ballet. Debut 1965 with Washington Ballet; joined Capitol Ballet 1968: Dance Theatre of Harlem 1971.

JOHNSON, WILLIAM. Born Aug. 13, 1943 in Ashland, Kan. Attended San Francisco City Col., SF Ballet School. Debut 1961 with San Francisco Ballet; joined NYC Ballet 1970.

JONES, BETTY. Born in Meadville, Pa. Studied with Ted Shawn, Alicia Markova, La Meri, Doris Humphrey, and Jose Limon. Debut 1947 with Limon Co. and toured world with it. Has own lecture-performance, and teaches master classes throughout U.S. Has appeared in Bdwy musicals.

JONES, MARILYN. Born Feb. 17, 1940 in Newcastle, Australia. Studied with Tessa Maunder, Lorraine Norton, Royal Ballet School. Debut 1956 with Royal Ballet, subsequently with Borovansky Ballet, Marquis de Cuevas, London Festival, and Australian Ballets.

JONES, SUSAN. Born June 22, 1952 in York, Pa. Studied at Washington School of Ballet. Joined Joffrey company 1968, NYC Opera Ballet 1969, Am. Ballet Theatre 1971.

JORGENSEN, NELS. Born in New Jersey in 1938. Studied with Rose Lischner, and toured with her co. before beginning studies at School of American Ballet in 1953. Appeared in musicals and on TV before joining Joffrey Ballet as soloist in 1958. Artistic director Louisville Ballet.

JURKOWSKI, KRYSTYNA. Born Jan. 15, 1954 in Nottingham, Eng. Appeared with Joffrey II, NJ Ballet, before joining City Center Joffrey Ballet in 1973.

KAGE, JONAS. Born in Stockholm, Swed. Began training at 9 in Royal Swedish Ballet School, and joined company in 1967. Joined ABT in 1971, rising to principal in 1973; Stuttgart 1975.

KAHN, ROBERT. Born May 31, 1954 in Detroit, Mich. Attended NYU. Made debut 1975 with Jose Limon Co., subsequently joined Paul Taylor Co.

KAHN, WILLA. Born May 4, 1947 in NYC. Attended Bklyn Col., CCNY. Studied with Paul Sanasardo, Mia Slavenska, Karoly Zsedbnyi. Debut 1959 with Paul Sanasardo Dance Co.

KAIN, KAREN. Born in 1952 in Hamilton, Ontario, Can. Trained at Ntl. Ballet School, and joined Ntl. Ballet of Canada in 1969; promoted to principal in 1971.

KARNILOVA, MARIA. Born in Hartford, Conn., Aug. 3, 1920. Studied with Mordkin, Fokine, Charisse, and Craske. First appeared with Met corps de ballet (1927–34). Became soloist with Ballet Theatre, and Met Opera Ballet. Recently in several Bdwy musicals.

KATAYEN, LELIA. Born in N.Y.C.: studied with Francesca de Cotelet, Sybil Shearer, Nanette Charisse, Joseph Pilates. In 1960 formed Katayen Dance Theatre Co, for which she is director-choreographer. Head of Southampton College Dance Dept.

KATO, MIYOKO. Born Sept. 26, 1943 in Hiroshima, Japan. Studied at Tachibana Ballet School. Made U.S. debut in 1965 with Met. Opera Ballet. Member of Harkness Ballet; joined Joffrey 1975.

KAYE, NORA. Born in N.Y.C. Jan. 17, 1920. Studied at Ballet School of Met Opera, and with Michel Fokine. Debut at 7 with Met's children's corps de ballet. Joined American Ballet Theatre as soloist in 1940 and N.Y.C. Ballet in 1950. Now assistant to her husband, choreographer Herbert Ross.

KEAN, FIORELLA. Born in Rome, Italy. Studied at Royal Acad., Sadler's Wells. Debut 1946 with Sadler's Wells Theatre Ballet; Sadler's Wells Ballet 1948–54; teacher 1959–69. Ballet Mistress Juilliard (1966–69), Dance Rep. Co. (1969–72), Ailey Co. (1972–3); ABT (1973).

KEHLET, NIELS. Born in 1938 in Copenhagen where he began studies at 6, subsequently going to Royal Danish Ballet School. Teachers include Vera Volkova, Stanley Williams, Nora Kiss, and Melissa Hayden. First solo at 16 in Royal Danish Ballet's "Sleeping Beauty." Made concert tour of Africa, and guest artist with de Cuevas' Ballet, London Festival Ballet, and ABT (1971).

KEHR, DOLORES. Born May 11, 1935 in Boston. Studied with Fokine, Danielian, Doukodovsky, Vikzak. Made debut in 1952 with Ballet Russe; former ballerina with National Ballet. Now has school in Ft. Lauderdale. Fla., and is director of "Classiques."

KEIL, BIRGIT. Born Sept. 22, 1944 in Kowarschen, Sudetanland. Studied at Royal Ballet School. Made debut 1961 with Stuttgart Ballet.

KELLY, DESMOND. Born in 1945 in Bulawayo, Rhodesia. Studied at London's Royal Acad. Joined London Festival Ballet, becoming principal in 1963; subsequently with New Zealand Ballet, Zurich Opera Ballet, National Ballet 1968, Royal Ballet as principal in 1970.

KELLY, GENE. Born Aug. 23, 1912 in Pittsburgh. Graduate of U. Pittsburgh. Teacher and choreographer before appearing in Bdwy musicals and films. Currently choreographing and directing films.

KELLY, KAREN. Born Feb. 1, 1951 in Philadelphia. Trained at Thomas-Fallis School. Debut 1969 with American Ballet Co.

KENT, ALLEGRA. Born Aug. 11, 1938 in Los Angeles where she began her studies. At 13 went to School of American Ballet, and 2 years later joined N.Y.C. Ballet. Quickly rose to one of company's leading ballerinas.

KENT, HELEN. Born Dec. 30, 1949 in N.Y.C. U. Wisc. graduate. Studied with Waring, Cunningham, Nikolais. Made debut in 1971 with Murray Louis Co.

KENT, LINDA. Born Sept. 21, 1946 in Buffalo, N.Y. Juilliard graduate. Studied with Graham, Limon, Sokolow, Craske, Corvino, Tudor. Joined Alvin Ailey Co. in 1968, Paul Taylor Co. 1975.

KESSLER, DAGMAR. Born in 1946 in Merchantville. N.J. Studied with Thomas Cannon. Joined Penn. Ballet 1965, Hamburg State Opera 1966, London's Festival Ballet in 1967, Pittsburgh Ballet 1973.

KEUTER, CLIFF. Born in 1940 in Boise, Idaho. Studied with Welland Lathrop, Graham, Farnworth, Slavenska, Sanasardo. Debut in 1962 with Tamiris-Nagrin Co. Formed own company in 1969 for which he choreographs.

Finis Jhung

Virginia Johnson

Robert Kahn

Hava Kohav

Dane LaFontsee

KIDD, MICHAEL. Born in N.Y.C. Aug. 12, 1919. Attended City College, and School of American Ballet. Studied with Blanche Evan, Ludmila Scholler, Muriel Stewart, and Anatole Vitzak. Appeared as soloist with Ballet Caravan in 1938, and with Eugene Loring Co. Solo dancer with Ballet Theatre (1942–47), before becoming popular choreographer for musicals and films.

KIM, HAE-SHIK. Born Apr. 29, 1944 in Seoul, Korea. Graduate of Ewha U. Studied at Royal Ballet, London. Made debut in 1959 with Lim Sung Nam: subsequently with Zurich Opera Ballet (1967) and from 1969 with Les Grands Ballets Canadiens; promoted to soloist in 1970.

KIMBALL, CHRISTINA. Born Dec. 22, 1954 in Otsu, Japan. Debut 1972 with Alvin Ailey Co.

KINCH, MYRA. Born in Los Angeles. Graduate of U. of Calif. Solo and concert dancer, and choreographer of satirical ballets. Also teaches.

KING, BRUCE. Born in Oakland, Calif. Graduate of U. Calif. and NYU. Studied at Holm, Met Opera Ballet and Cunningham Schools. Debut 1950 with Henry St. Playhouse Dance Co. Toured with Merce Cunningham and is choreographer and teacher.

KIRKLAND, GELSEY. Born in 1953 in Bethlehem, Pa. Studied at School of American Ballet. Joined N.Y.C. Ballet in 1968, promoted to soloist in 1969, principal in 1972. Joined ABT 1974.

KIRPICH, BILLIE. Born in N.Y.C., graduate of NYU. Studied with Graham, and at American School of Ballet. Debut 1942 with Pittsburgh Dance Co. Has appeared with New Dance Group, NYC Opera Ballet, on TV, and in musicals.

KITCHELL, IVA. Born in Junction City, Kan., March 31, 1912. Appeared with Chicago Opera Ballet before making solo debut as dance satirist in 1940. Has continued as concert artist and teacher.

KIVITT, TED. Born in Miami, Fla., Dec. 21, 1942. Studied with Alexander Gavriloff, Thomas Armour, Jo Anna Kneeland, and George Milenoff. Debut 1958 in night club revue. Appeared in Bdwy musicals before joining American Ballet Theatre in 1961. Elevated to soloist in 1964, principal dancer in 1967.

KLOS, VLADIMIR. Born July 1, 1946 in Prague. Studied at Koncervatory Prag. Joined Stuttgart Ballet and quickly rose to principal.

KNAPP, MONICA. Born Jan. 23, 1946 in Germany. Made debut in 1963, and appeared with several companies before joining Stuttgart Ballet in 1971; promoted to principal.

KOESUN, RUTH ANN. Born May 15, 1928 in Chicago. Studied with Suoboda, Nijinksa, Tudor, and Stone-Camryn. Debut with Ballet Theatre in 1946, and became one of its principal dancers. Retired in 1968 but makes guest appearances.

KOLPAKOVA, IRINA. Born in 1933 in Leningrad. Studied with Kirov company and made debut at 18. Elevated to principal ballerina. Now prima ballerina for Leningrad Kirov Co.

KONDRATÝEVA, MARINA. Born Feb. 1, 1933 in Kazan, Russia. Enrolled in Bolshoi School in 1943; graduated into company in 1953. One of company's principal ballerinas.

KONER, PAULINE. Born 1912 in NYC. Studied with Fokine, Michio Ito, Angel Cansino. Debut 1926 with Fokine Ballet. Debut as choreographer-solo dancer 1930. Formed own company (1949–1964). In addition to solo-performances, now teaches and choreographs.

KONING, LEON. Born July 5, 1947 in Zandvoort, Netherlands. Studied with Peter Leoneff, Benjamin Harkarvy, Richard Gibson, Hans Brenner. Debut 1967 with Netherlands Dance Theater.

KOSMINSKY, JANE. Born in Jersey City, N.J. in 1944. Attended Juilliard, CCNY. Debut 1960 with May O'Donnell. Joined Paul Taylor Co. in 1965. Has appeared with Helen Tamiris, Daniel Nagrin, and Norman Walker.

KRASSOVSKA, NATHALIE. Born June 3, 1918 in Leningrad. Studied with Preobrajenska, Fokine, Massine, Balanchine, and Nijinska. Prima ballerina with Ballet Russe de Monte Carlo and London Festival Ballet. Currently teaches and dances with Dallas Civic Ballet, and appears with other companies as guest artist.

KRONSTAM, HENNING. Born in Copenhagen in 1934. Studied at Royal Danish Ballet School and joined company in 1952. Became premier danseur in 1956. Has appeared as guest artist with many companies.

KRUPSKA, DANIA. Born Aug. 13, 1923 in Fall River, Mass. Studied at Ethel Phillips, and Mordkin Ballet Schools. Began dancing at 6 in Europe as Dania Darling. On return to U.S., joined Catherine Littlefield Ballet. Became member of American Ballet Co. in 1938. More recently has been busy as choreographer.

KUCHERA, LINDA M. Born Jan. 28, 1952 in Monongahela, Pa. Studied at Wash. School of Ballet. Debut 1970 with NYC Opera Ballet; Joffrey II 1970, Ballet Brio 1972–3, ABT 1973.

KUNI, MASANI. Started career in Japan at 13. Gained international fame in solo recitals throughout Europe. Graduate of German Dance College, and studied with Mary Wigman and Max Terpis. Has taught and choreographed in Berlin, London, Copenhagen, Italy, Argentina, and Israel. Is currently director of Kuni Inst. of Creative Dance in Tokyo and Los Angeles.

LAERKESEN, ANNA. Born in 1942 in Copenhagen. Studied at Royal Danish Ballet School and joined company in 1959. Became soloist in 1961.

LaFONTSEE, DANE. Born Nov. 9, 1946 in Lansing, Mich. Studied at School of Am. Ballet. Debut in 1966 with National Ballet; joined Pa. Ballet in 1967, promoted to soloist in 1972.

LAING, HUGH. Born in Barbados, B.W.I. Studied in London with Craske and Rambert. Long career with Ballet Rambert, and Ballet Theatre, before joining N.Y.C. Ballet in 1950. Now a commercial photographer.

LA MERI. Born Russell Meriwether Hughes in Louisville, Ky., May 13, 1899. Professional debut in 1928. Annual tours throughout world until 1957. Established Ethnologic Dance Center and Theater in 1943, which she closed in 1956, and retired in 1960. Has written several books on dance, and teaches. Organized Festival of Ethnic Dance 1970.

LAMHUT, PHYLLIS. Born Nov. 14, 1933 in N.Y.C. where she began her studies in Henry St. Settlement Playhouse. Also studied with Cunningham, and at American Ballet Center. Debut in title role of Nikolais' "Alice in Wonderland." In 1957 gave concert of own works, and has appeared with Murray Louis. In addition to dancing, teaches and choreographs.

LAMONT, DENI. Born in 1932 in St. Louis, Mo. Appeared in musicals before joining Ballet Russe de Monte Carlo in 1951, Ballet Theatre 1953, N.Y.C. Ballet in 1954, now soloist.

LANDER, TONI. Born June 19, 1931 in Copenhagen, and studied there with Leif Ornberg, and in School of Royal Danish Ballet. Became member of its company at 17. In 1951, joined Paris Opera Ballet. Later joined London Festival Ballet, Ballet Theatre Francais; ABT in 1960 becoming principal ballerina. Rejoined Royal Danish 1971.

LANDON, JANE. Born Jan. 4, 1947 in Perth, Australia. Attended Royal Ballet School, London. Joined company in 1963 rising to principal dancer in 1969. Member of Stuttgart Ballet from 1970.

LANG, HAROLD. Born Dec. 21, 1920 in Daly City, Calif. Debut with S.F. Opera Co., subsequently dancing with Ballet Russe de Monte Carlo, and Ballet Theatre. More recently has appeared in musicals, and teaches.

LANG, PEARL. Born May 29, 1922 in Chicago. Attended U. of Chicago, and studied at Frances Allis, Martha Graham, American Ballet, Nenette Charisse, and Vicente Celli Schools. Debut with Ukrainian Folk Dance Co. in 1938, subsequently appearing with Ruth Page, Martha Graham companies before forming her own. Became active choreographer and teacher and has appeared on Bdwy.

LANNER, JORG. Born Mar. 15, 1939 in Berlin. Studied with Kurt Jooss, Nora Kiss, Menia Martinez. Debut 1958 in Ballet Babilee; joined Bejart in 1959.

LANOVA, MERRIEM. Born in California. Attended San Francisco State, and U. Cal. Studied with Nijinska, Lichine, Danilova, and at School of Am. Ballet, and Ballet Arts. Appeared with Ballet International, and Ballet Russe de Monte Carlo. Now operates own school, choreographs for and directs Ballet Celeste International.

LAPZESON, NOEMI. Born in Buenos Aires, Argentina, June 28, 1940. Studied at Juilliard, and with Corvino, Tudor, Limon, Nikolais, and Graham. Debut in Buenos Aires in 1955. Has appeared with Yuriko, Sophie Maslow, Helen McGehee, Bertram Ross, and Martha Graham. Has appeared in several musicals, and teaches.

LARSEN, GERD. Born in Oslo in 1921. Studied with Tudor. Debut with London Ballet, followed with Ballet Rambert, International Ballet, Sadler's Wells (now Royal) becoming soloist in 1954. Also teaches.

LASCOE, MATTI. Born Feb. 24, 1932. Graduate UCal. Trained with New Dance Group, Merce Cunningham, Herbert Ross. Premiered her own Dance Theatre Co. in 1972.

LATIMER, LENORE. Born July 10, 1935 in Washington, D.C. Graduate Juilliard. Joined Jose Limon Co. in 1959. Has appeared with Valerie Bettis, Anna Sokolow. Also teaches.

LAVROVSKY, MIKHAIL. Born Oct. 29, 1941. Studied at Bolshoi and graduated into company, rapidly rising to principal.

LAYTON, JOE. Born May 3, 1931 in N.Y.C. Studied with Joseph Levinoff. Bdwy debut in 1947. After many musicals, joined Ballet Ho de George Reich in Paris (1945-6). Returned to N.Y. and has become popular director and choreographer.

LECHNER, GUDRUN. Born Nov. 7, 1944 in Stuttgart, Ger. Studied at Stuttgart, and Royal Ballet School, London. Debut 1962 with Stuttgart Ballet; promoted to principal.

LEDIAKH, GENNADI. Born in 1928 in Russia. Entered Bolshoi School in 1946, and was graduated into company in 1949.

LEE, ELIZABETH. Born Jan. 14, 1946 in San Francisco. Studied with Harriet DeRea. Wilson Morelli, Richard Thomas. Debut 1964 with Pennsylvania Ballet. Joined American Ballet Theatre in 1967. American Ballet Co. 1969. Rejoined ABT in 1971; Eliot Feld Ballet 1974.

LEE, KEITH. Born Jan. 15, 1951 in the Bronx. Studied at Harkness, and Ballet Theatre Schools. Has danced with Norman Walker, Harkness Youth Co., and own company. Joined ABT in 1969; became soloist in 1971.

LEES, MICHELLE. Born Mar. 18, 1947 in Virginia. Studied at Wash. School of Ballet. Made debut 1964 with National Ballet.

LEIGH, VICTORIA. Born July 3, 1941, in Brockton, Mass. Studied with Georges Milenoff and at JoAnna-Imperial Studio. Debut 1958 with Palm Beach Ballet. Joined American Ballet Theatre in 1961, and became soloist in 1964.

LELAND, SARA. Born Aug. 2, 1941 in Melrose, Mass. Studied with E. Virginia Williams, Robert Joffrey, and at School of Am. Ballet. Debut with New England Civic Ballet, and subsequently with N.Y.C. Opera (1959), Joffrey Ballet (1960), N.Y.C. Ballet from 1960. Appointed principal in 1972.

LERITZ, LARRY. Born Sept. 26, 1955 in Alton, Ill. Trained with Harkness, Joffrey, and School of Am. Ballet. Debut 1974 with Harkness Ballet. With NY Dance Ensemble (1974-75), American Chamber Ballet 1975.

LERNER, JUDITH. Born in Philadelphia, Dec. 30, 1944. Attended Hunter College, American Ballet School, Ballet Theatre School, and studied with Nenette Charisse and Antony Tudor. Debut as soloist with Eglevsky Ballet in 1961, and joined American Ballet Theatre same year.

LESINS, MARCIS. Born Jan. 6, 1946 in Neustadt, WGer. Studied with Elisabeth Curland, Helen Uraus-Natschewa, Leonid Gonta. Debut 1963 with Munich Opera Ballet; joined Stuttgart Ballet 1970; promoted to principal.

LEVANS, DANIEL. Born Oct. 7, 1953 in Ticonderoga, N.Y. Studied at HS Performing Arts, N.Y. School of Ballet. Debut in 1969 with American Ballet Co. Joined ABT in 1971, promoted to soloist in 1972, principal 1973. Joined NYCB 1974, U.S. Terpsichore Co. 1975.

LEVINE, MICHELLE. Born Jan. 24, 1946 in Detroit, Mich. NYU graduate. Studied with Nenette Charisse, Gladys Bailin, Jean Erdman. Debut 1970 with Erdman Co.

LEWIS, DANIEL. Born July 12, 1944 in Bklyn. Juilliard graduate. Joined Limon Co. in 1963. Has appeared with Ruth Currier, Felix Fibich, Anna Sokolow companies.

LEWIS, JAMES J. Born July 30, 1946 in Denver, Colo. Graduate U. Mich. Studied with Sandra Severo. Debut 1969 with Boston Ballet. Joined American Ballet Co. in 1970.

LEWIS, MARILYN. Born June 15, 1947 in Winnipeg, Can. Attended United Col. Debut in 1966 with Royal Winnipeg Ballet; subsequently with Deutsche Operam Phein, and Wuppertal Opera in Germany, Netherlands Dans Theatre.

LIEPA, MARIS. Born July 27, 1930 in Riga, Latvia. Studied at Riga, and Bolshoi schools. Joined Bolshoi in 1961, quickly rising to principal.

LINDEN, ANYA. Born Jan. 3, 1933 in Manchester, Eng. Studied in U.S. with Theodore Koslov, entered Sadler's Wells School in 1947; joined company (now Royal) in 1951; ballerina in 1958. Now retired.

LINDGREN, ROBERT. Born in 1923 in Vancouver, Can. Studied with Vilzak, Swoboda, Preobrajenska. Joined Ballet Russe in 1942, N.Y.C. Ballet in 1957. Retired to teach.

LINN, BAMBI. Born in Brooklyn. April 26, 1926. Studied with Mikhail Mordkin, Helen Oakes, Hanya Holm, Agnes de Mille, and Helene Platava. Debut 1943 in "Oklahoma!" Subsequently danced with Ballet Theatre, Met Opera Ballet, Dance Jubilee Co., and American Ballet Co.

LISTER, MERLE. Born in Toronto, Can., where she began training and had own dance troupe. After moving to N.Y.C., organized dance company in 1964 with which she has appeared in N.Y. and on tour. Also teaches.

LITZ, KATHERINE. Born in 1918 in Denver, Colo. Studied with Humphrey, Weidman, Horst, Platova, Thomas. Debut with Humphrey-Weidman Co. in 1936. Soloist with Agnes de Mille Co. (1940-42), and in Bdwy musicals. Debut as choreographer in 1948 in Ballet Ballads, followed by solo and group works. Also teaches.

LLAND, MICHAEL. Born in Bishopville, S.C. Graduate U.S. Car. Studied with Margaret Foster. Debut 1944 in "Song of Norway." Joined Teatro Municipal Rio de Janeiro (1945), ABT (1948) rising to principal in 1957, Ballet Master Houston Ballet (1968), ABT (1971).

LOKEY, BEN. Born Dec. 15, 1944 in Birmingham, Ala. Graduate U. Utah. Studied with Wm. Christensen, Caton, Peryoslavic, Weisberger, Morawski, Patricia Wilde. Made debut in 1966. Principal with Ballet West, and soloist with Pa. Ballet.

LOMBARDI, JOAN. Born Nov. 18, 1944 in Teaneck, N.J. Parsons graduate. Studied with Raoul Gelebert, Igor Schwezoff, Paul Sanasardo, Richard Thomas. Debut 1967 with Sanasardo Co. Has appeared with N.Y.C. Opera Ballet, and John Butler.

LOMMEL, DANIEL. Born March 26 in Paris. Studied with Joseph Lazzini, Nora Kiss. Made debut in 1966 with Grand Ballet Marquis de Cuevas. Joined Bejart Ballet in 1967 and is now a principal dancer.

LORING, EUGENE. Born in Milwaukee in 1914. Studied at School of American Ballet, and with Balanchine, Muriel Stuart, Anatole Vilzak, and Ludmilla Schollar. Debut 1934 in "Carnival." Subsequently with Met Opera Ballet, and Ballet Caravan, for whom he choreographed and starred in "Billy The Kid." Has become a leading choreographer for all media. Owns and operates American School of Dance in Hollywood.

LORRAYNE, VYVYAN. Born April 20, 1939 in Pretoria, South Africa. Entered Royal Ballet School in 1956 and company in 1957. Became principal in 1967.

LOSCH, TILLY. Born in Vienna, Aust., Nov. 15, 1907. Studied ballet with Vienna State Opera, later becoming its premiere danseuse. Toured Europe as dance soloist, and with Harold Kreutzberg. Joined Balanchine Ballets in Paris, and later formed own company "Les Ballets." In additon to choreographing, has appeared on Bdwy and is successful painter.

LOUIS, MURRAY. Born Nov. 4, 1926 in N.Y.C. Graduate of NYU. Studied with Alwin Nikolais, and made debut in 1953. Has appeared annually in concerts and on tour with Nikolais, and own company, for which he also choreographs. Co-director of Chimera Foundatuon for Dance.

LOUTHER, WILLIAM. Born 1942 in Brooklyn. Attended Juilliard. Studied with Kitty Carson, Martha Graham, May O'Donnell, Antony Tudor, Gertrude Schurr. Debut with O'Donnell Co. in 1958. Has appeared in musicals, and in Donald McKayle Co. Joined Graham Co. in 1964. Artistic director Batsheva Co. 1972.

LOVE, EDWARD. Born June 29, 1950. Graduate Ohio U. Debut 1973 with Alvin Ailey Dance Theatre.

LOVELLE, LAURA. Born May 6, 1958 in Brooklyn, NY. Studied at Dance Theatre of Harlem and made debut with company in 1973.

LOVELLE, SUSAN. Born May 22, 1954 in NYC. Attended Barnard, SUNY. Studied at Dance Theatre of Harlem, and made debut with company in 1968.

LOWSKI, WOYTEK. Born Oct. 11, 1939 in Brzesc, Poland. Studied in Warsaw and Leningrad. Debut 1958 with Warsaw Ballet, joined Bejart Ballet 1966, Cologne Ballet 1971, Roland Petit Co. in 1972; Boston Ballet 1973 as premier danseur.

LOYD, SUE. Born May 26, 1940 in Reno, Nev. Studied with Harold and Lew Christensen, Vilzak, Scolar, Danielian, Zerapse, Bruson, and Joffrey. Debut with San Francisco Ballet in 1954. Joined Joffrey Ballet in 1967. Now Ballet Mistress for Cincinnati Ballet.

Sara Leland

Daniel Levans

Laura Lovelle

Maris Liepa

Merle Marsicano

LUBOVITCH, LAR. Born in Chicago; attended Art Inst., U. Iowa, Juilliard, ABT School, and studied with Martha Graham, Margaret Black. Debut 1962 with Pearl Lang, subsequently with Glen Tetley, John Butler, Donald McKayle, Manhattan Festival Ballet, Harkness, before forming own company. Also designs and choreographs for other companies.

LUCAS, JONATHAN. Born Aug. 14, 1922 in Sherman, Tex. Gradute of Southern Methodist U. Studied at American Ballet School. Debut 1945 in "A Lady Says Yes," followed by many Bdwy musicals. Became choreographer in 1956.

LUCCI, MICHELLE. Born Apr. 26, 1950 in Buffalo, NY. Studied at Banff School, with Joffrey, Caton, Lazowski, and Harkarvy. Debut 1968 with Royal Winnipeg Ballet. Joined Pennsylvania Ballet in 1969.

LUDLOW, CONRAD. Born in Hamilton, Mont. in 1935. Began studies in San Francisco, and became member of its ballet company where he attained rank of soloist before joining N.Y.C. Ballet in 1957. Retired in 1973.

LUPPESCU, CAROLE. Born April 18, 1944 in Brooklyn. Attended Ind. U. Studied at Met Opera Ballet School. Joined Pennsylvania Ballet in 1964. Has performed with Ballet Rambert. Now retired.

LUSBY, VERNON. Born in New Orleans, La. Studied with Leila Haller, Dolin, Caron, Craske, Nijinska, Tudor. Appeared with ABT, Grands Ballets de Marquis de Cuevas, Natl. Ballet of Brazil. Also dancer and choreographer on Bdwy. Now associate director Royal Winnipeg Ballet.

LYMAN, PEGGY. Born June 28, 1950 in Cincinnati, Ohio. Studied at Stone-Camryn, Martha Graham, and Joffrey schools. Debut 1969 with NYC Opera Ballet. Joined Martha Graham Co. in 1973.

LYNN, ENID. Born in Manchester, Conn. Studied with Joseph Albano, Martha Graham, Sigurd Leeder. Director-Choreographer for Hartford Modern Dance Theatre, and Hartford Ballet.

LYNN, ROSAMOND. Born Dec. 31, 1944 in Palo Alto, Calif. Studied with Bill Griffith, Vincenzo Celli, Richard Thomas, Patricia Wilde. Debut 1964 with Philadelphia Lyric Opera, subsequently with ABT (1965), Alvin Ailey Co. (1970)

MacDONALD, BRIAN. Born May 14, 1928 in Montreal, Canada where he began choreographing for television. In 1958 became choreographer for Royal Winnepeg Ballet, and commuted to Norwegian and Royal Swedish Ballets where he held positions as director. Joined Harkness Ballet as director in 1967, left in 1968.

MacLEARY, DONALD. Born in Iverness, Scot., Aug. 22, 1937. Trained at Royal Ballet School. Joined company in 1954, became soloist in 1955 and premier danseur in 1959. Has partnered Beriosova on most of her appearances.

MacMILLAN, KENNETH. Born Dec. 11, 1930 in Scotland. Studied at Sadler's Wells and joined company (now Royal) in 1948. Debut as choreographer with Sadler's Wells Choreographers Group in 1953 with "Somnambulism." Subsequently created dances for Theatre Ballet, Royal Ballet, American Ballet Theatre, Royal Danish Stuttgart, and German Opera Ballet. Perhaps most famous are "Romeo and Juliet" and "The Invitation." Director Royal Ballet from 1970.

MADSEN, EGON. Born Aug. 24, 1944 in Copenhagen. Appeared with Pantomime Theatre and Scandinavian Ballet before joining Stuttgart Ballet in 1961. Promoted to soloist in 1963. Now principal.

MADSEN, JORN. Born Dec. 7, 1939 in Copenhagen. Studied at Royal Danish Ballet School; joined company in 1961; appointed soloist in 1961. Guest with Royal Ballet in 1965. Now retired.

MAGALLANES, NICHOLAS. Born Nov. 27 in Chihuahua, Mex. Studied at School of American Ballet. Danced with Littlefield Ballet, American Ballet Caravan, Ballet Russe de Monte Carlo. Principal dancer with N.Y.C. Ballet from its inception in 1946.

MAGNO, SUSAN. Born in 1946 in Melrose, Mass. Studied with Margaret Craske, Alice Langford, Virginia Williams. Appeared with Boston Ballet before joining Joffrey Ballet in 1965. Lar Lubovitch Co. in 1972.

MAHLER, RONI. Born in N.Y.C. in 1942. Studied with Maria Swoboda and at Ballet Russe School. Debut with Ballet Russe de Monte Carlo in 1960. Joined National Ballet in 1962 and became leading soloist in 1963. Joined ABT as soloist in 1969.

MAKAROVA, NATALIA. Born Nov. 21, 1940 in Leningrad. Studied at Kirov School and joined company in 1959. Had triumph with her first "Giselle" in 1961. Defected in 1970 and joined ABT in 1970 as principal, making debut in "Giselle."

MANN, BURCH. Born in Texas: Studied with Adolph Bolm, Mordkin, and Fokine. Operates studio in Pasadena, Calif. Organized "Burch Mann Concert Group" that has become The American Folk Ballet.

MARCEAU, MARCEL. Born March 22, 1923 in Strasbourg, France. Studied with Charles Dullen and Etienne Decroux. Debut with Barrault-Renaud Co. in 1946. In 1947 formed own company, and among other works, presented "Bip" with whom he has become identified. Subsequently toured Europe, and U.S.

MARCHOWSKY, MARIE. Studied with Martha Graham: became member of company 1934–40. With own company, and as soloist, performing own choreography, has appeared in U.S. and abroad.

MARINACCIO, GENE. Born 1931 in Newark, NJ. Studied with Bupesh Guha, Michael Brigante. Appeared with Lichine's Ballet, Petit's Ballet de Paris, Ballet Russe Monte Carlo, Ballet de Cuba. Now teaches and formed own company American Concert Ballet.

MARKO, IVAN. Born Mar. 29, 1947 in Hungary. Studied at Allami Ballet Intezet. Debut 1967 with Budapest Opera Ballet. Joined Ballet of 20th Century 1968.

MARKOVA, ALICIA. Born in London, Dec. 1, 1910. Studied with Seraphina Astafieva and Enrico Cecchetti. Appeared with Diaghilieff Ballet (1925–29). Vic-Wells Ballet (1932–5), Markova-Dolin Ballet (1935–7), Monte Carlo Ballet Russe (1938–41), prima ballerina Ballet Theatre (1941–5). Original Ballet Russe 1946, Markova-Dolin Co. (1947–8), co-founder and prima ballerina London Festival Ballet (1950–2), and has appeared as guest artist with companies throughout the world. Director of Met Opera Ballet 1963–9. Teaches at U. Cinn.

MARKS, BRUCE. Born in N.Y.C. in 1937 and studied at Met Opera School of Ballet with Tudor and Craske. Joined Met Opera Ballet in 1957, rising to rank of first dancer; joined American Ballet Theatre in 1961 as a principal dancer, and became premier danseur. Appeared as guest in 1963 with Royal Swedish Ballet, and in 1965 with London Festival Ballet. Joined Royal Danish Ballet in 1971; ABT 1974 summer season.

MARKS, J. Born in Los Angeles, Feb. 14, 1942. Founder of San Francisco Contemporary Dancers Foundation. Has choreographed over 200 works. Founder-Director of First National Nothing.

MARSICANO, MERLE. Born in Philadelphia. Studied with Ethel Phillips, Mordkin, Ruth St. Denis, Mary Wigman, Martha Graham, Louis Horst. Debut with Pennsylvania Opera. Since 1952 has presented own program of solos which she choreographs.

MARTIN, KEITH. Born June 15, 1943 in Yorkshire, Eng. Joined Royal Ballet School in 1958 and company in 1961. Appointed soloist in 1967. Joined Pa. Ballet in 1971, and now a principal.

MARTIN, YON. Born Sept. 12, 1945 in Washington, D.C. Studied with Erika Thimey, Paul Sanasardo, and at Washington School of Ballet. Debut with Dance Theatre of Wash. Joined Sanasardo Co. in 1966.

MARTINEZ, ENRIQUE. Born 1926 in Havana, Cuba where he studied with Alonso and danced with Ballet Alicia Alonso. In addition to appearing with American Ballet Theatre has created several ballets, and in 1964 served as ballet master of Bellas Artes Ballet de Mexico.

MARTINEZ, MENIA. Born Sept. 27, 1938 In Havana, Cuba. Studied at Alonso School. Made debut with Alicia Alonso Ballet in 1959; subsequently with Bolshoi (1965), Kirov (1966), and Bejart from 1969.

| Peter Martins | Patricia McBride | Kevin McKenzie | Teena McConnell | Arthur Mitchell |

MARTINS, PETER. Born 1947 in Copenhagen. Trained at Royal Danish Ballet School and joined company in 1965. Granted leave to appear with N.Y.C. Ballet. Joined company in 1970 as principal.

MARTIN-VISCOUNT, BILL. Born in Winnipeg, Can. Began study at 12 with Royal Winnipeg Ballet, subsequently studied at Royal Ballet, American Ballet Theatre, and Bolshoi Schools. Joined Royal Winnipeg Ballet in 1959; took leave to appear with London Festival Ballet, and returned in 1962. Appeared with Joffrey as principal in 1969, Rio de Janeiro Ballet in 1970. In demand as guest artist with regional companies. Artistic director Memphis Ballet 1974.

MASLOW, SOPHIE. Born in N.Y.C. where she studied with Blanche Talmund, and Martha Graham. Joined Graham company and became soloist. Debut as choreographer 1934. Joined Jane Dudley, William Bales to form Dudley-Maslow-Bales Trio. Helped found American Dance Festival at Conn. College. Has choreographed and appeared in many of her works. On Board of Directors and teaches for New Dance Group Studio.

MASON, KENNETH. Born April 17, 1942 in Bartford, Eng. Attended Royal Ballet School and joined company in 1959. Became principal in 1968.

MASON, MONICA. Born Sept. 6, 1941 in Johannesburg, S.A. Studied at Royal Ballet School, and joined company in 1958, rising to soloist, and principal in 1967.

MASSINE, LEONIDE. Born in Moscow, Aug. 9, 1896. Studied at Imperial Ballet School and with Domashoff Checchetti, and Legat. Discovered by Diaghilev; joined his company in 1914; became principal dancer and choreographer; Ballet de Monte Carlo 1932–41; Ballet National Theatre 1941–4, organized Ballet Russe Highlights 1945–6; subsequently appearing as guest artist and/or choreographer with almost every important company, and in films.

MATHIS, BONNIE. Born Sept. 8, 1942 in Milwaukee, Wisc. Attended Juilliard. Studied with Tudor and Anderson. Performed with Radio City Music Hall, Paul Taylor, Norman Walker, before joining Harkness Ballet. ABT (1971) as soloist; promoted to principal in 1974.

MATTEO (VITTUCCI). Born in Utica, N.Y. Graduate of Cornell. Studied at Met Opera School, with La Meri, LaQuica, Esparsa, Azuma, Guneya, Baiasaraswati. Member Met Opera Ballet (1947–51); solo debut in 1953; formed partnership with Carola Goya in 1954. Teaches, and organized Indo-American Dance Group with which he appears.

MATTHEWS, LAURENCE. Born in Hollywood, Cal. Studied with Lew and Harold Christensen, Anatole Vizak, Ted Howard, Paul Curtis, Richard Gibson, Royal Cons. Den Hag. Debut with San Francisco Ballet 1968. Joined Penn. Ballet 1973 as soloist; NYCB 1974.

MATTOX, MATT. Born Aug. 18, 1921 in Tulsa, Okla. Attended San Bernardino College; studied with Ernest Belcher, Nico Charisso, Eugene Loring, Louis Da Pron, Evelyn Bruns, Teddy Kerr, and Jack Cole. Debut 1946 in "Are You With It?," subsequently appearing in many musicals. First choreography in 1958 for "Say, Darling," followed by several Bdwy productions, and Met Opera Ballet.

MAULE, MICHAEL. Born Oct. 31, 1926 in Durban, S.Af. Studied with Vincenzo Celli and made debut in 1946 in "Annie Get Your Gun." Joined Ballet Theatre, then Ballet Alicia Alonso (1949–50), N.Y.C. Ballet (1950–53), Ballets; U.S.A. (1959), Ballet Ensemble (1960–61). In 1964 organized own touring group. Now teaches.

MAULE, SARA. Born June 27, 1951 in Tokyo, Japan. Studied at UCal., San Francisco Ballet School. Joined SFB in 1965; became soloist 1970; Am. Ballet Theatre 1972.

MAXIMOVA, YEKATERINA. Born in Russia in 1939. Entered Bolshoi School at 10, and joined company in 1958, rising to ballerina.

MAXWELL, CARLA. Born Oct. 25, 1945 in Glendale, Calif. Juilliard graduate; debut 1965 with Limon Co. (now soloist), also appears with Louis Falco, and in concert with Clyde Morgan.

MAYBARDUK, LINDA. Born in1951 in Orlando, Fla. Studied at Natl. Ballet School of Canada and graduated into company in 1969; promoted to soloist.

MAZZO, KAY. Born Jan. 17, 1947 in Chicago. Studied with Bernadene Hayes, and at School of American Ballet. In 1961 appeared with Ballets U.S.A. before joining N.Y.C. Ballet corps in 1962, became soloist in 1965, ballerina in 1969.

McBRIDE, PATRICIA. Born Aug. 23, 1942, in Teaneck, N.J., and studied at School of American Ballet. Joined N.Y.C. Ballet in 1959 and became principal dancer before leaving teens; ballerina in 1961.

McCONNELL, TEENA. Born in Montclair, NJ. Attended Columbia U. Studied at School of Am. Ballet. Joined NYCBallet in 1961; promoted to soloist in 1966.

McFALL, JOHN. Born in Kansas City, Mo.; studied at San Francisco Ballet, and joined company in 1965.

McGEHEE, HELEN. Born in Lynchburg, Va. Graduate Randolph-Macon College. Studied at Graham School and joined company; became first dancer in 1954. Among her choreographic works are "Undine," "Metamorphosis," "Nightmare," "Cassandra," and "Oresteia." Also teaches, and dances with own company.

McKAYLE, DONALD. Born in N.Y.C., July 6, 1930. Attended NYCC; studied at New Dance Group Studio, Graham School, with Nenette Charisse, Karel Shook, and Pearl Primus. Debut with New Dance Group in 1948, subsequently appeared with Dudley-Maslow-Bales, Jean Erdman, N.Y.C. Dance Theatre, Anna Sokolow, and Martha Graham. Formed own company in 1951, and in addition to choreographing, teaches.

McKENZIE, KEVIN. Born Apr. 29, 1954 in Burlington, Vt. Trained at Washington School of Ballet. Debut 1972 with National Ballet. Joined Joffrey Ballet 1974.

McLEOD, ANNE. (formerly Anne Ditson) Born Dec. 20, 1944 in Baton Rouge, La. Graduate UCLA. Studied at Louis-Nicholais School. Joined Murray Louis Co. 1970.

McKINNEY, GAYLE. Born Aug. 26, 1949 in NYC. Attended Juilliard. Made debut 1968 with Dance Theatre of Harlem.

McLERIE, ALLYN ANN. Born Dec. 1, 1926 in Grand Mere, Can. Studied with Nemchinova, Caton, De Mille, Yeichi Nimura, Holm, Graham, and Forte. First performed in ballet corps of San Carlo Opera in 1942. Bdwy debut 1943 in "One Touch of Venus" followed by many musicals. Now in films.

MEAD, ROBERT. Born April 17, 1940 in Bristol, Eng. Studied at Royal Ballet School, and joined company in 1958. Made principal dancer in 1967. Joined Hamburg Opera Ballet in 1971.

MEDEIROS, JOHN. Born June 5, 1944 in Winston Salem, N.C. Studied at Boston Cons., with Ailey, Beatty, and Segarra. Has appeared in musicals and with Alvin Ailey Co.

MEEHAN, NANCY. born in San Francisco. Graduate U. Cal. Studied with Halprin, Lathrop, Graham, and Hawkins. Debut 1953 with Halprin company. Joined Erick Hawkins in 1962.

MEISTER, HANS. Born in Schaffhausen on the Rhine. Studied at Zurich Opera Ballet, Royal Ballet, Leningrad Kirov Schools. Joined Ntl. Ballet of Canada 1957; Met Opera Ballet (1962–6); Zurich Opera 1966; founder-member Swiss Chamber Ballet; now principal and teacher for Finnish Natl. Opera Ballet.

MENENDEZ, JOLINDA. Born Nov. 17, 1954 in NYC. Studied at Ntl. Academy of Ballet. Made debut with Ballet Repertory Co. Joined American Ballet Theatre 1972; promoted to soloist 1974.

MERCIER, MARGARET. Born in Montreal. Studied at Sadler's Wells School, graduating into company in 1954. Joined Les Grands Ballets Canadiens in 1958; Joffrey Ballet 1963; Harkness Ballet 1964.

MERRICK, IRIS. Born in 1915 in N.Y.C. Studied with Fokine, Fedorova, Vladimiroff Decroux, Egorova. Is now director and choreographer of Westchester Ballet Co. which she founded in 1950.

MEYER, LYNDA. Born in Texas. Studied at San Francisco Ballet School and joined company in 1962. Became principal dancer in 1966.

MILLER, BUZZ. Born in 1928 in Snowflake, Ariz. Graduate Ariz. State College. Debut 1948 in "Magdalena." In addition to Bdwy musicals, has appeared with Jack Cole Dancers, Ballets de Paris, and is choreographer.

| Meredith Monk | Jack Moore | Hilda Morales | Karl Musil | Victoria More |

MILLER, JANE. Born Mar. 19, 1945 in NYC. Studied at School of American Ballet. Debut 1964 with Pennsylvania Ballet; subsequently with Harkness Ballet, National Ballet as principal.

MILLER, LINDA. Born Sept. 7, 1953 in Washington, DC. Attended N.C. School of Arts, School of Am. Ballet. Debut 1972 with North Carolina Dance Theatre. Joined Eliot Feld Co. in 1974.

MINAMI, ROGER. Born in Hawaii, reared in Calif. Left Long Beach State College to attend Eugene Loring's American School of Dance. Became member of Loring's Dance Players, and now teaches in Loring's school.

MITCHELL, ARTHUR. Born in N.Y.C. Mar. 27, 1934. Studied at School of American Ballet. Joined N.Y.C. Ballet in 1955 and rapidly rose to principal. Was choreographer at Spoleto, Italy, Festival for one season. Founder-director-choreographer for Dance Theatre of Harlem.

MITCHELL, JAMES. Born Feb. 29, 1920 in Sacramento, Calif. Graduate of LACC. Debut 1944 in "Bloomer Girl." Joined Ballet Theatre in 1950, subsequently danced with Met Opera, De Mille Dance Theatre, and on Bdwy.

MITCHELL, LUCINDA. Born Feb. 18, 1946 in Takoma Park, Md. Graduate Smith Col. Studied with Martha Graham. Debut 1970 with Bertram Ross Co.; Kazuko Hirabayashi Dance Theatre 1971; Martha Graham Co. 1972.

MLAKAR, VERONIKA. Born in 1935 in Zurich, Switzerland. Appeared with Roland Petit, Ruth Page, Milorad Miskovitch, Janine Charat, John Butler, and Jerome Robbins before joining American Ballet Theatre in 1964.

MOFSIE, LOUIS. Born in N.Y.C., May 3, 1936. Graduate of SUNY at Buffalo. Training on Hopi and Winnebago Indian reservations. Debut at 10. In 1950, organized, directed and appeared with own group performing native Indian dances, both in N.Y.C. and on tour.

MOLINA, JOSE. Born in Madrid, Spain, Nov. 19, 1937. Studied with Pilar Monterde. Debut 1953 with Soledad Mirales Co., subsequently joined Pilar Mirales, Jose Greco, and in 1962 premiered own company in the U.S. Has since made international tours.

MONCION, FRANCISCO. Born in Dominican Republic, July 6. Studied at School of American Ballet. Danced with New Opera Co., Ballet International, Ballet Russe de Monte Carlo, and Ballet Society which became N.Y.C. Ballet. Is now a principal. First choreographic work "Pastorale" performed by company in 1957. Is also a painter.

MONK, MEREDITH. Born Nov. 20, 1943 in Lima, Peru. Graduate of Sarah Lawrence. Studied with Tarassova, Slavenska, Cunningham, Graham, Mata and Hari. Debut 1964, subsequently choreographed for herself and company.

MONTALBANO, GEORGE. Born in Bklyn. Studied with Mme. Deinitzen, Natalia Branitska., ABC. Appeared with Westchester Ballet, and in musicals, before joining Joffrey Ballet; Eliot Feld Ballet 1974.

MONTERO, LUIS. Born in Granada in 1939. Debut at 15 with Mariemma company. Joined Pilar Lopez, then Jose Greco, Victor Albarez. Became first dancer with Jose Molina Bailes Espanoles in 1961; also choreographs for company.

MOONEY, ELINA. Born Nov. 28, 1942 in New Orleans. Attended Sarah Lawrence Col. Studied with Evelyn Davis, Weidman, Cunningham, Tamiris, Sanasardo. Debut 1961 with Tamiris-Nagrin Co., subsequently with Weidman, Marion Scott, Paul Sanasardo, Cliff Keuter, Don Redlich, and own company.

MOORE, GARY. Born Jan. 29, 1950 in Washington, D.C. Studied with Mavis Murry, Tania Rousseau, Oleg Tupine. Debut with Harkness Youth Co. in 1969, after which joined Pa. Ballet.

MOORE, JACK. Born Mar. 18, 1926 in Monticello, Ind. Graduate U. Iowa. Studied at Graham School, School of American Ballet, Conn. College, and Cunningham Studio. Debut 1951, subsequently with Nina Fonaroff, Helen McGehee, Pearl Lang, Katherine Litz, Martha Graham, Anna Sokolow, and NYC Opera, in musicals, and his own works annually since 1957. Has taught at Conn. College, Bennington, Juilliard, UCLA, and Adelphi.

MORALES, HILDA. Born June 17, 1946 in Puerto Rico. Studied at San Juan Ballet School and American School of Ballet. Debut with N.Y.C. Ballet, then joined Penn. Ballet in 1965, becoming principal. Guest with Les Grands Ballets Canadiens, ABT 1973 as soloist.

MORAWSKI, MIECZYSLAW. Born Jan. 1, 1932 in Wilno, Poland. Studied at Warsaw Ballet School, Bolshoi and Kirov schools, and graduated as teacher. Now director of Virginia Beach Ballet.

MORDAUNT, JOANNA. Born Feb. 13, 1950 in London. Trained at Royal Ballet School; joined company in 1968; London Festival Ballet in 1970.

MORDENTE, TONY. Born in Brooklyn in 1935. Studied with Farnworth. Has appeared on Bdwy and TV, and been assistant to Gower Champion and Michael Kidd. Has also directed and choreographed musicals.

MORE, VICTORIA. Born in Los Angeles. Attended School of American Ballet. Debut with N.Y.C. Opera and joined Joffrey Ballet in 1969.

MORGAN, CLYDE. Born Jan. 30, 1940 in Cincinnati. Graduate Cleveland State Col. Studied at Bennington, Karamu House, Ballet Russe, New Dance Group. Debut 1961 with Karamu Dance Theatre; joined Limon 1965 (now soloist), also appears with Anna Sokolow, Pearl Lang, Olatunji, and in concert with Carla Maxwell.

MORGAN, EARNEST. Born Dec. 3, 1947 in Waihjwa, Hawaii. Attended Northwestern U. Studied with Jene Sugano, Gus Giordano, Ed Parish. Debut 1966 with Gus Giordano Co., subsequently in musicals before joining Paul Taylor Co. in 1969.

MORGAN, VICTORIA. Born Mar. 18, 1951 in Salt Lake City, U. Graduate UUtah with training under Willam Christensen. Joined Ballet West in 1970; principal since 1972.

MORRIS, MARNEE. Born Apr. 2, 1946 in Schenectady, N.Y. Studied with Phyllis Marmein, Cornelia Thayer, Vladimir Dokoudovsky, and at School of Am. Ballet. Joined N.Y.C. Ballet in 1961. Is now a soloist.

MORRIS, MONICA. Born Sept. 23, 1946 in Eustis, Fla. Attended Oglethorpe U. Debut 1966 with Harkness Ballet; subsequently with Martha Graham Co., Paul Taylor Co. 1972.

MOYLAN, MARY ELLEN. Born in 1926 in Cincinnati. Studied at School of American Ballet, and made debut at 16 as leading dancer in operetta "Rosalinda." In 1943 joined Ballet Russe de Monte Carlo as soloist. In 1950 became ballerina with Ballet Theatre. Retired in 1957.

MUELLER, CHRISTA. Born Dec. 20, 1950 in Cincinnati, O. Studied with Merce Cunningham, Ben Harkarvy, Harkness House. Debut 1972 with Dance Repertory Co. Joined Alvin Ailey Co. 1973.

MULLER, JENNIFER. Born Oct. 16, 1944 in Yonkers, N.Y. Graduate Juilliard. Studied with Limon, Graham, Lang, Tudor, Corvino, Craske, Horst, Sokolow. Has danced with Pearl Lang, Sophie Maslow, N.Y.C. Opera, Frances Alenikoff, Louis Falco. Member of Jose Limon Company from 1963. Teaches, and choreographs. Associate director of Falco Co.

MUMAW, BARTON. Born in 1912 in Hazelton, Pa Studied with Ted Shawn; debut with Shawn's company in 1931 and danced with group until it disbanded. Now makes guest appearances, teaches, and appears in musicals.

MUNRO, RICHARD. Born Aug. 8, 1944, in Camberley, Eng. Trained at Hardie Ballet School. Debut with Zurich Opera Ballet, subsequently with London Festival Ballet, American Ballet Co. Now co-director of Louisville Ballet and teaches.

MURPHY, SEAMUS. Born in Hong Kong. Attended Juilliard. Appeared on Bdwy before forming own company. Also teaches.

MURRAY-WHITE, MELVA. Born May 24, 1950 in Philadelphia, Pa. Attended Md. State, Ohio State U. Studied with Marion Cuyjet, Bettye Robinson. Debut 1971 with Dance Theatre of Harlem.

MUSGROVE, TRACI. Born Feb. 7, 1948 in Carlysle, Pa. Graduate SMU. Studied with Graham, Limon, Hoving, Kuch, Yuriko. Debut 1970 with Yuriko, subsequently with Pearl Lang, Martha Graham.

MUSIL, KARL. Born Nov. 3, in Austria. Studied at Vienna State Opera School; joined company in 1953; promoted to soloist in 1958. Has appeared as guest artist with many companies.

MUSSMAN, MARJORIE. Born Feb. 19, 1943 in Columbus, O. Attended Smith College, and Sorbonne, Paris. Studied with Reznikoff, Marmein, Limon, and Joffrey. Debut with Paris Festival Ballet in 1964, and U.S. debut with Jose Limon in 1964. Member of Joffrey Ballet 1965. Currently with First Chamber Dance Co.

NAGRIN, DANIEL. Born May 22 in N.Y.C., graduate of CCNY. Studied with Graham, Tamiris, Holm, and Sokolow. Debut in 1945 in "Marianne," followed by several Bdwy musicals and choreography for Off-Bdwy productions. Now appears in solo concerts, and teaches.

NAGY, IVAN. Born Apr. 28, 1943 in Debrecen, Hungary. Studied at Budapest Opera Ballet School and joined company. Came to U.S. and National Ballet in 1965. One season with N.Y.C. Ballet; joined ABT in 1968 as soloist. Became principal in 1969.

NAHAT, DENNIS. Born Feb. 20, 1947 in Detroit, Mich. Studied at Juilliard. Debut 1965 with Joffrey Ballet. Appeared and choreographed on Bdwy before joining ABT in 1968; Soloist 1970, Principal 1973.

NAULT, FERNAND. Born Dec. 27, 1921 in Montreal, Can. Studied with Craske, Tudor, Preobrajenska, Volkova, Pereyaslavic, Leese. Debut with American Ballet Theatre in 1944, for which he has been ballet master 20 years. Artistic Director of Louisville Ballet, and associate director of Les Grands Ballets Canadiens.

NEARHOOF, PAMELA. Born May 12, 1955 in Indiana, Pa. Studied at American Ballet Center, Sulik School. Joined Joffrey Ballet 1971.

NEARY, PATRICIA. Born Oct. 27, 1942 in Miami, Fla. Studied with Georges Milenoff and Thomas Armour, at Natl. Ballet School, School of American Ballet. From 1960 to 1968 was soloist with N.Y.C. Ballet. Now makes guest appearances. Co-director Berlin State Opera Ballet 1970. Director Le Grand Theatre du Geneve 1972.

NEELS, SANDRA. Born Sept. 21, 1942 in Las Vegas, Nev. Studied with Nicholas Vasilieff, Martha Nishitani, Richard Thomas. Debut with Merle Marsicano in 1962. Teacher at Cunningham School since 1965.

NELSON, TED. Born May 17, 1949 in San Pedro, Cal. Studied at San Francisco Ballet, School of American Ballet. Debut 1970 with San Francisco Ballet. Joined Joffrey Ballet 1973.

NERINA, NADIA. Born Oct. 21, 1927 in Cape Town, South Africa where she received training. Joined Sadler's Wells Ballet in 1946, subsequently becoming one of its leading ballerinas. Now retired.

NEUMEIR, JOHN. Born Feb. 24, 1942 in Milwaukee. Studied at Stone-Camryn, and Royal Ballet (London) schools, and with Sybil Shearer, Vera Volkova. Debut 1961 with Sybil Shearer. With Stuttgart Ballet from 1963. Director Frankfurt Opera Ballet 1969; Hamburg Opera Ballet 1973.

NIGHTINGALE, JOHN. Born Oct. 21, 1943 in Salisbury, Southern Rhodesia. Studied at London School of Contemporary Dance. Joined Paul Taylor Company in 1967.

NIKOLAIS, ALWIN. Born Nov. 25, 1912 in Southington, Conn. Studied with Graham, Humphrey, Holm, Horst, Martin, and at Bennington Summer Dance School. Professional debut 1939. Designs, composes, and choreographs for own company that tours U.S. and abroad. Was co-director of Henry St. Playhouse School of Dance and Theatre. Now co-director of Chimera Foundation for Dance.

NILES, MARY ANN. Born May 2, 1933 in N.Y.C. Studied with Nenette Charisse, Ernest Carlos, Frances Cole, and Roye Dodge. Appeared with American Dance Theatre in U.S. and abroad. Was half of Fosse-Niles dance team that toured U.S. and appeared in Bdwy musicals. Currently teaching, dancing and choreographing.

NILLO, DAVID. Born July 13, 1917 in Goldsboro. N.C. Debut with Ballet Theatre in 1940, then with Ballet Caravan, and Chicago Opera Ballet before appearing in and choreographing musicals.

NIMURA, YEICHI. Born in Suwa, Japan March 25, 1908. First appeared with Operetta Taza. Soloist Manhattan Opera House 1928. Choreographed for musicals and Met Opera. Currently teaches.

NOBLE, CHERIE. Born Dec. 11, 1947 in Philadelphia. Studied with Ethel Phillips, Michael Lopuszanski, Edmund Novak, Pa. Ballet School. Debut with Novak Ballet in 1961 before joining Pennsylvania Ballet in 1962. Now artistic director Delaware Regional Ballet.

NUCHTERN, JEANNE. Born in N.Y.C. Nov. 20, 1939. Studied with Craske, and Graham. Debut 1965 in "The King and I" followed by appearances with Martha Graham, Yuriko, Sophie Maslow, and Bertram Ross.

NUREYEV, RUDOLF. Born Mar. 17, 1938 in Russia; reared in Tartary, Bashkir. Admitted to Kirov Ballet school at 17; joined company and became premier danseur. Defected during 1961 appearance in Paris. Invited to join Royal Ballet as co-star and partner of Margot Fonteyn in 1962. Has choreographed several ballets. Considered by many as world's greatest male dancer. Has appeared with ABT, National Ballet of Canada, Australian Ballet, Paul Taylor.

O'BRIEN, SHAUN. Born Nov. 28, 1930. Studied with Fokine, Schwezoff, Diaghilev, Balanchine, School of American Ballet. Debut 1944 with Ballet International, subsequently with Ballet for America, Grand Ballet de Monte Carlo, Ballet Da Cuba, Conn. Ballet. N.Y.C. Ballet from 1949.

ODA, BONNIE. Born Sept. 15, 1951 in Honolulu, Hawaii. Graduate UHawaii. Apeared with UHawaii Dance Theater (1968–73), Ethel Winter (1971), Met. Opera Ballet (1971). Joined Martha Graham Co. 1973.

O'DONNELL, MAY. Born in Sacramento, Calif., in 1909. Debut with Estelle Reed Concert Group in San Francisco; lead dancer with Martha Graham Co. 1932–44. Formed own school and company for which she dances and choreographs.

OHARA, ORIE. Born June 18, 1945 in Tokyo. Studied at Tokyo Ballet School. Debut 1960 with Tokyo Ballet before joining Bejart Ballet.

OHMAN, FRANK. Born Jan. 7, 1939 in Los Angeles. Studied with Christensens in San Francisco, and appeared with S.F. Ballet. Joined N.Y.C. Ballet in 1962. Now soloist.

OLRICH, APRIL. Born in Zanzibar, E. Africa in 1931. Studied with Borovsky, and Tchernicheva. Joined Original Ballet Russe in 1944. Appeared on Bdwy.

O'NEAL, CHRISTINE. (formerly Christine Knoblauch) Born Feb. 25, 1949 in St. Louis, Mo. Made debut in 1966 with St. Louis Municipal Opera. Subsequently joined National Ballet, and Harkness Ballet as principal; ABT 1974.

ONSTAD, MICHAEL. Born Feb. 18, 1949 in Spokane, Wash. Studied with Robert Irwin, Anatol Joukowski, Willam Christensen, Gordon Paxman, Philip Keeler. Joined Ballet West as soloist in 1966.

ORIO, DIANE. Born Feb. 9, 1947 in Newark, N.J. Trained at Newark Ballet Academy, School of American Ballet, American Ballet Center. Joined Joffrey Ballet in 1968.

ORMISTON, GALE. Born April 14, 1944 in Kansas. Studied with Hanya Holm, Shirlee Dodge, and at Henry St. Playhouse. Debut 1966 with Nikolais Co. Appeared with Mimi Garrard, and formed own company in 1972.

ORR, TERRY. Born Mar. 12, 1943 in Berkeley, Calif. Studied at San Francisco Ballet School; joined company in 1959; American Ballet Theatre in 1965, became principal in 1972.

OSATO, SONO. Born Aug. 29, 1919 in Omaha, Neb. Studied with Egorova, Oboukhoff, Caton, Bolm and Bernice Holmes. Member of corps de ballet and soloist with Ballet Russe de Monte Carlo (1934–40), Ballet Theatre (1940–43), followed by Bdwy musicals.

OSSOSKY, SHELDON. Born Brooklyn, June 10, 1932. Attended Juilliard, and studied with Nikolais, Graham, Limon, Tudor, and Craske. Debut 1950, subsequently appeared in musicals and with Pearl Lang, Sophie Maslow, Fred Berke, and at Henry St. Playhouse.

OSTERGAARD, SOLVEIG. Born Jan. 7, 1939 in Denmark. Studied at Royal Danish Ballet School; joined company in 1957; appointed soloist in 1962.

OUMANSKY, VALENTINA. Born in Los Angeles; graduate of Mills College. Studied with Oumansky, de Mille, Vladimiroff, Horst, Cunningham, Graham, and Maracci. Debut with Marquis de Cuevas' Ballet International, subsequently in Bdwy musicals, before devoting full time to choreography, concert work, and teaching.

OWENS, HAYNES. Born in Montgomery, Ala. Studied with Elinor Someth, Molly Brumbly; appeared with Montgomery Civic Ballet. Attended ABC, and joined Joffrey Ballet in 1966.

OXENHAM, ANDREW. Born Oct. 12, 1945 in London, Eng. Studied with Gwenneth Lloyd, Rosella Hightower, Franchetti. Debut 1964 with Ntl. Ballet of Canada; joined Stuttgart Ballet 1969; National Ballet of Canada 1973 as soloist.

PADOW, JUDY. Born Jan. 10, 1943 in N.Y.C. Studied with Don Farnworth, Marvis Walter, Trisha Brown Schlicter, Ann Halprin. Has danced with Yvonne Rainer, and in own works.

PAGE, ANNETTE. Born Dec. 18, 1932 in Manchester, Eng. Entered Royal Ballet School in 1945, and joined company in 1950. Became ballerina in 1959. Has toured with Margot Fonteyn, and made guest appearances at Stockholm's Royal Opera. Retired in 1967.

PAGE, RUTH. Born in Indianapolis, Ind. Studied with Cecchetti, Bolm, and Pavlowa. Debut 1919 with Chicago Opera Co. Toured S. America with Pavlowa, leading dancer on Bdwy, and premier danseuse with Met Opera. Danced with Diaghilev Ballet Russe, and Ballet Russe de Monte Carlo. Formed own company with Bently Stone and toured U.S., Europe, and S. America for 8 years. In Chicago, has been first dancer, choreographer, director for Allied Arts, Grand Opera Co., Federal Theatre, Ravinia Opera Festival. Currently ballet director of both Chicago Opera Ballet, Lyric Opera of Chicago, and Chicago Ballet.

Alwin Nikolais

Diane Orio

Terry Orr

Merle Park

John Parks

PANAIEFF, MICHAEL. Born in 1913 in Novgorod, Russia. Studied with Legat, Egorova. Debut with Belgrade Royal Opera Ballet, becoming first dancer in two years; later joined Blum Ballet, Ballet Russe, and Original Ballet Russe. Now has school and performing group in Los Angeles.

PANOV, VALERY. Born in 1939 in Vilnius, Lithuania. Made debut at 15. Joined Leningrad Maly Ballet 1958; Kirov 1963 and became its lead dancer. U.S. debut 1974.

PAPA, PHYLLIS. Born Jan. 30, 1950 in Trenton, N.J. Studied at Joffrey, Harkness, and Ballet Theatre schools. Debut with Harkness Ballet in 1967. Joined ABT in 1968. Royal Danish Ballet 1970.

PAREDES, MARCOS. Born in Aguascalientes, Mex. Trained at Academia de la Danza. Danced with Ballet Contemperaneo, and Ballet Classico de Mexico before joining American Ballet Theatre in 1965. Became soloist 1968, principal 1973.

PARK, MERLE. Born Oct. 8, 1937 in Salisbury, Rhodesia. Joined Sadler's Wells (now Royal) Ballet in 1954, becoming soloist in 1958. Now a leading ballerina.

PARKER, ELLEN. Born Feb. 18 in Columbus, O. Attended NC Sch. of Arts, UPa. Studied with Tatiana Akinfieva, Josephine Schwarz, Oleg Briansky, Deborah Jowitt, Sonja Tyven, Job Sanders, Pauline Koner, Duncan Noble, Edward Caton, Valentina Pereyaslavec, Hector Zaraspe. Appeared in musicals before joining NY. Ballet in 1968. Retired in 1972. First Dance Intern in Arts Admin., Consultant NYS Council on the Arts.

PARKES, ROSS. Born June 17, 1940 in Sydney, Australia. Studied with Valrene Tweedie, Peggy Watson, Audrey de Vos, Martha Graham. Debut 1959 with Ballet Francais. Has danced with Ethel Winter, Bertram Ross, Helen McGehee, Martha Graham, Sophie Maslow, Glen Tetley, Mary Anthony, Carmen de Lavallade, Jeff Duncan companies. Joined Pennsylvania Ballet in 1966; Martha Graham 1973. Associate Director Mary Anthony Dance Co.

PARKINSON, GEORGINA. Born Aug. 20, 1938 in Brighton, Eng. Studied at Sadler's Wells School. Joined Royal Ballet in 1957, became soloist in 1959. Now a principal ballerina.

PARKS, JOHN E. Born Aug. 4, 1945 in the Bronx. Studied at Juilliard. Teacher-dancer-choreographer for Movements Black: Dance Repertory Theatre. Joined Alvin Ailey Co. in 1970; left in 1974 for Bdwy musical.

PARRA, MARIANO. Born in Ambridge, Pa. Mar. 10, 1933. Studied with La Meri, Juan Martinez, La Quica, and Luisa Pericet in Spain. Debut 1957. Has organized and appeared with own company in N.Y.C. and on tour.

PATAROZZI, JACQUES. Born Apr. 28, 1947 in Ajallio, France. Studied with Paul Sanasardo and joined his company in 1972.

PAUL, MIMI. Born in Nashville, Tenn., Feb. 3, 1943. Studied at Washington (D.C.) School of Ballet and School of American Ballet. Debut 1960 in N.Y.C. Ballet in "Nutcracker," and became soloist in 1963. Joined ABT in 1969 as principal.

PEARSON, JERRY. Born Mar. 17, 1949 in St. Paul, Minn. Attended UMinn. Studied and appeared with Nancy Hauser before joining Murray Louis Co.

PEARSON, SARA. Born Apr. 22, 1949 in St. Paul, Minn. Attended UMinn. Studied and appeared with Nancy Hauser before joining Murray Louis Co.

PENNEY, JENNIFER. Born Apr. 5, 1946 in Vancouver, Can. Studied at Royal Ballet School, London, and graduated into company. Is now a principal.

PEREZ, RUDY. Born in N.Y.C. Studied with New Dance Group, Graham, Cunningham, Hawkins, Anthony, on faculty at DTW. Choreographer-Director Rudy Perez Dance Theatre, and artist-in-residence at Marymount Manhattan Col.

PERI, RIA. Born Aug. 20, 1944 in Eger, Hungary. Trained at Hungary State Ballet School, London Royal Ballet School. Debut 1964 with Royal Ballet.

PERRY, PAMARA. Born Feb. 8, 1948 in Cleveland, Ohio. Studied at School of American Ballet. Debut 1966 with Western Ballet Association of Los Angeles. With Eglevsky Ballet (1966–7), joined Joffrey Ballet in 1967. Retired in 1969.

PERRY, RONALD. Born Mar. 17, 1955 in NYC. Studied at Dance Theatre of Harlem, and made debut with company in 1969.

PERUSSE, SONIA. Born in 1954 in Longueil, Quebec, Can. Attended Ntl. Ballet School, and graduated into company in 1972. Promoted to soloist 1973.

PETERS, DELIA L. Born May 9, 1947 in N.Y.C. Attended School of American Ballet. Joined N.Y.C. Ballet in 1963.

PETERSON, CAROLYN. Born July 23, 1946 in Los Angeles. Studied with Marjorie Peterson, Irina Kosmouska, Carmelita Maracci, and at School of American Ballet. Debut 1966 with N.Y.C. Ballet.

PETERSON, STANZE. Born in Houston, Tex. Has appeared with Syvilla Fort, Edith Stephen, Charles Weidman, Eve Gentry, and Gloria Contreras. In 1963 organized Stanze Peterson Dance Theatre with which he has appeared in N.Y.C. and on tour.

PETIT, ROLAND. Born in Paris Jan. 13, 1924. Studied at Paris Opera School; became member of corps in 1939, and began choreographing. In 1945 was co-founder, ballet master, and premier danseur of Les Ballets des Champs-Elysees. In 1948 formed own company Les Ballets de Paris, for which he danced and choreographs.

PETROFF, PAUL. Born in Denmark: Studied with Katja Lindhart; Debut 1930 with Violet Fischer. Became premier danseur of de Basil's Ballet Russe; later joined Original Ballet Russe, Ballet Theatre (1943) and International Ballet. Now teaches.

PETROV, NICOLAS. Born in 1933 in Yugoslavia; studied with Ureobrajenska, Gsowsky, Massine. Appeared with Yugoslav Ntl. Theatre, Ballet de France, Theatre d'Art Ballet; lead dancer with Massine Ballet. Came to U.S. in 1967 and founded Pittsburgh Ballet Theatre in 1969; also teaches.

PHIPPS, CHARLES. Born Nov. 23, 1946 in Newton, Miss. Studied with Graham, Cunningham, and at Ballet Theatre School. Debut 1968 with Pearl Lang, subsequently with Louis Falco, Lucas Hoving.

PIERSON, ROSALIND. Born in Salt Lake City. Bennington graduate. Studied at Thomas-Fallis School, American Ballet Center. Has appeared with Ruth Currier, Charles Weidman, Ballet Concepts, Anne Wilson, DTW, Garden State Ballet.

PIKSER, ROBERTA. Born Sept. 3, 1941 in Chicago. Graduate U. Chicago. Studied with Erika Thimey, Paul Sanasardo. Debut 1951 with Dance Theatre of Washington; subsequently with Edith Stephen, Paul Sanasardo, Eleo Pomare.

PLATOFF, MARC. Born in Seattle, Wash., in 1915. Debut with de Basil's Ballet Russe; soloist with Ballet Russe de Monte Carlo 1938–42 and choreographed for them. As Marc Platt made Bdwy bow in 1943, subsequently in and choreographing for films. Was director of Radio City Ballet.

PLEVIN, MARCIA. Born Oct. 26, 1945 in Columbus, O. Graduate U. Wisc. Studied with Lang, Graham, Cohan, Yuriko. Debut 1968 with Pearl Lang, subsequently with Sophie Maslow. New Dance Group, Ethel Winter.

PLISETSKAYA, MAYA. Born in Russia Nov. 20, 1925. Began studies at Moscow State School of Ballet at 8 and joined Bolshoi company in 1943, rising to prima ballerina. Internationally famous for her "Swan Lake." Awarded Lenin Prize in 1964. In addition to dancing with Bolshoi, is now teaching. Considered one of world's greatest ballerinas.

PLUMADORE, PAUL. Born Nov. 5, 1949 in Springfield, Mass. Studied at NYU and with Kelly Holt, Jean Erdman, Nenette Charisse, Gladys Bailin. Debut 1969 with Katherine Litz, with Jean Erdman in 1970, and in concert.

POMARE, ELEO. Born in Cartagena, Colombia Oct. 22, 1937. Studied with Jose Limon, Luis Horst, Curtis James, Geoffrey Holder, and Kurt Jooss. In 1958 organized and has appeared with the Eleo Pomare Dance Co. in N.Y.C., abroad, and on tour in the U.S.

POOLE, DENNIS. Born Dec. 27, 1951 in Dallas, Tex. Trained at Harkness School, and joined company in 1968; soloist 1970; National Ballet 1971–74 as principal.

POPOVA, NINA. Born in 1922 in Russia. Studied in Paris with Preobrajenska and Egorova. Debut 1937 with Ballet de la Jeunesse. Later with Original Ballet Russe, Ballet Theatre, and Ballet Russe de Monte Carlo. Now teaches.

POSIN, KATHRYN. Born Mar. 23, 1944 in Butte, Mont. Bennington graduate. Studied with Fonaroff, Cunningham, Graham, Thomas-Fallis. Debut with Dance Theatre Workshop in 1965. Has danced with Anna Sokolow, Valerie Bettis, Lotte Goslar, American Dance Theatre, and in own works.

POWELL, GRAHAM. Born in Cardiff, Wales. Aug. 2, 1948. Studied at Royal Ballet School; joined company in 1965, then Australian Ballet

POWELL, ROBERT. Born in Hawaii in 1941; graduate of HS Performing Arts. Has been featured dancer with all major American modern dance companies, and appeared with N.Y.C. Opera Ballet. Soloist with Graham Co., associate artistic director 1973.

PRICE, MARY. Born May 20, 1945 in Fort Bragg, N.C. Graduate U. Okla. Studied with Mary Anthony, Martha Graham. Debut 1970 with Mary Anthony, subsequently with Pearl Lang, Richard Gain, Larry Richardson.

PRIMUS, PEARL. Born Nov. 29, 1919 in Trinidad, B.W.I. N.Y. debut in YMHA in 1943; first solo performance 1944. Has since choreographed and performed in West Indian, African, and primitive dances throughout the world. Also teaches.

PRINZ, JOHN. Born in Chicago May 14, 1945. Studied with Comiacoff, Allegro School, American Ballet Center, School of American Ballet. Joined N.Y.C. Ballet in 1964; Munich Ballet, then ABT in 1970. Appointed principal in 1971.

PROKOVSKY, ANDRE. Born Jan. 13, 1939 in Paris, and achieved recognition in Europe with Grand Ballet du Marquis de Cuevas and London Festival Ballet; made world tour with "Stars of the French Ballet." Joined N.Y.C. Ballet as principal dancer in 1963; London's Festival Ballet in 1967.

PROVANCHA, LEIGH. Born Mar. 22, 1953 in St. John's, Newfoundland. Studied at Wash. Ntl. School of Ballet, NC Sch. of Arts, Sch. of Am. Ballet. Debut 1972 with Ballet Repertory Co. Joined ABT 1973.

QUITMAN, CLEO. Born in Detroit. Attended Weinstein U. Studied with Martha Graham, Alfredo Corvino, Maria Nevelska. Formed N.Y. Negro Ballet Co. that toured Europe. Had appeared with Joffrey Ballet and is founder-director-choreographer of Cleo Quitman's Dance Generale.

RADIUS, ALEXANDRA. Born July 3, 1942 in Amsterdam, Holland. Studied with Benjamin Harkarvy. Debut with Nederlands Dans Theatre in 1957. Joined American Ballet Theatre in 1968 as soloist. Became principal in 1969. Joined Dutch National Ballet in 1970.

RAGOZINA, GALINA. Born in 1949 in Archangel, Russia. Joined Kirov Ballet in 1967, and rose to soloist. U.S. debut 1974.

RAIMONDO, ROBERT. Born June 18, 1945 in Jersey City, NJ. Studied at Harkness House, American Ballet Theatre School. Debut 1965 with American Festival Ballet; with Garden State Ballet (1967–70), Houston Ballet from 1972.

RAINER, YVONNE. Born in 1934 in San Francisco. Studied with Graham, Cunningham, Halprin, Stephen. Has performed with James Waring, Aileen Passloff, Beverly Schmidt, Judith Dunn. Started Judson Dance Workshop in 1962, and choreographs for own company.

RAINES, WALTER. Born Aug. 16, 1940 in Braddock, Pa. Attended Carnegie-Mellon U. Studied at Pittsburgh Playhouse, School of American Ballet, Dance Theatre of Harlem. Debut 1952 with Pittsburgh Opera Ballet; subsequently with Pennsylvania Ballet 1962, Stuttgart Ballet 1964, Dance Theatre of Harlem 1969.

RALL, TOMMY. Born Dec. 27, 1929 in Kansas City, Mo. Attended Chouinard Art Inst. Studied with Carmelita Maracci, David Lichine, and Oboukhoff of School of American Ballet. Joined Ballet Theatre in 1944, and became soloist in 1945. Has appeared in musicals, films, and choreographed for TV.

RAPP, RICHARD. Born in Milwaukee, Wisc. Studied with Adele Artinian, Ann Barzel, School of American Ballet. Joined N.Y.C. Ballet in 1958; became soloist in 1961.

RAUP, FLORITA. Born in Havana, Cuba; attended school in Springfield, O. Has studied with Holm, Limon, Humphrey, Tamiris, and Julia Berashkova. Debut in 1951. Has appeared in concert and with own group since 1953, in N.Y.C. and on tour.

REBEAUD, MICHELE. Born Jan. 24, 1948 in Paris, France. Debut 1972 with Paul Sanasardo Co.

REDLICH, DON. Born in Winona, Minn., Aug. 17, 1933. Attended U. Wisc., studied with Holm, and Humphrey. Debut in 1954 musical "The Golden Apple." Has danced with Hanya Holm, Doris Humphrey, Anna Sokolow, Murray Louis, John Butler, and in own concert program. Is teacher, choreographer, and tours with own co.

REED, JANET. Born in Tolo, Ore., Sept. 15, 1916. Studied with Willam Christensen, Tudor, and Balanchine. Member of San Francisco Ballet 1937–41, Ballet Theatre 1943–6, N.Y.C. Ballet from 1949. Has been teaching since 1965.

REESE, GAIL. Born Aug. 13, 1946 in Queens, N.Y. Studied with Syvilla Fort, Hector Zaraspe, Marianne Balin. Debut with Cleo Quitman in 1967, and then with Talley Beatty, Lar Lubovitch, and Alvin Ailey from 1970.

REID, ALBERT. Born July 12, 1934 in Niagara Falls, N.Y. Graduate Stanford U. Studied with Nikolais, Cunningham, Lillian Moore, Richard Thomas, Margaret Craske. Debut 1959 with Nikolais Co., with Murray Louis, Erick Hawkins, Katherine Litz, and Yvonne Rainer.

REIN, RICHARD A. Born May 10, 1944 in N.Y.C. Attended Adelphi U. School of Am. Ballet. Debut 1965 with Atlanta Ballet, subsequently with Ruth Page's Chicago Ballet, Pa. Ballet, joined ABT in 1970, Pa. Ballet 1973.

REMINGTON, BARBARA. Born in 1936 in Windsor, Can. Studied with Sandra Severo, School of American Ballet, Ballet Theatre School, Royal Ballet School. Joined Royal Ballet in 1959, followed by American Ballet Theatre, Joffrey Ballet.

RENCHER, DEREK. Born June 6, 1932 in Birmingham, Eng. Studied at Royal Ballet school and joined company in 1952, rising to principal in 1969.

REVENE, NADINE. Born in N.Y.C. Studied with Helen Platova. In musicals before joining Ballet Theatre. Subsequently member of N.Y.C. Ballet, prima ballerina of Bremen Opera in Germany, and First Chamber Dance Quartet. Joined Pa. Ballet in 1970 as soloist. Now assistant ballet mistress.

REY, FRANK. Born in 1931 in Tampa, Fla. Made debut with Chicago Opera Ballet. Founder-Director Florida Dance Camp, Choreographer-in-residence for Florida Ballet Theatre. Is noted as choreographer for outdoor dramas.

REYES, RAMON DE LOS. Born in Madrid and started dancing at 9. Debut at 17 after studying with Antonio Marin. Formed own company and toured Spain, Europe, and U.S. Joined Ximenez-Vargas Co., later Roberto Iglesias Co. as leading dancer. With Maria Alba, formed Alba-Reyes Spanish Dance Co. in 1964.

REYN, JUDITH. Born Dec. 28, 1943 in Rhodesia. Studied at Royal Ballet School, London, and joined company in 1963. Member of Stuttgart Ballet since 1967; promoted to principal.

RHODES, CATHRYN. Born in 1958 in Westchester, NY. Studied with Iris Merrick, Don Farnsworth, at Manhattan Ballet School, Manhattan School of Dance, Am. Ballet Theatre School. Joined ABT 1973.

RHODES, LAWRENCE. Born in Mt. Hope, W. Va., Nov. 24, 1939. Studied with Violette Armand. Debut with Ballet Russe de Monte Carlo. Joined Joffrey Ballet in 1960, Harkness Ballet in 1964. Became its director in 1969. Joined Netherlands National Ballet in 1970, Pa. Ballet 1972. Appeared with Eliot Feld Ballet 1974.

RIABOUCHINSKA, TATIANA. Born May 23, 1916 in Moscow. Studied with Alexandre Volinin, and Mathilda Kchesinska. Debut in London in 1932. With Monte Carlo Ballet Russe de Basil (1933–43), Ballet Theatre, London Festival Ballet, Theatre Colon (Buenos Aires, 1946–47). Also appeared in musicals. Now teaches.

RICHARDSON, DORENE. Born in N.Y.C., Oct. 5, 1934. Studied at NYU and Juilliard. Debut in 1953. In addition to musicals has appeared with Natanya Neumann, Sophie Maslow, Donald McKayle, and Alvin Ailey.

RICHARDSON, LARRY. Born Jan. 6, 1941 in Minerva, O. Graduate of Ohio State U. Studied with Louis Horst, Jose Limon. Has danced at Kauffman Hall, Hunter College, in musicals, and with Pearl Lang. Also choreographs and tours own company.

RIOJA, PILAR. Born Sept. 13, 1932 in Torreon, Mex. Studied with Pericet, Estampio, Ortega, Tarriba. Debut 1969 in Madrid, Spain. Carnegie Hall 1973. Tours with her own company.

RIVERA, CHITA. Born Jan. 23, 1933 in Washington, D.C. Studied at School of American Ballet. Has become popular star of musicals and TV.

RIVERA, LUIS. Born in Los Angeles. Studied with Michael Brigante, Martin Vargas, Luisa Triana, Mercedes & Albano, Alberto Lorca. Appeared with several companies before forming his own company.

ROBBINS, JEROME. Born Oct. 11, 1918 in N.Y.C. Attended NYU. Studied with Daganova, Platova, Loring, Tudor, New Dance League, and Helen Veola. Debut in 1937 with Sandor-Sorel Co. Subsequently in musicals before joining Ballet Theater in 1940, for which he first choreographed "Fancy Free." Joined N.Y.C. Ballet in 1949 and became its associate artistic director in 1950. Formed Ballets: U.S.A. which toured Europe and U.S. (1958–1961). Has choreographed and directed many Bdwy productions and ballets.

ROBERSON, LAR. Born May 18, 1947 in Oakland, Calif. Attended Cal. State College, and Graham School. Debut 1968 with Sophie Maslow Company. Joined Graham Company in 1969. Also appeared with Pearl Lang.

Raymond Serrano

Tonia Shimin

Daniel Simmons

Donna Silva

Samuel Smalls

SHIMIN, TONIA. Born Sept. 16, 1942 in N.Y.C. Attended Met Opera Ballet, Royal Ballet, Graham schools. Debut 1965 with Martha Graham, subsequently with Pearl Lang, Gus Solomons, Anna Sokolow, Mary Anthony. Joined Jose Limon Co. 1975.

SHIMOFF, KAREL. Born in Los Angeles where she began studies with Irina Kosmovska. Appeared with L.A. Junior Ballet and N.Y.C. Ballet's "Nutcracker" in L.A. in 1961. Studied at School of American Ballet, and joined N.Y.C. Ballet for 2 years, before returning as principal dancer with Ballet of Los Angeles.

SHULER, ARLENE. Born Oct. 18, 1947 in Cleveland, O. Studied at School of American Ballet, and American Ballet Center. Debut with N.Y.C. Ballet in 1960, and joined Joffrey Ballet in 1965.

SHURR, GERTRUDE. Born in Riga, Latvia. Studied at Denishawn, and with Humphrey, Weidman, and Graham. Has appeared with Denishawn Co., Humphrey-Weidman Concert Co., and Martha Graham. Now teaches.

SIBLEY, ANTOINETTE. Born in Bromley, Eng., Feb. 27, 1939. Studied at Royal Ballet School, and made debut with them in 1956, becoming soloist in 1959, principal in 1960.

SIDIMUS, JOYSANNE. Born June 21 in NYC. Attended Barnard Col., School of Am. Ballet, Joffrey School. Debut 1958 with NYC-Ballet. Subsequently with London Festival Ballet, National Ballet of Canada, Pennsylvania Ballet. Ballet Mistress Grands Ballets de Geneve (1971), Ballet Repertory Co. from 1973. Also teaches.

SIMMONS, DANIEL. Born in Edinburg, Tex. Studied at Pan American U., San Francisco Ballet School. Debut with SF Ballet 1967.

SIMON, VICTORIA. Born in 1939 in N.Y.C. Studied at School of American Ballet, American Ballet Center, Ballet Theatre School. Joined N.Y.C. Ballet in 1958, promoted to soloist in 1963.

SIMONE, KIRSTEN. Born July 1, 1934 in Copenhagen. Studied at School of Royal Theatre; made debut with Royal Danish Ballet in 1952, subsequently becoming principal dancer. Has appeared with Ruth Page Opera Ballet, Royal Winnipeg Ballet, Royal Swedish Ballet.

SIMONEN-SVANSTROM, SEIJA. Born in Helsinki, Finland, Sept. 7, 1935. Studied at Finnish Natl. Opera Ballet School, and with Nikitina, Baltazcheva, Semjonowa, Lopuchkina, Karnakoski, Stahlberg, Northcote, Franzel, and Craske. Debut 1952 with Helsinki Natl. Opera. Has appeared with Finnish Natl. Ballet, and London Festival Ballet.

SINGLETON, SARAH. Born Apr. 21, 1951 in Morgantown, WVa. Graduate Stephens Col. Studied with Susan Abbey, Rebecca Harris, Karel Shook, Paul Sanasardo. Debut 1972 with Sanasardo Dance Co.

SINGLETON, TRINETTE. Born in Beverly, Mass., Nov. 20, 1945. Studied with Harriet James, and at American Ballet Center. Debut with Joffrey Ballet in 1965.

SIZOVA, ALLA. Born in Moscow in 1939. Studied at Leningrad Ballet School. Joined Kirov Co. in 1958, and became its youngest ballerina.

SKIBINE, GEORGE. Born Jan. 17, 1920 in Russia. Studied with Preobrajenska, and Oboukhoff. Debut with Ballet de Monte Carlo in 1937, and with company until 1939. Original Ballet Russe (1939–40). American Ballet Theatre (1940–1942). Marquis de Cuevas Grand Ballet (1947–56), Theatre National de Opera Paris (1956–64), artistic director of Harkness Ballet 1964–66. Currently works with regional companies. Director Dallas Civic Ballet.

SLAVENSKA, MIA. Born in 1916 in Yugoslavia. At 12 made debut and toured Europe with Anton Vyanc, subsequently with Lifar and Dolin, and prima ballerina with Ballet Russe de Monte Carlo, before forming own company Ballet Variant that toured Americas and Europe. Has worked with many regional companies, toured with Slavinska-Franklin Co. Currently teaches at UCLA.

SLAYTON, JEFF. Born Sept. 5, 1945 in Richmond, Va. Attended Adelphi U. Studied with Merce Cunningham and made debut with his company in 1968. Appears with Viola Farber Co.

SLEEP, WAYNE. Born July 17, 1948 in Plymouth, England. Attended Royal Ballet School, and was graduated into the company in 1966.

SMALL, ROBERT. Born Dec. 19, 1949 in Moline, Ill. UCLA graduate. Studied with Gloria Newman. Murray Louis, Nikolais, and at Am. School of Ballet. Debut in 1971 with Murray Louis Co.

SMALLS, SAMUEL. Born Feb. 17, 1951 in N.Y.C. Attended CCNY. Studied with Lester Wilson, Jamie Rodgers, Harkness House. Debut 1969 with Dance Theatre of Harlem.

SMUIN, MICHAEL. Born Oct. 13, 1929 in Missoula, Mont. Studied with Christensen brothers, William Dollar and Richard Thomas. Joined San Francisco Ballet in 1957, and made choreographic debut in 1961. Has choreographed for Harkness and Ballet Theatre. A principal with American Ballet Theatre since 1969. Associate director San Francisco Ballet 1973.

SOKOLOW, ANNA. Born in 1912 in Hartford, Conn. Studied with Graham and Horst. Became member of Graham Co. but left to form own in 1938. Internationally known as choreographer, and her works include many modern classics. Formed Lyric Theatre Co. in Israel in 1962. Has taught at major studios and universities, and choreographed for Broadway, TV, and opera.

SOLINO, LOUIS. Born Feb. 7, 1942 in Philadelphia. Studied with Graham, O'Donnell, Schurr, Walker, Anthony, Farnworth. Has performed with Glen Tetley, Mary Anthony, Sophie Maslow, Norman Walker, Arthur Bauman, Seamus Murphy, and Jose Limon.

SOLOMON, ROBERT. Born Feb. 13, 1945 in The Bronx. Studied at Henry Street Playhouse. Has appeared with Henry Street Playhouse Company, and Nikolais.

SOLOMON, RUTH. Born June 10, 1936 in N.Y.C. Studied with Jean Erdman and joined company in 1957, still appears with her between teaching. Now head of Dance-Theatre program at U. Cal. at Santa Cruz.

SOLOMONS, GUS, Jr. Born in Boston where he studied with Jan Veen and Robert Cohan. Danced with Donald McKayle, Joyce Trisler, Pearl Lang, Martha Graham, Merce Cunningham. Formed own company in 1971.

SOLOV, ZACHARY. Born in 1923 in Philadelphia. Studied with Littlefield, Preobrajenska, Carlos, Holm, and Humphrey and at American Ballet School. Debut with Catherine Littlefield Ballet Co. Later joined American Ballet, New Opera Co., Loring Dance Players, and Ballet Theatre. In 1951 became choreographer for Met Opera Ballet. Toured own company 1961–1962. Also appeared on Bdwy and with regional companies.

SOLOVYOV, YURI. Born Aug. 10, 1940. Graduated from Leningrad Ballet School and into Kirov Co. in 1958. Has become one of its leading soloists.

SOMBERT, CLAIRE. Born in 1935 in Courbevoie, France. A pupil of Brieux, made debut in 1950. Has appeared with Ballets de Paris. Ballets Jean Babilee, Miskovitch Co. Toured U.S. with Michel Bruel.

SOMES, MICHAEL. Born Sept. 28, 1917 in Horsley, Eng. Attended Sadler's Wells School; joined company (now Royal) in 1937, and became lead dancer in 1938. For many years, partner for Margot Fonteyn, and creator of many famous roles. In 1962 appointed assistant director of company, and still performs character roles.

SORKIN, NAOMI. Born Oct. 23, 1948 in Chicago. Studied at Stone-Camryn School. Debut with Chicago Lyric Opera Ballet in 1963. Joined ABT in 1966; promoted to soloist in 1971. Joined San Francisco Ballet 1973.; Eliot Feld Ballet 1974.

SPASSOFF, BOJAN. Born in Oslo, Norway. Appeared with Ntl. Ballet of Holland, Royal Danish Ballet, ABT, and joined San Francisco Ballet 1973.

SPIZZO, CHRISTINE. Born Apr. 3, 1953 in Belleville, Ill. Attended N.C. School of Arts, San Francisco Ballet Sch., Sch. of Am. Ballet. Debut 1971 with National Ballet.

SPOHR, ARNOLD. Born in Saskatchewan, Can. Joined Winnipeg company in 1945, rising to leading dancer, and appeared in England partnering Markova. Began choreographing in 1950. In 1958 was appointed director of Royal Winnipeg Ballet for which he choreographs.

195

SPURLOCK, ESTELLE. Born May 9, 1949 in Jersey City, N.J. Graduate Boston Cons. Studied with Sonia Wilson, Lar Lubovitch, James Truitte. Debut 1971 with Alvin Ailey Co.

STACKHOUSE, SARAH. (formerly Sally). Born in Chicago, Graduate U. Wisc. Studied with Arrby Blinn, Steffi Nossen, Perry-Mansfield School, John Begg, Limon, Graham, and Nagrin. Joined Limon company in 1959. Also appeared with Alvin Ailey Co. Teaches at Juilliard and Conn. College.

STARBUCK, JAMES. Born in Albuquerque, New Mex. Attended College of Pacific. Debut 1934 with Ballet Modern, subsequently appearing with San Francisco Opera Ballet. Ballet Russe de Monte Carlo (1939–44). On Bdwy in musicals before first choreography for "Fanny." Has since choreographed and directed for theatre and TV.

STEELE, MICHAEL. Born in Roanoke, Va. Studied at American Ballet School, and made debut with N.Y.C. Ballet.

STEELE, ROBERT. Born June 22, 1946 in Erie, Pa. Attended Boston Cons. Studied with Statia Sublette, Virginia Williams, Stanley Williams, Vera Volkova. Debut 1974 with Boston Ballet; subsequently with Pennsylvania Ballet 1964, American Festival Ballet 1965, Royal Danish Ballet 1966, Boston Ballet 1968.

STEFANSCHI, SERGIU. Born Mar. 2, 1941 in Roumania. Graduate of Academie Ballet. Debut 1962 with Bucharest Opera Ballet; subsequently with Theatre Francais de la Dance, National Ballet of Canada 1971 as principal.

STEPHEN, EDITH. Born in Salamanca, N.Y. Studied with Doris Humphrey, Jose Limon, Mary Wigman, Rudolf Laban. Debut in 1962 with own company and choreography. Has toured U.S. and Europe.

STEVENSON, BEN. Born April 4 in Portsmouth, Eng. Was principal dancer for many years with London's Festival Ballet. Retired to teach but makes guest appearances. Directed Harkness Youth Co., National Ballet, and currently Chicago Ballet.

STEWART, DELIA WEDDINGTON. Born in Meridian, Miss. Studied at Ballet Arts Center, Ballet Theatre, and International Dance Schools. Appeared in Bdwy musicals. Director of Dixie Darling Dance Group. In 1963 became artistic director of Mississippi Coast Ballet.

STIRLING, CRISTINA. Born May 22, 1940 in London. Trained at Audrey de Vos and Andrew Hardie School. Debut with Sadler's Wells Opera Ballet, Subsequently with Netherlands Ballet, London Festival Ballet, American Ballet Co. Now co-director of Louisville Ballet and teacher.

STONE, BENTLEY. Born in Plankinston, S.Dak. Studied with Severn, Caskey, Albertieri, Novikoff, and Rambert. After dancing in musicals joined Chicago Civic Opera, becoming premier danseur. Also danced with Ballet Rambert, Ballet Russe, and Page-Stone Ballet for which he choreographed many works.

STRICKLER, ILENE. Born July 5, 1952 in NYC. Studied at Met Opera Ballet School. Debut 1969 with Manhattan Festival Ballet; subsequently with Yuriko Co., Boston Ballet 1973.

STRIPLING, JAN. Born Sept 27, 1947 in Essen, Ger. Studied with Volkova, Tudor, Jooss, Hoving, and Jean Lebron. Joined Stuttgart Ballet in 1963; promoted to principal.

STROGANOVA, NINA. Born in Copenhagen, and studied at Royal Danish Ballet with Preobrajenska and Dokoudovsky. Appeared with Ballet de L'Opera Comique Paris, Mordkin Ballet, National Ballet Theatre, de Basil's Original Ballet Russe, Ballet Russe de Monte Carlo, and Danish Royal Ballet. Was co-director and ballerina of Dokoudovsky-Stroganova Ballet. Is now a teacher.

STRUCHKOVA, RAISSA. Born in 1925 in Moscow; graduate of Bolshoi School in 1944. Became soloist in 1946 with company; now a prima ballerina. Has appeared in almost every ballet performed in Bolshoi repertoire.

SULTZBACH, RUSSELL. Born in Gainesville, Fla. Studied at Royal School, and American Ballet Center. Debut 1972 with Joffrey Ballet.

SUMNER, CAROL. Born Feb. 24, 1940 in Brooklyn. Studied with Eileen O'Connor and at School of American Ballet. Joined N.Y.C. Ballet, becoming soloist in 1963.

SURMEYAN, HAZAROS. Born in 1942 in Yugoslavia. Began training at 13. Made debut with Skopje Opera Ballet; subsequently with Belgrade Opera Ballet, Mannheim Opera Ballet, Cologne Opera Ballet. Joined National Ballet of Canada in 1966. Is now a principal and teacher.

SUTHERLAND, DAVID. Born Sept. 18, 1941 in Santa Ana, Cal. Studied with Michel Panaieff, Aaron Girard. Debut 1959 with Ballet de Cuba. Joined Stuttgart Ballet in 1965; promoted to principal.

SUTHERLAND, PAUL. Born in 1935 in Louisville, Ky. Joined Ballet Theatre in 1957, subsequently dancing with Royal Winnipeg Ballet, and Joffrey Ballet. Rejoined American Ballet Theatre as soloist in 1964; promoted to principal 1966; Harkness in 1969, Joffrey 1971.

SUTOWSKI, THOR. Born in Trenton, NJ. in Jan. 1945. Studied with Rosella Hightower, Franchette, Williams, Franklin, Tupine, Pereyaslavec. Debut with San Diego Ballet; then with San Francisco Ballet, National Ballet, Hamburg Opera Ballet, Norwegian Opera Ballet where he became premier soloist. Now co-director of San Diego Ballet.

SUZUKI, DAWN. Born in Slocan, B.C., Can. Graduate U. Toronto; studied at Canadian Royal Academy of Dance, Banff and Martha Graham Schools. Debut with Yuriko in 1967, followed by performances with Pearl Lang. Joined Graham Co. in 1968.

SVETLOVA, MARINA. Born May 3, 1922 in Paris. Studied with Trefilova, Egorova, and Vilzak. With Original Ballet Russe (1939–41). Ballet Theatre (1942), prima ballerina Met Opera Ballet (1943–50), N.Y.C. Ballet (1950–52), own concert group (1944–58), and as guest with most important European companies. Artistic Director of Dallas Civic Ballet; choreographer for Dallas, Seattle, and Houston Operas; Teaches at Indiana U.

SWANSON, BRITT. Born June 6, 1947 in Fargo, N.Dak. Studied at S.F. Ballet Sch., N.Y. School of Ballet. Debut 1963 with Chicago Opera Ballet, subsequently with S.F. Ballet, on Bdwy with Paul Sanasardo, Paul Taylor (1969).

TALIAFERRO, CLAY. Born Apr. 5, 1940 in Lynchburg, Va. Attended Boston Consv. Debut 1964 with Emily Frankel Co. Has appeared with companies of Donald McKayle, Sophie Maslow, Buzz Miller, Stuart Hodes, Jose Limon.

TALLCHIEF, MARIA. Born Jan. 24, 1925 in Fairfax, Okla. After studying with Nijinska, joined Ballet Russe de Monte Carlo in 1942, and became leading dancer. In 1948 joined N.Y.C. Ballet as prima ballerina, and excelled in classic roles. Has appeared as guest artist with Paris Opera and other European companies. Retired in 1965.

TALLCHIEF, MARJORIE. Born Oct. 19, 1927 on Indian reservation in Oklahoma. Studied with Nijinska, and Lichine, Debut with American Ballet Theatre in 1945, subsequently with Marquis de Cuevas Ballet (1947–56), Theatre National Opera de Paris (1956–64), Bolshoi (1964), and Harkness Ballet in 1964. Resigned in 1966. Now teaches. Associate director Dallas Civic Ballet.

TALMAGE, ROBERT. Born June 24, 1943 in Washington, D.C. Attended S.F. State Col. Studied with Eugene Loring. Appeared with Atlanta Ballet, in musicals, before joining Joffrey Ballet in 1968.

TANNER, RICHARD. Born Oct. 28, 1949 in Phoenix, Ariz. Graduate U. Utah. Studied at School of Am. Ballet. Made debut with N.Y.C. Ballet in 1968.

TARAS, JOHN. Born in N.Y.C. Apr. 18, 1919. Studied with Fokine, Vilzak, Shollar, and at School of American Ballet. Appeared in musicals and with Ballet Caravan, Littlefield Ballet, American Ballet, and Ballet Theatre with which he became soloist, ballet master, and choreographed first ballet "Graziana" in 1945. Joined Marquis de Cuevas' Grand Ballet in 1948. Returned to N.Y.C. Ballet in 1959 as assistant to Balanchine. Has created and staged ballets for companies throughout the world.

TAVERNER, SONIA. Born in Byfleet, Eng., in 1936. Studied at Sadler's Wells, and joined company before moving to Canada where she became member of Royal Winnipeg Ballet, developing into its premiere danseuse. Joined Pa. Ballet as principal in 1971; left in 1972.

TAYLOR, BURTON. Born Aug. 19, 1943 in White Plains, N.Y. Studied with Danielian, and at Ballet Theatre School. Debut with Eglevsky Ballet in 1959 before joining American Ballet Theatre, Joffrey Co. in 1969.

TAYLOR, JUNE. Born in 1918 in Chicago. Studied with Merriel Abbott. Debut in "George White's Scandals of 1931." Choreographer for June Taylor Dancers and director of own school.

TAYLOR, PAUL. Born in Allegheny County, Pa., July 29, 1930. Attended Syracuse U., Juilliard., Met Opera Ballet, and Graham Schools. Studied with Craske and Tudor. Member of Graham Co. for 6 years, and appeared with Merce Cunningham, Pearl Lang, Anna Sokolow, and N.Y.C. Ballet. In 1960 formed and choreographs for own company that tours U.S. and Europe annually.

TCHERINA, LUDMILLA. Born in Paris in 1925. Trained with d'Allesandri, Clustine, Preobrajenska. Has appeared with Monte Carlo Opera, Ballets des Champs-Elysees. Nouveau Ballet de Monte Carlo. Toured with own company, and now appears in films.

TCHERKASSKY, MARIANNA. Born 1955 in Glen Cove, N.Y. Studied with her mother Lillian Tcherkassky; made debut with Eglevsky Ballet; joined ABT in 1970; soloist in 1972.

TENNANT, VERONICA. Born Jan. 15, 1947 in London, Eng. Studied in Eng., and Ntl. Ballet School of Canada. Debut 1964 with Ntl. Ballet of Canada., and rapidly rose to principal.

TETLEY, GLEN. Born Feb. 3, 1926 in Cleveland, Ohio. Attended Franklin and Marshall College, and NYU graduate. Studied with Holm, Graham, Tudor, and Craske. Debut in 1946 in "On The Town," subsequently with Hanya Holm (1946–9), John Butler (1951–9), N.Y.C. Opera (1951–66), Robert Joffrey (1955–6), Martha Graham (1957–60). American Ballet Theatre (1958–60), Ballets; U.S.A. (1960–1), Nederlands Dans Theatre (1962–5). Formed own company in 1961, and choreographs. Director of Stuttgart Ballet 1974.

THARP, TWYLA. Graduate Barnard College. Studied with Collonette, Schwetzoff, Farnworth, Louis, Mattox, Graham, Nikolais, Taylor, and Cunningham. Debut with Paul Taylor in 1965. Has organized, choreographed, and appeared with own company in N.Y.C. and on tour.

Ben Stevenson   **Veronica Tennant**   **Glen Tetley**   **Jan Van Dyke**   **Antony Tudor**

THOMAS, ROBERT. Born Mar. 5, 1948 in Iowa City. Studied with Anne Kirksen, and at Harkness School. Joined Harkness Ballet in 1968. Joffrey Ballet 1970.

THOMPSON, BASIL. Born in Newcasle-on-Tyne, Eng. Studied at Sadler's Wells. Joined Covent Garden Ballet in 1954, the Royal Ballet, ABT in 1960. Currently ballet master of Joffrey Ballet.

THOMPSON, CLIVE. Born in Kingston, Jamaica, B.W.I., Oct. 20. Studied with and joined Ivy Baxter's Dance Co. Attended Soohih School of Classical Dance, and University College of West Indies. In 1958 represented Jamaica at Federal Festival of Arts. Won Jamaican award for choreography and contribution to dance. Came to U.S. in 1960, studied with Graham, and joined company in 1961. Also with Talley Beatty, Pearl Lang, Yuriko, Geoffrey Holder, and Alvin Ailey.

THORESEN, TERJE. Born in 1945 in Stockholm. Debut in 1959. Appeared with Royal Dramatic Theatre, Stockholm Dance Theatre, Syvilla Fort African Dance Group.

TIMOFEYEVA, NINA. Born in 1935 in Russia. Entered Leningrad Ballet School and graduated with Kirov Co. in 1953. Joined Bolshoi in 1956 and is a principal ballerina.

TIPPET, CLARK. Born Oct. 5, 1954 in Parsons, Kan. Trained at National Academy of Ballet. Made debut with American Ballet Theatre 1972.

TOMASSON, HELGI. Born Oct. 8, in Reykjavik, Iceland. Studied with Sigidur Arman, Erik Bidsted, Vera Volkova, and American Ballet School. Debut in Copenhagen's Pantomine Theatre in 1958. In 1961 joined Joffrey Ballet; Harkness Ballet in 1964; N.Y.C. Ballet in 1970, becoming principal.

TOMLINSON, MEL A. Born Jan. 3, 1954 in Raleigh, NC. Attended NC School of Arts, Dance Theatre of Harlem. Debut 1973 with Agnes deMille's Heritage Dance Theatre. Joined Dance Theatre of Harlem 1974.

TORRES, JULIO. Born in Ponce, PR. Attended NY High School of Performing Arts. Appeared with Jose Greco, Carmen Amaya, Vienna Volksopera, Pilar Lopez. Founder-Director-Choreographer of Puerto Rican Dance Theatre.

TOTH, EDRA. Born in 1952 in Budapest, Hungary. Trained with Alda Marova, E. Virginia Williams. Joined Boston Ballet in 1965, rising to principal.

TOUMANOVA, TAMARA. Born in 1919. Protege of Pavlowa; danced first leading role with Paris Opera at 10; ballerina with Ballet Russe de Monte Carlo at 16. Joined Rene Blum Co. in 1939; returned to Paris Opera in 1947, and to London with de Cuevas Ballet in 1949. More recently in films.

TRACY, PAULA. Born Feb. 25 in San Francisco where she studied with Lew and Harold Christensen. Debut with San Francisco Ballet in 1956. Joined American Ballet Theatre in 1967, San Francisco Ballet 1973.

TRISLER, JOYCE. Born in Los Angeles in 1934. Graduate of Juilliard. Studied with Horton, Maracci, Tudor, Holm, Joffrey, Caton. Debut with Horton Co. in 1951. Became member of Juilliard Dance Theater, and performed with own group, for which she choreographed. Has also choreographed for musicals and operas. Now teaches.

TROUNSON, MARILYN. Born Sept. 30, 1947 in San Francisco. Graduated from Royal Ballet School and joined company in 1966. Joined Stuttgart as principal.

TUDOR, ANTONY. Born Aug. 4, 1908 in London. Studied with Marie Rambert, and made debut with her in 1930, when he also choreographed his first work. Joined Vic-Wells Ballet (1933–5), and became choreographer. Formed own company, London Ballet, in N.Y. in 1938. In 1940 joined American Ballet Theatre as soloist and choreographer. Has produced ballets for N.Y.C. Ballet, Theatre Colon, Deutsche Opera, and Komaki Ballet. Was in charge of Met Opera Ballet School (1957–63); artistic director Royal Swedish Ballet 1963–64. Considered one of world's greatest choreographers. Associate director Am. Ballet Theatre 1974.

TUNE, TOMMY. Born Feb. 28, 1939 in Wichita Falls, Tex. Graduate UTex. Has been featured dancer in films and on Bdwy.

TUPINE, OLEG. Born in 1920 aboard ship off Istanbul. Studied with Egorova and made debut with her company. Joined Original Ballet Russe in 1938, Markova-Dolin Co. in 1947. Ballet Russe de Monte Carlo in 1951, then formed own company. Now teaches.

TURKO, PATRICIA. Born May 22, 1942 in Pittsburgh. Studied at School of American Ballet. Danced with Pittsburgh and Philadelphia Opera companies and in musicals before joining Pennsylvania Ballet in 1964. Now retired.

TURNEY, MATT. Born in Americus, Ga. Joined Martha Graham Co. in 1951. Also danced with Donald McKayle, Alvin Ailey, Paul Taylor, and Pearl Lang.

TUROFF, CAROL. Born Jan. 14, 1947 in New Jersey. NYU graduate; studied with Jean Erdman, Erick Hawkins. Debut 1968 with Hawkins Co., subsequently appearing with Jean Erdman, and in concert.

TUZER, TANJU. Born May 17, 1944 in Istanbul, Turkey. Trained at State Conservatory. Made debut with Turkish State Ballet 1961. Joined Hamburg State Opera Ballet 1969, Harkness Ballet 1972.

UCHIDA, CHRISTINE. Born in Chicago, Ill. Studied with Vincenzo Celli, School of American Ballet, American Ballet Center. Debut 1972 with Joffrey Ballet.

UCHIYAMA, AYAKO. Born in Japan in 1925. Began studies in Tokyo with Masami Kuni, Aiko Yuzaki and Takaya Eguchi. In 1950 organized Uchiyama Art Dance School. Awarded scholarship to study in U.S. with Graham, Horst, Limon, Cunningham, Joffrey, Ballet Russe School, and Luigi's Jazz Center. Has given many concerts and recitals in Japan, and U.S. under sponsorship of Japan and Asia Societies.

ULANOVA, GALINA. Born in Russia, Jan. 8, 1910. Studied with Vagonova. Graduate of Leningrad State School of Ballet. Joined Bolshoi Company and became Russia's greatest lyric ballerina. Now in retirement, but coaches for Bolshoi.

ULLATE, VICTOR. Born in Spain. Studied with Rosella Hightower, Maria de Avila. Debut with Antonio. At 18 joined Bejart Ballet.

UTHOFF, MICHAEL. Born in Santiago, Chile, Nov. 5, 1943. Graduate of U. Chile. Studied at Juilliard, School of American Ballet, American Ballet Center, and with Tudor, and Limon. Debut with Limon's company in 1964. Appeared with American Dance Theatre before he joined Joffrey Ballet in 1965, First Chamber Dance Co. (1969). Since 1972 artistic director of Hartford Ballet, and teacher at SUNY in Purchase N.Y.

VALDOR, ANTONY. Began career with Marquis de Cuevas Company, subsequently appearing with Jose Torres' Ballet Espagnol, Opera de Marseille, Theatre du Chatelet, Theatre Massimo de Palermo. Currently ballet master of San Francisco Ballet.

VALENTINE, PAUL. Born March 23, 1919 in N.Y.C. Began career at 14 with Ballet Russe de Monte Carlo, subsequently as Val Valentinoff with Fokine Ballet, and Mordkin Ballet. Since 1937 has appeared in theatre, TV, and night clubs.

VAN DYKE, JAN. Born April 15, 1941, in Washington, D.C. Studied with Ethel Butler, Martha Graham, Merce Cunningham, and at Conn. College, Henry St. Playhouse, Dancer-choreographer-director of Church St. Dance Co., and appeared with DTW.

VAN HAMEL, MARTINE. Born Nov. 16, 1945 in Brussels. Attended Natl. Ballet School of Canada. Debut 1963 with Natl. Ballet of Can. Guest with Royal Swedish Ballet, Royal Winnipeg Ballet, Joffrey Ballet, before joining ABT. Became soloist in 1971, principal 1973.

VARDI, YAIR. Born May 29, 1948 in Israel. Studied at Batsheva Dance Studio, and joined Batsheva Dance Co.

VARGAS, GEORGE. Born Apr. 19, 1949 in Barranquilla, Col. Studied with Thomas Armour, School of American Ballet. Debut 1968 with Eglevsky Ballet; joined Boston Ballet 1969.

VASSILIEV, VLADIMIR. Born in Russia in 1940. Studied at Bolshoi School and joined company in 1958, becoming soloist in 1959, then principal.

principal 1970.

VERED, AVNER. Born Feb. 3, 1938 in Israel. Debut 1965 with Bertram Ross, subsequently with Jose Limon, Pearl Lang.

VERSO, EDWARD. Born Oct. 25, 1941 in N.Y.C. Studied with Vincenzo Celli. Appeared on Bdwy and with Ballets U.S.A., before joining American Ballet Theatre in 1962, Joffrey Ballet in 1969. Directs his own school, and Festival Dance Theatre in N.J.

VEST, VANE. Born in Vienna. Studied with Larry Boyette. Debut with Denver Civic Ballet; subsequently with Ballet Theatre Players, ABT 1968, San Francisco Ballet 1972.

VETRA, VIJA. Born Feb. 6 in Latvia. Studied in Vienna, and India. Debut 1945 in Burgertheatre, Vienna. Since 1955 has toured world in solo concerts, and teaches in own N.Y. studio.

VIKULOV, SERGEI. Trained at Leningrad Ballet School. Joined Kirov Company in 1956.

VILLELLA, EDWARD. Born Oct. 1, 1936, in Bayside, Queens, N.Y. Began studies at School of American Ballet at 10. Graduate of Maritime College. Joined N.Y.C. Ballet in 1957, and rapidly rose to leading dancer. First male guest artist to appear with Royal Danish Ballet. Appeared in N.Y.C. Center productions of "Brigadoon," and on TV. Recently choreographed for N.Y.C. Ballet and own ensemble.

VODEHNAL, ANDREA. Born in 1938 in Oak Park, Ill. Studied at Ballet Russe School, and School of American Ballet, and with Semenova and Danilova. Joined Ballet Russe de Monte Carlo in 1957, and became soloist in 1961. Joined National Ballet in 1962 as ballerina.

VOLLMAR, JOCELYN. Entered native San Francisco Ballet School at 12 and joined company at 17 in 1943. Later with N.Y.C. Ballet, American Ballet Theatre, de Cuevas Ballet, and Borovansky Australian Ballet. Rejoined S.F. Ballet in 1957, and has choreographed several ballets.

VON AROLDINGEN, KARIN. Born July 9, 1941 in Germany. Studied with Edwardsca, Gsovsky. Debut 1958 in Frankfurt. Joined N.Y.C. Ballet in 1961, soloist 1967, principal 1972.

VONDERSAAR, JEANETTE. Born May 17, 1951 in Indianapolis, Ind. Trained at Harkness School, and made debut with company in 1969.

WAGNER, RICHARD. Born Jan. 30, 1939 in Atlantic City, N.J. Studied with Antony Tudor. Debut with Ballet Russe de Monte Carlo in 1957; joined American Ballet Theatre in 1960, and Harkness Ballet in 1964 as dancer and choreographer.

WAGONER, DAN. Born July 13, 1932 in Springfield. W.Va. Attended U.W.Va. Studied with Ethel Butler, Martha Graham. Debut 1958 with Graham, subsequently with Merce Cunningham, Paul Taylor, and in own choreography and concerts.

WALKER, DAVID HATCH. Born Mar. 14, 1949 in Edmonton, Can. Studied at Natl. Ballet School. Toronto Dance Theatre, Martha Graham. Debut 1968 with Ballet Rambert, London, subsequently with Donald McKayle, Lar Lubovitch, Martha Graham.

WALKER, NORMAN. Born in N.Y.C. in 1934. Studied at HS Performing Arts. Appeared with May O'Donnell, Yuriko, Pauline Koner, and Pearl Lang. Began choreographing while in army, and afterward taught at Utah State U., Choreographed for musicals and festivals throughout U.S. Now appears with own company, and choreographs for it as well as others. Also teaches, and was artistic director of Batsheva Co., and Jacob's Pillow.

WALL, DAVID. Born in London, March 15, 1946. Attended Royal Ballet School, and made debut with company in 1962. Now a principal.

WALLSTROM, GAY. Born Mar. 9, 1949 in Beaumont, Tex. Studied at American Ballet Center and joined Joffrey Ballet in 1968.

WARD, CHARLES. Born Oct. 24, 1952 in Los Angeles, Cal. Studied with Audrey Share, Stanley Holden, Michael Lland, Ballet Theatre School, Gene Marinaccio. Debut 1970 with Houston Ballet; joined ABT 1972; promoted to soloist 1974.

WARDELL, MARCIA. Born Dec. 22, 1948 in Lansing, Mich. Studied with Elizabeth Wiel Bergmann, Betty Jones, Ethel Winter, Alfredo Corvino, Murray Louis, Nikolais, Gladys Bailin. Debut in 1971 with Murray Louis Co.

WARNER, DENISE. Born Mar. 24, 1951 in Meriden, Conn. Studied with Vera Nikitins, American Ballet Theatre School. Debut 1968 with Hartford Ballet; joined ABT 1972.

VEGA, ANTONIO. Born in Huelva, Spain. Studied with Pericet and Antonio Marin. Has performed with Jose Molina, Luisillo, Mariemma, Antonio, and Jose Greco. Joined Ballet Granada in 1968 as soloist.

VERDON, GWEN. Born Jan. 13, 1926 in Culver City, Calif. Studied various styles of dancing, including ballet with Ernest Belcher and Carmelita Maracci. Danced with Aida Brodbent company, and Jack Cole. Became assistant choreographer to Cole on several films, before becoming star in Bdwy musicals.

VERDY, VIOLETTE. Born in Brittany, Dec. 1, 1933. Debut in 1944 with Roland Petit. Has appeared with major European ballet companies, including England's Royal Ballet, Petit's Co., and Paris Opera Ballet. Joined ABT in 1957, N.Y.C. Ballet in 1958 as a principal.

VERE, DIANA. Born Sept. 29, 1942 in Trinidad. Studied at Royal Ballet School; joined company in 1962; promoted to soloist in 1968,

WARREN, GRETCHEN. Born Apr. 7, 1945 in Princeton, N.J. Attended Aparri School, School of Ballet, Royal Ballet, and National Ballet Schools. Debut in 1964 with Covent Garden Opera Ballet; subsequently with Icelandic Natl. Opera Ballet, National Ballet (1964–5), Pa. Ballet from 1965. Made soloist in 1968.

WARREN, VINCENT. Born Aug. 31, 1938 in Jacksonville, Fla. Studied at Ballet Theatre School. Debut 1957 with Met Opera Ballet, subsequently with Santa Fe Opera, James Waring, Aileen Pasloff, Guatemala Natl. Ballet, Penn. Ballet, Cologne Opera Ballet, Les Grands Ballets Canadiens.

WATANABE, MIYOKO. Born in Japan and began training at 6. Joined all-girls Kabuki Troupe and became one of its leading performers. Came to U.S. in 1960 as announcer-interpreter for Kabuki troupe, and remained to perform in concert and teach classic Japanese dances.

WATTS, JONATHAN. Born in 1933 in Cheyenne, Wyo. Studied with Joffrey, Shurr, and O'Donnell. Debut with Joffrey before joining N.Y.C. Ballet in 1954, Australian Ballet 1962, and Cologne Opera Ballet as premier danseur in 1965. Now director Am. Ballet Center.

WAYNE, DENNIS. Born July 19, 1945 in St. Petersburg, Fla. Debut 1962 with Norman Walker Co.; subsequently with Harkness Ballet 1963, Joffrey Ballet 1970; ABT as soloist 1974.

WEBER, DIANA. Born Jan. 16, in Passaic, N.J. Studied at Ballet Theatre School. Joined ABT in 1962; became soloist in 1966; San Francisco Ballet 1973.

WEISS, JEROME. Born in Florida; graduate Juilliard. Debut with Miami Ballet; subsequently with Atlanta Ballet, Netherlands Dans Theatre 1968, Harkness Ballet 1971, San Francisco Ballet 1973.

WELCH, GARTH. Born Apr. 14, 1936 in Brisbane, Aust. Studied with Phyllis Danaher, Victor Gzovsky, Anna Northcote, Zaraspe, Martha Graham. Debut 1955 with Borovansky Ballet, subsequently with Western Theatre Ballet, Marquis de Cuevas Ballet, Australian Ballet (1962).

WELLS, BRUCE. Born Jan. 17, 1950 in Tacoma, Wash. Studied with Patricia Cairns, Banff School, School of American Ballet. Joined N.Y.C. Ballet in 1967, dancing soloist and principal roles since 1969.

WELLS, DORREN. Born June 25, 1937 in London. Studied at Royal Ballet School and made debut with company in 1955, rising to ballerina.

WENGERD, TIM. Born Jan. 4, 1945 in Boston. Graduate U. Utah. Studied with Elizabeth Waters, Yuriko, Ethel Winter, Merce Cunningham, Viola Farber, Donald McKayle. Debut in 1966 with Ririe-Woodbury Co. Dancer-choreographer with Repertory Dance Theatre from 1966. Joined Graham Co. 1972.

WESCHE, PATRICIA. Born Oct. 13, 1952 in West Islip, N.Y. Attended American Ballet Theatre School. Debut 1969 with ABT.

WESLOW, WILLIAM. Born Mar. 20, 1925 in Seattle, Wash. Studied with Mary Ann Wells. Appeared on Bdwy and TV before joining Ballet Theatre in 1949. Joined N.Y.C. Ballet in 1958.

WHELAN, SUSAN. Born Feb. 26, 1948 in N.Y.C. Studied with Eglevsky, at Ballet Theatre, and Harkness schools. Joined Harkness Ballet in 1966, ABT 1971.

WHITE, FRANKLIN. Born in 1924 in Shoreham, Kent, Eng. After 3 years with Ballet Rambert, joined Royal Ballet in 1942. Is also well known as lecturer on ballet.

WHITE, GLENN. Born Aug. 6, 1949 in Pittsburg, Calif. Studied at Norfolk Ballet Academy. American Ballet Center, Debut 1967 with N.Y.C. Opera, joined Joffrey Company in 1969.

WHITE, ONNA. Born in 1925 in Cape Breton Island, Nova Scotia. Debut with San Francisco Opera Ballet Co. Became assistant choreographer to Michael Kidd, and subsequently choreographer for Bdwy, Hollywood, and London productions.

WHITENER, WILLIAM. Born Aug. 17, 1951 in Seattle, Wash. Studied with Karen Irvin, Mary Staton, Hector Zaraspe, Perry Brunson. Debut 1969 with City Center Joffrey Ballet.

WILDE, PATRICIA. Born in Ottawa, Can. July 16, 1928 where she studied before joining Marquis de Cuevas' Ballet International and continuing studies at School of American Ballet. Joined N.Y.C. Ballet in 1950 and became one of its leading ballerinas, having danced almost every role in the company's repertoire. Director of Harkness School. Now teaches. Ballet mistress for ABT.

WILLIAMS, ANTHONY. Born June 11, 1946 in Naples, Italy. Studied with Virginia Williams and Joffrey. Debut 1964 with Boston Ballet. Joined Joffrey company 1968; rejoined Boston Ballet in 1969. Soloist with Royal Winnipeg Ballet 1973.

WILLIAMS, DANIEL. Born in 1943 in San Francisco. Studied with Welland Lathrop, Gloria Unti, May O'Donnell, Gertrude Shurr, Nina Fonaroff, Wishmary Hunt, Paul Taylor. Joined Taylor company in 1963 and appears in most of its repertoire.

WILLIAMS, DEREK. Born Dec. 14, 1945 in Jamaica, WI. Studied at Harkness House, Martha Graham School. Debut with Jamaica Ntl. Dance Co. Joined Dance Theatre of Harlem 1968.

WILLIAMS, DUDLEY. Born in N.Y.C. where he began dance lessons at 6. Studied with Shook, O'Donnell, Tudor, Graham, and at Juilliard. Has appeared with May O'Donnell, Martha Graham, Donald McKayle, Talley Beatty, and Alvin Ailey from 1964.

Sallie Wilson   **Edward Verso**   **Lynda Fourth**   **Dan Wagoner**   **Maria Youskevitch**

WILLIAMS, KERRY. Born in Philadelphia; studied at San Francisco Ballet School, and made debut with company. Joined American Ballet Co., and returned to SF Ballet in 1972.

WILLIAMS, STANLEY. Born in 1925 in Chappel, Eng. Studied at Royal Danish Ballet and joined company in 1943. Became soloist in 1949. Teacher and guest artist since 1950. Ballet master and leading dancer with Ballet Comique (1953–4). Knighted by King of Denmark. Since 1964, on staff of School of Am Ballet.

WILSON, ANNE. Born in Philadelphia. Graduate of U. of Chicago. Studied with Fokine, Tudor, Weidman, Elizabeth Anderson, Etienne Decroux, and Heinz Poll. Debut 1940 with American Ballet Theatre. Also with Weidman, and in 1964 formed own co. Noted for solo concert-lecture "The Ballet Story" which she has toured extensively.

WILSON, JOHN. Born in 1927 in Los Angeles. Studied with Katherine Dunham. Toured with Harriette Ann Gray, appeared in concert with own group, and Joyce Trisler. Joined Joffrey Ballet in 1956, Harkness Ballet in 1964.

WILSON, PAUL. Born Oct. 19, 1949 in Carbondale, Pa. Studied with Barbara Doerffer, Charles Weidman, Zena Rommett. Joined Weidman Co. 1971. Also danced with Jan Wodynski, Jeff Duncan, Xoregos Co. Formed Theatre-dance Asylum 1975. Also teaches.

WILSON, SALLIE. Born Apr. 18, 1932 in Ft. Worth, Tex. Studied with Tudor and Craske. Joined American Ballet Theatre in 1959, and in 1963 became principal dancer. Has also appeared with Met Opera and N.Y.C. Ballets.

WILSON, ZANE. Born Feb. 25, 1951 in Elkton, Md. Attended UMd. Trained at Harkness School and joined Harkness Ballet in 1970.

WINTER, ETHEL. Born in Wrentham, Mass., June 18, 1924. Graduate of Bennington College, Soloist with Martha Graham Co. since 1964. Has taught Graham Method in various schools in Eng. and appeared as lecture-demonstrator. Her own choreography has received recognition, and is included in repertoire of Batsheva Co. Also appeared with N.Y.C. Opera, and Sophie Maslow.

WOLENSKI, CHESTER. Born Nov. 16, 1931 in New Jersey. Attended Juilliard, and American School of Ballet. Debut 1956 with Jose Limon, subsequently with Anna Sokolow, Donald McKayle, John Butler, American Dance Theatre, Juilliard Dance Theatre, Jack Moore, Bill Frank and Ruth Currier. Also appeared in musicals.

WONG, MEL. Born Dec. 2, 1938 in Oakland, Cal. Graduate UCLA. Studied at Academy of Ballet. SF Ballet School, School of Am. Ballet, Cunningham Studio. Debut in 1968 with Merce Cunningham Co.

WOOD, DONNA. Born Nov. 21, 1954 in NYC. Joined Alvin Ailey Dance Theatre 1972.

WOODIN, PETER. Born in Tucson, Ariz. Graduate Wesleyan U. Debut 1971 with Lucas Hoving Co.; subsequently with Utah Repertory Dance Theatre, Gus Solomons, Chamber Arts Dance Players, Alvin Ailey Dance Theatre 1973.

WRIGHT, REBECCA. Born Dec. 5, 1947 in Springfield, Ohio. Studied with David McLain and Josephine Schwarz. Joined Joffrey Ballet in 1966.

YOHN, ROBERT. Born Sept. 23, 1943 in Fresno, Calif. Studied at Fresno State Col., New Dance Group, and with Charles Kelley, Perry Brunson. Has appeared with New Dance Group, Bruce King, and joined Erick Hawkins Company in 1968.

YOUNG, CYNTHIA. Born Dec. 16, 1954 in Salt Lake City, U. Studied with Carol Reed, Ben Lokey, Willam Christensen, Anatole Vilzak, Gordon Paxman. Joined Ballet West in 1970; promoted to soloist 1973; principal 1974.

YOUNG, GAYLE. Born Nov. 7, in Lexington, Ky. Began study with Dorothy Pring at U. Calif. Studied at Ballet Theatre School, and joined Joffrey Ballet. Appeared on Bdwy and with N.Y.C. Ballet before joining American Ballet Theatre in 1960. Became principal in 1964.

YOURTH, LINDA. Born in Maplewood, N.J. in 1944. Studied at Sch. of Am. Ballet. At 14 joined Eglevsky's Ballet; NYCB at 16, rising to soloist. Joined Ballet du Grand Theatre de Geneve (1968–71). Returned to NYCB in 1971.

YOUSKEVITCH, IGOR. Born in Moscow, Mar. 13, 1912. Studied with Preobrajenska. Debut in Paris with Nijinska company; joined De Basil's Ballet, then, Ballet Russe de Monte Carlo. In 1946 became premier danseur with Ballet Theatre. Currently operating own school in N.Y.C.

YOUSKEVITCH, MARIA. Born Dec. 11, 1945 in N.Y.C. Studied with father, Igor Youskevitch, and made debut with his company in 1963. Appeared with Met Opera Ballet before joining American Ballet Theatre in 1967. Promoted to soloist 1973.

YUAN, TINA. Born Oct. 9, 1947 in Shanghai, China. Attended Juilliard, Martha Graham School. Debut 1969 with Pearl Lang; subsequently Yuriko 1970, Chinese Dance Co. 1972, Alvin Ailey Co. 1972.

YUDENICH, ALEXEI. Born July 5, 1943 in Sarajevo, Yugoslavia. Studied at Sarajevo Opera Ballet School, and made debut with company. Guest artist with Sagreb Opera Ballet before joining Pennsylvania Ballet in 1964 as principal dancer; retired in 1973 and now teaches.

YURIKO. Born Feb. 2, 1920 in San Jose, Calif. Began professional career at 6 with group that toured Japan for 7 years. Studied with Martha Graham, and joined company in 1944, becoming soloist, and choreographer. Formed own company in 1948 with which she has appeared in N.Y. and on tour. Also appeared in musicals.

ZAMIR, BATYA. Studied and appeared with Alwin Nikolais, Gladys Bailin, Phyllis Lamhut, Murray Louis, Mimi Garrard, Rachel Fibish, Joy Boutilier, and in own concerts and choreography. Also teaches.

ZHDANOV, YURI. Born in Moscow in 1925. Began career at 12 before attending Bolshoi School. Joined Company in 1944, became Ulanova's partner in 1951. Is now retired.

ZIDE, ROCHELLE. Born in Boston, Ap. 21, 1938. Studied with Hoctor, Williams, Pereyaslavec, Joffrey, Danielian, and at Ballet Russe School. Debut in 1954 with Ballet Russe de Monte Carlo, subsequently appearing with Joffrey Ballet (1958), Ballets U.S.A. (1961), American Dances (1963), N.Y.C. Opera Ballet (1958–63), Ballet Spectaculars (1963), and became ballet mistress of Joffrey Ballet in 1965.

ZIMMERMANN, GERDA. Born Mar. 26, in Cuxhaven, Ger. Studied with Georgi, Wigman, Horst, Zena Rommett. Soloist with Landestheater Hannover 1959–62. Choreographer from 1967. Solo recitals in U.S. from 1967 and in Ger. formed Kammertanz Theatre. Teaches.

ZITO, DOROTHY. Born in Jersey City, N.J. Attended Juilliard. Studied at Graham, Harkness schools, and N.Y. School of Ballet. Debut 1969 with New Dance Group, subsequently with Pearl Lang.

ZOMPAKOS, STANLEY. Born in N.Y.C. May 12, 1925. Studied with Balanchine and at School of American Ballet. Debut 1942 with New Opera Co. In Bdwy musicals, with Ballet Russe de Monte Carlo (1954–6), and became artistic director of Charleston, S.C., Civic Ballet.

ZORINA, VERA. Born Jan. 2, 1917 in Berlin, Ger. Studied with Edwardova, Tatiana and Victor Gsovsky, Dolin, and Legat. Debut 1930 in Berlin. Toured with Ballet Russe de Monte Carlo (1934–6). Made N.Y.C. debut in "I Married An Angel" in 1938. Joined Ballet Theatre in 1943. Subsequently, appeared in Bdwy productions, films.

ZORITCH, GEORGE. Born in Moscow June 6, 1919. Studied in Lithuania, Paris, and N.Y., with Preobrajenska, Vilzak, Vladimiroff, and Oboukhoff. Debut 1933 with Ida Rubenstein Co. in Paris. Joined de Basil Ballet Russe 1936. Ballet Russe de Monte Carlo 1938, Grand Ballet de Marquis de Cuevas (1951–8), Marina Svetlova Co. (1961), then formed own company. A favorite teacher and choreographer for regional ballet companies. Operates own school in Los Angeles.

OBITUARIES

JOSEPHINE BAKER, 68, St. Louis-born dancer and singer, died Apr. 12, 1975 of a cerebral hemorrhage in her adopted Paris, where she had lived since 1925. She became a French citizen in 1937. She was appearing in a revue celebrating her 50 years as an entertainer when she died. She was separated from her third husband, musician Jo Bouillon. Surviving are her 12 adopted orphans of various nationalities.

JULIA BARASHKOVA, Russian-born teacher and former dancer, died Oct. 14, 1974 in NYC. After the revolution, she lived in China before coming to the U.S. Joined Chicago Opera Ballet, and later Metropolitan Opera Ballet. Because of her analysis of body placement and movement impulse, and her exercise-based corrections she became known as a "dance doctor." No reported survivors.

RUDOLF BENESH, 59, inventor of system of movement notation, died May 3, 1975 in London. A gifted painter, he became interested in movement notation after his marriage to Joan Rothwell, a soloist with Sadler's Wells Ballet. Today more than 25 companies throughout the world use the Benesh notation system. He was director of London's Institute of Choreology, and a founder of the American Institute of Choreology in New York. He is survived by his widow and his son.

HEINZ BOSL, 29, first solo dancer of the Bavarian State Opera died June 12, 1975 of a virus infection in Munich, WGer. No reported survivors.

BETTY BRUCE, 54, dancer and comedienne on stage, screen and tv, died in NYC July 18, 1974 of cancer. From the ballet companies of Michael Fokine and George Balanchine, she moved to Broadway and appeared in several productions. She is survived by her mother and a son, Louis Satenstein.

MARIAN KNIGHTON BRYAN, 74, died Dec. 9, 1974 in NYC. She started the modern dance program at Sarah Lawrence College, was assistant director of the Yorkville Youth Center, and also taught at Columbia U., Skidmore, NYU, and Horace Mann School. She was the widow of documentary film photographer Julien H. Bryan. A son survives.

MARY WATKINS CUSHING, America's first fulltime daily newspaper dance critic, died Oct. 4, 1974 in NYC. In 1927 she was appointed dance critic of the NY Herald Tribune, and retired in 1934. A daughter survives.

ELIDA WEBB DAWSON, 79, a dancer and choreographer at Harlem's Cotton Club (1923–34), died May 1, 1975 in NYC. She also danced and choreographed for Broadway. Surviving is her husband, retired dancer George "The Strutter" Dawson.

RAYMOND CLAY, artistic director-founder of the Contemporary Ballet Dance Theatre of Nashville, died July 12, 1974 in Nashville, Tenn. Had studied at Rambert School, and London School of Contemporary Dance, and Juilliard. Had performed with Boscoe Holder, Murray Louis, Phyllis Lamhut, Rod Rodgers, Pepsi Bethel, Lilliam Harmel, and Yuriko. No reported survivors.

ROGER PRYOR DODGE, 76, Paris-born critic, dancer and choreographer, died June 2, 1974 in NYC. Began training in Paris before coming to U.S. In 1925 joined Adolf Bolm's company. Became noted for his translations of jazz dances into ballet format, and appeared in "Skyscraper" (1926), the first jazz ballet. He later became a critic on dance and jazz. His widow and son survive.

RUTH HARRISON FISHER, 62, Nebraska-born half of the internationally famous Harrison and Fisher dance team, died Aug. 12, 1974 of a coronary attack in her NYC home. Studied ballet in Omaha and left at 15 to join Chicago Civic Opera Ballet, where she met Alex Fisher, a dancer, with whom she teamed to begin a career that spanned three decades. They appeared on Broadway and in all of Europe's major cities. They were noted for their witty and satirical routines that were a skillful blend of ballet, ballroom and adagio dancing. They were regularly featured at Radio City Music Hall, and on the Ed Sullivan tv show. She is survived by her husband who is on the staff of Dance Magazine.

SONIA GASKELL, Russian-born founder of Het Nederlands Ballet, died July 9, 1974 in Paris. She became director of the Het Nederlands Ballet in 1958, and three years later fused into the Dutch National Ballet. She served as its director until 1968. No reported survivors.

YVONNE GEORGI, 72, dancer, choreographer and ballet mistress, died Jan. 25, 1975 in Hanover, Ger. As an exponent of German dance expressionism, she had appeared in many countries, including the U.S. with Harald Kreutzberg. For 15 years was ballet director of the Hanover State Theater. Her last U.S. appearance was in 1939 with her own ensemble. No reported survivors.

ROKUKA HANAYAGI, 56, Japanese-born teacher-dancer, died Sept. 23, 1974 in Los Angeles, Ca. With her own troupe, she had toured widely, including the Orient. No reported survivors.

GYULA HARANGOZO, 66, Hungarian dancer and choreographer, died in October of 1974 in Budapest. He became a principal dancer with the Hungarian National Ballet in 1928, and its choreographer 'n 1936. No reported survivors.

ALBERT KOZLOVSKY, 72, Latvia-born dancer and teacher, died Sept. 16, 1974 in his home in Lidingo, Swed. Moscow-trained, he danced with several European companies, and formed his own. In 1944 he escaped to Sweden with his dancer-wife Nina Dombrovska and opened a private ballet school. In 1949 he was engaged to take over the Royal Swedish Ballet School, and remained its head until he retired in 1969. No reported survivors.

EUGENIE OUROUSSOW LEHOVICH, 66, director of the School of American Ballet (official school of the NYC Ballet) died of cancer Jan. 7, 1975 in NYC. She had been associated with the school since its founding in 1934 by George Balanchine and Lincoln Kirstein. After study in Paris, she came to the U.S. and graduated from Parsons School of Design. Surviving are her husband, writer Dimitri Lehovich, a son, and a daughter.

KATHERINE MANNING, former dancer, died Aug. 13, 1974 in Chicago, Ill. She had been a soloist with the Doris Humphrey-Charles Weidman Dance Co., and was Emeritus Professor of Women's Physical Education at UChicago. No reported survivors.

MORAYMA MUNOZ, 30, a member of the Rosario Galan Spanish Dance Co., was killed instantly in a NYC traffic accident on Mar. 30, 1975. She had been a featured dancer at the Chateau Madrid in NYC and was scheduled to open in Puerto Rico on April 7. She had also danced with Ballets de San Juan, and taught at Jose Greco's school. She is survived by her husband, contractor, Tom Foldy.

PAUL NICKEL, 35, Detroit-born ballet soloist, died June 24, 1975 in NYC. He joined American Ballet Theatre in 1961 and became a soloist in 1967, and assistant stage manager in 1972. Before joining ABT he had appeared with NYC Ballet, and Andre Englevsky's company. His parents survive.

JOE PRICE, 73, national executive director of the Professional Dance Teachers Association, and a teacher of acrobatics, died June 6, 1974 in NYC. He had an international reputation as a teacher of acrobatics. Surviving are his widow, two sons and a daughter.

ANNA KNAPTON POVITCH, dancer and teacher, died Dec. 11, 1974 in West Roxbury, Mass. She had danced with Anna Pavlova's company, and with the Diaghilev's Ballets Russes. She had taught ballet for 55 years in NYC. She is survived by a son and a daughter.

JANE KISER ROBBINS, 53, former dancer with the Ballet Russe de Monte Carlo, died from heart failure June 24, 1974 in Doylestown, Pa. Her husband, musician William Robbins, survives.

MANZELL SENTERS, 27, Dallas-born former member of Salt Lake City's Repertory Dance Theatre, died Nov. 1, 1974 in Salt Lake City, Utah. No reported survivors.

GERRY SEVERN, 67, Moscow-born German Sevatianov, former managing director of Ballet Theatre and other ballet companies, died June 26, 1974 in Switzerland. No reported survivors.

FORREST THORNBURG, 69, teacher and former dancer, died Sept. 13, 1974 in Los Angeles, Ca. He was long affiliated with the Denishawn company, and was also known for his lyric and religious dances. His son and daughter survive.

GRAHAM USHER, 36, former principal with The Royal Ballet, died in his sleep Feb. 3, 1975 in London. He joined the company in 1955 but he was forced to retire in 1970 because of his health. No reported survivors.

VERA VOLKOVA, 71, Russian-born teacher and former dancer, died May 5, 1975 in her home in Copenhagen, Den. Soon after making her debut in Russia, she went to China where she danced, until she joined the International Ballet in London. She retired from dancing in 1943 and opened a studio that attracted many dancers, including Margot Fonteyn. Since 1952 she had been teacher and artistic adviser for the Royal Danish Ballet. She is survived by her husband, Hugh Williams, the English painter.

CHARLES WEIDMAN, 73, a pioneer and leading figure in modern dance for over 50 years, died July 15, 1975 in his NYC home. His last performance was given on July 13 at his studio where he had danced almost every weekend since 1960. He was a student of the Denishawn School with Doris Humphrey, and a soloist with the company for 8 years. With Miss Humphrey formed a company and school that trained many important modern dancers from 1927 to 1945. In 1948 he organized his own company and school, producing such dancers as Jose Limon, Jack Cole, Bob Fosse, Sybil Shearer and Tony Charmoli. His "Atavisms," "Lynch Town," "Fables of Our Time," "A House Divided," and "The War between Men and Women" are among his best known works. He had also choreographed for several Broadway musicals. He was very influential in increasing the participation of men in modern dance. No reported survivors.

JOE WEIL, 57, a member of "The Three Wiles" dance team, died Dec. 29, 1974 in Brooklyn, NY. Together with his wife and brother they worked vaudeville and nightclubs for over 30 years. Surviving are his wife and brother, and another brother, comedian Larry Wyle.

INDEX

203

205

207

213

216

219